GLOBAL PERSPECTIVES ON COUNTERTERRORISM

ASPEN COURSEBOOK SERIES

GLOBAL PERSPECTIVES ON COUNTERTERRORISM

Third Edition

Amos N. Guiora
Professor of Law
S.J. Quinney College of Law
University of Utah

ASPEN
PUBLISHING

Cover image: Bastian Herre, Veronika Samborska, Hannah Ritchie, Joe Hasell, Edouard Mathieu, and Max Roser (2023). "Terrorism." Published online at OurWorldInData.org. Retrieved from: https://ourworldindata.org/terrorism.

To contact Customer Service, e-mail customer.service@aspenpublishing.com, call 1-800-950-5259, or mail correspondence to:

Aspen Publishing
Attn: Order Department
1 Wall Street
Burlington, MA 01803

Printed in the United States of America.

1 2 3 4 5 6 7 8 9 0

ISBN 979-8-8861-4394-2

Library of Congress Cataloging-in-Publication Data

Names: Guiora, Amos N., 1957– author.
Title: Global perspectives on counterterrorism / Amos N. Guiora, Professor of Law, S. J. Quinney College of Law, University of Utah.
Description: Third edition. | Burlington: Aspen Publishing, 2024. |
Series: Aspen coursebook series | Includes index. | Summary: "Elective book on global counterterrorism"—Provided by publisher.
Identifiers: LCCN 2024011849 | ISBN 9798886143942 (paperback) | ISBN 9798886143959 (ebook)
Subjects: LCSH: Terrorism—Prevention—Law and legislation. | Terrorism (International law) | LCGFT: Casebooks (Law).
Classification: LCC KZ7220 .G857 2024 | DDC 363.325/17—dc22
LC record available at https://lccn.loc.gov/2024011849

About Aspen Publishing

Aspen Publishing is a leading provider of educational content and digital learning solutions to law schools in the U.S. and around the world. Aspen provides best-in-class solutions for legal education through authoritative textbooks, written by renowned authors, and breakthrough products such as Connected eBooks, Connected Quizzing, and PracticePerfect.

The Aspen Casebook Series (famously known among law faculty and students as the "red and black" casebooks) encompasses hundreds of highly regarded textbooks in more than eighty disciplines, from large enrollment courses, such as Torts and Contracts to emerging electives such as Sustainability and the Law of Policing. Study aids such as the *Examples & Explanations* and the *Emanuel Law Outlines* series, both highly popular collections, help law students master complex subject matter.

Major products, programs, and initiatives include:

- **Connected eBooks** are enhanced digital textbooks and study aids that come with a suite of online content and learning tools designed to maximize student success. Designed in collaboration with hundreds of faculty and students, the Connected eBook is a significant leap forward in the legal education learning tools available to students.

- **Connected Quizzing** is an easy-to-use formative assessment tool that tests law students' understanding and provides timely feedback to improve learning outcomes. Delivered through CasebookConnect.com, the learning platform already used by students to access their Aspen casebooks, Connected Quizzing is simple to implement and integrates seamlessly with law school course curricula.

- **PracticePerfect** is a visually engaging, interactive study aid to explain commonly encountered legal doctrines through easy-to-understand animated videos, illustrative examples, and numerous practice questions. Developed by a team of experts, PracticePerfect is the ideal study companion for today's law students.

- The **Aspen Learning Library** enables law schools to provide their students with access to the most popular study aids on the market across all of their courses. Available through an annual subscription, the online library consists of study aids in e-book, audio, and video formats with full text search, note-taking, and highlighting capabilities.

- Aspen's **Digital Bookshelf** is an institutional-level online education bookshelf, consolidating everything students and professors need to ensure success. This program ensures that every student has access to affordable course materials from day one.

- **Leading Edge** is a community centered on thinking differently about legal education and putting those thoughts into actionable strategies. At the core of the program is the Leading Edge Conference, an annual gathering of legal education thought leaders looking to pool ideas and identify promising directions of exploration.

To my wife, Hagit, whose extraordinary support throughout the years is unparalleled, and to our three children, their partners, and our grandchildren

BIOGRAPHY

Amos N. Guiora

Amos N. Guiora is Professor of Law at the S.J. Quinney College of Law, the University of Utah. He is a Distinguished Fellow at The Consortium for the Research and Study of Holocaust and the Law at Chicago-Kent College of Law, and a Distinguished Fellow and Counselor at the International Center for Conflict Resolution, Katz School of Business, University of Pittsburgh. Professor Guiora is on the Board of the Lauren McCluskey Foundation.

Professor Guiora is the recipient of the University of Utah's Distinguished Faculty Service award (https://sjquinney.utah.edu/news-articles/prof-amos-guiora-wins-distinguished-faculty-service-award-for-bystander-initiative/).

For the past 10 years, Professor Guiora has been researching, writing, and lecturing on the question of bystanders (originally in the Holocaust), resulting in his books, *The Crime of Complicity: The Bystander in the Holocaust* and *Armies of Enablers: Survivor Stories of Complicity and Betrayal in Sexual Assaults* (https://armiesofenablers.com).

Professor Guiora's most recent article, "Holding Enablers of Child Sexual Abuse Accountable: The Case of Jeremy Bell" (https://papers.ssrn.com/sol3/papers.cfm?abstract_id=4366186), addresses the role of enablers in sexual assault of children.

Professor Guiora directs the S.J. Quinney College of Law Bystander Initiative (https://tinyurl.com/3dfxsmp8).

Professor Guiora has an A.B. in history from Kenyon College, a J.D. from Case Western Reserve University School of Law, and a Ph.D. from Leiden University.

SUMMARY OF CONTENTS

CONTENTS

PREFACE

In the opening lines of the first edition's Preface I wrote: This book was a labor of love. It was born during a short conversation with my colleague and good friend, Professor Craig Nard, in the fall of 2004, who urged I write a book on terrorism. Urged would be the polite term; "ordered" would be more descriptive of the conversation. For that, I will be forever thankful. As inspiration, I strategically placed Craig's casebook, along with one of the many academic publications written by my late father, Professor A.Z. Guiora, on my bookshelf in such a manner that they were the first things I would see every morning.

In addition, my then Dean Gerry Korngold was a constant supporter—providing both words of encouragement and generous summer stipends. For both, I am very grateful. In addition, almost 20 years later I still owe a huge debt to my then editor John Devins and my then publisher Steve Errick (both then at Aspen Publishing) who believed in me, even though this was my first book, and have remained great friends throughout the years.

While Nard and Korngold are no longer my colleagues, they are to this day amongst my closest friends.

The second edition was framed by feedback to the first edition. The feedback emphasized the value and uniqueness of comparatively analyzing counterterrorism in an interdisciplinary manner. A recurring theme was the need to incorporate additional countries. For that reason, the second edition remained true to the pedagogical approach of the first edition while adding two countries, China and Colombia.

In retrospect, both were obvious choices: China because of its extraordinary geopolitical power and relevance; Colombia because of the unique combination of threats it faces. With China, I was very fortunate that American and Chinese academics were gracious with their time and cooperation. The new material on Colombia enormously benefited from insight offered by American and Colombian experts who graciously responded to my many questions.

With the five previously surveyed countries—the U.S., Israel, Russia, India, and Spain—significant additions have been made that reflect the developments of recent years. I have sought to present to the reader a continuum of events between each edition. Terrorism cannot be viewed in a vacuum; rather, historical appreciation enormously facilitates understanding it. The four-legged approach that drives this book—law, policy, operations, and intelligence—requires both geopolitical and historical sensitivity to events, trends, and responses.

It was very important for me to approach counterterrorism from an interdisciplinary perspective. This decision reflects my 19-year career in the Israel Defense Forces, where I was exposed to some of the most complicated and complex decision making that commanders could face in the realm of operational counterterrorism.

What struck me throughout my career was that counterterrorism decisions require the incorporation of different disciplines—in particular, law, policy, tactics and operations, and intelligence gathering. As the Judge Advocate to senior commanders, I was expected to provide legal advice in an area of law best described by Israel as operational international law. This is not an area of law that was studied when I was in law school in the early- to mid-1980s; nor were there an enormous number of "guides" or "checklists." What could be considered benchmarks were the decisions rendered by the Israel Supreme Court sitting as the High Court of Justice—international law and a moral compass combined with instinct.

I soon realized I had to provide advice beyond the realm of law; a Major General asked me to participate in a meeting where legal issues were not to be discussed. When I asked why, his response was succinct: because I expect you to provide *both* legal and policy advice. From that point on, integrating operational considerations with legal and policy matters was a given, as was my increasing understanding that the soul of counterterrorism is intelligence gathering. To that extent, I worked closely—and obviously not always in agreement—with commanders and intelligence officials alike. Recommending operational decisions steeped in the law while being mindful of additional valid considerations is the essence of legal advice for military commanders. That was my role.

That professional experience serves as the backdrop for this book. I am convinced that the only way counterterrorism can truly be studied and understood is through an interdisciplinary approach. Otherwise, an extremely complicated subject will be given short shrift.

As to why I initially chose to examine the U.S., Israel, Russia, India, and Spain, the answer is relatively simple. I felt they were interesting unto themselves, and I also recognized that each conducted counterterrorism sufficiently differently from one another to enable effective comparison.

While on some matters the five—now seven—nations have similar approaches, on a significant number of issues their differences facilitate examining and learning from the contrasts. Different regimes have different laws and policies, and civil democratic societies also have significant similarities and differences. Those similarities and distinctions, in the context of the four subject areas—law, policy, operations, and intelligence—are the essence of this book.

When writing the first edition, I tried out various chapters at both the law school and collegiate levels to gauge the relevancy and applicability of my four-subject approach with respect to the five nations. My conviction, based on courses I have taught at both levels, is that the approach resonates with students. To all those students who were the initial "adopters": my many thanks for your honest feedback during and after the respective courses.

As to this third edition: when I began, the intent was to undertake a traditional revision of a casebook. As noted in the Prologue, that significantly changed on October 7, 2023. The events in Israel and the Gaza Strip raise important questions regarding terrorism and counterterrorism as traditionally understood. While the results of the conflict are unknown at this time, their importance to this book cannot be sufficiently stated.

Amos Guiora
November 2023

ACKNOWLEDGEMENTS

Obviously, a project of this nature is not a one-man show. Many thanks are due. I have benefited from the endless and tireless support of several people, without whom this project would not have reached the end zone. The words below with respect to the first edition were true then and are true now. The vibrancy of the students who worked with me then is as relevant and important to this edition as it was to the first two.

At Case Western Reserve University School of Law, I was extraordinarily fortunate to have a team of remarkable student research assistants: two students—Erin Page and Sam Riotte—truly became collaborators; their endless and tireless determination made the book a reality. I benefited enormously not only from their research and editing, but also from their insistence that the student be the focus of the book and that I keep my "eye on this ball" at all times. Rounding out the remarkable team were Niki Dorsky Schaefer, Matt Ezzo, Brian Field, and Rebecca Slazinski, who all made significant contributions to this book. Anne Hollander and Jeff Lowe provided additional assistance in securing copyright permissions.

I am truly indebted to Case Western Reserve University School of Law research librarian Andrew Dorchak. His ability to consistently find "needles in haystacks" made much of this book possible. The IT staff at Case was patient to a fault; in particular, Suparerk (Sami) Janjarasjitt was literally there every step of the way.

In 2007 I moved to the S.J. Quinney College of Law, University of Utah. This book very much benefited from that move for the same spirit of extraordinary collaboration is true for the SJQ law students who worked on the second edition. Katee Tyler took it upon herself to create a timetable predicated on meeting tight deadlines, keeping our collective eye on the ball, and integrating an enormous amount of new research information.

With respect to that complicated effort, I am enormously in debt to Katee, Lena Cetvi, and Amra Ferhathegovic. Without their individual and collective efforts, the finished product would be drastically different than it is.

With respect to this third edition: I am deeply indebted to Landon Moore and Cait McKee (SJQ, 2024) who worked with me "step for step" on a project which had significant challenges, given its topic and never ending "current events" which directly impacted our timetable. Both Landon and Cait were gracious, understanding, dedicated, and engaged. For that, they have my deepest gratitude.

Landon's work was under the auspices of the S.J. Quinney, Quinney Fellowship. Cait graciously agreed to continue her efforts for a second year to see this project to its completion. For that, I am deeply indebted and most appreciative, as it was crucial to a timely conclusion of our efforts. The reader is the ultimate beneficiary of that. It goes without saying, all errors are solely mine.

This book reflects the collaborative atmosphere at the S.J. Quinney College of Law, the University of Utah that Dean Elizabeth Kronk Warner fosters and deeply encourages.

I gratefully acknowledge the permission granted by the authors, publishers, and organizations to reprint the following materials:

"Committee Against Torture Examines Russian Federation's Report." United Nations Office of the High Commissioner for Human Rights, 27 July 2018, https://www.ohchr.org/en/press-releases/2018/07/committee-against-torture-examines-russian-federations-report. Press release.

"Defence conceals a satellite spy station in the Sierra* of Madrid." Cryptome, 28 Jan. 2003, cryptome.org/echelon-es.htm.

"JuM Ultras Get Life Term for Murder." *The Tribune,* The Tribune Trust, 3 February 2003, www.tribuneindia.com/2003/20030203/nation.htm#4.

"Nur-Pashi Kulayev." Wikipedia, Wikimedia Foundation, 1 April 2024, https://en.wikipedia.org/wiki/Nur-Pashi_Kulayev.

bin Laden, Osama. *A Call for Jihad to Stop the Gaza Assault.* www.nefafoundation.org/miscellaneous/FeaturedDocs/nefabinladen0109.pdf.

Breaking the Grip? Obstacles to Justice for Paramilitary Mafias in Colombia. Human Rights Watch, 16 October 2008, www.hrw.org/report/2008/10/16/breaking-grip/obstacles-justice-paramilitary-mafias-colombia. Licensed under CC BY-NC-ND 4.0 DEED, https://creativecommons.org/licenses/by-nc-nd/4.0/deed.en.

Center for Strategic & International Studies. *U.S. Terrorist Attacks and Plots and Fatalities, 1994-2021*. Graph, 17 May 2022, www.csis.org/analysis/pushed-extremes-domestic-terrorism-amid-polarization-and-protest. Reprinted with permission.

Cohen, Stanley, and Daphna Golan. *The Interrogation of Palestinians during the Intifada: Ill-Treatment, "Moderate Physical Pressure" or Torture?* B'Tselem–The Israeli Information Center for Human Rights in the Occupied Territories, March 1991, www.btselem.org/Download/199103_Torture_Eng.doc.

Cole, David and James X. Dempsey. *Terrorism and the Constitution.* The New Press, 2002.

Davis, Maia. "A Painful Reminder for Japanese-Americans." The Record, 20 September 2001.

Dickinson, Laura. "Using Legal Process to Fight Terrorism: Detentions, Military Commissions, International Tribunals, and the Rule of Law." Southern

California Law Review, Vol. 75, 2002. USC Gould School of Law. Reprinted with permission from the author.

Dorf, Michael C. "Why the Military Commissions Act Is No Moderate Compromise." FindLaw, Thomson Reuters, 11 October 2006, supreme.findlaw.com/legal-commentary/why-the-military-commissions-act-is-no-moderate-compromise.html.

Fitzpatrick, Joan. "Jurisdiction of Military Commissions and the Ambiguous War on Terrorism." The American Journal of International Law, Vol. 96, No. 2, April 2002. American Society of International Law.

Foreign Interrogators in Guantanamo Bay. Center for Constitutional Rights, 21 May 2008, ccrjustice.org/home/get-involved/tools-resources/fact-sheets-and-faqs/foreign-interrogators-guantanamo-bay.

Gaeta, Paola. "The Armed Conflict in Chechnya before the Russian Constitutional Court." European Journal of International Law, Vol. 7, No. 4, 1996. Oxford University Press on behalf of EJIL Ltd. Reprinted with permission from the European Journal of International Law.

Golding, Peter. *The Transformation of Counter Terrorism: USAWC Strategy Research Project.* U.S. Army War College, 9 April 2002.

Guiora, Amos N. *American Counterterrorism: The Triangle of Detention, Interrogation and Trial.* Magna Carta Institute's Symposium, Towards a Global Legal Counter-Terrorism Model: Transatlantic Perspectives, 2010

Herre, Bastian, et al. *Number of Terrorist Attacks, 2021.* Chart, 2022, ourworldindata.org/terrorism#all-charts. Licensed under CC BY 4.0 DEED, https://creativecommons.org/licenses/by/4.0/.

Human Rights in Palestine and Other Occupied Arab Territories: Report of the United Nations Fact Finding Mission on the Gaza Conflict. United Nations General Assembly, 25 September 2009, www2.ohchr.org/english/bodies/hrcouncil/docs/12session/a-hrc-12-48.pdf.

In the Name of Counter-Terrorism: Human Rights Abuses Worldwide. Human Rights Watch, 25 Mar. 2003, www.hrw.org/en/reports/2003/03/25/name-counter-terrorism-human-rights-abuses-worldwide. Licensed under CC BY-NC-ND 4.0 DEED, https://creativecommons.org/licenses/by-nc-nd/4.0/deed.en.

India: Punitive use of preventive detention legislation in Jammu and Kashmir. Amnesty International, 16 May 2000, https://www.amnesty.org/en/wp-content/uploads/2021/06/asa200102000en.pdf. Licensed under CC BY-NC-ND 4.0, https://creativecommons.org/licenses/by-nc-nd/4.0/legalcode.

Kaplan, Eben, and Jayshree Bajoria. *Counterterrorism in India.* Council on Foreign Relations, 27 November 2008, www.cfr.org/backgrounder/counterterrorism-india.

Kellman, Barry. "Regulation of Biological Research in the Terrorism Era." Health Matrix: The Journal of Law-Medicine, Vol. 13, No. 1, January 2003. Case Western Reserve University School of Law.

Levit, Kenneth J. "The CIA and the Torture Controversy: Interrogation Authorities and Practices in the War on Terror." Journal of National Security Law and Policy, vol. 1, 2005. Syracuse University and Georgetown Law.

Limitations on Challenging the Lawfulness of the Detention. Human Rights Watch, January 2005, https://www.hrw.org/reports/2005/spain0105/7.htm.

Licensed under CC BY-NC-ND 4.0 DEED, https://creativecommons.org/licenses/by-nc-nd/4.0/deed.en.

Maiti, Prasenjit. "Human Rights Violation in Kashmir." Peace Magazine (January-March 2002). Canadian Disarmanent Information Service.

Mehta, Sachin. Repeal of POTA - Justified. Legal Service India, www.legalservicesindia.com/articles/pota.htm.

Newton, Michael A. "International Criminal Law Aspects of the War Against Terrorism." International Law Studies, Vol. 79, 2003. U.S. Naval War College. Reprinted with permission from the author.

Omelicheva, Mariya Y. "Russia's Counterterrorism Policy: Variations on an Imperial Theme." Perspectives on Terrorism, Vol. III, Issue 1, April 2009. International Centre for Counter-Terrorism. Reprinted with permission from the author.

Paul, Solil. *Counter-Terrorism Laws: The Supreme Court on Confessions*. South Asia Terrorism Portal, 2001, www.satp.org/satporgtp/publication/faultlines/volume16/Article2.htm.

Phares, Walid. "Moussaoui, Wrong Court, Wrong Debate." Foundation for Defense of Democracies, 4 May 2006.

Riedel, Bruce. "Terrorism in India and the Global Jihad." The Brookings Institution, 30 November 2008, www.brookings.edu/articles/terrorism-in-india-and-the-global-jihad/.

Rosand, Eric. "Security Council Resolution 1373, the Counter-Terrorism Committee, and the Fight against Terrorism." The American Journal of International Law, Vol. 97, No. 2, April 2003. Cambridge University Press.

Roth, Kenneth. *Obama & Counterterror: The Ignored Record*. Human Rights Watch, 5 February 2015, www.hrw.org/news/2015/02/05/obama-counterterror-ignored-record. Licensed under CC BY-NC-ND 4.0 DEED, https://creativecommons.org/licenses/by-nc-nd/4.0/deed.en.

Schnell, Jonathan. "The Atlantic Divide over Fighting Terrorism." YaleGlobal Online, Yale University, 16 March 2005, archive-yaleglobal.yale.edu/content/atlantic-divide-over-fighting-terrorism.

Stewart, James G. "The Military Commissions Act of 2006 Inconsistency with the Geneva Conventions." Journal of International Criminal Justice, Vol. 5, No. 1, 2007. Oxford University Press.

The Failed Military Commissions. Center for Victims of Torture, 19 July 2023, www.cvt.org/what-we-do/advocating-for-change/legacy-of-us-torture/the-failed-military-commissions/. Reprinted with permission.

The Prevention of Terrorism Act, 2002. South Asia Terrorism Portal, www.satp.org/satporgtp/countries/india/document/actandordinances/POTA.htm.

Torture by the United States. World Organization for Human Rights USA, January 2005, www2.ohchr.org/english/bodies/hrc/docs/ngos/wohr.pdf.

Touron, Candido Conde-Pumpido. *Judicial Response to Terrorism: National Venues, the Spanish Model*. 10th International Judicial Conference in Strasbourg.

Trahan, Jennifer. "Trying a Bin Laden and Others: Evaluating the Options for Terrorist Trials." Houston Journal of International Law, no. 24, 2002. University of Houston Law Center.

Widespread Torture in the Chechen Republic: Torture by Personnel of the Second Operational Investigative Bureau (ORB-2). Human Rights Watch, hrw.org

/backgrounder/eca/chechnya1106/2.htm#_Toc150776963. Licensed under CC BY-NC-ND 4.0 DEED, https://creativecommons.org/licenses/by-nc-nd/4.0/deed .en.

Xu, Beina, and Eleanor Albert. *Media Censorship in China*. Council on Foreign Relations, 17 February 2017, www.cfr.org/backgrounder/media-censorship-china.

Amos N. Guiora
Salt Lake City
November, 2023

PROLOGUE: OCTOBER 7TH

As these lines are written, certain sections of this book are directly related to the conflict between Israel and Hamas. For the past months Cait McKee, editor Kathy Langone, and I have been engaged in intensive conversations regarding the rewriting of this book, particularly Chapter 5 (Judicial Review). Those discussions reflected the "judicial reform" movement in Israel as the Israeli government focused on eviscerating the independence of the judiciary. In full disclosure, the author of the book has been an active participant in the demonstrations against the so-called "judicial reform" and has done interviews and written op-eds in response to the government's efforts.

On September 12, 2023, the Israeli Supreme Court—sitting as the High Court of Justice—heard a series of petitions that had been submitted against the Government's efforts.[1] This edition was undertaken with the expectation that its completion would be postponed until the Supreme Court issued its ruling. However, the judicial reform, for important reasons, has taken a back-seat. Because the events on October 7, 2023 and its aftermath are of particular relevance to this book, we then asked ourselves whether chapters should be rewritten to highlight the dilemma introduced. The discussion below focuses exclusively on the aftermath of October 7; while acknowledging the humanitarian crisis, the discussion is restricted to the conflict between Hamas and Israel.

In the immediate aftermath of October 7, at the behest of Prime Minister Benjamin Netanyahu, the Israeli government declared "war" against Hamas. Except for President Bush's reaction to 9/11 when declaring "war on

1. On January 1st, 2024, by a vote of 8-7, the Israeli Supreme Court invalidated the Government's aim to repeal the reasonableness clause. The legislation was a component of the Government's judicial overhaul efforts. Further information *available at* https://www.jpost.com/breaking-news/article-780303 and https://www.washingtonpost.com/world/2024/01/01/israel-supreme-court-judicial-reform-netanyahu/?utm_source=alert&utm_medium=email&utm_campaign=wp_news_alert_revere&location=alert.

terrorism," this is the first time a government has declared "war" against a terrorist organization. Whether this was meant rhetorically, politically, or had legal connotations is an open question. Distinct from the traditional operation counterterrorism model—the heart of the first and second editions of this book—which was predicated on person-specific counterterrorism, declaring war would suggest an expansive view of the operational reach. In the previous editions, Israel's targeted killing policy was addressed at length along with the U.S. drone policy established by President Bush post-9/11, and later adopted by President Obama as articulated in the White Papers. The Israeli government's decision to declare war on Hamas is distinct from its targeted killing operations. That has raised important questions regarding the definition and application of international law—in particular, legitimate targets and collateral damage. Furthermore, Israel's decision to kill the members of Hamas involved in the October 7 attack regardless of knowledge of future involvement in terrorism does not, prima facie, meet international law requirements, which condemn attacks devoid of information regarding future acts of terrorism.

Over the course of the years, the author of this book has argued that terrorist organizations cannot be defeated. Critics have suggested that the American military operation campaign against ISIS and al Qaeda resulted in all but defeat. That model, to the best of our understanding, reflects the Israeli's approach to Hamas after October 7. On more than one occasion, Prime Minister Netanyahu and Defense Minister Yoav Gallant have clearly articulated that the exclusive goal of Operation Iron Swords—the operation launched in response to October 7—is the destruction of Hamas. Such a clear announcement is reflected in the operational decision making which is predicated on an all-out effort to eradicate Hamas operatives, leadership, and infrastructure. That effort indicates an expansive view of self-defense under Article 51 of the United Nations Charter. This view is not without cost, particularly as it applies to innocent Palestinians living in the Gaza Strip. From an operational perspective, the complexity of conducting an aggressive campaign against a terrorist organization is exacerbated when innocent civilians in a densely populated area are being used as human shields, whether in their homes, neighborhoods, or in hospitals. The humanitarian crisis that confronts the innocent Palestinians living in Gaza has drawn international concern, if not condemnation, of Israeli operation decision making and measures.

Distinct from person-specific counterterrorism, the declaration of war reflects a significantly different approach to how nation-states respond to terrorism. Unlike previously understood terrorism, Hamas operatives who attacked on October 7 conducted themselves like soldiers in a brigade. The 3,000 members of Hamas who penetrated Israel via land, air, and sea resembled a military rather than a traditional terrorist organization. The lack of linguistic clarity regarding Hamas, whether terrorists, militants, combatants, illegal combatants, or soldiers, reflects the challenges in developing an operational response. Hamas is no longer organized as the commonly understood terrorist organization that they previously were. As these lines are written the expectation is that the Israeli Defense Forces, acting in accordance with the government's orders, will all but eradicate Hamas. The question is then what happens "the day after." While important, this question is beyond the purview of this book.

What is not beyond our discussion, and to which we turn our attention, is seeking to understand what led to Hamas' unparalleled achievement on October 7 and the profound failure of Israeli leadership, IDF command, and intelligence community. It is widely expected that commissions of inquiry will find that all three levels failed and will impose significant repercussions on government, military, and intelligence officials. In particular, it is expected that in addition to Prime Minister Netanyahu and perhaps Defense Minister Gallant, senior IDF officials, including the Head of IDF intelligence Aharon Haliva, IDF Chief of Staff Herzi Halevi, and the Head of Israel Security Agency Ronen Bar, will be held personally and professionally accountable.

Hamas' overwhelming success on October 7 raises important questions regarding Israel's overreliance on technology (SIGINT) rather than human intelligence (HUMINT) and the consequences of that significant operational-intelligence decision. In the traditional counterterrorism model, intelligence gathering is based on three legs: HUMINT, SIGINT, and open sources. Hamas' success included cyber-attacks on Israeli technology intelligence gathering infrastructure, such as shutting down the balloon-like mechanisms monitoring the Gaza/Israel border.

In addition, Hamas' ability to infiltrate Israeli airspace and attack from the sea, along with the land attack, is suggestive of at least two years of planning and execution that recalls, if not exceeds, Al-Qaeda's attack on 9/11. A cyber-attack by Hamas had never been done before October 7. Hamas' clear success—and, simultaneously, the failure of the IDF and the costs incurred—suggest that October 7 and its aftermath constitute a distinctly different paradigm exceeding traditional terrorism. It is for that reason that the traditional models discussed in this book must be understood in concert with the different lessons learned from the Israel/Gaza war.

This unprecedented paradigm has led to the creation of the operational unit NILI, whose sole operational mandate—according to the Israeli media—is to identify through observations of video and other social media, locate, and kill those responsible for October 7, with no knowledge of future plans of terrorism. This is akin to Operation Wrath of God, which was implemented by then Prime Minister of Israel Golda Meir to find and kill the members of the Black September organization responsible for the murder of Israeli Olympians at the 1972 Munich Olympics. As further discussed in Chapter 4, this is relevant only in the understanding of Israel's actions under international law.

> Operation Wrath of God poses the dilemma requiring us to differentiate between punishment and retribution. In deciding to kill those responsible for the murder of 11 Israeli athletes, Prime Minister Meir ordered the Mossad to kill—not capture—the Black September operatives. Had she ordered their detention leading to a trial in Israel (or in Germany) that decision would have resulted in the punishment of those responsible. In choosing to order the Mossad to kill them, Prime Minister Meir engaged in retributive conduct. There is no indication of available material that consideration was given to

> arrest those responsible for Munich and bring them to trial in Israel as was done with Adolf Eichmann.[2]

With respect to the judicial reform efforts, it is unclear when and how the Israeli Supreme Court will rule and what the Government's reaction to a holding will be if it accepts the petitions filed against the judicial reform. Similarly, it is unclear how the Israeli government will, if at all, re-engage with judicial reform efforts in the aftermath of October 7.

The recent attacks emphasize the evolving realm of terrorism and counterterrorism. The means, methods, and organization, while different between terrorist groups, has drastically changed within Hamas. It is unknown how and when the Israel/Gaza conflict will cease and to what extent the collateral damage will be. Israel's overreliance on technology and delayed response to re-enforce the infrastructure has left them even more vulnerable to Hamas' thorough planning and flawless execution of their attacks.

2. Amos Guiora's chapter *Operation Wrath of God: Illegal but Necessary* in Eric Patterson and Marc LiVecche, *Military Necessity and Just War Statecraft: The Principle of National Security Stewardship (War, Conflict and Ethics)*, 170 (1st ed. 2023).

CHAPTER 1

INTRODUCTION

This third edition analyzes terrorism and counterterrorism by surveying the approach seven different nations use to conduct operational counterterrorism. Its aim is to analyze the four Counterterrorism Pillars—**law, policy, operations,** and **intelligence**—as implemented by the United States, Israel, Russia, India, Spain, China, and Colombia. Distinct from the first two editions, this edition will have a greater focus on domestic terrorism, particularly in the United States. Specific acts of terrorism in nations outside of the seven discussed in the book will also be addressed.

Expanding beyond the first two editions (2007 and 2011), this edition addresses significant developments in the years 2011-2024 including, but not limited to, the following:

a) 2011 killing of Osama bin Laden;
b) Rise of ISIS;
c) U.S. withdrawal from Iraq and Afghanistan;
d) Election of U.S. Presidents Trump and Biden;
e) Release of the Department of Justice White Paper on U.S. drone policy;
f) Rise of white nationalism/supremacy in the U.S.;
g) Decrease in Islamic extremism attacks;
h) Impact of social media;
i) Evolution of technology use by terrorists;

Attention will also be paid to crossover terrorism—the 2013 Boston Marathon attack, which killed 3 and injured over 260, is a prime example—reflecting a melding of training in one country and acting in a second country. In that sense, this third edition reflects a transition from the primary focus on international-based terrorism in the first two editions to a more broad-based, multilevel terrorism reflecting the blurring of distinct lines. An early indication of the hazy distinction between domestic and international terrorism was the 2004 Madrid train bombing, in which al Qaeda detonated 10 bombs in 4 trains, killing 191 people and injuring more than 1,800. This attack took place just three days before Spain's general elections, causing major political consequences.

Examining actual terrorist attacks over time and geography contributes to a better understanding of operational measures, government policy, and judicial holdings. By focusing on those three disparate elements, the reader will gain a deeper understanding of counterterrorism enhanced by the comparative analysis of the surveyed nations. That said, the treatment of the seven countries will not be "equal," as more emphasis will be placed on certain nations. A particular important event, such as the Madrid train bombing, may serve as the focal point when examining a particular country. While there is an ebb and flow to how nations understand terrorist threats, regardless of whether the threats are domestic, international, or "crossover," the source of restraint—if any—is the nation's judiciary. That is why it is important to pay particular attention to judicial oversight-review-intervention of the executive branch. For example, in the more than 20 years since the attacks in New York City and Washington, D.C. on September 11, 2001, the U.S. Congress has largely been relegated to a non-player, filling the role of active cheerleader or cautious critic. Neither of these roles puts the legislator in a position to engage with the executive branch and both reflect passivity, whether rooted in deference to the executive branch, or from a concern of being accused of preventing aggressive measures in the name of national security. Under both circumstances, the executive need not be concerned with aggressive legislative oversight.

That is the case whether the President is a Democrat or a Republican, and regardless of whether the majority party is in the Senate and/or House of Representatives. That same model applies in the other nations surveyed, raising important questions regarding the degree to which restraints are imposed on the executive branch. For the democratic nations surveyed in this book, the degree of restraints is particularly relevant to how counterterrorism is conducted. In contrast, national leaders not beholden to democratic norms and limits have freer rein in how they conduct operational counterterrorism. Whether that is more effective, short- or long-term, is an open question that will be considered in this book.

The challenges decision makers face in addressing terrorism—whether proactive or reactive—have been magnified in recent years by the power, reach, and speed of social media. In years past, decision makers were able to control the narrative more effectively. That apparent advantage, sometimes used with great effect, has given way to a new reality that poses significant challenges to efforts to galvanize public opinion. In the 1960s, America tuned into Walter Cronkite (CBS News) or the Huntley–Brinkley Report (NBC); later, the country tuned into cable television (CNN). That model has since been replaced by social media, which has had a direct impact on how counterterrorism is conducted because the battle over the narrative is far more complex, sophisticated, and challenging than in previous years. When Cronkite would end his evening broadcast with the iconic, "and that's the way it is,"[1] America nodded its collective head. Cronkite's knowledgeable reassurance

1. Witnify, *Walter Cronkite on His Famous Sign Off "That's the Way It Is"*, YouTube, March 5, 2022, *available at* https://www.youtube.com/watch?v=E1oiywM09h4 (last visited February 15, 2024).

has given way to a full-on battle in which non-state actors are no less adept than state actors in asserting their message, information, misinformation, and disinformation.

Additionally, social media has become a primary mechanism for terrorist organizations recruiting new members from beyond what would otherwise be considered areas of immediate reach; one noteworthy example is ISIS's success in recruiting so-called "ISIS brides." Another example is the wide usage by ISIS of beheadings conducted by "Jihadi John."[2]

Certain core concepts are integral to any discussion of terrorism/counterterrorism, whether the focus is domestic, international, or a hybrid. These core concepts, regardless of the nation-state's form of government, focus on the extent to which state power can be utilized against a threat, whether perceived or actual. The oft-repeated assumption that terrorism can be defeated reflects a significant misunderstanding of terrorists, terrorism, and state power. Terrorist organizations can absorb significant firepower without being dissuaded from their missions. This is a reality that national leaders have confronted over the years, despite operational successes such as the killing of Osama bin Laden by SEAL Team 6.

Terrorism is a conflict between a nation-state and a non-state actor. This is distinct from traditional war between nation-states, which are largely regulated by the laws of war, international treaties and conventions, and accepted prosecutorial channels. In terrorism, unlike traditional war, there is no "white flag" of surrender. The notion of "winners/losers" is alien to terrorism-counterterrorism, predicated on either the next attack or preventing the next attack. Unlike war, there is no final battle followed by a victory parade. National leaders hoping for a photo image reflecting operational success are often disappointed; President Obama's White House address in front of cameras and microphones in the immediate aftermath of the bin Laden killing is an outlier, as is the widely-disseminated picture of Obama, members of his cabinet, and others closely watching a TV monitor as SEAL Team Six approached bin Laden. While the political considerations were understandable, a more measured-strategic approach suggests that effective counterterrorism avoids the public glare, notwithstanding clamor for "something to be done" in the aftermath of an attack.

As we shall come to see, terrorism-counterterrorism is complex, complicated, and perhaps murky. In many ways, there are more unknowns than knowns, and more questions than answers. To best understand terrorism and counterterrorism, this book will focus on the following:

a) Defining key concepts and terms, such as terrorism, counterterrorism, threats, self-defense, and "legitimate targets";

b) The relationship between strategic and tactical dilemmas when countering terrorism;

2. Dominic Casciani, *Islamic State: Profile of Mohammed Emwazi aka 'Jihadi John'*, BBC News, November 13, 2015, *available at* https://www.bbc.com/news/uk-31641569 (last visited February 15, 2024).

c) The extent of self-defense;
d) Defining international law concepts, particularly proportionality, military necessity, alternatives, and collateral damage;
e) Balancing legitimate national security considerations with equally legitimate individual rights;
f) The cost of not responding to terrorist attacks;
g) The limits of operational counterterrorism;
h) The means, and limits, of intelligence gathering and interrogation methods;
i) Motivations for terrorism;
j) Judicial review;
k) Executive decision-making;
l) The role of the media (including social media);
m) The limits of power;
n) Which judicial regime is appropriate for bringing terrorists to trial;
o) The status and rights of suspected terrorists

Chapters are divided by subject matter with each of the surveyed nations' approach to that issue presented as a basis for discussion. In addition, "Issues to Consider" are presented throughout the chapters to stimulate debate and discussion. Unlike other areas of the law, the legal and policy aspects of counterterrorism are often amorphous. While this book seeks to address complex counterterrorism issues, many of the questions presented do not have easy answers. That is the reality of counterterrorism.

I. BACKGROUND

What is effective counterterrorism? Lawyers provide the legal justification for a wide variety of counterterrorism measures; sociologists explain the origins of terrorism in the context of human misery, ethno-nationalism, and religion; political scientists explain trends and developments related to terrorism in the field of government; and philosophers and psychologists discuss the existential motives for terrorism. However, none of these disciplines alone can explain the cause of terrorism or how to combat it effectively. Accordingly, a multitrack approach to the study of terrorism is most effective.

The study of counterterrorism from a comparative and interdisciplinary perspective requires consideration of geopolitical forces. That, in turn, requires an appreciation for different, if not competing, definitions of effectiveness; an understanding of the limits of power; recognition of the attraction of religion, hatred, and ideology; respect for the determination and dedication of the individual terrorist; and an appreciation of historical, political, and social forces. Understanding terrorism requires both a reading of history and a sophisticated analysis of current events, particularly when examining differing ideas and motivations that might exist beyond the world of accepted norms. Furthermore, various tools can be used to attempt to understand terrorism, including simulations, role-playing, and war games.

Successful counterterrorism strategy incorporates all four pillars referenced above. While the pillars can be studied separately, decision makers must successfully integrate them. Otherwise, operational decisions will neither be predicated on the rule of law nor subjected to a rigorous cost-benefit analysis regarding their effectiveness. Similarly, counterterrorism requires intelligence gathering and analysis of information received; together, these two are the backbone of operational decisions. Ultimately, operational counterterrorism is dependent on correct analysis of intelligence gathered from single or multiple sources. However, even when operational counterterrorism decisions are based on reliable, corroborated intelligence, success is not guaranteed.

Addressing counterterrorism from a global perspective, this book is comparative both in structure and purpose. A word about "comparative" is in order: successful policy for one nation is not necessarily effective for another. However, by examining how different nations respond to similar dilemmas, decision makers can adopt measures relevant to their paradigm. Comparativism can be applied to all four pillars of counterterrorism; that integrated approach is at this book's core.

No one nation has the answer to counterterrorism, as evidenced by the inability of any country to eradicate terrorism. In analyzing different national policies, either to proactively prevent terrorism or reactively respond to it, the book analyzes decisions from a legal and policy perspective alike. The two are intertwined and cannot be considered separately. Furthermore, counterterrorism must be viewed through the lens of practicality. Unlike other areas of the law predicated on abstract theoretical analysis, counterterrorism does not lend itself to such an approach. Effective counterterrorism strategy requires operationally viable policy and considerations rooted in the rule of law.

II. DEFINING TERRORISM

One of the greatest challenges in studying terrorism and counterterrorism is a lack of clear, concise universal definitions. Even different government agencies within the United States have varying definitions of terrorism. Consider, for example, the definitions used by the Department of State, Federal Bureau of Investigation (FBI), and Department of Defense.

The Department of State definition is based on 22 U.S.C. §2656f(d), which states:

> (1) the term "international terrorism" means terrorism involving citizens or the territory of more than 1 country;
>
> (2) the term "terrorism" means premeditated, politically motivated violence perpetrated against noncombatant targets by subnational groups or clandestine agents;
>
> (3) the term "terrorist group" means any group practicing, or which has significant subgroups which practice, international terrorism[.][3]

---

3. 22 U.S.C. §2656f(d)(1)–(3).

The FBI takes its definitions of domestic and international terrorism from 18 U.S.C. §2331(5) and §2331(1), respectively:

> [T]he term "domestic terrorism" means activities that—
>
> (A) involve acts dangerous to human life that are a violation of the criminal laws of the United States or of any State;
> (B) appear to be intended--
> (i) to intimidate or coerce a civilian population;
> (ii) to influence the policy of a government by intimidation or coercion; or
> (iii) to affect the conduct of a government by mass destruction, assassination, or kidnapping; and
> (C) occur primarily within the territorial jurisdiction of the United States[.]
>
> [T]he term "international terrorism" means activities that—
>
> (A) involve violent acts or acts dangerous to human life that are a violation of the criminal laws of the United States or of any State, or that would be a criminal violation if committed within the jurisdiction of the United States or of any State;
> (B) appear to be intended—
> (i) to intimidate or coerce a civilian population;
> (ii) to influence the policy of a government by intimidation or coercion; or
> (iii) to affect the conduct of a government by mass destruction, assassination, or kidnapping; and
> (C) occur primarily outside the territorial jurisdiction of the United States, or transcend national boundaries in terms of the means by which they are accomplished, the persons they appear intended to intimidate or coerce, or the locale in which their perpetrators operate or seek asylum[.][4]

The Department of Defense defines terrorism as the "unlawful use of violence or threat of violence, often motivated by religious, political, or other ideological beliefs, to instill fear and coerce governments or societies in pursuit of goals that are usually political."[5]

While these definitions have obvious and easily recognizable similarities, the *essence* of each definition is different. As noted by Simonsen and Spindlove, the State Department looks to motives, the FBI emphasizes methods, and the Department of Defense focuses on the objectives or goals.[6] Therefore, from the perspective of the United States, one might argue that these three elements are fundamental to the definition of terrorism.

Limiting the definition to its necessary elements, however, fails to include the broader elements of terrorism. In their classic book on the subject, *Political Terrorism,* Schmid and Jongman surveyed international scholars and received 109 definitions of terrorism (today, more than 260 definitions have been

---

4. 18 U.S.C. §2331.
5. DOD Dictionary of Military and Associated Terms (January 2020).
6. C.E. Simonsen & J.R. Spindlove, *Terrorism Today: The Past, the Players, the Future* (2000).

created).[7] Similar to Simonsen and Spindlove's analysis, Schmid and Jongman's analysis identified 22 elements common to the 109 definitions.[8] These elements included violence and force, terrorism's clandestine nature, its arbitrariness, and the terrorist's intent to use civilians as victims.

Ultimately, Schmid and Jongman proposed the following comprehensive definition:

> Terrorism is an anxiety-inspiring method of repeated violent action, employed by (semi-clandestine) individual, group, or state actors, for idiosyncratic, criminal, or political reasons, whereby—in contrast to assassination—the direct targets of violence are not the main targets. The immediate human victims of violence are generally chosen randomly (targets of opportunity) or selectively (representative symbolic targets) from a target population and serve as message generators. Threat- and violence-based communication processes between terrorist (organization), (imperiled) victims, and main target (audience(s)), turning it into a target of terror, a target of demands, or a target of attention, depending on whether intimidation, coercion, or propaganda is primarily sought.[9]

While the rigor of such a definition is impressive, it remains unwieldy, complex, and potentially unworkable. To include as many elements as possible, it may have rendered itself overly inclusive. But, definitions that fail to consider elements such as terrorism's political nature, its intent to target civilians, and the use of threats and intimidation may be seen as under-inclusive. For this reason, the most effective definitions of terrorism are often direct and straightforward. Scholars have noted definitions put forth separately by Bruce Hoffman and Walter Laqueur that emphasize using "illegitimate force to achieve political ends by targeting innocent people." Determining what is "illegitimate," what a "political end" might include, and whether someone is "innocent" provides numerous opportunities for academic and popular debate without suggesting resolution of the question. As the frequently expressed idea goes, one man's terrorist is another man's freedom fighter.[10]

Indeed, the debate over an appropriate definition of terrorism also requires consideration of another issue: who is doing the talking? As Schmid recognized, distinct arenas speak differently about terrorism. That is, the definition of terrorism potentially changes depending upon whether an academic, a government, or the media is leading the discussion.[11] Academics need a definition to support rigorous research and its conclusions, the state employs

---

7. Alex P. Schmid & Albert J. Jongman, *Political Terrorism: A New Guide to Actors, Authors, Concepts, Data Bases, Theories and Literature,* 5-6 (1988).

8. *Id.*

9. *Id.* at 28.

10. *See* Thomas R. O'Connor, "The Criminology of Terrorism: History, Law, Definitions, Typologies," (2014). This is a lecture from Professor O'Connor at North Carolina Wesleyan College, where he is the Program Manager of C.J. and Homeland Security. He is also the Director at Institute for Global Security Studies, Austin Peay State University Ctr. at Ft. Campell.

11. Alex Schmid, *The Response Problem as a Definitional Problem,* 4 Terrorism and Political Violence, 1992, 7-25.

another definition to serve its goals of promulgating laws and advancing strategy (domestic and foreign), and the media uses yet another to provide easily digestible information to the general public.

To navigate these differing motives, scholars such as Jonathan White forgo creating definitions and instead rely on making distinctions between various conflicts found in society.[12] White attempts to place terrorism in a continuum somewhere between low-level "folkway violations" and all encompassing "mass destruction." His efforts rely on identifying and distinguishing sometimes similar and overlapping concepts, such as "riot," "terrorism," and "guerilla war." While effective, such an analysis still begs the question: what defines each of the concepts that are employed, and what distinguishes them?

Yet another school of thought suggests that any internationally agreed upon definition of terrorism hampers counterterrorism operations, and therefore the discussion is superfluous. However, to ensure lawful counterterrorism, terrorism must be defined. For the purposes of this book, "terrorism" shall be defined as:

> Acts of violence intended to advance a cause—political, social, religious, or economic—aimed at innocent civilians defined as legitimate targets with the intent to cause physical harm, including death, and/or conducting psychological warfare against a population aimed at intimidating it from conducting its daily life in a normal fashion.

This definition captures the essence of terrorism without becoming over- or under-inclusive. When reviewing both scholarship and terrorists' writings, the overwhelming impression is that causing harm (physical or psychological) to the innocent civilian population is the core characteristic of terrorist action. Harming civilians is the most effective manner for terrorists to achieve their goals. Accordingly, it is the centerpiece of this book's definition.

While causing death or injury to the innocent civilian population is the "means to the end," intimidation of the population is of equal importance from the terrorist's perspective. Whether resulting in death, injury, or property damage, the attack itself is successful if it results in intimidation. The importance of understanding how terrorism impacts daily life cannot—and should not—be underestimated. Terrorism is endemic. It must be understood in the context of daily attacks in addition to one-time, dramatic attacks (e.g., 9/11). Smaller, more frequent attacks have a much greater long-term effect on an innocent civilian population than does a one-time major event whose undeniable short-term effect may not linger. Therefore, the book's proposed definition emphasizes the effect on the *daily life* of an innocent civilian population and the commensurate requirement imposed on the state to respond to the continuous, constant threats that are the reality of modern-day terrorism.

---

12. *See* Jonathan White, *Terrorism and Homeland Security* (2006).

III. THE TERRORIST

In many cases, the terrorist views himself or herself as making a significant contribution to a cause—be it Palestinian nationalism, profound hatred of the West, the desire to create an independent Kashmir, white supremacy in the U.S., establishing a free Chechnya, etc. The "cause" is at the heart of the terrorist's actions; the requisite follow-up query is how far the individual terrorist will go in support of this cause. After all, not everyone is willing to be a suicide bomber, take innocent civilian hostage in a Moscow opera house,[13] turn planes into guided missiles, or attack tourists in Mumbai over the course of several days.[14]

Herein lies the fundamental question: is the cause enough, or does another intangible exist that leads terrorists to deliberately and consciously endanger themselves and others?

Issues to Consider

1. Who becomes a terrorist?
2. How do terrorists define their aims/goals/mission?
3. What does success mean for the terrorists, the public, legislators, politicians, and the military?
4. Are terrorists calculated or spontaneous?
5. Do terrorists adhere to a code of conduct including self-imposed limits?
6. How is terrorism distinguished from other forms of violence?

IV. TYPES OF TERRORISM

Understanding terrorism requires appreciating distinct categories of terrorism and terrorists. Policy and decision makers make a critical mistake lumping terrorists into one catchall category. It is important to recognize different categories and to develop policies intended to address specific groups rather than rely on a generalized response. While particularized responses do not guarantee success, they represent the most effective approaches to lawful, and effective, operational counterterrorism.

A. ETHNO-NATIONALIST TERRORISTS

Ethno-nationalist terrorist organizations are dedicated to the establishment of an independent state, based on a specific ethnic, religious, and/or national

13. Artem Krechetnikov, *Moscow Theatre Siege: Questions Remain Unanswered*, BBC, October 24, 2012, *available at* https://www.bbc.com/news/world-europe-20067384 (last visited February 15, 2024).

14. *Mumbai Terror Attacks Fast Facts*, CNN, November 11, 2022, *available at* https://www.cnn.com/2013/09/18/world/asia/mumbai-terror-attacks/index.html (last visited February 15, 2024).

identity. Ethno-nationalist terrorists may be disfavored ethnic groups or dominant ethnic groups using nationalism to enforce their legitimacy (e.g., Adolf Hitler).[15] Ethno-nationalist terrorism is defined as seeking to achieve a limited goal, specific to a particular geographic region. In certain cases, ethno-nationalism is strongly influenced by religion. The decision to restrict the geographical range of terrorist acts is predicated on a number of factors, including limited operational capability, financial constraints, and ideological considerations.

In subsequent chapters, we will examine two ethno-nationalist, religious terrorist organizations: Hamas and the Chechen rebels. Hamas seeks to establish a Palestinian state based on Islam and nationalism in the Gaza Strip, the West Bank, and Israeli territory.[16] Chechen rebels seek to create an independent Chechen state, free of Russian control. To quote Charles De Gaulle, "patriotism is when love of your own people comes first; nationalism, when hate for people other than your own comes first." The promotion of "us" vs. "them" ideology by nationalist leaders can lead to violence.[17]

B. RELIGIOUS EXTREMISM

1. Al Qaeda

Global terrorists are a second category of terrorists. These groups conduct terrorist attacks on an international scale rather than limiting themselves to a specific geographic location. However, similar to ethno-nationalist terrorists whose specific goal is the creation of an independent state, global terrorists unite around specific goals. Al Qaeda, both before 9/11 and afterwards,[18] is clearly relevant to this category as it practices terrorism on a global scale. The organization seeks to ensure destruction of its enemy, defined both as Western society and its Arab supporters (primary targets include Egypt, Jordan, and Saudi Arabia), on whom it has openly declared war predicated on religious doctrine. The goals bin Laden articulated when creating the organization have survived his killing by SEAL Team 6.

Osama bin Laden, in his fatwa, wrote:

> The ruling to kill the Americans and their allies—civilians and military—is an individual duty for every Muslim who can do it in any country in which it is possible to do it, in order to liberate the al-Aqsa Mosque and the holy mosque (Mecca) from their grip, and in order for their armies to move out of the lands of Islam, defeated and unable to threaten any Muslims. This is

15. Seung-Whan Choi, *Leader Nationalism, Ethnic Identity, and Terrorist Violence*, 52 British J. Pol. Sci. 1151, 2022, https://www.cambridge.org/core/services/aop-cambridge-core/content/view/69709AC18950A90D044E8CE73C44555F/S0007123421000144a.pdf/leader-nationalism-ethnic-identity-and-terrorist-violence.pdf (last visited February 15, 2024).

16. Israel Proper pre-1967 boundaries.

17. *Id.*

18. For a listing of al Qaeda attacks after 9/11, *see* Timeline: al-Qaeda, BBC, August 7, 2008, *available at* http://news.bbc.co.uk/2/hi/7546355.stm (last visited December 22, 2023).

> in accordance with the words of Almighty Allah, and "fight the pagans all together as they fight you all together" and "fight them until there is no more tumult or oppression, and there prevail justice and faith in Allah."[19]

Al Qaeda is not a nationalist movement with aspirations of self-determination; rather, the organization's stated aspiration is to bring about the destruction of those identified either as the infidel or its supporters. According to scholars and observers alike, al Qaeda's ultimate objective is to replace secular Arab regimes with Sharia-based Islamic states.

It is instructive to quote from the "Minimanual" of the Brazilian revolutionary Carlos Marigella because it sheds light on bin Laden's similar design to create a new social order.

> The urban guerilla is not afraid of dismantling and destroying the present Brazilian economic, political, and social system, for his aim is to help the rural guerilla and to collaborate in the creation of a totally new and revolutionary social and political structure, with the armed people in power.[20]

Bin Laden's declaration of war against all things American ultimately required an attack on the scale of 9/11. Anything less would have been inadequate. The totality of al Qaeda's approach regarding the United States is evident in a missive drafted by Ramzi bin al-Shibh, who participated in planning 9/11:

> Concerning the operations of the blessed Tuesday (9/11) . . . they are legally legitimate, because they are committed against a country at war with us, and the people in that country are combatants. Someone might say that it is the innocent, the elderly, the women, and the children who are victims, so how can these operations be legitimate according to *sharia*? And we say that the sanctity of women, children, and the elderly is not absolute. There are special cases . . . Muslims may respond in kind if infidels have targeted women and children and elderly Muslims, (or if) they are being invaded, (or if) the non-combatants are helping with the fight, whether in action, word, or any other type of assistance, (or if they) need to attack with heavy weapons, which do not differentiate between combatants and non-combatants. . . . In killing Americans who are ordinarily off limits, Muslims should not exceed four million non-combatants, or render more than ten million of them homeless. We should avoid this, to make sure the penalty (that we are inflicting) is no more than reciprocal.[21]

Terrorism may be both discriminate and indiscriminate. In the case of political assassination, it is discriminate; killers of leaders have identified person-specific targets. By contrast, bin Laden's global terrorism is indiscriminate; the physical target is the West and secular Arab regimes, but the identity and ethnicity of actual victims is irrelevant. According to bin Laden's worldview,

---

19. For a complete transcript of bin Laden's fatwa, *see* International Institute of Counter-terrorism, https://ict.org.il/the-saudi-fatwah-against-suicide-terrorism/ (last visited December 22, 2023); *see generally* Walter Laqueur ed., *Voices of Terror: Manifestos, Writings and Manuals of Al Qaeda, Hamas, and Other Terrorists from Around the World and Throughout the Ages* (2004).

20. *See* Laqueur, *supra* note 19.

21. Alan Cullison, *Inside Al Qaeda's Hard Drive,* The Atlantic Monthly, September 2004.

Muslims killed on 9/11 were sympathizers, or even collaborators, with the Great Satan (the United States), and their deaths, therefore, are not regrettable.

The globalization of terrorism requires vast resources and a commitment to conducting the campaign widely. It also requires a unifying factor. For al Qaeda, the unifying factor is religion. Religious-based terrorism divides the world into easily recognizable factions: believers and non-believers. According to bin Laden:

> We—with Allah's help—call on every Muslim who believes in Allah and wishes to be rewarded to comply with Allah's order to kill the Americans and plunder their money wherever and whenever they find it. We also call on Muslim ulema, leaders, youths, and soldiers to launch the raid on Satan's U.S. troops and the devil's supporters allying with them, and to displace those who are behind them so that they may learn a lesson.[22]

Religious-based terrorism espouses limitless, indiscriminate violence based on theological doctrine. By addressing issues such as redemption, martyrdom, and salvation, religious-based terrorism appeals to a wider audience than secular terrorism does. Violence stemming from these beliefs is legitimized by reference to religious scripture and by approval of religious leaders. The core of religious terrorism is extremist interpretations of religious texts, predicated on religious absolutism.

Appreciating the influence of religious absolutism is essential to understanding the link between global terrorism and "homegrown" terrorist groups influenced by the teachings of al Qaeda but not operating in concert with the organization. It is important to note that the bombing of the Madrid train station (March 2004) was the handiwork of "homegrown" Islamic terrorism. This stands in contrast to 9/11 and the attempted Christmas Day bombing of Northwest Flight 253 (Detroit),[23] both executed by individuals specifically brought to the United States for their respective missions. The London train bombing (July 2005),[24] the attempted blowing up of commercial airlines from the U.K. to the U.S. (August 2006),[25] the Fort Hood massacre (November 2009),[26] and the attempted Times Square bombing (May 2010)[27] follow the Madrid pattern, rather than 9/11 and Detroit.

---

22. *See* Laqueur, *supra* note 19; Al-Qaeda Messaging/Attacks Timeline, Intel Center, Tempest Publishing, LLC, (2008).

23. *Umar Farouk Abdulmutallab Sentenced to Life in Prison for Attempted Bombing of Flight 253 on Christmas Day 2009*, U.S. Dept. of Justice, February 16, 2012, *available at* https://www.justice.gov/opa/pr/umar-farouk-abdulmutallab-sentenced-life-prison-attempted-bombing-flight-253-christmas-day (last visited February 15, 2024).

24. *London Bombings of 2005*, Britannica, Britannica.org, (last visited December 22, 2023).

25. Aki Peritz, *How the U.S., U.K., and Pakistan Teamed Up to Stop Another 9/11*, Politico, January 2, 2022, *available at* https://www.politico.com/news/magazine/2022/01/02/liquid-bomber-plot-counterterrorism-international-cooperation-526246 (last visited February 15, 2024).

26. Deborah Tedford, *Fort Hood Suspect Charged with 13 Counts of Murder*, NPR, November 12, 2009, *available at* https://www.npr.org/2009/11/12/120352222/fort-hood-suspect-charged-with-13-counts-of-murder (last visited February 15, 2024).

27. *Faisal Shahzad Indicted for Attempted Car Bombing in Times Square*, U.S. Dept. of Justice, June 17, 2010, *available at* https://www.justice.gov/opa/pr/faisal-shahzad-indicted-attempted-car-bombing-times-square (last visited February 15, 2024).

These incidents emphasize an important development in terrorism: the rise in what can be most accurately described as "bin Laden and his progeny,"[28] demonstrating the localization of terrorism *predicated* on themes of commonality, particularly religious extremism. From a geopolitical perspective, the distinction is enormous; a previously external-only threat has become internal. Though some homegrown actors lack the necessary skills to carry out successful attacks, al Qaeda "franchises" have survived bin Laden's death and still maintain power throughout various countries.

The list of attacks carried out by al Qaeda and its progeny over the years is proof of a commitment to a sustained ideology: Riyadh, November 1995; Khobhar Towers, June 1996; Tanzanina and Kenya, August 1998; *U.S.S. Cole,* October 2000; 9/11, September 2001; Bali, October 2002;[29] Madrid, March 2004; London, June 2005; Mumbai, November 2008.

All these attacks, regardless of where they occurred, targeted Western society or its supporters. This indicates what Ajami labels a desire to create a "radical order free from foreign entanglements"[30] with the clear aim (in the case of the attacks in Saudi Arabia) of driving the United States from Saudi Arabia; in essence, as Ajami suggests, this is xenophobia of a murderous kind dressed up in religious garb.[31]

2. The Islamic State

The Islamic State of Iraq and Syria (ISIS) seeks war of attrition with the West in the Middle East using local conflicts and sectarian tensions.[32] ISIS, descended from al Qaeda, differs in that its primary goal is capturing and directly governing territories. In 2014, ISIS established a caliphate—a government under a chief Muslim ruler—following its strict interpretations of Islam; however, the reign was short-lived as the self-declared caliphate was defeated in 2019. Though ISIS claims to defend Sunni communities, its army has brutalized its own Sunni communities and massacred Yazidis, Shiites, and other minority groups they viewed as apostates.[33]

As ISIS has focused its attacks on ridding the Middle East of any Western influence, it has maintained a large presence in Africa and Central and South Asia. Cultural cleansing, sexual violence, and military attacks have caused political crises, mass casualties, and international intervention.

---

28. *See al Qaeda,* https://www.cia.gov/the-world-factbook/references/terrorist-organizations/ (list of terrorist organizations including al Qaeda affiliated groups around the world).

29. One of the fundamental differences between al Qaeda and ethno-nationalist terrorism is scale; bin Laden's self-perception is of an international actor, whereas the Hamas or Chechen focus is on local goals. An example of the global scale of al Qaeda's terrorism is the bombing of a Bali disco frequented by Australians. The location itself held no political value. Perhaps more than any other terrorist attack, Bali illustrates the internationalization of al Qaeda's modus operandi.

30. Fouad Ajami, *The Sentry's Solitude,* Foreign Affairs, Nov./Dec. 2001.

31. Fouad Ajami, *The Sentry's Solitude,* Foreign Affairs, Nov./Dec. 2001.

32. Robin Wright, et al., *The Jihadi Threat: ISIS, al-Qaeda, and Beyond,* 2016, *available at* https://www.usip.org/publications/2016/12/jihadi-threat-isis-al-qaeda-and-beyond (last visited February 15, 2024).

33. *Id*

In addition to carrying out these numerous attacks, ISIS has also claimed credit for those which the group is believed to have inspired. ISIS will credit "a soldier of the caliphate" for an attack even if it was just carried out in the group's name. It is rare for ISIS to issue a statement with no intermediary. ISIS claims attacks through its own news outlet—Amaq News Agency—or through the Nashir Media Foundation, which is considered the official channel for ISIS.[34] Among the deadliest attacks planned by the Islamic State are the Paris attacks in November 2015, which killed 130 people and injured more than 350, and the Brussels airport bombing. In Paris a team of gunmen began coordinated attacks on popular nightspots, which cumulated in mass killing and hostage-taking at the Bataclan theatre and concert hall.[35] In March 2016, ISIS suicide bombers detonated explosives in departure terminals at the Brussels international airport killing a dozen people within seconds. An hour later, the next suicide bomber attacked the middle of a subway network serving the European Union Headquarters and associated offices. The attacks killed 32 people and injured more than 300.[36]

Other attacks credited by or connected to ISIS (but not planned by ISIS) have included a truck plowing through crowds in Berlin, December 2016; a truck attack at Westminster, March 2017; and a suicide bombing at the Ariana Grande concert in Manchester, May 2017. Many of these attacks have been "lone wolf" attacks.

3. Islamic State of Khorasan

The Islamic State of Khorasan Province (ISIS-K) emerged in 2015 as the Afghanistan affiliate of ISIS. ISIS-K was founded by disaffected Pakistani Taliban members who did not view their jihad as extreme enough. ISIS-K's goal is to "purify" the Islamic system in Afghanistan by forcing out the Afghan Taliban and implementing violent means to punish religious minorities.[37] More extreme and violent than other jihadist militant groups in Afghanistan, the group does not stop its violence at the country's borders. Enemies of ISIS-K include the U.S. and NATO forces, international agencies, and civilians, as well as other terrorist organizations like the Taliban.[38]

---

34. Greg Myre & Camila Domonoske, *What Does it Mean When ISIS Claims Responsibility for an Attack?*, NPR, May 24, 2017, 7:00 AM, *available at* https://www.npr.org/sections/thetwo-way/2017/05/24/529685951/what-does-it-mean-when-isis-claims-responsibility-for-an-attack (last visited February 15, 2024).

35. *Francois Hollande*, Encyclopedia Britannica, *available at* https://www.britannica.com/biography/Francois-Hollande (last visited May 15, 2023).

36. Hannah Bloch & Ariel Zambelich, *Brussels Attacks: What Happened, in Photos and Maps*, NPR, March 22, 2016, 5:23 PM, *available at* https://www.npr.org/2016/03/22/471423692/brussels-attacks-what-happened-in-photos-and-maps (last visited February 15, 2024).

37. Asfandyar Mir, *The ISIS-K Resurgence*, Wilson Ctr., October 8, 2021, *available at* https://www.wilsoncenter.org/article/isis-k-resurgence (last visited February 15, 2024); Azi Paybarah, *What Is the Islamic State Khorasan, a.k.a. ISIS-K?*, last updated October 2, 2021, *available at* https://www.nytimes.com/2021/08/27/world/asia/who-isis-k-afghanistan.html (last visited February 15, 2024).

38. Frank Gardner, *Afghanistan: Who Are Islamic State Khorasan Province Militants?*, BBC, October 11, 2021, *available at* https://www.bbc.com/news/world-asia-58333533 (last visited February 15, 2024).

ISIS-K is blamed for some of the most heartless attacks in recent years, including attacks on girls' schools and hospitals (including maternity wards). A suicide bombing at Kabul's international airport in August 2021, claiming the lives of more than 170 civilians and 13 U.S. soldiers, was the work of ISIS-K. Although there is a strong local focus, international threats continue, evidenced by the suicide bombing as well as detections of plots in Europe connected to ISIS-K that have been reported by the United Nations.[39]

Since the Taliban's takeover of Afghanistan, new opportunities have become possible for ISIS-K. With the former Afghan government falling to the Taliban's control, new resources have been made available to ISIS-K, furthering the organization's capabilities. There is a possibility for violence to increase as an attempt by ISIS-K to distinguish itself as more militant and hardline than the Taliban. Membership tactics may improve with anti-Taliban Afghans and newly released or escaped ISIS-K prisoners who may now rejoin the group.

4. Lehava

Israel's far-right Jewish supremacist organization is anti-Arab and anti-Muslim and strongly opposes personal relations between Jews and non-Jews. Lehava has incited violence against Arabs during marches and individual attacks throughout the years. During protests, the group's attacks on Arabs include shouting racist chants such as "death to Arabs" and "Muhammad is dead." Lehava has targeted churches and mixed Arab-Jewish schools and is regularly violent towards Arab men.[40]

At the Jerusalem Day flag march in May of 2022, Lehava and La Familia—another far-right organization—chanted violent anti-Arab slogans resulting in violent clashes between Jews and Arabs in multiple locations around east Jerusalem.[41] In advance of Jerusalem Day festivities, activists on the Temple Mount, where the al-Aqsa Mosque is under the protection of Israeli forces, protested the status quo—forbidding Jewish prayer at the site—by flying Israeli flags, chanting slogans, and praying. The UAE and Turkey have condemned these actions by Jewish extremists, calling on the Israeli government to take measures to preserve the Muslim holy places. Israeli politicians have also condemned the organization and have requested that Lehava be outlawed and designated as a terrorist organization.[42]

---

39. Asfandyar Mir, *supra* note 48.

40. Carrie Keller-Lynn & Judah Ari Gross, *After Extremism at March, Gantz Weights Terror Label for Far-Right La Familia, Lehava*, Times Israel, last updated May 30, 2022, 7:40 PM, *available at* https://www.timesofisrael.com/gantz-time-to-consider-terror-label-for-far-right-la-familia-lehava / (last visited February 15, 2024).

41. *Gantz: Lehava, La Familia Should Be Defined as Terrorist Organizations*, Jerusalem Post, May 30, 2022, 9:12 PM, *available at* https://www.jpost.com/breaking-news/article-708070 (last visited February 15, 2024).

42. Carrie Keller-Lynn & Judah Ari Gross, *supra* note 40.

C. SECULAR TERRORISM

1. White Supremacists

White supremacy is a complicated area to decipher because it involves both terrorist and other forms of criminal activity. White supremacists are defined as people who believe that the white race is superior to all other races and that white people should have control over people of other races. White supremacist groups have conducted numerous high-profile attacks as well as inspired individuals to participate in violence to further their cause. There is an important distinction between terrorist attacks and hate crimes or politically motivated violence. Hate crimes are defined as a prejudice motivated crime against a victim because they are a member—or perceived member—of a certain racial demographic or social group. Many acts by white supremacists amount to hate crimes and are considered criminal, while other actions surpass this level of crime and pose a greater threat to national security.

Far-right extremism has exploded over the past couple of years, with increased violence and growing support.[43] While a lot of focus has been on the U.S., white supremacist ideals have historically had a global reach. Right-wing extremists pose a significant risk in Western countries, where numerous violent attacks have occurred since World War II.[44] Extremist ideals and movements, such as the Great Replacement Theory—a conspiracy, popularized by French writer Renaud Camus in 2012, that white populations are being replaced by non-European immigrants—have continued to grow in popularity among Western populations.[45] Fears of a "white genocide" pushed by the Great Replacement Theory have been used by white supremacists to justify their violent acts against immigrants, non-Christians, and ethnic minorities, and have motivated attacks such as a mass shooting at two mosques in Christchurch, New Zealand resulting in 51 deaths; a mass shooting in a Walmart in El Paso, Texas killing 23; a mass shooting in Buffalo, New York, killing 10; a mass shooting in the Tree of Life synagogue that killed 11 in Pittsburgh, Pennsylvania; and a violent riot over the removal of a confederate statute in Charlottesville, Virginia that killed 1 and seriously injured 19.[46]

---

43. *Homeland Security Emerging Threats: Domestic Terrorism and White Supremacy*, Council Foreign Relations, December 8, 2020, *available at* https://www.cfr.org/event/homeland-security-emerging-threats-domestic-terrorism-and-white-supremacy (last visited February 15, 2024).

44. Daniel Koehler, Right-Wing Extremism and Terrorism in Europe: Current Developments and Issues for the Future, 6 J. Complex Operations 2, 2016, https://cco.ndu.edu/PRISM/PRISM-Volume-6-no-2/Article/839011/right-wing-extremism-and-terrorism-in-europe-current-developments-and-issues-fo/

45. *Great Replacement Theory*, Counter Extremism Project, *available at* https://www.counterextremism.com/content/great-replacement-theory (last visited May 15, 2023).

46. *Id.*; *European Ethno-Nationalist and White Supremacy Groups*, Counter Extremism Project, *available at* https://www.counterextremism.com/content/european-ethno-nationalist-and-white-supremacy-groups (last visited May 15, 2023); Khaleda Rahman, *'Great Replacement Theory' Has Inspired 4 Mass Shootings in Recent Years*, Newsweek, May 16, 2022, 12:23 PM, *available at* https://www.newsweek.com/great-replacement-theory-inspired-terror-attacks-recent-years-1706953 (last visited February 15, 2024).

The attack on the U.S. Capitol on January 6, 2021 included many white supremacist organizations with a strong presence throughout the U.S., including the Proud Boys, the Three Percenters, and the Oath Keepers. The Capitol riot was specifically planned to stop the counting of electoral votes for the 2020 presidential election by physically invading and threatening the safety of the politicians and staff members inside, while violent attacks on Capitol police officers occurred outside. At least seven people lost their lives in connection to the attack, with many more injured. Congress has enacted a statute defining domestic terrorism as a criminal offense imposing a danger to human life, lack of a foreign nexus, and which appears to be seeking to "influence the policy of a government by intimidation or coercion."[47] Some of the events on January 6 may be categorized as domestic terrorism under this definition; however, there is no federal criminal provision that expressly prohibits "domestic terrorism," leaving prosecutors to charge individuals under different—though related—statutes.[48]

The U.S. has not labeled many of these groups as terrorists, even when their actions fall within the federal definition of domestic terrorism. Other countries including Canada, New Zealand, and Australia have added U.S.-based ring-wing groups such as the Proud Boys and the Base to their list of terrorist organizations.[49]

2. Left-Wing Anarchists

In 2016, there were 27 attacks in the EU carried out by left-wing and anarchist terrorist groups or individuals.[50] Italy, Greece, and Spain were the EU states to experience most of these attacks. Violent protests have occurred all over Europe and in Turkey targeting governmental property and law enforcement. Left-wing extremism has also grown in popularity around the world, but in some countries, it is not as large of a concern as right-wing terrorism.[51] While many far-left segments do not believe that violence is necessary or helpful

47. Charlie Savage, *Was the Jan. 6 Attack on the Capitol an Act of 'Terrorism'?*, N.Y. Times, January 7, 2022, *available at* https://www.nytimes.com/2022/01/07/us/politics/jan-6-terrorism-explainer.html (last visited February 15, 2024).

48. Peter G. Berris et al., Cong. Rsch. Serv., Domestic Terrorism: Overview of Federal Criminal Law and Constitutional Issues 2021, https://sgp.fas.org/crs/terror/R46829.pdf.

49. Ayana Archie, *New Zealand's Government Classifieds the Proud Boys as a Terrorist Organization*, NPR, June 30, 2022, 4:32 AM, *available at* https://www.npr.org/2022/06/30/1108841462/new-zealands-government-classifies-the-proud-boys-as-a-terrorist-organization (last visited February 15, 2024); Daveed Gartenstein-Ross, *America Drops the Ball on White Supremacist Groups*, Foreign Pol'y, December 21, 2021, 4:12 AM, *available at* https://foreignpolicy.com/2021/12/21/white-supremacist-terror-groups-the-base-australia-designation/ (last visited February 15, 2024); Emma Jacobs, *Proud Boys Named 'Terrorist Entity' in Canada*, NPR, May 2, 2021, 8:00 AM, *available at* https://www.npr.org/2021/05/02/992846086/proud-boys-named-terrorist-entity-in-canada (last visited February 15, 2024).

50. Europol, *European Union Terrorism Situation and Trend Report* 4, 2017, https://www.europol.europa.eu/tesat/2017/4.LEFT-WING_AND_ANARCHIST_TERRORISM.html

51. Teun van Dongen, *We Need to Talk about Left-Wing Extremism. Or Do We?*, Int'l Ctr. for Counter-Terrorism, November 24, 2021, *available at* https://www.icct.nl/publication/we-need-talk-about-left-wing-extremism-or-do-we (last visited February 15, 2024).

in achieving political goals, there are various extremist movements such as Antifa and the New Black Panther Party.[52]

Antifa or "anti-fascist" is a decentralized network composed of far-left militants who oppose right-wing extremism. Antifa uses the method they refer to as "direct action" against right-wing extremist groups and individuals.[53] Antifa attends many protests and marches for movements they agree with, such as the Black Lives Matter protests, as well as rallies of their political enemies to counterprotest—often instigating violence.[54]

Homemade weapons, explosive devices, and vandalism are common methods used by Antifa. An attempt to bomb the U.S. Immigration and Customs Enforcement was attempted by Antifa member William Van Spronsen.[55] While assaults perpetuated by Antifa have occurred and are still a potential threat, the U.S. has not categorized Antifa as a domestic terrorist organization as the small-scale attacks pose a relatively small threat.[56]

The New Black Panther Party (NBPP), a Black power movement, was founded in 1989. The NBPP has been heavily criticized by the original Black Panther Party, with which it has no connection. The militant group engages in armed protests against police brutality, violent confrontations with white supremacist groups, and "hate marches" across the country. NBPP encourages violence against whites, Jews, and law enforcement, and believes that Black Americans should have their own nation.[57] The Nationalist Manifesto from the NBPP claims that white people have secret plans for genocide against all non-white races.[58]

The NBPP believes Black Americans should receive reparations as victims of what they describe as the "Black holocaust" of slavery and Jim Crow. The organization has taken their own measures to further their movement through voter intimidation (which brought charges by the Department of Justice) and backing politicians they deem to fit their values. The organization has even placed bounties on individuals who have killed Black victims—such as George Zimmerman, who killed Trayvon Martin.[59]

The NBPP's moral judgment is "an eye for an eye and a tooth for a tooth." The organization has spent many years protesting police brutality, which has escalated to killing police officers. Micah Johnson—a Black nationalist who

---

52. *Id.*

53. Alex Riggins, *Southern California Anti-Fascists Charged with Violently Countering pro-Trump 'Patriot March'*, L.A. Times, December 7, 2021, 7:33 PM, *available at* https://www.latimes.com/california/story/2021-12-07/southern-california-antifa-groups-charged-patriot-march (last visited February 15, 2024).

54. *Id.*

55. Seth G. Jones, *Who Are Antifa, and Are They a Threat?*, Ctr. for Strategic & Int'l Studies, June 4, 2020, *available at* https://www.csis.org/analysis/who-are-antifa-and-are-they-threat (last visited February 15, 2024).

56. *Id.*

57. *New Black Panther Party*, S. Poverty L. Ctr., *available at* https://www.splcenter.org/fighting-hate/extremist-files/group/new-black-panther-party (last visited May 15, 2023).

58. Carlos A. Cooks, *The Nationalist Manifesto*, New Black Panther Party Canada, October 28, 2009, *available at* http://newblackpantherpartycanada.blogspot.com/2009/10/nationalist-manifesto.html?m=0 (last visited February 15, 2024).

59. S. Poverty L. Ctr., *supra* note 57.

was praised and endorsed by the NBPP leader—killed five police officers in 2016 while attending a rally protesting police shootings in Dallas, Texas.[60] Many rallies that NBPP members have attended or organized themselves have resulted in multiple arrests.

D. LONE OFFENDERS

Lone offenders or "lone wolves" present interesting issues in that they are decentralized from terrorist organizations but may still be motivated by terrorist propaganda. Some may consider themselves acting for or being inspired by a terrorist organization but often have no direct connections to the organization. An example of an attack by a lone offender is the Pulse nightclub shooting which targeted LGBTQ+ individuals. In June 2016, Omar Mateen entered the LGBTQ+ nightclub and opened fire, killing 49 people and wounding 53. Mateen claimed allegiance to the Islamic State and said he was triggered by the killing of Abu Waheeb in Iraq.

As discussed above, motivation is a large factor in terrorism. But with a lone wolf, determining whether the individual is categorized as a terrorist is more complicated when the category is far less clear-cut now than in the past.[61] There is a difference between terrorizing people and being a terrorist, especially when an individual is acting alone when committing mass atrocities. School shootings are a large concern in American public-school systems, and while many individuals are killed with even more being "terrorized," should we consider the shooter a terrorist when their motive arises from bullying, mental health, or other more personal issues? Should Kyle Rittenhouse be considered a terrorist when he crossed state lines and killed protestors? Would the mass shooting at a music festival in Las Vegas, Nevada, be considered terrorism when it was planned and carried out alone by Stephen Paddock? The U.S. Office of Justice Programs categorizes lone wolf attacks as terrorism when the violent act is done on a political basis.[62] If terrorism is not as clear-cut as it used to be, does this mean the process of defining and categorizing it should be adjusted to consider other possible motives and factors?

E. DOMESTIC TERRORISM

The first two editions of this book focused primarily on terrorism that was not domestic in nature, whether international/global (e.g., Al-Qaeda) or geographically specific (albeit not originating internally, e.g., India). This third edition reflects the changing face of terrorism, suggesting the need for an increased focus on domestic extremism. The specter of domestic terrorism

60. *Id.*

61. Colin P. Clarke, *Five Trends Driving the Future of Terrorism*, Foreign Pol'y Rsch. Inst., September 2, 2022, *available at* https://www.fpri.org/article/2022/09/five-trends-driving-the-future-of-terrorism/ (last visited February 15, 2024).

62. *Lone Wolf Terrorism in America*, U.S. Dep't of Justice, February 2013, *available at* https://www.ojp.gov/ncjrs/virtual-library/abstracts/lone-wolf-terrorism-america (last visited February 15, 2024).

raises different concerns and challenges to decision makers, requiring, or at least giving pause to, the need for reprioritization of resources and priorities. There is, of course, risk in doing so.

Re-allocation can result in unintended consequences, whether in the short-term or long-term, creating—or exposing—national security vulnerabilities that can be exploited. On the other hand, as evidenced by the events of January 6, 2021, the threat posed by domestic extremism, if not terrorism, cannot be denied. While the events of January 6 took place in Washington, D.C., the date can be metaphorically understood as applying to domestic terrorism not only in the U.S. but throughout the world.

Domestic terrorism imposes acute challenges for decision makers, tasked with public safety while, simultaneously, upholding the rule of law and ensuring guaranteed rights, privileges, and protections. In many ways, countering external threats—while still challenging—is easier. The notion of a common enemy and the perception that "they" are attacking "us" creates a paradigm whereby "we" are rallying around the flag. Abraham Lincoln's words, "a house divided against itself cannot stand," is particularly apt when considering the threat posed by domestic, as compared to external, terrorism. Without minimizing the consequences of a potential attack, the threat of "a house divided" extends beyond the physical attack, for it cuts into the core of society—its norms, principles, and structure. Domestic terrorism undermines civil society and poses risks and dangers that are very different from any threat posed by an external entity.

That is not to suggest that external threats are to be dismissed or that radical measures be implemented that undermine democracy in the name of protecting it. Dismissing external threats and overstating the danger posed by domestic threats is dangerous, as is underestimating domestic threats and overstating external threats.

More than anything else, perhaps what has been learned in the aftermath of January 6 is that the domestic threat cannot be ignored. Democracies rest on the bedrock of freedom of speech and freedom of assembly. However, no state can tolerate violence that endangers state institutions, seeks to undermine democracy, and harms innocent people.

Furthermore, as the events of January 6 made clear, violence (domestic) does not happen in a vacuum; to understand what happened at the US Capitol requires acknowledging—to what degree is a matter of controversy—that speech encourages action. While the primary encourager, if not inciter, was President Donald Trump, it remains to be seen if he or any other actor will be held liable for incitement. That is distinct from indictments, prosecutions, convictions, and incarcerations for those who committed crimes inside the Capitol themselves.

Those individuals were acting, directly or indirectly, with a variety of white nationalist groups. Their primary motivation was a belief that Trump had won the 2020 election: certifying the election results whereby former Vice President Joe Biden would be recognized as the winner would be "stealing" the election from Trump. The election "deniers" motivated and encouraged (incited according to some) by Trump committed serious crimes for which they have been held accountable before a court of law. Words such as "insurrection" and "coup" have been used to describe their intentions and actions, whether they were acting in concert with a particular group or individually.

The basis for the terms is violence accompanying a refusal to accept certified election results. Their actions on January 6 left nine individuals dead, more than 300 injured, and $1.5 million in damages. The following convictions—approximately 485—resulted in home detentions and prison sentences ranging from 2 months to 18 years.

While January 6 has become the focus of much of the contemporary discussion in the U.S., this event is not the first time domestic extremism or terrorism has been part of the American landscape. The delineation between extremism and terrorism is difficult under any circumstance; examining an event/circumstance with the perspective of time and distance does not alleviate that challenge.

The expression "one man's freedom fighter is another man's terrorist" is applicable to the extremist/terrorist debate. Perhaps we can understand the terms to be interchangeable, reflecting a commitment that includes (and justifies) violence in advancing an identified goal in the name of ideology and belief.

Writing this edition—particularly the discussion regarding domestic actors—requires asking, in the name of intellectual honesty, whether U.S.-based groups such as the Ku Klux Klan, the Black Panthers, the Students for a Democratic Society (SDS), or the Weathermen meet the test of extremism and/or terrorism, or whether they "merely" challenge society, regardless of their means and goals. That same question applies to domestic groups in other countries.

Ku Klux Klan	U.S. hate group advancing white supremacy through intimidation and violence predominately aimed at Black Americans, but also attacks other people of color, Jewish people, immigrants, and the LGBTQ+ community. Active 1865-current.
Black Panther Party	African American Marxist revolutionary party created for various reasons, including protection of Black communities from police brutality, arming of all Black Americans, and exemption from the draft and from all sanctions of white America. Active 1966-1982.
Students for a Democratic Society	American student organization against the Vietnam War and the draft, which grew increasingly militant. Active 1960-1974.
Weather Underground	Split from the SDS, an anti-war militant group that sought to advance communism through a violent revolution. Active 1969-1977.
Proud Boys	U.S.-based white nationalist organization that uses violence to further far-right ideology, following the Q-Anon and the Great Replacement Theory. Active 2016-current.
Three Percenters	A sub-ideology within the larger anti-government militias, named after the belief that only 3 percent of American colonists fought against the British during the American Revolution. Active 2008-current.

Oath Keepers	Far-right American militia group that is anti-government and views themselves as defenders of the U.S. Constitution as they interpret it. The group uses intimidation, including violence, to advance their goals. Active 2009-current.
Jewish Underground	A far right-wing organization in Israel that committed violent attacks against Palestinians. Active from 1979-1984.
Q-Anon	Conspiracy theory and political movement espousing, among other beliefs, that there are satanic cannibalistic pedophiles within Hollywood and the Democratic Party, against whom former President Donald Trump has been waging a secret war. The conspiracies have led to believers committing violent crimes, including the events on January 6th in Washington, D.C. Active from 2017-current.

The intention of this third edition, in addition to continuing the focus of the first two editions, is to raise the specter of domestic-based terrorism and extremism. One form of terrorism must not be understood as replacing another form, but rather quite the opposite. Decision makers must often confront three forms of terrorism at once: domestic; international; and crossover, which reflects a combination of the first two.

An example of crossover terrorism is the Tsarnaev brothers, who were responsible for the Boston Marathon terrorist attack. The brothers were raised in the U.S., radicalized in Dagestan in the Northern Caucasian region of Russia, and trained to commit an act of terrorism in the U.S. That same model applies to second-generation Somali-Americans who traveled to Somalia, where they were radicalized and trained for the purpose of committing acts of terrorism in the U.S.

This third edition, then, reflects the changing nature of terrorism national decision makers confront. If the first two editions primarily focused on what is referred to as the post-9/11 world, then this edition suggests that additional challenges demand the attention of counterterrorism officials. The more nuanced, and perhaps more multi-layered, forms of terrorism present dilemmas more complex than single-form terrorism. Without minimizing their danger, terrorist attacks and threats emanating from a different country present less complex paradigms for the question of protecting domestic civil liberties; they are not at the forefront of the discussion. Such is not the case when the primary actors are domestic actors, whose rights are established in the Constitution and consistently upheld by courts, including the Supreme Court.

For example, notwithstanding debate regarding the applicability of Miranda rights to suspected terrorists, no U.S. court has weighed in on the possibility of denying this basic right to an American suspected of involvement in terrorism. The Supreme Court decision in *Miranda*—guaranteeing all suspects the right to silence, the right to an attorney, and access to an attorney if they cannot afford one—has been addressed by the Court in innumerable subsequent cases.

The most important exception, created by the Court in *Quarles v. New York*, created a public safety exception (unrelated to terrorism), whereby a suspect need not be "Mirandized" when there is a public safety consideration. With that one clearly articulated exception—despite the facts in the case, which did not suggest law enforcement were confronted with a public safety dilemma—there has never been a willingness by the Supreme Court to minimize the rights of suspected terrorists.

That is particularly relevant when we consider in the pages ahead how decision makers, whether in the U.S. or in any of the surveyed countries, address domestic terrorist threats as compared to international or even crossover terrorism. The challenge posed by domestic terrorism—whether January 6 in Washington, D.C, the Tree of Life synagogue in Pittsburgh, the Charlie Hebdo office in Paris, or the mosques in Christchurch, New Zealand—is that it forces the traditional domestic law enforcement model to be applied to a paradigm that suggests, implicitly or explicitly, a distinct threat to public order and safety.

V. MEASURING EFFECTIVENESS

Experts suggest terrorist organizations define effectiveness through the prism of long-term strategic considerations. Israel's disengagement from the Gaza Strip in 2005 was, according to some analysts, a result—directly or indirectly—of Palestinian terrorism.[63] This theory rests on the assumption that Prime Minister Rabin, initially, and Prime Minister Sharon, subsequently, determined that the Israeli public had wearied of constant attacks by Palestinian terrorists, and postulated that disengagement would contribute to a sharp downturn in terrorism.[64]

Similarly, the bombing of the Madrid train station directly contributed to the newly elected Spanish government's decision to withdraw from Iraq. Much to the surprise of many commentators, the government's decision did not have the expected effect of directly contributing to additional acts of terrorism. Whether or not the government would have withdrawn from Iraq regardless of the attack is a matter of speculation; what is clear is that in the aftermath of the attack, Spain withdrew. Conversely, brutal attacks by Chechen terrorists did not contribute to a change in Russian tactical counterterrorism policy largely marked by significant violations of human rights. However, Russian declaration of victory in Chechnya represents a significant strategic decision extending beyond tactical considerations.

Meanwhile the effectiveness of various attacks in India must be analyzed through multiple prisms reflecting three terrorist threats: (1) internal threats based on historical enmity involving Hindus, Muslims, and Sikhs; (2) external-internal threats resulting from Pakistan's support of Muslims in Kashmir who seek independence; and (3) external threats arising out of Pakistani-Indian relations and the fact that both nations have nuclear capability.

---

63. PM Sharon's Statement on the Day of the Implementation of the Disengagement Plan, August 15, 2005, *available at* https://www.gov.il/en/Departments/news/speech150805 (last visited February 15, 2024).

64. *Id*

To understand terrorist behavior, it is necessary to appreciate the terrorist's determination and resilience. Terrorists are willing to engage in a "war of attrition," imposing enormous hardship on the individual and his or her immediate family to achieve goals the family may or may not share; family members may be indirect victims of operational counterterrorism measures. Counterterrorism, both strategically and tactically, must be premised on recognition that self-sacrifice is inherent to terrorist behavior. Engaging in a never-ending cycle of violence is one means by which terrorist organizations signal to distinct audiences (the general public, followers, and relevant governments) their commitment to the cause. From the perspective of terrorist organizations, the results from the pressures placed on decision makers, exerted by an attacked and frightened public, justifies continued attacks on innocent civilians.

Terrorists play to their public to signal resiliency, progress, and determination. "Blowback" is the term used for terrorists' responses to government action against them. For example, if in response to the targeted killing of a terrorist leader, terrorists perform a suicide bombing, the latter attack would be "blowback." This *modus operandi* demonstrates to audiences that aggressive government action is an ineffective counterterrorism policy and that a political response to terrorist demands (though others might call this capitulation) is the preferred course.

How terrorist leaders view the effectiveness of their actions is critical; e-mails from bin Laden suggest how he defines effectiveness and highlights the dilemmas U.S. policy faces.

> If it refrains from responding to jihad operations, its prestige will collapse, thus forcing it to withdraw its troops abroad and restrict itself to U.S. internal affairs. This will transform it from a major power to a third-rate power, similar to Russia.[65]
>
> And, this simply means that Obama and his administration have instilled new seeds to increase the hatred and revenge towards America. The number of those seeds is the number of harmed and destitute people from Swat valley and the tribal regions in Northern and Southern Waziristan, and the number of their sympathizers. And, with that Obama has walked like his predecessors in increasing hostility towards Muslims . . . establishing long-term wars, so the American public must get ready to continue harvesting what is instilled by the leaders of the White House during the next years and decades.[66]
>
> O' my Islamic nation, the discussion of the weakness and decline of American hegemony and the collapse of the American economy is not based upon mere hope alone. It has been acknowledged by their senior leaders what they can no longer hide. Incoming [U.S.] Vice President Biden has stated, "The crisis is worse than we expected. The entire American economy is in danger of collapse."[67]

The effectiveness of counterterrorism must be viewed from the perspective of government and terrorist alike. Defining effectiveness is one of the most

---

65. *See* Cullison, *supra* note 21.

66. Osama bin Laden: "Speech to the Pakistani Nation", June 3, 2009, *available at* https://slate.com/news-and-politics/2010/08/the-gingrich-bin-laden-alliance.html (last visited December 30, 2023).

67. Osama bin Laden: "A Call for Jihad to Stop the Gaza Assault", June 14, 2009, *available at* https://gtrp.haverford.edu/statement/OBL20090114/ (last visited December 30, 2023).

difficult aspects of counterterrorism because it requires an analysis of strategic and tactical goals, means, capabilities, and realistic expectations. In October 2003, then U.S. Secretary of Defense Donald Rumsfeld stated that there are "no metrics enabling the government to determine if it is winning or losing the war on terrorism."[68] Perhaps the frustration expressed by Rumsfeld best articulates the nebulousness associated with counterterrorism. Terrorists may well share a similar sentiment. Did 9/11 contribute to bin Laden's final endgame? Did killing hundreds of school children in Beslan advance the struggle for Chechen independence? Did killing hundreds of Indian businessmen on a Mumbai train contribute to a particular goal?

Each new threat evokes distinct philosophies. Former Israeli Prime Minister Yitzhak Rabin described a two-track approach: "We will work for peace as if there is no terrorism; and fight terrorism as if there is no peace."[69] President Bush's declaration of "war on terror" reflected a contrasting approach to Rabin's, allowing no room for a middle ground. President Obama articulated a more nuanced approach: "Where terrorists offer only the injustice of disorder and destruction, America must demonstrate that our values and our institutions are more resilient than a hateful ideology."[70]

Issues to Consider

1. How do governments define counterterrorism effectiveness?
2. How do terrorist organizations define effectiveness?
3. What would be appropriate guidelines to determine effectiveness of operational counterterrorism?
4. What weight should be given to the rule of law in ascertaining counterterrorism policy effectiveness?
5. What should be the appropriate balance between human rights, operational considerations, and the determination of effectiveness?
6. What are effective means to counter a terrorist's willingness to commit acts in the name of a "cause"?
7. How should governments respond—proactively and reactively—to the absoluteness articulated in bin Laden's fatwa?
8. Should school shootings be considered an act of terrorism? Do the motives of the shooter meet the defined motives of terrorism?
9. What about Kyle Rittenhouse's fatal shooting of two people at a civil rights protest? Is this an act of terrorism?

---

68. *See Are We Winning in Iraq: Testimony Before the H. Comm. on Armed Serv.,* 109th Cong. (2005) (testimony of Andrew F. Krepinevich).

69. AIJAC Staff, *Issues in Renewed Israeli-Palestinian Negotiations*, December 19, 2007, *available at* https://aijac.org.au/update/issues-in-renewed-israeli-palestinian-negotiatio/ (last visited February 15, 2024).

70. Remarks by the President on National Security, May 21, 2009, *available at* https://obamawhitehouse.archives.gov/the-press-office/remarks-President-national-security-5-21-09#:~:text=We're%20investing%20in%20the,to%20the%20world's%20deadliest%20weapons (last visited December 30, 2023).

CHAPTER 2

INTERNATIONAL LAW

I. INTRODUCTION

International law is a set of agreements, sometimes called conventions, freely entered into by states to regulate relations between themselves on particular issues including extradition, trade relations, and mutual defense. In addition, international agreements can establish an organization, such as the United Nations, in which like-minded states seek to resolve issues of mutual concern.

When international law was developing over the centuries, the world was composed largely of nation-states. Non-state actors, such as al Qaeda, ISIS, Hamas, and Hezbollah were not a factor in the development of international law. Furthermore, customary international law—universally binding but not codified law, developed from the general and consistent practice of states and adhered to from a sense of legal obligation—was predicated on nation-states developing and implementing agreed-upon rules. Customary international law consists of two elements: an agreed practice of several states, and practice consistent with prevailing law. Customary international law is included in Article 38 of the statute of the International Court of Justice (ICJ), which defines what law ICJ can apply.

According to the 1868 St. Petersburg Declaration,[1] the only legitimate object states should endeavor to accomplish during war is to weaken the military force of the enemy. The declaration's limitation on the use of exploding projectiles attempted to ensure that such weapons would reduce the number of soldiers fighting the war while preventing unnecessary and prolonged injury, pain, and suffering among the combatants.

The question of whether international law applies to terrorism is often asked. It is generally framed from two perspectives: (1) the applicability of a

1. National Security Strategy, May 2010, *available at* http://www.whitehouse.gov/sites/default/files/ rss_viewer/national_security_strategy.pdf (last visited June 1, 2010).

state/non-state paradigm, rather than the state/state relationship that is the core of international law, and (2) the relevance of principles imposed on only one actor—the state—rather than on both actors (which is distinct from traditional war conducted by two states obligated to international law agreements, conventions, and accountability before international tribunals). In addressing the role of international law in counterterrorism, the working assumption—despite understandable criticism and voices suggesting otherwise—is that the nation-state conducts operational counterterrorism in accordance with the principles established in concert with international law's initial iteration. As that is the basis for the discussion ahead, our focus is on how the nation-state applies aspects of international law while developing and conducting operational counterterrorism.

Therefore, the relationship between terrorism and international law is analyzed by examining international agreements and conventions as well as the conduct of states and non-state actors, predicated on the understanding that international law directly affects policies developed by decision makers and, most importantly, decisions implemented by commanders. While several conventions and agreements regarding terrorism have been signed over the years,[2] this chapter focuses on how the U.N. Charter and Geneva Conventions affect operational counterterrorism.

II. TERRORISM CONVENTIONS

The United Nations has drafted 19 multinational conventions and protocols relevant to terrorism, addressing the roles and responsibilities of member nations, but marked by one important omission: terrorism is not defined. As noted in Chapter 1, the question of how to define terrorism has consistently beguiled decision makers, law makers, courts, military commanders, and the public. The fact that international law has, similarly, failed to agree on a uniformly acceptable definition should come as no surprise.

Of the 19 conventions and protocols, we shall focus our attention primarily on the International Convention for the Suppression of Terrorist Bombings (1997)[3] because of the centrality of bombings to contemporary terrorism. This is not to disregard other acts of terrorism, nor to minimize their impact, but rather to recognize that—other attacks notwithstanding—bombing is the preferred tactic for terrorist organizations.

Types of terror bombing include the following: dirty bombs, suicide bombings, bombs triggered by remote control from a safe distance, and vehicle bombs. Particular attention must be given to the indiscriminate killing of innocent civilians accomplished by these bombing methods. "[B]y its sheer nature, [terror bombing] depends on such 'isolated' incidents to achieve its

---

2. *United Nations Treaty Collection: Conventions on Terrorism, available at* http://untreaty.un.org/English/Terrorism.asp (last visited July 11, 2010).

3. *Nations Treaty Collection International Convention for the Suppression of Terrorist Bombings,* U.N.T.S. 2149.

goals. The fragmented nature of most terrorist organizations makes it virtually impossible for the organizations to conduct anything other than small-scale acts."[4]

Terror bombings clearly differ from other forms of terrorist attacks. Because of their indiscriminate nature, their increasingly widespread use, their ease of success, and the difficulty of identifying the perpetrator and preventing attacks, terror bombings warrant special attention.

The Convention for the Suppression of Terrorist Bombings is a United States initiative in response to the 1996 bombing of American military personnel in Saudi Arabia.[5] The convention has two important provisions: (1) it establishes universal jurisdiction over those using explosives and other devices in public places with the intent to kill, cause serious bodily injury, or cause extensive destruction of a public place; and (2) it obliges nations to extradite for prosecution persons accused of committing or aiding such offenses. The convention became effective on May 23, 2001; today, 58 nations are signatories.

Because the drafters wanted a legal framework whereby nations could prosecute those involved in bombings, the convention established universal jurisdiction over terror bombings and further sought to contribute to international cooperation in the effort to combat terror bombings. According to Professor Whitten, "it is anticipated that these additional offenses [noted in Convention Art. 2] will strengthen the ability of the international community to investigate, prosecute and extradite conspirators or those who otherwise direct or contribute to the commission of offenses defined in the Convention."[6]

Issues to Consider

1. How is the effectiveness of an international convention determined?
2. What is the significance of universal jurisdiction in the context of counterterrorism?
3. What is the significance of distinguishing terrorism from criminal activity in prosecuting individuals involved in terror bombings?
4. How has the lack of a universally accepted definition of terrorism affected prosecution?
5. Do international conventions contribute to counterterrorism?

---

4. Frank A. Biggio, *Neutralizing the Threat: Reconsidering Existing Doctrines in the Emerging War on Terrorism,* 34 Case W. Res. J. Int'l L. 1 (2002).

5. H.R. Rep. No. 107-307, at 7 (2001) ("The International Convention for the Suppression of Terrorist Bombings was conceived by the United States in the wake of the bombing attack of the U.S. military personnel in Saudi Arabia in 1996.").

6. Whitten, *The International Convention for the Suppression of Terrorist Bombings,* 92 American Journal of International Law, 1998, 774-75.

III. SELF-DEFENSE

Nation-states primarily define operational counterterrorism through the parameter of self-defense; in doing so, they "position" themselves as either responding to an attack or preventing a planned attack. For this reason, this discussion places particular emphasis on self-defense. While international law principles impose limits on the scope and application of self-defense, a question that emerges is whether decision makers should apply a broad or narrow understanding of those principles. There is a lack of across-the-board uniformity on this question because it involves various considerations, including the severity of the attack, domestic political calculations, operational capability, geopolitical concerns, history between the nation-states, and the particular terrorist organization responsible for the attack (if known). However, when these considerations are assessed, national decision makers frame their response under the umbrella of self-defense. As we will discuss in subsequent chapters, this framing applies to preemptive operational measures, including—but not limited to—targeted killing (e.g., Israel) and drone attacks (e.g., U.S.). The application of self-defense, in accordance with international law, must be predicated on proportionality, military necessity, collateral damage, and exhaustion or unavailability of peaceful alternatives.

A. U.N. CHARTER

According to Article 2(4) of the U.N. Charter, "all Members shall refrain in their international relations from the threat or use of force against the territorial integrity or political independence of any state, or in any other manner inconsistent with the Purposes of the United Nations."[7] This article expresses one of the primary tenets of international law: prevention of war between member states. That principle, however, is moderated by Article 51, which articulates the framework for self-defense. The two Articles must be considered together and in juxtaposition. While 2(4) limits the power of the nation-state, Article 51 articulates under what conditions the nation-state may act. There is a tension between the two principals—one restricting, the other creating the circumstances under which actions may be taken. How the apparent dissonance is resolved is at the core of much of the discussion surrounding nation-state decision making.

According to Article 51:

> [n]othing in the present Charter shall impair the inherent right of individual or collective self-defence if an armed attack occurs against a Member of the United Nations, until the Security Council has taken measures necessary to maintain international peace and security. Measures taken by Members in the exercise of this right of self-defence shall be immediately reported to the Security Council and shall not in any way affect the authority and responsibility of the Security Council under the present Charter to take at any time such action as it deems necessary in order to maintain or restore international peace and security.[8]

7. U.N. Charter art. 2.
8. U.N. Charter art. 51.

Determining the extent of self-defense is critical to a discussion examining the relationship between international law and counterterrorism. Unlike traditional warfare in which militaries face off with planes, tanks, and warships, counterterrorism is characterized by an unseen enemy; battles take place in "back alleys with dark shadows." Self-defense in this environment is enormously complicated. The operational decision to preemptively attack a highly elusive target and their infrastructure, often in close proximity to civilians, is based on intelligence information gleaned from sources, the veracity of which is critical to the success or failure of any counterterrorism initiative.

B. THE LIMITS OF STATE SOVEREIGNTY IN SELF-DEFENSE

In 1837, U.S. Secretary of State Daniel Webster articulated a definition of self-defense, which evolved into customary international law. Webster's definition followed what has come to be known as the *Caroline* incident. The *Caroline* was a U.S. steamboat attempting to transport supplies to Canadian insurgents. A British force interrupted the *Caroline*'s voyage, shot at it, set it on fire, and let it wash over Niagara Falls. Webster said that Britain's act did not qualify as self-defense because self-defense is only justified "if the necessity of that self-defense is instant, overwhelming, and leaving no choice of means, and no moment for deliberation." According to Webster, Britain could have dealt with the *Caroline* in a more diplomatic manner. He limited the right to self-defense to situations in which the threat is real, the response is essential and proportional, and all peaceful means of resolving the dispute have been exhausted. The concept known as the *Caroline* doctrine was considered customary international law until a competing definition of self-defense arose in Article 51 of the U.N. Charter, which authorizes self-defense only if an armed attack "occurs."[9]

When can preemptive actions be undertaken? Preemptive action requires that intelligence information meets a four-part test of reliability, credibility, time sensitivity, and corroboration. As shall be discussed in a subsequent chapter, the requirement for corroborating intelligence prior to a decision to act pre-emptively is, sometimes, aspirational rather than realistic. In such circumstances, decision makers need to decide whether an operational decision is justified based on a single source of information. Furthermore, in order to be legitimate, preemptive action must be proportionate to the attack it seeks to prevent. In determining proportionality, decision makers must take into consideration both the immediacy of the threat and its severity. There is an important distinction between two types of threats: (1) immediate and real, and (2) perceived. When examining the preemptive use of force in the face of a threat, decision makers must distinguish between the two. Acting in the face of a perceived threat may reflect an unwarranted application of self-defense, therefore violating Article 51. In addition, given the significant disparity in the operational capability of the nation-state in comparison to the non-state actor, the question of proportionality must be examined through a different

9. *Id.*

lens than in the state/state paradigm. The state/non-state paradigm requires analyzing whether the state used the force at its means proportionate to the threat, rather than whether the state used force proportionate to the state with which it is in conflict. In this sense, proportionality has become more of an internal, rather than external, analysis. The concept of proportionality, however, is not intended to forbid the state's use of force, but rather to impose limits on when—and how—force may be used against a non-state actor.

The intent of Article 51 was to limit the invocation of the right to self-defense, while providing the justification for the nation-state to act preemptively. Any limitation, however, required a discussion regarding the right to engage in anticipatory self-defense. "The United Nations, and the international community, are wary of potential abuses of the rights inherent under Article 51 and has established four standards to prevent nations from abusing those rights."[10] States need to not only defend themselves against ongoing attacks, but also to act preemptively to prevent aggressive acts from being carried out. Customary international law permits a nation-state to respond to a threat and infringe on the territorial sovereignty of another nation-state when four criteria are met: (1) the state is acting in self-defense; (2) the attack is substantial and military (i.e., not an isolated armed incident); (3) the offending nation is complicit, unwilling, or unable to prevent further attacks; and (4) the attack is widespread and imminent.[11]

Issues to Consider

1. Decision makers often are confronted with intelligence that paints a less than full picture; in determining whether to strike preemptively against an imminent attack, how is "imminent" best defined?
2. How should nation-states justify preemptive self-defense in the context of Article 51?
3. Why, and how, was the *Caroline* doctrine narrowed by the United Nations?
4. Can an isolated terrorist attack be "substantial?"

In undertaking operational counterterrorism, decision makers are increasingly faced with the following dilemma: whether an action—be it preventative or responsive—can be undertaken if it may involve violating the sovereignty of another nation-state.

In response to terror attacks in Israel, the Israel Defense Forces (IDF) continually targeted terrorist cells in Syria. Though Israel has been widely criticized, the government has explained that the target was not Syria; rather, the IDF was targeting terrorists located in Syria with no intent to violate Syrian sovereignty. This argument appears disingenuous as Syrian sovereignty was clearly violated by the penetration of Syrian airspace by the IDF.

10. *See* Biggio, *supra* note 4.
11. *Id.*

Other nations have accused the U.S. of similarly violating another nation's sovereignty in the killing of Osama bin Laden in Pakistan (a clear violation of Pakistan's sovereignty), counterterrorism operations in Africa, and the killing of Qassim Suleimani (violating Iraq's sovereignty).

Similarly, the United States violated Sudan's and Afghanistan's sovereignty when the U.S. military, in response to the 1998 al Qaeda bombing attacks on the U.S. embassies in Kenya and Tanzania, attacked terrorist targets in the two countries. The U.S. fired 79 Tomahawk missiles at alleged bin Laden outposts in Sudan and Afghanistan, including a factory believed to produce chemical weapons. While the attack may be considered to have been retaliatory rather than self-defensive in nature, the question of anticipatory self-defense is relevant: if, as had been reported, the factory was indeed producing chemical weapons, then an argument could be made that America and its allies would potentially be in danger.

President Clinton relied on a traditional understanding of self-defense under Article 51 in justifying the attack on the chemical factories, adding that the strikes "were a necessary and proportionate response to the imminent threat of further terrorist attacks against U.S. personnel and facilities."[12] Article 51 was also relied on by President Obama in 2011 and President Trump in 2020 as justification for violating another nation's sovereignty.

The American drone policy directed against targets in Afghanistan, Pakistan, and Yemen has also violated the sovereignty of the three nation-states, which are all U.S. allies. U.S. decision makers have been careful to characterize the attacks as targeted exclusively against the Taliban and al Qaeda and not Pakistan or Yemen. Nevertheless, the bombings represented a violation of national sovereignty and also directly resulted in grace collateral damage—the deaths of innocent civilians, citizens of the attacked countries. While self-defense was the justification for the policy, the violation of national sovereignty raises questions regarding both the policy's legality and effectiveness.

Issues to Consider

1. What is the significance of the phrase "if an armed attack occurs" in Article 51?
2. Does Article 51 impose obligations on states that are irrelevant in the age of terrorism?
3. What obligations would be relevant in the age of terrorism?
4. Is a preemptive strike justified if intelligence information indicates a forthcoming attack?
5. According to international law, how reliable must intelligence be for it to be deemed operational?
6. What is anticipatory self-defense, and when is it legitimate?

12. Lucy Martinez, *September 11th, Iraq, and the Doctrine of Anticipatory Self-Defense,* 72 UMKC L. Rev. 123, 143 (2003).

C. FAILED STATE

In conjunction with self-defense, international law must also consider the question of failed states providing material support to terrorism. When the United States attacked al Qaeda and the Taliban in Afghanistan following the terrorist attacks of 9/11, it was attacking a sovereign nation. An argument emerged asserting that Afghanistan was not strong enough to try to control or limit terrorists within their borders; therefore, other nations affected by the terrorist groups could take action. The United States warned the Taliban regarding the consequences of cooperating with al Qaeda. However, as the Taliban government failed to take steps against al Qaeda, the United States and its coalition partners claimed self-defense in attacking Afghanistan. The same argument—albeit problematic—has been used by U.S. decision makers to justify American attacks in Yemen and Pakistan.

It has been suggested that the attacks are occurring with compliance—tacit or direct—of the three nation-states (Afghanistan, Yemen, and Pakistan). While this argument addresses the violation of sovereignty, it begs the question of a failed state. The U.S. killing of bin Laden in Pakistan may be justified by the failed state argument, which suggests that the region is a legitimate target because the Pakistani government (or elements within the government) had either proactively facilitated his safety or turned a blind eye. In either case, the U.S.'s interpretation of self-defense justified the attacks, despite the risk of violating Pakistani sovereignty. In a further attempt to justify the attacks, some experts have espoused the theory of Pakistan as a partially failed state, which has borne minimal impact.

Israel has also made a similar argument, maintaining that targeted attacks in Syria and Lebanon do not signal attacks on either country, but rather, that Israel is attacking terrorist targets located in these countries. However, given that any number of countries—including Turkey and Iran, among others—have a presence in Syria, one could argue that Syria is, at the least, a partially failed state.[13] Lebanon may also be viewed as a failed state due to the lack of government control. In southern Lebanon, Hezbollah—a Shia Islamist political party and militant group—has de facto control over the area that borders Syria. Hezbollah, with its many political actors, also has a large control over the government, and continues to exploit the government's weaknesses.[14] This hybrid-like status that Hezbollah currently holds in controlling Lebanon allows them to maintain power without being held accountable to the state and without the threat of international sanctions on the country.[15]

13. Failed States are characterized by their inability to fulfill their social contract with their citizens and the international community.

14. Lina Khatib, *How Hezbollah Holds Sway over the Lebanese State* (2021), https://www.chathamhouse.org/sites/default/files/2021-06/2021-06-30-how-hezbollah-holds-sway-over-the-lebanese-state-khatib.pdf (last visited February 15, 2024).

15. *Id.*

Issues to Consider

1. In attacking a sovereign nation that, at best, was marginally involved in 9/11, did the U.S. significantly expand the definition of self-defense?
2. What warning must be given either to terrorists or to the state providing material support to terrorists before undertaking an attack?
3. How much support must the sovereign nation provide to terrorists in order to justify attacks such as those carried out by the U.S. in Afghanistan, Pakistan, and Yemen?
4. When is a state defined as failed? How is that determination made, and by whom?
5. What are the rights of the failed state?

IV. CIVILIAN COMBATANT

In the aftermath of the horrors of World War II, the Geneva Conventions were drafted. The Conventions directly address the protection of the civilian population by clearly defining the rights and obligations of both combatants and civilians.

According to Article 43 of the First Protocol Additional to the Geneva Conventions, "members of the armed forces of a Party to a conflict are combatants," suggesting they have the right to participate directly in hostilities.[16] Article 44 stipulates:

> 1. Any combatant, as defined in Article 43, who falls into the power of an adverse Party shall be a prisoner of war.
>
> 2. While all combatants are obliged to comply with the rules of international law applicable in armed conflict, violations of these rules shall not deprive a combatant of his right to be a combatant or, if he falls into the power of an adverse Party, of his right to be a prisoner of war, except as provided in paragraphs 3 and 4.
>
> 3. In order to promote the protection of the civilian population from the effects of hostilities, combatants are obliged to distinguish themselves from the civilian population while they are engaged in an attack or in a military operation preparatory to an attack. Recognizing, however, that there are situations in armed conflicts where, owing to the nature of the hostilities an armed combatant cannot so distinguish himself, he shall retain his status as a combatant, provided that, in such situations, he carries his arms openly:
>
> a. During each military engagement, and
>
> b. During such time as he is visible to the adversary while he is engaged in a military deployment preceding the launching of an attack in which he is to participate.

16. Protocol Additional to the Geneva Conventions of 12 August 1949, and relating to the Protection of Victims of International Armed Conflicts (Protocol 1), 1125 U.N.T.S 135 [*hereinafter* Protocol 1].

> 4. A combatant who falls into the power of an adverse Party while failing to meet the requirements set forth in the second sentence of paragraph 3 shall forfeit his right to be a prisoner of war, but he shall, nevertheless, be given protections equivalent in all respects to those accorded to prisoners of war by the Third Convention and by this Protocol. This protection includes protections equivalent to those accorded to prisoners of war by the Third Convention in the case where such a person is tried and punished for any offences he has committed.[17]

Counterterrorism conducted by civil democratic society is necessarily predicated on principles outlined in the Geneva Conventions. To that end, one of the most important principles established by the Geneva Conventions is the requirement to distinguish between combatants and non-combatants.[18]

Unlike in traditional warfare, which pits army against army, military commanders confront terrorists who dress and look like civilians. The responsibility to distinguish between combatants and non-combatants remains a critical principle of international law that commanders are obligated to honor. These obligations are codified in the Geneva Convention Protocols, sometimes referred to as the "laws of war." The foremost principle is the following: "when in doubt whether person is a civilian, that person shall be considered to be a civilian."[19] An additional principle commanders are required to honor is protection of the civilian population:

> In order to ensure respect for and protection of the civilian population and civilian objects, the Parties to the conflict shall at all times distinguish between the civilian population and combatants and between civilian objects and military objectives and accordingly shall direct their operations only against military objectives.[20]

The obligation to protect non-combatants consists of the following: (1) the civilian population shall not be the target of attacks; (2) civilians shall enjoy protections unless they take part in attacks; (3) indiscriminate attacks on a civilian population are prohibited; (4) attacks shall be limited to military targets; (5) cultural objects shall be protected; (6) objects indispensable to a population's survival shall be protected; and (7) the natural environment shall be protected. According to the 4th Hague Convention, the right to use weapons is not unlimited; weapons that cause unnecessary suffering are prohibited.

Furthermore, the following international law principles must guide commanders in their operational decision making: (1) collateral damage should be minimized; (2) the action to be taken must meet the test of military necessity; (3) the damage—whether loss of life or damage to property—should be proportional to the threat posed by the individual whom the state intends to attack; and (4) all reasonable alternatives must be considered prior to the undertaking of a military operation.

---

17. *Id.*
18. *Id.* art. 48.
19. *Id.* art. 50.
20. *Id.* art. 48.

V. OBLIGATIONS OF STATES

According to international law, non-state actors (combatants, not innocent civilians) have neither rights nor obligations. However, states are obligated to act in accordance with international law even if other parties to the conflict do not. Does international law provide a category under which non-state actors may be held accountable for their actions? As discussed earlier, when international law was developed, the dominant institution was the nation-state; accordingly, no provisions were made for the non-state actor.

A. GENEVA CONVENTIONS

Although the Geneva Conventions obligate the state to distinguish between combatants and civilians, the lines are blurred when the combatant is not wearing a uniform, does not carry a weapon openly, and has no identifying insignia. While a chain of command in a terrorist infrastructure arguably exists, that is the sole condition of a lawful combatant that terrorism meets. According to Article 28 of the Fourth Geneva Convention, human shielding—defined as the deliberate placement of civilians in or around targets to deter an enemy; willful endangerment of an innocent civilian by a combatant by hiding behind them—is unlawful. Nevertheless, terrorist organizations use innocent civilians as human shields for a number of reasons, primarily to protect themselves, with the underlying assumption that states will not attack them if there is a possibility that innocent civilians will be killed as a result. In that vein, the Israeli High Court of Justice ruled in *Adalah — The Legal Center for Arab Minority Rights in Israel v. GOC Central Command, IDF*[21] that commanders may not use Palestinians as human shields. Although the IDF attempted to sidestep this requirement using alternatives, the Court was adamant: human shielding is a violation of international law and therefore forbidden.

Nevertheless, terrorist organizations, not beholden to law, act in direct contravention of this article of the Geneva Conventions, and often use innocent civilians, particularly children, as human shields.[22] Since terrorist organizations are not subject to international sanctions, should nation-states apply similar principles when responding to threatening non-state actors? This question suggests a fundamental weakness in international law since terrorist organizations assume immunity regarding their actions.

B. HUMAN RIGHTS LAW

Human rights are the nation-state's obligations to the individuals within the nation-state's jurisdiction. The Universal Declaration of Human Rights provided the first framework for protecting human rights—though the declaration is not legally binding. While human rights are still recognized in

21. HCJ 3799/02, Adalah—The Legal Center for Arab Minority Rights in Israel v. GOC Central Command, IDF [2005] (Isr.).

22. Chris Bury, *Battle of Jenin: The Search for Truth,* ABC News, Apr. 30, 2002.

international law, nation-states differ on what constitutes a human right. There are, however, generally agreed upon rights such as the prohibition of torture or cruel, inhuman or degrading treatment or punishment, prohibition of slavery and the slave trade, prohibition of arbitrary arrest, detention or exile, and freedom from discrimination. Some human rights have been deemed so important and fundamental that these rights have risen to the level of a peremptory norm—fundamental principles of international law from which no derogation is permitted.

Differing from the Geneva Conventions and other international laws and treaties which regulate nation-states only during times of conflict, human rights law also applies during times of peace. However, there are exceptions for when human rights may be derogated from, which include reasons for national security and public emergency, though some rights—that are viewed as a peremptory norm—are never justified in derogation.

Terrorists are not obligated to protect human rights—like other international laws and customs. Terrorist organizations often violate individual rights in an attempt to further their cause or as a result of collateral damage. Although terrorists pose a major threat to a state's national security, the state is obligated to protect individual rights. The protection of these rights may further restrict the abilities and effectiveness of a state's operatives as a result. While there is a strong moral obligation for states to uphold human rights of all individuals—including the rights of terrorists—the enforcement of legal obligations proves to be difficult and often unavailable or overlooked.

Issues to Consider

1. Is the United Nations the appropriate forum for resolving violations of international law by non-state actors?
2. What sanctions can be imposed on terrorists?
3. What is the role of states that either provide haven or support to terrorists?
4. Should international law be adapted to reflect attacks by terrorists and their violations of international law?
5. Should the restriction regarding human shielding be waived to enable states to more effectively conduct counterterrorism?
6. Do states have an obligation to protect individual or human rights in other states?
7. Does counterterrorism justify a stronger limitation on terrorists' rights compared to non-combatants?
8. What rights may the nation-state restrict in the name of national security?

VI. IMPACT OF 9/11

In the immediate aftermath of 9/11, the United Nations Security Council passed Resolutions 1368 and 1373, intended, in part, to redefine the limits of self-defense.[23] Resolution 1368 specifically recognized the "inherent right of individual or collective self-defence," articulating determination to "combat by all means threats to international peace and security caused by terrorist acts."[24]

> Resolution 1373 requires all states to take steps to combat terrorism; it creates uniform obligations for all 191 member states to the United Nations, thus going beyond the existing international counterterrorism conventions and protocols binding only those that have become parties to them. This is an unprecedented step for the Security Council to take. The Council has taken provisions from a variety of international legal instruments that do not yet have universal support, such as the Terrorism Financing Convention, and incorporated them into a resolution that is binding on all UN member states. Some mistakenly think Resolution 1373 is directed mainly at terrorist financing. It does address this crucial area, but it also requires or urges other steps by states against terrorists, their organizations, and supporters—for example, to update laws and to bring terrorists to justice, improve border security and control traffic in arms, cooperate and exchange information with other states concerning terrorists, and provide judicial assistance to other states in criminal proceedings related to terrorism. More generally, it requires all member states to review their domestic laws and practices to ensure that terrorists cannot finance themselves or find safe havens for their adherents or their operations on these states' territory.[25]

In the post-9/11 world, nations such as the United States have encouraged a broader reading of international law to justify a policy of aggression either following an attack or in an attempt to thwart a suspected threat. The broad latitude sought by the U.S. was used by the Bush administration to justify attacking Iraq and Afghanistan and used by the Obama administration for aggressive implementation of the drone policy in Afghanistan, Pakistan, and Yemen. To that end, self-defense as expressed in Article 51 of the UN Charter and the inherent limitations placed on states under Article 2(4) have been clearly challenged by the U.S.'s post-9/11 actions.

Issues to Consider

1. Has an expanded interpretation of self-defense served the policy interests of the United States?
2. What have been the legal or policy considerations of nations who have not adopted a similar approach?
3. Does U.S. policy suggest that international law is irrelevant?
4. What flexibility does international law allow for?
5. What safeguards, if any, does international law provide for in the face of such a broad re-interpretation of basic principles?
6. How expansively can self-defense be defined?

---

23. S.C. Res. 1368, U.N. SCOR, 56th Sess., 4370th mtg., U.N. Doc. S/RES/1368 (2001); S.C. Res. 1373, U.N. SCOR, 56th Sess., 4385th mtg., U.N. Doc. S/RES/1373 (2001).

24. S.C. Res. 1368, U.N. SCOR, 56th Sess., 4370th mtg., U.N. Doc. S/RES/1368 (2001).

25. Eric Rosand, *Security Council Resolution 1373, the Counter-Terrorism Committee, and the Fight Against Terrorism,* 97 A.J.I. L. 333, 334 (April 2003).

VII. CONCLUSION

U.N. resolution 1373 and other terror-related agreements and conventions address a variety of counterterrorism issues. The failure of the international community to develop an agreed-upon definition of terrorism is but one symptom of a larger issue that directly affects how the world both prevents and responds to terrorism. For international law to impact how nations conduct counterterrorism efforts while protecting innocent civilians, traditional principles must be modified to reflect the new reality.

Collateral damage is an inevitable byproduct of counterterrorism;[26] the principle of the Geneva Conventions that collateral damage be held to a minimum is conceivably an impractical obligation when terrorists surround themselves with innocent civilians. As will be discussed in forthcoming chapters, targeting specific individuals suspected of involvement in acts of terrorism inevitably results in loss of innocent life. It is a reasonable assumption that targeting individuals will continue; similarly, one of the predictable results is continued loss of innocent lives.

Distinct from traditional warfare, which implies large armies engaged in mutual attack and counterattack with infantry, planes, and warships, sophisticated counterterrorism is far more target-specific and localized. Military commanders and decision makers must determine what risks and costs are acceptable according to both domestic and international law.

26. *See* Amos N. Guiora & Martha Minow, *Guess Who's Coming to Dinner?*, Boston Globe, January 21, 2006.

CHAPTER 3

BALANCING NATIONAL SECURITY AND INDIVIDUAL RIGHTS

I. INTRODUCTION

Balancing legitimate national security rights and equally legitimate individual civil and political rights is the most significant issue faced by liberal democratic nations developing a counterterrorism strategy. Without balancing these two needs, democratic societies lose the very ethos for which they fight. As Benjamin Franklin once said, "Those who would give up essential liberty, to purchase a little temporary safety, deserve neither liberty nor safety."[1] While it is imperative for democracies to avoid infringing on political freedoms and civil liberties, a government's ultimate responsibility is protecting its citizens.

How—and whether—each of the following seven surveyed nations balances these competing interests is the focus of the chapter. To that extent, how—and whether—each struggles with the self-imposed restraints that inherently limit their response to terrorism is examined. Regimes that act with impunity and disregard norms are distinguishable from nations that internalize the reality of limits of state power. In that vein, the discussion that follows considers responses to major terror attacks in each of the reviewed countries, illustrating how—and whether—national security and individual rights are balanced. In the United States, both the Bush and Obama administrations struggled to play catch-up. The treatment of undocumented immigrants in the United States demonstrates the tenuous balance between national security and individual rights. Israel's balancing efforts are analyzed by examining the implementation of its house-demolition policy. Both Russia and China have action-oriented policies, responding to attacks with an instantaneous narrowing of individual rights intended to protect national security. India's balancing is analyzed by examining legislative actions favoring national security over

1. Benjamin Franklin, *Pennsylvania Assembly: Reply to the Governor, Nov. 11, 1755, in* The Papers of Benjamin Franklin 242 (Leonard W. Labaree ed., 1963).

individual civil rights in the wake of terrorist attacks. Spain's balancing efforts are examined by addressing the issue of incommunicado detention, whereby individual rights are minimized for a limited time in the interest of national security. Colombia has chosen to favor national security, providing little protection for individual rights, and focusing almost exclusively on eliminating the terrorist threat.

Issues to Consider

1. How far should democracies go with self-imposed restraints in the context of counterterrorism?
2. What price are democracies willing to pay for freedom? How much should they be willing to pay?
3. Does surrendering liberty guarantee security?
4. Should nations adopt special/emergency legislation in response to terrorism?
5. Should the government be able to monitor conversations of federally incarcerated persons if there is a reasonable suspicion that the communication might further terrorism?
6. Are there other circumstances in which the government would want to listen in on conversations of those in federal prison?
7. How do we distinguish between actions and thoughts?
8. When are nations allowed to impinge upon certain liberties, including, for example, the right to contribute to a charity of one's choice?

II. UNITED STATES

A. HISTORICAL DISCRIMINATION AND ETHNIC PROFILING

Though the United States is a nation of immigrants, many of whom having traveled far and wide to reach America's shores and achieve the American dream, U.S. history is replete with examples of their mistreatment. Until the mid-1800s, employment ads and "help wanted" signs in many cities included notations saying, "No Irish Need Apply," and several states refused to allow Jewish immigrants to vote. Mistreatment of immigrants extended beyond private actions; the U.S. government implemented policies that limited immigrants' rights. In the Palmer Raids following World War I, suspected radicals were rounded up, held without bail, and often deported without trial.[2] These "radicals" were often Eastern European Jews; the raids resulted in the deportation of more than 3,000 immigrants.[3] During World War I, the government imprisoned dissidents for "merely speaking out against the war"; most of those imprisoned were immigrants.[4] In the immediate aftermath of Pearl Harbor,

2. Haynes Johnson, *The Age of Anxiety: McCarthyism to Terrorism* 107-10 (2005).
3. Laura K. Donohue, *Terrorist Speech and the Future of Free Expression,* 27 Cardozo L. Rev. 233, 245 (2005).
4. David Cole & James X. Dempsey, *Terrorism and the Constitution* 150 (2002).

more than 120,000 Japanese Americans were interned in camps solely because of their ancestry. Individual determinations of national security threats were not made prior to internment.[5]

Over the years, the Supreme Court has ruled on several issues related to immigrants. In *Yick Wo v. Hopkins,* the Supreme Court held that discrimination based on race and nationality was illegal and "all persons within the jurisdiction of the United States shall have the same right in every State and Territory . . . to the full and equal benefit of all laws and proceedings for the security of persons and property as is enjoyed by white citizens."[6] However, within 60 years, the Supreme Court allowed these very rights to be taken away. In *Korematsu v. United States,* the Supreme Court upheld President Roosevelt's decision to place innocent American citizens of Japanese ancestry in internment camps following the Japanese attack on Pearl Harbor.[7] While those responsible for 9/11 were not from the United States, not all people of international origin living in the United States were involved in planning and executing the attack.

Furthermore, not all immigrants supported the attack; immediately after the attacks, many immigrant groups, including the American-Arab Anti-Discrimination Committee, publicly expressed their outrage.[8] Yet, the United States continues to use ethnic profiling to identify national security risks while infringing on the rights of innocent individuals.

Recent examples of ethnic profiling include President Trump's Muslim and refugee ban[9] signed into order on January 27, 2017. This executive order banned people from seven Muslim-majority countries from entering the U.S.—including refugees fleeing war, among other hardships—to prevent terrorism. The discriminatory order was upheld by the U.S. Supreme Court in the case *Trump v. Hawaii,* which found that the Immigration and Nationality Act granted this power to the President.[10]

> Whenever the President finds that the entry of any aliens or of any class of aliens into the United States would be detrimental to the interests of the United States, he may by proclamation, and for such period as he shall deem necessary, suspend the entry of all aliens or any class of aliens as immigrants or nonimmigrants or impose on the entry of aliens any restrictions he may deem to be appropriate.

---

5. *Id.*
6. Yick Wo v. Hopkins, 118 U.S. 356, 369 (1882).
7. Korematsu v. U.S., 323 U.S. 214, 65 S. Ct. 193 (1944). The number of people interned ranges from 110,000 to 120,000. *See* http://www.sfmuseum.org/war/evactxt.html. Executive Order 9066 requiring the internment of Americans of Japanese heritage was signed on February 19, 1942. The Order was rescinded by President Franklin D. Roosevelt in 1944 and by the end of 1945 the last internment camp was closed. *Available at* http://www.infoplease.com/spot/internment1.html (last visited February 15, 2024).
8. ADC Press Release, *ADC Joins Fellow Americans in Remembering 9/11 Attacks, Mourning Victims,* March 11, 2002, *available at* http://www.adc.org/index.php?id=147&no_cache=1&sword_list[ ]=9%2F11 (last visited February 15, 2024).
9. Executive Order 13769, titled Protecting the Nation from Foreign Terrorist Entry into the United States, was labeled the "Muslim ban" or the "Trump travel ban" by those criticizing the Order.
10. 8 U.S.C. §1182(f); *Trump v. Hawaii,* 585 U.S. 667, 684-685 (2018).

> By its terms, §1182(f) exudes deference to the President in every clause. It entrusts the President the decisions whether and when to suspend entry ("[w]henver [he] finds that the entry" of aliens "would be detrimental" to the national interest); whose entry to suspend ("all aliens or any class of aliens"); for how long ("for such period as he shall deem necessary"); and on what conditions ("any restrictions he may deem to be appropriate"). It is therefore unsurprising that we have previously observed that §1182(f) vests the President with "ample power" to impose entry restrictions in addition to those elsewhere enumerated in the INA. . . .
>
> The Proclamation falls well within this comprehensive delegation. The sole prerequisite set forth in §1182(f) is that the President "find[]" that the entry of the covered aliens "would be detrimental to the interests of the United States."[11]

Amnesty International UK called this unfortunate decision by the Supreme Court "essentially a license to discriminate, disguised as a 'national security measure,'" stating that it was "cruel, inhumane, and violated international law."[12] While the Trump administration viewed this as a victory for them, the Court's decision sparked protests around the country.

B. ETHNIC PROFILING

In the weeks after 9/11, Gallup polls showed almost 60 percent of Americans favored "requiring people of Arab descent to undergo special, more intensive security checks when flying on American planes," and approximately 50 percent said that "they should have to carry special identification cards with them at all times."[13]

> Before September 11, about 80 percent of the American public considered racial profiling wrong. State legislatures, local police departments, and the President had all ordered data collection on the racial patterns of stops and searches. The U.S. Customs Service, sued for racial profiling, had instituted measures to counter racial and ethnic profiling at the borders. And a federal law on racial profiling seemed likely.
>
> After September 11, however, polls reported that 60 percent of the American public favored ethnic profiling, at least as long as it was directed at Arabs and Muslims. The fact that the perpetrators of the September 11 attack were all Arab men, and that the attack appears to have been orchestrated by al Qaeda, led many to believe that it is only common sense to pay closer attention to Arab-looking men boarding airplanes and elsewhere. And the high stakes—there is reason to believe that we will be subjected to further terrorist attacks—make the case for engaging in profiling stronger here than in routine drug interdiction stops on highways. . . .
>
> Press accounts made clear that whether as a matter of official policy or not, law enforcement officials were paying closer attention to those who appear to

---

11. *Trump v. Hawaii*, 128 S.Ct. 2392, 2408 (2018).

12. *A Licence to Discriminate: Trump's Muslim & Refugee Ban*, Amnesty Int'l U.K., October 6, 2020, 6:12 AM, *available at* https://www.amnesty.org.uk/licence-discriminate-trumps-muslim-refugee-ban (last visited February 15, 2024).

13. Maia Davis, *A Painful Reminder for Japanese-Americans*, The Record (Bergen County, NJ), Sept. 20, 2001, at A15.

be Arabs and Muslims. And in November, the Justice Department announced its intention to interview 5,000 young immigrant men, based solely on their age, immigrant status, and the country from which they came.[14]

Historically, racial profiling has not worked, regardless of whether its purpose has been fighting crime or countering terrorism. Professor David Harris argues that when race or ethnic appearance is used in law enforcement, the accuracy of catching criminals actually decreases.[15] In the late 1990s, the New York City police department initiated a "stop and frisk" campaign whereby police would regularly stop people on the street in order to confiscate illegal weapons and reduce crime. Minority communities felt they were unfairly targeted, a belief that turned out to be correct.[16] Only after Amadou Diallo, an unarmed West African immigrant, was killed during such a stop was it demonstrated, according to a study ordered by New York Attorney General Eliot Spitzer, that minorities were unfairly targeted.[17]

However, the federal government did not learn from New York City's experience; in November 2001, Attorney General Ashcroft announced that the FBI and other law enforcement agencies would interview more than 5,000 men, mostly from the Middle East, all in the United States on temporary visas.[18] Of the 5,000 individuals initially sought for interviews, only about half could be located.[19] Additionally, interviews that the FBI was able to conduct revealed very little information.[20] In fact, this tactic has been greatly criticized by former FBI agents, claiming that it is ineffective and "guts the values of our society."[21]

The ultimate question is whether such a policy, however negatively it may impact a particular population group, contributes to national security. If the policy lacks a balanced approach, then it is, in all probability, ineffective, decidedly problematic, and potentially unconstitutional.

According to David Cole:

> The government has detained over 1200 persons in connection with its investigation of the attacks of September 11, yet as of late December only one had been charged with any involvement in the crimes under investigation, and the government claims that only ten or twelve of the detained are members of al Qaeda, the organization said to be responsible for the attacks. The vast majority are being held on routine immigration charges under unprecedented secrecy. The government will not disclose most of their names, their trials are held in secret, and their cases are not listed on any public docket.
>
> At the same time, ethnic profiling is being broadly engaged in, and widely defended as reasonable. Already, we fear, the government has overreacted in a time of fear, assuming powers in the name of fighting terrorism that are in

14. *See* Cole & Dempsey, *supra* note 4, at 168.
15. David Harris, *Profiles in Injustice: Why Racial Profiling Cannot Work* (2002).
16. *Id.*
17. *Id.*
18. Jena Heath, *Bush Defends Anti-Terror Fight, Military Courts,* Atlanta J. & Const., Nov. 30, 2001, at A17.
19. Michael Ratner, *Making Us Less Free: War on Terrorism or War on Liberty?,* (2003).
20. *Id.*
21. Jim McGee, *Ex-FBI Officials Criticize Tactics on Terrorism,* Wash. Post, Nov. 28, 2001, at A1.

> no way limited to counterterrorist investigations. It has not shown that the new powers it has asserted are necessary to fight terrorism. And it has targeted the lion's share of its infringements on liberty at immigrants, and particularly Arab and Muslim immigrants.[22]

Racial profiling implies guilt by association, a concept abhorrent to American democratic values that raises profound constitutional questions and reflects an imbalance between national security considerations and personal rights. Guilt by association suggests that mere membership in a particular religious, ethnic, or social group is sufficient to determine guilt. The Supreme Court, on several occasions, has expressly stated the unconstitutionality of guilt by association.[23] In *NAACP v. Claiborne Hardware Co.*, the Court held that the First Amendment "restricts the ability of the State to impose liability on an individual solely because of his association with another."[24] The Court wrote that to "punish association with such a group, there must be 'clear proof that a defendant specifically intends to accomplish the aims of the organization by resort to violence.'"[25]

However, the Supreme Court has upheld the convictions of individuals for membership in a group that advocates overthrowing the U.S. government by force or violence.[26] For membership to be illegal, the Court held that the membership must be knowing, active, and purposive as to the organization's criminal ends.[27]

During Barack Obama's presidency, he was roundly criticized for much of his rhetoric regarding terrorism. Criticism was particularly acute in his refusal to articulate the phrase "Islamic terrorism" when speaking about terrorists who have self-proclaimed Islamic religious motives.[28] This avoidance of "Islamic terrorism," which seemingly seeks to mitigate racial, ethnic, and religious profiling of Muslim men who commit acts of terrorism, fails to reflect the reality of religiously motivated violence. This was particularly highlighted in December 2009 when Umar Farouk Abdulmutallab—known as the underwear or Christmas Day bomber—attempted to detonate explosives while on board a Northwest Airlines flight from Amsterdam to Detroit, Michigan.[29] The bomb, which failed to detonate, started a small fire before Abdulmutallab was tackled by other passengers, thereby saving 290 lives. Al Qaeda organized the attack which they believed to be a "martyrdom mission."[30] The Justice Department maintains that "the racial profiling guidance recognizes that race and

22. *See* Cole & Dempsey, *supra* note 4, at 149.

23. *See, e.g.,* NAACP v. Claiborne Hardware Co., 458 U.S. 886, 932 (1982); United States v. Robel, 389 U.S. 258, 265 (1967); Keyishaian v. Board of Regents, 385 U.S. 589, 686 (1967).

24. *Claiborne,* at 918-19.

25. *Id.* at 919 (*citing* Scales v. United States, 367 U.S. 203, 229 (1961) and Noto v. United States, 367 U.S. 290, 299 (1961)).

26. Scales v. United States, 367 U.S. 203, 205-06 (1961).

27. *Id.* at 227.

28. Daniella Diaz, *Obama: Why I Won't Say 'Islamic Terrorism'*, CNN, last updated Sept. 29, 2016, 4:49 PM, *available at* https://www.cnn.com/2016/09/28/politics/obama-radical-islamic-terrorism-cnn-town-hall (last visited February 15, 2024).

29. Scott Shane, *Inside Al Qaeda's Plot to Blow Up an American Airline*, N.Y. Times, February 22, 2017, *available at* https://www.nytimes.com/2017/02/22/us/politics/anwar-awlaki-underwear-bomber-abdulmutallab.html (last visited February 15, 2024).

30. *Id.*

ethnicity may be used in terrorist identification, but only to the extent permitted by the nation's laws and the Constitution."[31]

Issues to Consider

1. Is racial profiling constitutional?
2. What are the dangers inherent to such a policy?
3. Does this policy reflect a failure to internalize the lessons suggested by *Korematsu?*
4. Does the policy of profiling and detaining suspects, as described by Cole and Dempsey, guarantee Americans' safety?
5. Has profiling prevented acts of terrorism?
6. Does this policy reflect American values and the democratic ethos?
7. Is this a balanced policy?

C. DETENTION vs. DUE PROCESS

The Foreign Intelligence Surveillance Act of 1978 (FISA) establishes judicial and congressional oversight of foreign intelligence surveillance activities while maintaining necessary secrecy for national security threats.[32] FISA provides authorization for electronic surveillance, use of pen registers and trap and trace devices, physical searches, and business records for the purpose of gathering foreign intelligence. Most relevant to this chapter are the FISA warrants. The Department of Justice must first obtain a warrant for an authorized electronic surveillance of foreign agents. The DOJ must provide demonstrative evidence that the "target of the surveillance is a foreign power or agent of a foreign power" and that "a significant purpose" of the surveillance is to obtain "foreign intelligence information."[33] FISA defines agents of foreign powers as "agents of foreign political organizations and groups engaged in international terrorism, as well as agents of foreign nations."[34] Court hearings to obtain FISA warrants are sealed and closed to the public. The Court in 2021 granted 431 warrants while denying only 4 applications in full.[35]

Requirements for the warrant are heightened when the targets are U.S. persons. The Act provides an exception to the court order required, stating that:

> The President may authorize electronic surveillance to acquire foreign intelligence information for periods of up to one year without FISC court order where the Attorney General certifies that there is "no substantial likelihood

---

31. Fact Sheet Racial Profiling, Dep't of Justice, June 17, 2003 (on file with author).
32. *The Foreign Intelligence Surveillance Act of 1978 (FISA)*, U.S. Dep't of Justice, *available at* https://bja.ojp.gov/program/it/privacy-civil-liberties/authorities/statutes/1286 (last visited May 15, 2023).
33. *Id.*
34. *Id.*
35. Roslynn R. Mauskopf, Report of the Director of the Administrative Office of the U.S. Courts on Activities of the foreign Intelligence Surveillance Courts for 2021 (2022), *available at* https://www.uscourts.gov/sites/default/files/fisc_annual_report_2021_0.pdf (last visited February 15, 2024).

> that the surveillance will acquire the contents of any communication to which a U.S. person is a party," provided the surveillance is directed solely at communications among or between foreign powers, or "the acquisition of technical intelligence . . . from property or premises under the open and exclusive control of a foreign power."[36]

The PATRIOT Act is relevant to this chapter, for immigrants' rights are directly affected by its provisions. Professor Cole argues the following:

> The PATRIOT Act gives the Attorney General unprecedented power to lock up any immigrant that he certifies as a "suspected terrorist." Such persons are subject to potentially indefinite detention. While "suspected terrorists" may sound like a class that should be locked up, there are several problems with this measure. It applies to "suspected" terrorists, not "proved" terrorists. It allows the Attorney General to lock up individuals where he has "reasonable grounds to believe" that they have committed any of a wide range of immigration violations, without a hearing to determine whether they actually pose any real threat. And the legislation defines "terrorist activity" so expansively that it includes virtually every immigrant who is suspected of being involved in a barroom brawl or domestic dispute, as well as aliens who have never committed an act of violence in their lives, and whose only "crime" is to have provided humanitarian aid to an organization disfavored by the government. The law further provides that such persons may be detained indefinitely, even if they are "granted relief from removal," and therefore have a legal right to remain here permanently. . . . [W]hat the new legislation adds is the authority to detain aliens who do not pose a current danger or flight risk, and who are not removable because they are entitled to asylum or some other form of relief. This provision raises several constitutional concerns.[37]

In the days following 9/11, many Muslim men were detained by the Immigration and Naturalization Service (INS) for a number of reasons, including possible violations of immigration laws, suspicion of terrorist activity, preexisting federal criminal charges, or for use as material witnesses. The Court of Appeals for the D.C. Circuit held that the government had a right to keep information about the detainees' names secret; subsequently, the Supreme Court refused to take the case on appeal.[38] Nevertheless, complaints were lodged that visitors to the United States were locked up for months in cells lit 24 hours a day simply because their visas had expired.

In the aftermath of 9/11, the Bush Administration seemed to implement a policy of guilt by association. The detention of thousands of immigrants and the decision to interview thousands of others amounted to a rounding up of people deemed to be the usual suspects—Muslim men.

The Obama administration struggled with the same dilemma. The PATRIOT Act allows the Department of Homeland Security to detain and deport immigrants based on an immigrant's support—including money, food,

---

36. U.S. Dep't of Justice, *supra*, note 32; 50 U.S.C. §1802.

37. *See* Cole & Dempsey, *supra* note 4, at 156.

38. Center for National Security v. U.S. Dept. of Justice, 331 F. 3d 918 (D.C. Cir. 2003), *cert. denied*, 124 S. Ct. 1041 (2004).

transportation, or supplies—of an organization defined by the United States as a terrorist organization. But what if someone desires to support the peaceful objectives of such an organization which are distinct from its more violent aims? This question was argued before the Supreme Court in *Holder v. Humanitarian Law Project.* Several plaintiffs challenged a federal statute that inhibited their ability to support two international groups the United States had designated as terrorist organizations: the Kurdistan Workers' Party in Turkey, and the Liberation Tigers of Tamil Eelam in Sri Lanka.[39] These groups sought independent Kurdish and Tamil states in their respective countries.[40] In its decision, the Supreme Court ruled that the government may block speech and other forms of advocacy that support groups officially labeled as terrorist organizations, even if the support is aimed at the terrorist groups' peaceful or humanitarian activities.[41] Therefore, an immigrant is assumed to be a national security risk even if the support was given to further the organization's nonviolent objectives.

In 2013, Edward Snowden leaked highly classified information from the National Security Agency (NSA). Snowden exposed privacy abuses by government intelligence agencies in data collection from cellphones, laptops, social media, chatrooms, and other sources. The biggest concern that Snowden raised with the quantities of data gathered is that a person does not have to be a suspected terrorist for their personal data to be analyzed by the NSA.[42] The NSA justifies its actions as a necessity to prevent another 9/11 when the chances of finding a real terror threat in the data collected are the same as finding a needle in the haystack.[43] The PATRIOT Act's power has only grown with the changes in technology and surveillance. While many of the laws the government has enacted are in publicly available records, the laws have been controversial.

The "second PATRIOT Act" was signed into law in 2015 by President Obama. This Act specifically included the text of the Cybersecurity Information Sharing Act (CISA) permitting private companies to directly share information with federal agencies, including the NSA.[44] The Act removed the previous requirements for information sharing when there are "imminent threats" to create "a voluntary cybersecurity information sharing process that will encourage public and private sector entities to share cyberthreat information, without legal barriers and the threat of unfounded litigation—while protecting private information."[45] The USA FREEDOM Reauthorization Act of 2020 broadens the criteria for when a FISA Court decision is classified and

39. 561 U.S. 1, 9-10 (2010)

40. *Id.* at 9.

41. *Id.* at 36-39.

42. Ewen Macaskill & Gabriel Dance, *NSA Files Decoded: Edward Snowden's Surveillance Revelations Explained*, Guardian, November 1, 2013, *available at* https://www.theguardian.com/world/interactive/2013/nov/01/snowden-nsa-files-surveillance-revelations-decoded#section/1 (last visited February 15, 2024).

43. *Id.*

44. Everett Rosenfeld, *The Controversial 'Surveillance' Act Obama Just Signed*, CNBC, last updated December 22, 2015, 2:50 PM, *available at* https://www.cnbc.com/2015/12/22/the-controversial-surveillance-act-obama-just-signed.html (last visited February 15, 2024).

45. *Id.*

when declassification review is to be issued.[46] The bill had bipartisan support until President Trump announced via Twitter that he would veto the bill, most likely because it would expand the Justice Department's power to investigate political candidates.[47] Privacy activists fought tirelessly against the bill, because the amendments would allow warrantless collection of internet search and web browsing data. While privacy advocates won when the bill was scrapped, government surveillance legislation is still a major concern, due to the history of abuses by the U.S. government.[48]

An effective counterterrorism strategy must be based on sophisticated risk assessment; an approach that views all threats as equal is both operationally unfeasible and ineffective. Mass detention predicated on association with a particular group, rather than on an individualized basis, does not better protect the public. Because of this, the policy adopted by the Bush administration in the aftermath of 9/11 reflects an improper balance between national security and individual rights. As technology has advanced, this imbalance has created new privacy concerns that must again be balanced with legitimate national security concerns.

Issues to Consider

1. Were the Bush administration's actions with respect to immigrants a justified response to 9/11?
2. Is guilt by association necessary to protect Americans?
3. When a person provides material support to a terrorist group, does guilt by association create an effective method of identifying national security risks?

III. ISRAEL

A. INTRODUCTION

The Israeli experience with terrorism has been extensively documented in academic research, media reports, and by international and Israeli human rights organizations. Many of Israel's counterterrorism methods have been criticized for violating the rights of Palestinians living in the West Bank, the Gaza Strip, and East Jerusalem. The question of balancing national security

46. Adi Robertson, *Senate Passes Surveillance Bill without Ban on Web History Snooping*, The Verge, May 14, 2020, 1:26 PM, *available at* https://www.theverge.com/2020/5/14/21257782/surveillance-bill-congress-senate-pass-usa-freedom-reauthorization-act (last visited February 15, 2024).

47. Aaron Holmes, *The House Just Ditched a Bill That Would Renew and Expand the FBI's Surveillances Powers after Trump Threatened to Veto It*, Business Insider, May 28, 2020, 10:01 AM, *available at* https://www.businessinsider.com/house-cancels-vote-fisa-patriot-act-bill-trump-veto-2020-5 (last visited February 15, 2024).

48. Adina Ailoaiei, *The Senate Has Voted to Reauthorize the USA Freedom Act*, last updated November 3, 2021), *available at* https://www.cyberghostvpn.com/en_US/privacyhub/freedom-act/ (last visited February 15, 2024).

and individual rights has come under judicial review throughout the years by the Israeli Supreme Court, sitting as the High Court of Justice.

An assessment of Israeli policy regarding the demolition of Palestinian homes and a discussion of the measure's effect on both terrorists and civilians will facilitate an understanding of how Israel balances national security considerations and individual rights. Focusing on the question of how—and whether—Israel balances these two equally legitimate considerations highlights the interplay between operational considerations, morality, and the rule of law. While the decision to implement the demolition policy was rooted in a legal regime (see below), the "price" for the actual act of demolition was paid by the suspected terrorists' families, rather than the individuals responsible for the act. This raises significant questions of morality and collective punishment as the families bear the burden of the decision. The prosecutorial decision regarding the suspected terrorist is distinct from the administrative policy regarding the sanction. In this way, Israeli policymakers created a bifurcated counterterrorism policy, applying criminal law and administrative sanctions. The former applies to the individual; the latter directly impacts the family.

The policy was consistently upheld by the Supreme Court, sitting as the High Court of Justice. The Court accepted the government's argument that deterrence served as the basis of the policy. This is particularly important when considering the effectiveness of counterterrorism measures deemed lawful by the nation's judiciary.

B. POLICY

To quell the Palestinian Intifada (1987-1993), the Israeli Government instituted several counterterrorism measures, including a policy of demolishing houses in which suspected terrorists resided, hoping this would deter other Palestinians from committing similar acts of terrorism. Israel viewed the policy as an administrative sanction in addition to the criminal law process, whereby a terrorist is tried in court. In applying the deterrence rationale, policy makers sought a mechanism—within the boundary of the law—to prevent future acts of terrorism. In this two-fold approach—criminal law and administrative action—Israel sought to expand the traditional means that focus exclusively on the actor. In doing so, the effort was made to take a more all-encompassing approach to combatting Palestinian terrorism by imposing a penalty on the terrorist's family.

C. THE PROCESS

In response to terrorist attacks, the General Security Services—today, Israel Security Agency (ISA)—recommended demolition of the suspected terrorist's home to the Officer's Command (O.C.) of the West Bank or Gaza Strip, depending on where the home was located. In *Association for Civil Rights in Israel and Others v. Central District Commander,* the Israel High Court of Justice ordered the Israel Defense Forces to establish a mechanism whereby written notification would be given to the family of the intent to demolish the home.[49] The right to appeal the decision to the O.C. to reverse the demolition order.

Several criteria were established. For example, if the suspected terrorist committed an act resulting in the death of innocent civilians, a wall within the home would be immediately built to seal the individual room, and the family would be simultaneously notified of the O.C.'s intent to demolish the house. The purpose of immediately sealing the house was to deter others in the community from committing a similar act of terrorism. Simultaneous to the sealing, the relevant authorities gathered information—classified and unclassified—regarding the following issues: (1) whether the terrorist actually lived in the house; (2) the number of family members residing in the dwelling; (3) the owner of the house; (4) whether the terrorist received assistance—active or passive—from family members; (5) whether demolition of the house would cause structural damage to neighboring homes; and (6) the severity of the terrorist acts committed. After the decision was made to seal or demolish the house, the authorities would determine the extent of the sanction imposed. Written notice of the Commander's decision would be given to the family by an Arabic-speaking officer serving in the Civil Administration (an IDF unit).

The chart below illustrates what administrative sanctions were implemented in the West Bank and Gaza Strip during the Intifada.

Criteria for Imposing Administrative Sanctions

Result of Terrorist Act: Sanction:	*Injury, Not Death*	*Less than Five Individuals Killed*	*More than Five Individuals Killed*
Sealing	Yes, without intent to demolish	Yes, immediately	Yes, immediately—with intent to demolish
House Demolition	No	Yes, in some cases	Yes
Administrative Detention	No	No	No

D. LEGAL REGIME

Section 119 of the Emergency Defense Regulations 1945 authorizes house demolitions:

> (1) A Military Commander may by order direct the forfeiture to the Government of Palestine of any house, structure, or land from which he has reason to suspect that any firearm has been illegally discharged, or any bomb, grenade or explosive or incendiary article illegally thrown, or of any house, structure or land situated in any area, town, village, quarter or street the inhabitants or some of the inhabitants of which he is satisfied have committed, or attempted to commit, or abetted the commission of, or been accessories after the fact to

49. HCJ 358/88, The Association for Civil Rights in Israel and Others v. The Central District Commander and Another [1989].

> the commission of, any offence against these Regulations involving violence or intimidation or any Military Court offence; and when any house, structure or land is forfeited as aforesaid, the Military Commander may destroy the house or the structure or anything on growing on the land.
>
> (2) Members of His Majesty's forces or of the Police Force, acting under the authority of the Military Commander may seize and occupy, without compensation, any property in any such area, town, village, quarter or street as is referred to in sub regulation (1), after eviction without compensation, of the previous occupiers, if any.[50]

When the IDF entered the West Bank and the Gaza Strip in 1967, the British 1945 Defense Emergency Regulations were in effect; accordingly, commanders were authorized, according to section 119, to order the forfeiture, sealing, and demolition of houses.

Issues to Consider

1. What safeguards are required to ensure the judicious implementation of the house demolition policy?
2. Is the displacement of innocent family members reasonable?
3. Does the inherent and inevitable collective punishment contribute to counterterrorism?
4. Does the policy reflect a balance between national security and individual rights?
5. What are the effects on the Palestinian family?

From 1967 to 1989, IDF commanders would order the demolition of homes without granting prior notice to the homeowner or tenants. The High Court's ruling ordering due notice fundamentally changed the process both substantively and procedurally.[51] This ensured a more lawful process and a more balanced approach to the sanction.

The High Court of Justice forced Israeli decision makers to articulate a house demolitions policy; once the policy was in place, the High Court of Justice largely gave the IDF a free hand in implementing the house demolition sanction.[52] Therefore, the issue was not the policy's legality; the High Court of Justice had decided that. Rather, the relevant concern was the policy's effectiveness.

Because of this concern over effectiveness, a high-level IDF commission recommended to the Minister of Defense that the policy be frozen. The commission concluded that house demolitions had not acted as a deterrent and therefore did not meet its stated purpose. Subsequently, Prime Minister Sharon accepted the recommendation, indicating that the policy could be reactivated were there an extreme change in circumstances.

---

50. Yoram Dinstein, *Israel Yearbook of Human Rights* (1996).

51. HCJ 358/88, The Association for Civil Rights in Israel and Others v. The Central District Commander and Another.

52. *Id.*

Issues to Consider

1. What is the significance of the decision to freeze house demolitions?
2. Does Israel owe some form of compensation to Palestinians whose homes have been demolished, in essence, on false premises?
3. Can a state simply say, "sorry, we were wrong"?
4. Did the HCJ too hastily accept the deterrence argument without fully understanding Palestinian society?
5. Did the state truly consider the balancing required of liberal democracies?
6. Was the price of collective punishment and the human toll involved an instigator in encouraging Palestinian terrorism?

Many of the questions raised by house demolitions and the subsequent decision to suspend such tactics are open-ended, reflecting the enormous uncertainty involved in developing a counterterrorism strategy in the face of terror attacks. The balancing required, while difficult to implement, must reflect both a mature legal analysis and an equally sober, realistic policy analysis. While some would argue "better late than never," the ultimate question regarding the commission's findings is whether this policy, and the legal arguments designed to explain it, failed.

The cost paid by Palestinian families whose homes were demolished in response to the actions of a family member is unquestioned. The development of an effective, balanced counterterrorism strategy that does not collectively punish, and which deters others while minimizing blowback, is the true test facing policy and decision makers, who must be sensitive to active judicial review during armed conflict.[53]

The house demolition policy was developed and implemented as a deterrent. According to the internal IDF commission, the policy failed in its primary purpose. Over the years, though the High Court upheld commanders' decisions, human rights organizations strenuously argued that the policy reflected collective punishment and was, therefore, imbalanced. It is indisputable that family members paid a price for the terrorist activities of a child, sibling, or parent. If, according to the internal IDF commission, the house demolitions did not deter others, then the price paid by family members would ultimately represent imbalance and a failed policy.

IV. RUSSIA

Russia's approach to balancing national security and individual rights appears to be of greater concern to the international community than to Russian policymakers. In developing a strategy designed to respond to Chechen terrorism, the approach is primarily action-oriented, with significant costs to human

53. Amos N. Guiora & Erin M. Page, *The Unholy Trinity: Intelligence, Interrogation and Torture*, 37 Case W. Res. J. Int'l L. 2, 3 (2006).

rights. The issue of Russian counterterrorism cannot be viewed in a vacuum; discussion of Russia's counterterrorism strategy must be understood in the context of post-Soviet–era nascent democracy.

A. POST-SOVIET RUSSIA

Post-Soviet Union Russia initially failed to address the allocation of power between branches of government, including the President and the Parliament. Under the Soviet system, the judiciary furthered party policy, and independent judges and lawyers were not well regarded. While the Russian Constitution seeks to separate power between the three branches of government and provides that justice shall be administered only by courts of law, concerns exist regarding the judiciary's ability to adjudicate issues discussed in this chapter.

According to Article 121 of the Constitution, judges cannot be removed except for cause.[54] Supreme Court and Constitutional Court judges, as well as the judges of the other federal courts, have life tenure.[55] Justices of the peace are elected or appointed for an initial three-year term; if reelected or reappointed, they also gain life tenure.[56] Normally, an independent judiciary serves democratic ideals. However, the guarantees of the Russian constitution are not being enforced. An expert on the United Nations Human Rights Committee reports that regional and federal law enforcement agencies are under the direct control of the President, and that "[i]nvestigators, lawyers, and bailiffs [are] perceived as corrupt."[57] The president controls the appointment and removal of federal judges, who in 2019 acquitted just 0.36% of defendants.[58] The expert also said that only 50 to 60 percent of court rulings are actually implemented.[59] One writer describes judges' hesitancy to acquit a defendant this way:

> According to Supreme Court records, the average judge renders a not-guilty verdict once every seven years. Judges understand that such a verdict will always be appealed and often repealed. The repeal of a sentence is a stain on a judge's record that could lead to penalties and even dismissal.[60]

These accounts strongly suggest that judges' careers in Russia depend on whether they uphold or reject executive decisions. In analyzing the

---

54. Article 12.1.5 of the Law on the Status of Judges states the reasons a judge can be removed: "Disciplinary punishment in the form of removal may be imposed upon a judge in exceptional cases for a significant, culpable violation of provisions of substantive law and (or) procedural legislation, of provisions of this Law and (or) of the Code of Judicial Ethics, incompatible with the distinguished title of a judge." https://www.vsrf.ru/en/judicial_system/law_status_judges/

55. *Law on the Statute of Judges*, Supreme Court of the Russian Federation, https://www.vsrf.ru/en/judicial_system/law_status_judges/, Art. 11.

56. *Id.*

57. *Human Rights Committee Considers Report of the Russian Federation in the Absence of a Delegation, Experts Raise Issues on the Persecution of Journalists and the Arrests of Protesters*, UN, October 20, 2022, *available at* https://www.ohchr.org/en/news/2022/10/human-rights-committee-considers-report-russian-federation-absence-delegation-experts (last visited February 15, 2024).

58. *Id.*

59. *Id.*

60. Olga Romanova, *The Problem with the Russian Judiciary*, Carnegie Endowment for Int'l Peace, January 22, 2018, *available at* https://carnegiemoscow.org/commentary/75316 (last visited February 15, 2024).

balancing of rights in Russia, one must understand that the executive is clearly the dominant branch. Despite the constitution's language, the judiciary is beholden to the executive. Accordingly, Russian judicial review in armed conflict is significantly weaker than both the American and Israeli models, with Israel being the most rigorous. This truth was exemplified when the Constitutional Court declared that Russia's annexation of four Ukrainian territories in October 2022 was constitutional, despite the annexation being almost universally condemned as illegal under international law.[61] Another demonstration of the imbalance between national security concerns and the protection of individual rights—as well as the imbalance between the different branches of government, reflecting the "freedom" accorded to the Russian executive—is the number of significant human rights abuses in Chechnya committed by Russian forces.

B. CHECHNYA

The Chechen Republic (also called Chechnya) is a Muslim-majority region in southwest Russia that has repeatedly been a focal point of intense conflict. Russia conquered the area in the 1850s. When the Soviet Union collapsed, the native Chechen people sought independence from Russia, but Russia refused. This led to the First and Second Chechen Wars between 1994 and 2009. Though these wars occurred in Chechnya, Chechen fighters executed multiple bombings and other attacks throughout Russia during and even after these wars were declared over. In 2002, for example, Chechen attackers took up to 900 people hostage in a theater in Moscow and demanded that Russian troops withdraw from Chechnya. In response, Russian forces pumped a gas later revealed to be a derivative of fentanyl into the theater to disable the attackers. During the crisis, the attackers killed only two people, but the gas killed as many as 130 of the theater-goers. In short, the Chechen conflict in both Chechnya and Russia has been filled with violence.

According to the academic and former United States Ambassador to Russia Michael A. McFaul:

> Putin's armed forces continue to abuse the human rights of innocents on a massive scale in Chechnya. Russia may have had the right to use force to defend its borders. But the means deployed to fight this war—torture, including summary executions, bombings of villages, the rape of Chechen women, and the inhumane treatment of prisoners of war—cannot be defended. . . . [T]he gross violation of international norms by the Russian government in combating the problem has left a trail of devastation that will take years to overcome and has brought Russia no closer to ending this tragic conflict.[62]

---

61. Robyn Dixon, *In Two More Staged Votes, Russian Parliament Moves to Ratify Annexation*, Wash. Post, October 3, 2022, 12:51 PM, *available at* https://www.washingtonpost.com/world/2022/10/03/russia-duma-ratify-annexation-ukraine/ (last visited February 15, 2024).

62. *See Russia's Transition to Democracy and U.S.-Russia Relations: Unfinished Business;* Testimony before U.S. House of Representatives, Committee on International Relations, Subcommittee on Europe, September 30, 2003, *available at* http://commdocs.house.gov/committees/intlrel/hfa89668.000/hfa89668_0f.htm (last visited October 24, 2022).

McFaul addresses the issue of how this affects Russia's developing democracy as follows:

> The campaign to erect managed democracy (reforms intended to strengthen Putin's political power without undermining formally the democratic rules of the nation) has had serious negative[ ] consequences for the quality of democracy in Russia. . . . [T]here is no demand from society for a more liberal, democratic order.[63]

The Chechen terrorist attack on the Beslan schoolhouse in 2004 is the worst attack in modern Russian history.[64] Terrorists took 1,100 students, parents, and teachers hostage on the first day of school and sought to negotiate the independence of Chechnya. When the attack ended after Russian forces stormed the school, more than 330 people were dead, 186 of them children. President Vladimir Putin used the attack to further consolidate his power, which led to increased erosion of fundamental rights for Russian citizens.[65]

Even as the conflict in Chechnya entered its sixth year, the Russian government insisted that "it was successfully restoring peace in the republic."[66] However, Human Rights Watch reported that "Russian troops committed hundreds of enforced disappearances and extrajudicial executions, and tortured detainees on a large scale."[67] Chechens have attempted to enlist the help of the European Court of Human Rights to halt abuse by Russian troops. However, applying to the Court has proved to be difficult because Russian troops harass the Chechen applicants:

> Government forces continued to abuse individuals seeking accountability for earlier mistreatment in Chechnya and to harass persons who had applied to the ECHR for the redress of grievances. Amnesty International and other human rights groups reported that reprisals against applicants to the court, included killings, disappearances, and intimidation. According to press reports and human rights NGOs, as of September at least six applicants to the ECHR had been killed or abducted. In a 2007 ruling the court emphasized that the relatives of disappeared persons and witnesses should be protected from intimidation and revenge. However, this practice continued during the year. . . .
>
> An HRW report released in September concluded that the central government had failed to act on any of the ECHR rulings that called on it to investigate specific human rights violations in Chechnya. According to the report, the court had issued 115 rulings relating to Chechnya, almost all of which found the country responsible for serious human rights violations and for failure to investigate the crimes. HRW researched 33 of the cases and found that the government had not brought a single perpetrator to justice, even in cases where the court named the persons allegedly responsible.[68]

---

63. *Id.*
64. Human Rights Watch, World Report 2005, 406.
65. *Id.* At 406-407.
66. *Id.* At 409.
67. *Id.*
68. U.S. Department of State, Bureau of Democracy, Human Rights, and Labor, *2009 Country Reports on Human Rights Practices: Russia*, March 11, 2010, *available at* https://2009-2017.state.gov/j/drl/rls/hrrpt/2009/eur/136054.htm (last visited November 9, 2022).

The poor human rights conditions in Chechnya were explained in this report from the U.S. Department of State:

> The North Caucasus region of Russia remained an area of particular concern. The government's poor human rights record in the North Caucasus worsened, as the government fought insurgents, Islamist militants, and criminal forces. Local government and insurgent forces reportedly engaged in killing, torture, abuse, violence, politically motivated abductions, and other brutal or humiliating treatment, often with impunity. In Chechnya, Ingushetiya, and Dagestan, the number of extrajudicial killings and disappearances increased markedly, as did the number of attacks on law enforcement personnel. Authorities in the North Caucasus appeared to act outside of federal government control. Although the Chechen government announced a formal end to counterterrorist operations, there was an increase in violence during the summer, which continued through the remainder of the year.[69]

It is important to note, as the State Department report suggests, that Chechen fighters have similarly committed abuses:

> Chechen fighters planted landmines that killed or injured federal forces and often provoked federal counterattacks on civilian areas. In other incidents, the rebels took up positions in populated areas and fired on federal forces, thereby exposing the civilians to federal counterattack. When villagers protested, they sometimes were beaten or fired upon by the rebels. . . . Chechen fighters also reportedly abused, tortured, and killed captured soldiers from federal forces.[70]

Additionally, Chechen fighters have not limited their attacks or abuses to the Chechen territory; they have been responsible for numerous attacks on civilians both inside Chechnya and elsewhere in Russia. In addition, Chechen troops assassinated Akhmad Kadyrov and other local Chechen leaders who worked with the Russian authorities.

In the aftermath of an attack on the Moscow subway system in March 2010 by two Chechen suicide bombers that killed 40 people, a major concern was whether the Russian executive would respond disproportionately, as it had done after previous terrorist attacks.

Issues to Consider

1. On the assumption that the reports regarding the conduct of Russian troops are largely accurate, how does this benefit the state?
2. What controls have been instituted over the Russian forces?
3. How do these issues affect the general populace?
4. What is the importance and effect of international condemnation?
5. Is the imposition of Western human rights standards justified?
6. Does an attack such as Beslan justify a no-holds-barred response?

---

69. *Id.*
70. *Id.*

7. Does the fact that Russia is a managed democracy suggest that the executive is unchecked?
8. What legal standards are appropriate for such a democracy?
9. What institution will ensure balance in such a system?

Given the combination of weak institutions and a public apparently indifferent to brutal attacks committed against innocent civilians, the resulting lack of government accountability is inevitable. Has this accountability void contributed to the Russian counterterrorism effort?

In the managed democracy system where courts and the legislature do not exercise oversight or act as a restraining force, perhaps executive aggression is inevitable. Only a few days after the Beslan massacre, President Putin announced new political measures designed to "give the president de facto power to appoint governors, even more sway over the parliament, or state Duma, and increase the executive's influence over the judiciary."[71] Many Russians disagreed with the new proposals, but the authority and power of the other branches of government were so compromised that implementation of the measures could not be prevented.[72]

When Putin first came to power, political parties had great public debates regarding policy issues. The media published a wide variety of opinions, regional governors were strong, the courts had achieved a degree of independence from the executive, and involvement by nongovernmental organizations was growing. This is no longer the case today.

> Public debate on key policy issues has all but disappeared. The pro-presidential United Russia party controls more than two-thirds of all seats in the State Duma, enough to adopt any law or even change the constitution. Opposition parties have been either decimated or eliminated altogether, partially a result of the deeply flawed elections of December 2003. During this election campaign and the presidential election that followed, television media shamelessly promoted United Russia and a few other Kremlin-favored parties while constantly vilifying the opposition.
>
> After a two-year long assault on the independent electronic media, all television stations are firmly under Kremlin control, as are most radio stations. Television news has become monotone, perpetually portraying the president in a positive light and avoiding criticism of his policies. Most programs featuring live debate on political issues have been cut. Only a small number of newspapers and internet publications provide some plurality of opinion, but their readership is marginal.
>
> After convincing regional governors to give up their seats in Russia's senate as a concession to Putin early in his presidency, the Kremlin gradually destroyed them as an independent political force. Through intensive meddling in gubernatorial election campaigns, using its sway over television media

71. Human Rights Watch, World Report 2005, 406-407.
72. *Id.* at 407.

and its enormous administrative resources, the Kremlin effectively made the gubernatorial candidates dependent on its support. By September 2004, the governors' power had been reduced to such an extent that not one of them dared publicly to criticize Putin's proposal to scrap gubernatorial elections.[73]

Issues to Consider

1. Does the apparent disregard of both checks and balances and the rule of law in Russia contribute to a more effective counterterrorism policy?
2. Would unilateral executive action free of checks-and-balances restrictions be appropriate when Chechen terrorists commit acts such as the bombing of the Beslan schoolhouse?
3. What should be the limits of state power?

Though conflict in Chechnya has formally ended, there are still incidents of insurgents fighting against security forces and widespread abuses of human rights by the government. These abuses include violence against the LGBTQ+ population, kidnapping, extra-judicial killing, torture, incommunicado detention, false criminal charges, death threats, assault, and expulsion from the republic. Russia did not allow the Moscow Mechanism rapporteur from the Organization for Security and Co-operation in Europe to enter the country when the rapporteur attempted to investigate 2018 allegations of human rights violations in Chechnya. A report from the U.S. Department of State outlined some of the alleged abuses in Chechnya this way:

> Credible nongovernmental organizations (NGOs) and independent media outlets continued to publish reports indicating that, from December 2018 to January 2019, local authorities in the Republic of Chechnya renewed a campaign of violence against individuals perceived to be members of the lesbian, gay, bisexual, transgender, queer, and intersex (LGBTQI+) community. . . . [T]he news outlet Novaya Gazeta published information corroborating previous reports that Chechen security officials extrajudicially executed 27 residents of the Republic of Chechnya in 2017. As part of its investigation into the abuses, Novaya Gazeta interviewed former Chechen police sergeant Suleyman Gezmakhmayev, who testified that his police regiment, the Akhmat Kadyrov Police Patrol Service Regiment, carried out mass arrests and some of the extrajudicial killings of the 27 residents between December 2016 and January 2017. Media reported that Chechen police officers subsequently sought to force Gezmakhmayev to recant his testimony by putting pressure on relatives who remained in Chechnya. . . . [P]residential press secretary Dmitriy Peskov told reporters that the government was aware of Novaya Gazeta's investigations into the extrajudicial executions in Chechnya but did not have the prerogative to investigate. Media outlets reported that the former head of the regiment, Aslan Iraskhanov, was appointed head of Chechnya's police at the end of March [2021]. According to human rights organizations, as of December

73. *Id.* at 407-408.

authorities had failed to open investigations into the allegations or reports of extrajudicial killings and mass torture of LGBTQI+ persons in Chechnya and continued to deny there were any LGBTQI+ persons in the republic.[74]

In the context of balancing national security considerations and the rights of the individual, measuring effectiveness requires sensitivity to both international law and international opinion. An analysis of the Russian government's conduct in Chechnya suggests a willful disregard for both. Weak efforts on the part of domestic institutions, in clear contrast to the Israeli model of active judicial review in armed conflict, clearly contribute to the present state of affairs. Even an American model of circumspect judicial review could contribute to a more balanced, and therefore more effective, Russian counterterrorism strategy.

C. ASSAULT ON UKRAINE

After Russian troops invaded parts of Ukraine in February 2022, citizens of occupied areas reported that the troops committed egregious abuses of human rights. Upon investigation, a UN–appointed panel determined that Russian troops had committed war crimes.[75] The crimes included attacks on civilian targets such as hospitals, schools, and apartment buildings; indiscriminate attacks upon civilians, including with cluster munitions; executions of civilians and soldiers while in detention; beatings; electrocution; forced nudity; rape; torture; and forced displacement. Russian troops have also used missiles and drones to destroy civilian infrastructure such as power plants and water treatment facilities, causing blackouts and a lack of clean water. Though Russia's pretext for the war was to liberate Ukraine from Nazism and genocide, life for those under Russian occupation has been marked by oppression, violence, and death. Ukrainian courts have convicted multiple Russian soldiers of war crimes, though uncertainty remains over whether military leaders of higher rank or Russian state leaders will ever be held accountable, or to what extent.

V. INDIA

A. INTRODUCTION

The dominant reality is that India faces myriad external and domestic terrorist threats. In examining the development of India's counterterrorism strategy, the primary question is whether a nation as large and diverse as India is truly capable of a consistent and uniform policy, given its objective circumstances.

74. U.S. Department of State, Bureau of Democracy, Human Rights, and Labor, *2021 Country Reports on Human Rights Practices: Russia*, April 12, 2022, *available at* https://www.state.gov/reports/2021-country-reports-on-human-rights-practices/russia/ (last visited November 11, 2022).

75. Independent International Commission of Inquiry on Ukraine, statement before United Nations Human Rights Council, September 23, 2022, *available at* https://www.ohchr.org/en/statements/2022/09/update-chair-independent-international-commission-inquiry-ukraine-51st-session (last visited November 11, 2022).

This assessment is not meant to justify or defend human rights violations either perpetrated by the government or committed with its acquiescence; rather, it is to present a reality not faced by the other surveyed nations. India's history is rife with conflict and ethnic violence. Upon establishment of India's independence in 1947, neighboring Pakistan was created based on Muslim-majority areas in the eastern and western parts of India. Prior to independence, the land that is now India was mostly Hindu, with some Muslim areas. War between India and Pakistan broke out in 1948 over Kashmir—India wanted to maintain the status quo of its control and Pakistan refused to accept jurisdiction and control by India.

The historical tension between Hindus and Muslims has been the focal point of repeated horrific attacks and violence. Contemporary terrorism first occurred in Punjab in 1978 but "communal and ethnic violence has been a part of the Indian scene since independence in 1947."[76] However, that tension has been superimposed on the age in which we live—the age of terrorism. No longer can conflict between these two religions of India be considered a local one. The reality of the India-Pakistan relationship, and the primacy of Islamic terror in India, are such that interreligious conflict in India has an importance beyond the local arena.

Given these political and historical circumstances unique to India, is legislation balancing national security and individual rights realistic? India's religious tensions and strict policies in the wake of terrorist attacks do not offer much evidence in favor of individual rights. India's record of striking an appropriate balance is best analyzed by examining legislation promulgated in response to terrorism.

B. PREVENTION OF TERRORISM ACT

On March 26, 2002, India enacted the Prevention of Terrorism Act (POTA) as a response to the December 2001 attack on Parliament. The Act was intended to grant statewide powers in conducting operational counterterrorism. Indian and international human rights groups, journalists, opposition parties, and minority rights groups all condemned POTA; the Act was repealed two years later in response to this pressure.

Counterterrorism efforts in India are complicated because terrorism is both internally and externally driven. The internal threat involving disputes between Hindus and Muslims is, in large part, externally driven. Troubled relations with neighboring Pakistan exacerbate domestic terror and create circumstances in which internal disputes can lead to non-domestic terror threats. The suspected Pakistani involvement both in the December 2001 attack on the Indian Parliament and the November 2008 attacks in Mumbai are examples of situations where perceived threats to national security could dangerously escalate, a reality compounded by the nuclear capability of both nations.

---

76. Ved Marwah, India, in *Combating Terrorism* 301 (Yonah Alexander ed., 2002).

> . . . India needs to alter other dimensions of its policy [on terrorism]. The first is the approach to Pakistan, which must start with two premises—that there are limits to what the United States can do, and the impossibility of getting Islamabad to negotiate away its leverage on terrorism. That will lead a different set of options to the top of the Indian agenda vis-à-vis Pakistan.
>
> One is to develop an activist engagement with the Pakistani polity and society that aims at containing the negative forces in that nation. India's constant temptation has been to avoid dealing with Pakistan as a way of punishing those responsible for terrorism. That approach has not worked. Instead, India must actively intervene in the political dynamic inside Pakistan. Tied to this bold policy toward Pakistan must be comprehensive security sector reforms at home. Without a root and branch overhaul of the security forces, intelligence agencies, border management and the higher political command of internal security, India's own war on terrorism will not succeed. There has been too much rhetoric on the threat from terrorism and too little thought on recasting India's internal security strategy.[77]

The tension between Pakistan and India over Kashmir adds another factor to the equation confronting India. There have been widespread reports of serious human rights violations committed in Kashmir by India.[78] From the perspective of the Indian government, the conflict in Kashmir represents an additional threat.[79] Whether India has responded to this threat in a balanced manner is open to debate:

> There have been repeated cases of violation of the Geneva Convention in Jammu and Kashmir. Indian security forces have consistently violated humanitarian law, and do not often comply with its provisions regarding treatment of prisoners-of-war. There were more than 200 incidents of rape in Doda in January 1994 alone. Rape continues to be a major instrument of Indian repression against the Kashmiri people while the majority of casualties in Kashmir are civilians. The Indian authorities have also steadfastly refused to allow any independent monitoring of the situation.
>
> Human rights organizations are routinely denied permission to investigate in a free manner. Although India has recently permitted an assessment visit by the International Committee of the Red Cross and another by the International Commission of Jurists, other organizations have had difficulties conducting public investigation. The International Federation of Human Rights and the Amnesty International have also been denied permission to visit.
>
> Newspersons have been attacked and arrested. Humanitarian relief is limited as external agencies are not being allowed to provide medical assistance and other relief materials. There are incidents of destruction of revered

---

77. C. Raja Mohan, *India and the War on Terror,* The Hindu, September 12, 2003, *available at* http://www.hindu.com/thehindu/2003/09/12/stories/2003091201571000.htm (last visited March 26, 2006).

78. *See, e.g., Behind the Kashmir Conflict Abuses by Indian Security Forces and Militant Groups Continue,* Human Rights Watch Report, July 1999, *available at* http://www.hrw.org/reports/1999/kashmir/ (last visited February 15, 2024); *India's Secret Army in Kashmir New Patters of Abuse Emerge in the Conflict,* Human Rights Watch Report, May 1996, vol. 8, no. 4(c), *available at* http://www.hrw.org/campaigns/kashmir/ 1996/ (last visited February 15, 2024).

79. Kashmir, GlobalSecurity, *available at* https://www.globalsecurity.org/military/world/war/kashmir.htm (last visited December 22, 2023).

shrines and cultural places by the Indian forces. Villages have been razed to the ground.

Many cases of human rights violation stem from abuse of power under repressive laws and police/army brutality unleashed against the Kashmiri people. They are taken into custody for acts that are legitimized by international human rights standards of free speech, freedom of association and assembly, and freedom of the press. While many arrests are without any legal justification whatsoever, the Indian forces also depend on several laws to justify their acts of human rights violation.[80]

Issues to Consider

1. What effect do external threats have on a nation's internal balancing?
2. Does the fact that India's internal terror threat is, in part, externally driven suggest balancing is significantly more difficult?
3. Does the internal/external threat India faces suggest that different standards can or should be applied?
4. Does the size of India's population significantly complicate balancing?

According to Human Rights Watch, legislation enacted by India was imbalanced.[81] In addition, the government misused POTA, targeting minorities and political opponents in a manner similar to the misuse of the previous legislation, the Terrorist and Disruptive Activities Act (TADA). One of POTA's most problematic aspects was an overly broad definition of terror, enabling the government to detain suspects for up to three months without charging them. With the permission of a special judge, the suspect could be detained for an additional three months. The government tried to remedy some of these problems by implementing safeguards intended to protect due process rights. However, critics argued that safeguards intended to protect individual rights were insufficient and that the legislation was superfluous because existing laws were sufficient.

Human rights abuse, largely the result of a free hand granted to the security forces, continues to be reported, especially in Kashmir due to an executive branch subject to minimal scrutiny. While Public Interest Litigation increasingly enables a citizen aggrieved by government action to petition the Supreme Court, the Indian judiciary is not fully engaged in active judicial review during armed conflict.

The drafting, repealing, subsequent redrafting, and re-repealing of legislation curtailing the rights of the individual reflect legislative and executive uncertainty. India's effort to balance is clearly a work in progress; the Indian executive branch has been greatly affected by the powerful and persistent

80. Peace Magazine, Jan.-Mar. 2002, at 18; Prasenjit Maiti, *Human Rights Violation in Kashmir, available at* https://peacemagazine.org/archive/v18n1p18.htm (last visited February 15, 2024).

81. *Human Rights Watch, In the Name of Counter Terrorism: Human Rights Abuses World Wide* 15, March 25, 2003, *available at* https://www.hrw.org/reports/counter-terrorism-bck_0.pdf (last visited February 15, 2024).

enmity between Hindus and Muslims. A Hindu-controlled Indian government convinced that Pakistan and its overwhelmingly Muslim population are intent on military victory does not contribute to a balanced counterterrorism policy.

Perhaps the best example of this very complicated and fragile situation is the following account of recurrent tensions:

> On February 19, 2003, the Gujarat government charged 131 Muslims under POTA for allegedly attacking Hindus. A year earlier, a Muslim mob set fire to a train carrying Hindu activists in Godhra in the western state of Gujarat. Fifty-eight people were killed. In the days that followed, Hindu nationalist groups and their supporters killed more than 2,000 Muslims throughout the state. Muslims were branded as terrorists while armed gangs set out to systematically destroy Muslim homes, businesses and places of worship. Scores of Muslim women and girls were gang-raped before being mutilated and burnt to death. Human Rights Watch investigations revealed that attacks against Muslims were carried out with extensive state participation and support and planned months in advance of the Godhra attack. The Hindu nationalist Bharatiya Janata Party that heads the state government has not charged any Hindus under POTA for violence against Muslims.[82]

This horrific act of random ethnically-oriented violence and the tepid—at best—response of the Indian government speaks volumes regarding balance. The incident demonstrates the inability (or unwillingness) of the Indian government to provide measures necessary to protect the rights of all its citizens. The combination of threats, both internal and external in origin, presents a unique challenge; however, balancing requires protecting individuals from the government's inherent inclination to engage in excess regarding national security, despite the threats faced.

VI. SPAIN

A. INTRODUCTION

Spain has long faced domestic terrorism; Basque nationalists in the northern part of the nation have demanded an independent state for years. As a result, Euskadi Ta Askatasuna (ETA)[83] has presented a major challenge to Spanish governments and has taken a significant toll on Spanish life. But Spanish counterterrorism relating to Basque separatists is not discussed here; rather, the balanced response to the multiple bombings at the Madrid train station on March 11, 2004, is examined.

Spanish balancing is paradoxical. On the one hand, Spanish laws enable authorities to implement tough measures; on the other hand, the response of the Spanish government to the train bombing was, in large part, a

82. *Id*

83. ETA, whose name translates to Basque Homeland and Freedom, was established in 1959 and states its ultimate goal to be complete independence from Spain. Jean R. Tartter, *Spain: A Country Study* 345-53 (Eric Solsten & Sandra W. Meditz ed., 1990).

non-response. Unlike the United States, which responded to 9/11 by enacting legislation and implementing measures, some perhaps unconstitutional, and in contrast to Russia, Israel, and India, which clearly responded with force, the Spanish reaction was limited to implementing existing laws. Before September 11, 2001, Spain was one of only six European countries with specific counter-terrorism laws distinct from ordinary criminal codes. The tough statutes allow Spanish magistrates to be "among the most dogged pursuers of al Qaeda suspects."[84] It is important to note that the existing laws were in place precisely because Spain has, for years, experienced internal terrorism. Unlike the United States, which had to scramble and enact legislation in response to 9/11, Spain had at its disposal a full panoply of relevant laws.

B. INCOMMUNICADO DETENTION

According to Human Rights Watch,[85] current Spanish law enables the authorities to hold an individual in incommunicado detention for up to 13 days. Incommunicado detention deprives individuals of basic rights, including notifying family members of the detainee's whereabouts, the ability to seek legal counsel, and access to a judge for purposes of objective review of the evidence against the individual. According to Human Rights Watch, "virtually all terrorism suspects are held in incommunicado detention upon arrest. During this period, they do not have the right to hire a lawyer of their own choosing."[86]

Human Rights Watch further suggests that:

> The principle features of Spain's counterterrorism provisions are the extended period of detention in police custody allowed before the prisoner must be brought before a judge, and the use of the incommunicado detention . . . those detained on suspicion of membership or collaboration with an armed group (including terrorist organization) may be held for an additional 48 hours (others must be brought before a magistrate within 72 hours). This means that terrorism suspects may be under police custody for five days before being seen by a judge.[87]

Similar to concerns that arose regarding the status of detainees in Guantanamo Bay and Order 1500 in Israel, Spain has been criticized for legislation enabling authorities to hold a detainee incommunicado.

Issues to Consider

1. What is the benefit of holding a detainee incommunicado?
2. What rights are being violated?
3. How serious is such an infringement?
4. What have the costs and benefits of such a policy been historically?

---

84. Jonathan Stevenson, *How Europe and America Defend Themselves,* 82 Foreign Aff., 2003, 75, 81.

85. Human Rights Watch, *Setting an Example?* 27 (2005) (citing L.E. Crim. Art. 509).

86. *Id.* at 17.

87. *Id.* at 18-19.

5. Why do other nations not implement such a policy?
6. Is such a policy suitable for those suspected of terrorism?
7. How does such a policy reflect on a liberal democracy?

Given that incommunicado detention has been legislatively enacted, there are two issues to consider: its effectiveness and its possible violation of internationally recognized human rights.

The United Nations commented on Spain's practice of incommunicado detention in *Mikel Egibar Mitxelena v. Spain*:

> Incommunicado detention, when justified by insuperable problems in the investigation of the offence concerned, especially when crimes as serious as terrorism are involved, cannot in itself be regarded as contrary to the Covenant. Furthermore, the Body of Principles for the Protection of All Persons Under Any Form of Detention or Imprisonment authorizes incommunicado detention for a few days in exceptional cases (Principles 15, 16 and 18, paragraph 3), such as "exceptional needs of the investigation," or "exceptional circumstances, to be specified by law or lawful regulations, when it is considered indispensable by a judicial or other authority in order to maintain security and good order." The Group considers charges of terrorism and conspiracy to represent an exceptional circumstance which, according to Spanish legislation, authorizes incommunicado detention for a brief period. It should be added that the judge of Examining Court No. 3 of the National High Court took measures for the physical and psychological protection of the person under arrest, to the point where he received a medical examination daily.[88]

However, Human Rights Watch has expressed concern regarding incommunicado detention in terrorism cases.

> Spain's anti-terror laws permit the use of incommunicado detention, secret legal proceedings, and pre-trial detention for up to four years. The proceedings governing the detentions of suspected al Qaeda operatives apprehended in Spain in November 2001, July 2002, and January 2003, among others, have been declared secret (causa secreta). The investigating magistrate of the Audiencia Nacional, a special court that oversees terrorist cases, can request causa secreta for thirty days, consecutively renewable for the duration of the four-year pre-trial detention period. Secret proceedings bar the defense access to the prosecutor's evidence, except for information contained in the initial detention order. Without access to this evidence, detainees are severely hampered in mounting an adequate defense.[89]

Incommunicado detention reflects a policy of firmness verging on denial of basic human rights. In denying a detainee basic rights, such as informing

---

88. Adopted Nov. 29, 1999, E/CN.4/2001/14/Add.1, *available at* http://www1.umn.edu/humanrts/wgad/26-1999.html (last visited February 15, 2024).

89. *Supra*, note 81.

family members regarding the detention, the Spanish government is taking measures that seem to enact an imbalance. When the Israel Defense Forces invaded the West Bank, the relevant military order decreed that detainees must be brought to a judge within eight days of their detention. Though the military commander reached the conclusion that operational circumstances dictated extension to 18 days, the High Court of Justice held that logistical considerations are irrelevant and that basic rights may not be violated, even during conflict.[90] In a similar vein, the Presidential Order creating the military commissions in Guantanamo Bay, and the Department of Defense instructions subsequently promulgated, were heavily criticized because detainees were denied the right to be brought before an independent judge.

Furthermore, an analysis from an operational perspective suggests that the benefits of incommunicado detention are unclear. While there has not been another major Islamic-based terrorist attack on Spanish soil since the Madrid bombing, there is a lack of evidence as to whether this is a direct result of Spanish counterterrorism policies. Since balance requires that national security not outweigh civil liberties, the holding of a detainee under such conditions seemingly creates an imbalance.

A comparative transnational analysis would suggest that the policy is illegal, though statutorily enacted. If compared to court holdings in response to Order 1500 and Guantanamo Bay, then its illegality is quite evident. Incommunicado detention is still legal in Spain, although it has been limited in length of time and allows the right to an attorney and to medical treatment. These changes occurred after years of international criticism and a 2014 ruling by the European Court of Human Rights finding that Spain had violated article 3 of the European Convention on Human Rights.[91]

VII. CHINA

China's national security dilemmas have increasingly drawn international attention and criticism, primarily due to unrest in Xinjiang Province which stems in part from ethnic tensions; a majority of the population of Xinjiang are Muslim Uyghurs, an ethnic minority elsewhere in China. The unrest in the past decade has led to terrorist convictions and vocational training internment camps[92] predominantly holding Muslim Uyghurs.

---

90. HCJ 3239/02, Marab v. IDF Commander in the West Bank (2002) (Isr.).

91. *2020 Country Reports on Human Rights Practices: Spain*, U.S. Dep't of State, 2021, *available at* https://www.state.gov/reports/2020-country-reports-on-human-rights-practices/spain/ (last visited February 15, 2024); *Spain's Incommunicado Detention Violates Human Rights*, Rights Int'l Spain, October 27, 2014), *available at* https://www.liberties.eu/en/stories/spain-incommunicado-detention/2196 (last visited February 15, 2024).

92. The vocational training internment camps have also been referred to by outside sources as reeducation camps, internment camps, and even concentration camps.

A. HISTORY

During the Cultural Revolution, oppressive policies against the religious and cultural practices of ethnic minorities led to dramatic and draconian limits on individual rights, ruthlessly applied. In the 1980s, the practice was relaxed, allowing Uyghurs greater autonomy for their religious and cultural practices. However, this relaxation allowed radical Islamic beliefs to spread; the Chinese government alleges that radical Islamic separatists are primarily responsible for a majority of the terrorist attacks in Xinjiang province.

The Xinjiang Province is of importance to China due to significant economic, strategic, and military benefits. Xinjiang has vast natural resources, is the base of economic trade with Central Asian states, and has a border with eight countries, which magnifies its importance for border security purposes. The eight bordering states also share a common threat of domestic terrorism from radical Islamic groups.

The Chinese response to domestic terrorism has included strong law enforcement crackdown, especially in Xinjiang Province. In 1996, China implemented "Strike Hard, Maximum Pressure," an anti-crime campaign. The "Strike Hard" campaign was initially intended to crack down on corruption but included severe restrictions on the practice of religion. Amnesty International has reported serious violations of human rights committed against Uyghurs in the name of counterterrorism. These reported violations included imposition of the death penalty against 190 Uyghurs between January 1997 and April 1999. "Strike Hard" was re-launched in 2001, resulting in additional executions, arrests, and prison sentences.

Even with these strict policies in place, there have been numerous incidents of domestic terrorism in Xinjiang province. The Chinese government alleges that the acts are predominantly the responsibility of the East Turkestan Independence Movement (ETIM). In April 1990, an armed rebellion in Baren township resulted in the deaths of more than 100 protestors and police. In addition, there were numerous riots in 1997 and in July 2009; the riots reflect the constant tension and violence between the Uyghurs and the Chinese government. The response to the 2009 riots highlights China's struggle with balancing national security and individual rights.

B. CHINESE RESPONSE

During the unrest in July 2009, approximately 200 people were killed when Uyghurs and Hans clashed in Urumqi, the capital of Xinjiang Province. The violence occurred when protests by Uyghurs resulted in the destruction of shops and vehicles; subsequently, groups of Han in the province retaliated. In October 2009, several Uyghurs were sentenced for crimes committed during the riots, including murder, property damage, arson, and robbery. In November 2009, nine men were executed for various crimes, including murder and arson. According to a Chinese white paper on Xinjiang, Uyghur separatists promoting the independence of the region caused the riots.

When the riots began, thousands of security personnel poured into Urumqi in an attempt to end the riots. One correspondent stated that the city was under "martial law."[93] Immediately after the riots began, a curfew was imposed on the Urumqi, and mosques were ordered to remain closed. Additionally, the area was flooded with more troops and armed police, surrounding Uyghur neighborhoods. In the days following, over 1,400 individuals were arrested by the government; by the end of August, the police had arrested over 1,500 people. In November 2009, Chinese officials articulated an intention to implement another "Strike Hard" campaign, aimed at maintaining stability and eliminating security dangers.

China's response to the riots is in accordance with a well-documented pattern: the government sweeps into the region, arrests suspects, quickly holds trials, and executes those convicted. Thereafter, the government imposes restrictive policies for a few years intended to deter future violent actions. In times of crisis, China has responded with an instantaneous reduction in individual rights, which has been articulated as essential to national security. The Chinese response, in contrast with other countries, is less of a preemptive attempt intended to prevent terrorist attacks than an *ex post* response. Severe *ex post* restraints on individual rights, including the imposition of curfews and closing of mosques, raise important questions regarding both legitimacy and effectiveness as China fails to consistently balance national security and individual rights. China's heavy-handed security policies suggest long-term policy weakness, if not ineffectiveness, as these methods have exacerbated tensions with Uyghurs.[94]

In 2016 China's new Counterterrorism Law went into effect, changing how terrorism is defined through overly broad and vague language. The Human Rights Watch has repeatedly raised concerns with the new Counterterrorism Law and with China's approach to combatting and preventing extremism.[95] The Counterterrorism Law quickly allowed Chinese law enforcement to enact prompt prosecution, deprivation of liberty, or other restrictions without the requirement of actual action or violence on the part of the alleged terrorist.[96] A 2018 amendment to Xinjiang's de-extremify ordinance introduced the concept of "Vocational Skills Education Training Centers," which are estimated to be holding more than 1 million people.[97] These training centers—run by

93. *China Riot City Under Control,* BBC News, July 8, 2009, *available at* http://news.bbc.co.uk/2/hi/asia-pacific/8140492.stm (last visited February 15, 2024).

94. Chris Buckley, *Chinese Police Blame Religious Extremists for Violence in Region,* N.Y. Times, June 30, 2013, *available at* https://www.nytimes.com/2013/07/01/world/asia/china-blames-religious-extremists-for-violence-in-xinjiang.html (last visited February 15, 2024).

95. *China: Disclose Details of Terrorism Convictions,* Human Rights Watch, March 16, 2017, 7:45 PM, *available at* https://www.hrw.org/news/2017/03/16/china-disclose-details-terrorism-convictions (last visited February 15, 2024).

96. *Id.*

97. Adrian Zenz, *Brainwashing, Police Guards and Coercive Internment: Evidence from Chinese Government Documents about the Nature and Extent of Xinjiang's "Vocational Training Internment Camps",* 7 J. Pol. Risk, 2019, *available at* https://www.jpolrisk.com/brainwashing-police-guards-and-coercive-internment-evidence-from-chinese-government-documents-about-the-nature-and-extent-of-xinjiangs-vocational-training-internment-camps (last visited February 15, 2024); Anna Schecter, *New Details of Torture, Cover-Ups in China's Internment Camps Revealed in Amnesty International Report,* NBC News, June 10, 2021, 9:00 AM, *available at* https://www.nbcnews.com/news/world/new-details-torture-cover-ups-china-s-internment-camps-revealed-n1270014 (last visited February 15, 2024).

the Education and Training Bureau—are intended to transform the individual through political re-education, and are deemed necessary to prevent terrorism and root out Islamist extremism. Detainees are forced to study Chinese communist propaganda, renounce their religion—predominantly Islam—and are subjected to cruel treatment, including forced labor, mass sterilization of Uyghur women, and torture through methods such as waterboarding, sexual abuse, and sleep deprivation.[98]

Leaked official documents and first-hand accounts have allowed experts to piece together that the detention center resembles a maximum-security prison rather than a "boarding school," as government officials in Xinjiang have claimed. The Chinese government claims that the detainees can regularly ask for home leave and are not there involuntarily. No government documents, either outlining the procedure on establishing voluntary agreements with the "students," or processing requests to leave the center, have been found.[99] This extra-judicial detention has furthered the concerns of human rights groups. Detention centers are legally authorized to detain individuals for short-term education correction that is limited to 37 days, as an alternative to shorter prison sentences. The training centers can, in practice, detain individuals longer than the 37 days without a formal arrest or charges.[100] Many detainees have been subjected to long-term confinement in the name of national security and counterterrorism.

Issues to Consider

1. What is the benefit of an *ex post* response? Is there any situation in which it can be more beneficial to respond after an attack?
2. Can a preemptive limitation of rights prevent violence?
3. Is there a way to consistently limit some individual rights for the interest of national security?
4. Do short-term limitations on individual rights, such as freedom of movement or religion, impose a cost on society?

VIII. COLOMBIA

While other countries have attempted—with varying degrees of success—to balance national security and individual rights, Colombia's emphasis on national security at the expense of individual rights is palpable and institutionalized. That said, Colombia has been subjected to consistent attacks from violent organizations since the 1940s. Groups including the Revolutionary

98. Jen Kirby, *Concentration Camps and Forced Labor: China's Repression of the Uighurs, Explained*, Vox, last updated Sept. 25, 2020, 4:52 PM, *available at* https://www.vox.com/2020/7/28/21333345/uighurs-china-internment-camps-forced-labor-xinjiang (last visited February 15, 2024).

99. Adrian Zenz, *supra* note 97.

100. *Id.*

Armed Forces of Colombia (FARC) and the National Liberation Army (ELN) have been operating in Colombia for over 45 years; this has contributed directly to the near-exclusive focus on counterterrorism by Colombia's defense and security policies.

The Democratic Security and Defense Policy was implemented by President Uribe in 2003; its stated goals were to "reinstate the rule of law in Colombia and protect the population" through consolidation of state control by denying sanctuary to terrorists, increasing state presence, destroying illegal drugs, and maintaining a deterrence-based military.[101] Uribe's policy included granting the military a broad range of police power. Proponents of the policy point to the decrease in the number of people murdered and kidnapped between 2002 and 2006 as evidence of its effectiveness.[102] However, the numbers increased between 2008 and 2009.

The success of this policy has been measured both in the decline of crime as well as an increase in the number of terrorists killed or captured. This has led to "false positives," which directly contribute to violations of the individual rights of Colombian citizens. To create incentives for capturing or killing terrorists, various promotions and vacations for military personnel have been developed that depend on quotas of terrorists killed or captured. To maximize the numbers, military personal round up peasants, dress them in uniforms from FARC or other groups, and shoot them—allowing the military to count their deaths as successes.

The focus on national security contributing to a temporary decrease in the number of murders, kidnappings, and drugs has led to extreme violations of individual rights. The U.S. State Department Human Rights Report for Colombia asserted that the human rights abuses by the government included unlawful and extra-judicial killings, forced disappearances, torture and mistreatment of detainees, arbitrary arrest, and a high number of pretrial detainees.[103]

Colombia has consistently held national security to be more important than individual rights. This has left the population caught between the government, the military, and a terrorist organization, with little protection for their rights or lives. A peace deal signed by the Colombian state and FARC in 2016 outlined a plan to substitute illegal crops for legal crops to allow coca farmers to maintain their livelihood while addressing the drug problem. Unfortunately, the substitution program failed many farmers, whose wages were cut by more than half; the farmers resorted back to cultivating illegal crops.[104] Further issues arose from the peace deal when new and old illegal

101. Press Release, Embassy of Colombia, *The Uribe Administration's Democratic Security and Defense Policy*, *available at* http://www.presidencia.gov.co/sne/visita_bush/documentos/security.pdf (last visited November 14, 2009).

102. Michael Reid, *Forgotten Continent: The Battle for Latin America's Soul* 262 (2007).

103. Bureau of Democracy, Human Rights, and Labor, *2022 Country Reports on Human Rights Practices: Colombia,* Dep't of State, 2022, *available at* https://www.state.gov/reports/2022-country-reports-on-human-rights-practices/colombia/ (last visited February 15, 2024).

104. Christina Noriega, *Colombia's Radical New Approach to Cocaine*, Foreign Pol'y, October 30, 2022, 6:00 AM, *available at* https://foreignpolicy.com/2022/10/30/colombia-cocaine-coca-industry-policy-war-drugs-gustavo-petro/?utm_source=PostUp&utm_medium=email&utm_campaign=Flashpoints%20OC&utm_term=56591&tpcc=Flashpoints%20OC (last visited February 15, 2024).

groups replaced FARC in the drug business, continuing the violence in clashes for power. These violent groups even target community leaders who advocate for the substitution program.

Since President Gustavo Petro—an ex-guerrilla—was elected in 2022, the Colombian government has been pursuing new strategies as it recognizes that the war on drugs is a "categorical failure" that has "left a million Latin Americans dead" without ending the country's drug problem.[105] The leftist president has sparked debate over the decriminalization of cocaine and marijuana in order to decrease funding for organized crime groups. Petro's drug policy reform, which will largely affect the state's counterterrorism efforts, takes the focus away from farmers on the bottom rung who cultivate the illegal plants and instead targets the high-ranking drug traffickers that are continuing the violence.[106]

Issues to Consider

1. What is the price society can tolerate in the context of aggressive counterterrorism?
2. How is the effectiveness of aggressive counterterrorism defined?
3. What is the benefit of temporary relief from terrorism when accomplished by significant violations of human rights?
4. What is the significance of historical enmity between government and terrorist organizations?
5. Is balancing possible if the danger posed to society is constant and pervasive?
6. When, if at all, is aggressive counterterrorism justified?

IX. CONCLUSION

A comparative analysis of how the seven surveyed nations balance legitimate national security interests with equally legitimate individual rights reveals imbalanced approaches in the face of terrorism.

In spite of dissimilar threats, not to mention political, geographic, historical, and social differences, the responses of the seven nations are remarkably similar. The United States detains immigrants based on guilt by association; Israel justified house demolitions (a policy considered collective punishment by the international community) by arguing that the action deters potential terrorists, only to conclude that the policy, though upheld by the High Court of Justice, was ineffective; Russia's operational counterterrorism efforts are characterized by widespread human rights abuses; India enacts and repeals legislation severely curtailing individual rights while simultaneously committing military abuses in Kashmir; Spain imposes an incommunicado detention

105. *Id*
106. *Id.*

policy; China's counterterrorism strategy suggests an emphasis on short-term restrictions contributing to a temporary reduction in terrorism, followed by resurgence; and Colombia's policy is reflective of Russia's in that protections of human rights take a back seat to national security.

The balancing equation—as especially illustrated by Russia, Colombia, and China—reflects a clear emphasis on national security at the expense of human rights. The United States, Israel, India, and Spain's balancing is more nuanced, though all four impose limits on individual rights in an effort to conduct effective counterterrorism.

What are the legal and policy implications of this analysis, and what recommendations can be suggested? Fighting terrorism clearly requires developing policies that enable governments to respond to the threat of terrorism, in whatever form. Yet, the approach adopted by democracies must uphold democratic values and principles. The former president of the Israeli Supreme Court, Aharon Barak, suggests that democracies adopt "self-imposed restraints." Otherwise, according to Barak, the attacked will become like the attacker and lose moral superiority. In developing counterterrorism strategies, nations must be equally cognizant of operational and balancing requirements.

CHAPTER 4

EXECUTIVE AND LEGISLATIVE RESPONSES TO TERRORISM

I. INTRODUCTION

Modern-day terrorism was born on September 5, 1972. That is the date the Palestinian terrorist organization Black September killed 11 Israeli athletes at the 1972 Summer Olympics in Munich. In response, Israeli Prime Minister Golda Meir gave an order to kill those involved in the planning and execution of the attack, creating modern day counterterrorism.

Both the attack and response are of prime importance in understanding terrorism and counterterrorism discussed in this book, notwithstanding significant changes in both over the years. In analyzing this event and its aftermath, there is no attempt to gainsay previous counterterrorism but rather provide background relevant to understanding contemporary comparative counterterrorism.

The name Black September references the events of September 1970 when King Hussein of Jordan forcefully attacked Palestinian's living in Jordan, resulting in significant casualties and claims of torture at the hands of Jordanian forces. As a result of Hussein's actions, many Palestinians left Jordan, making their way to refugee camps in southern Lebanon.[1]

The 1972 Munich Olympics were supposed to mark the "new" Germany, and to erase memories of the heavily criticized 1936 Berlin Olympics when Hitler was provided an opportunity by the International Olympic Committee to present a positive, sanitized image of pre-World War II Nazi Germany. In an effort to show the world a "different" Germany, security at the Olympic village was lax, a matter of tragic significance when examining the events of September 5.

The decision to attack the Israeli athletes reflected Palestinian anger with respect to the events of September 1970, the Israeli-Arab War of 1948, and

1. Al Abed, Oroub. "Palestinian refugees in Jordan." *FMO Research Guide* (2004).

the 1967 Six-Day War primarily between Israel, Syria, Jordan, and Egypt.[2] In the aftermath of both wars, Palestinian refugees became a central issue in the politics and conflict of the Middle East.

To draw attention to their plight and condition, the leaders of Black September determined that the Munich Olympics presented a unique opportunity to put the Palestinian cause "front and center" on the global stage. They were absolutely correct.

As the world watched via live shots from ABC TV, German officials negotiated with the Black September terrorists demanding the release of Palestinians held by Israel. The official Israeli policy was not to negotiate with terrorists.[3] The crisis began with an early morning assault of the living quarters of the Israeli athletes resulting in several deaths. The demands and threats were clear: failure to guarantee release of prisoners would result in the killing of the athletes and coaches held hostage in their living quarters. While the deadline moved throughout the day, Prime Minister Meir was adamant in her position, though there was a lack of direct interaction between German and Israeli officials.

Late in the day, German officials agreed to transport via helicopter the athletes and terrorists to a local airport from which they would fly to an Arab country to effectuate an exchange thereafter.[4] The plan was a German ruse: at the airport, German snipers opened fire on the terrorists who in return killed all the Israelis. From an operational perspective, the operation was a resounding failure reflecting poor planning, ill-equipped forces, and problematic command and leadership.

The German officials refused to allow the participation of Israeli forces, eschewing advise and suggestions from senior Israelis who were on site at the airport. The IOC made the decision, after a memorial service and one day abeyance, to continue the Games. Several Black September terrorists were killed; others were later released when West Germany acceded to demands in the aftermath of the hijacking of a Lufthansa commercial plane.[5]

When ABC TV announcer Jim McKay, informed the world, "they are all gone," the operative question became what Israel would do in response. The answer has become known as "Operation Wrath of God" (Operation Bayonet in Israel), implementing a governmental decision reflecting a combination of retribution-revenge-deterrence.

The operation was conducted by the Mossad, the Israeli national intelligence service that operates outside of Israel's borders, distinct from the SHABAK that operates within Israel, the West Bank, and the Gaza Strip. An operation of this magnitude required teams working in Europe, Cyprus, and

---

2. *Arab-Israeli Wars*, Encyc. Britannica, *available at* https://www.britannica.com/event/Arab-Israeli-wars (last updated Jan. 4, 2024)

3. Calahan, Alexander B., *Countering terrorism: The Israeli response to the 1972 Munich Olympic massacre and the development of independent covert action teams*, PhD diss., Marine Corps Command and Staff College, 1995.

4. *Id.*

5. Carlton, David, and David Carlton. "Rewarding the Palestinians." *The West's Road to 9/11: Resisting, Appeasing and Encouraging Terrorism since 1970* (2005): 47-63.

the Middle East to track targets and to kill them.[6] There was no discussion of capturing-detaining-interrogating the identified Black September operatives. The operational goal was clear and concise, devoid of nuance: kill those deemed responsible for the murder of the 11 Israelis. The killings were conducted in a variety of ways, including shooting and bombs placed in telephones and under an individual's bed; the methods were intended both to kill the intended target but also to send a clear message to others. The operation was halted after a Moroccan waiter in Lillehammer, Norway, was killed due to misidentification.[7]

Notwithstanding this significant operational error, from an Israeli counterterrorism perspective the undertaking was both justified and effective, albeit warranting legitimate and significant critiques. As discussed in Chapter 2, international law does not tolerate revenge-based actions, as operational counterterrorism must reflect the principle of self-defense as articulated in Article 51 of the U.N. Charter. In Chapter 6, the discussion will primarily focus on U.S. drone and Israeli targeted killing policies; both are distinct from Operation Wrath of God as they are predicated on self-defense, rather than the retribution motivation.

Whether the Operation was a success depends on whether the analysis is short-term or long-term based; from a societal "morale" perspective—sending a clear message—the killings were, arguably, effective but received muted criticism from some of the families of the Israeli athletes. From the perspective of sending a clear message to terrorist organizations, the operation reflected significant capability in identifying, tracking, and killing identified targets.

In that sense, Israel achieved its immediate purpose. Whether that had a long-term impact on potential terrorists and future acts of terrorism is an open question. What is clear is that the rationale for operational counterterrorism was expanded by Israel from a self-defense model to a broader rationale, crossing into a "zone" not in accordance with a narrow interpretation of international law.

In later years, the then head of the Mossad, Zvi Zamir, argued that the operation did reflect self-defense rationale by suggesting there was intelligence information indicating future involvement in terrorist attacks by those killed. That argument was met with wide-spread skepticism and has largely been dismissed.[8]

While other attacks, some discussed in this book, exacted a greater price in terms of casualties, what makes Munich-Operation Wrath of God particularly relevant are the following:

- The fact that it was, literally, the first terrorist attack a world-wide audience could watch unfolding "live," including seeing one of the terrorists standing on the balcony;

---

6. *Id.*
7. *Id.*
8. Yair Galily (2022) *'We can only trust ourselves': Operation Wrath of God in Perspective,* Israel Affairs, 28:4, 589-596 (June 15, 2022).

- The comings and goings of German officials interacting with the terrorists;
- The bitter, historical irony of the location of the attack and its unique circumstance;
- Jim McKay's words which were heard by hundreds of millions;
- The clear determination by Israel to extract a steep price;
- The means by which Black September operatives were killed;
- The unapologetic motivation for the Operation.

The attack-operation serves as an important framework for the subsequent discussion in this chapter.

II. UNITED STATES

While Tuesday morning, September 11, 2001, would strike most Americans as the starting date for terrorism—at least as understood by an America that was just attacked—the truth is very different from both the national and international perspective. However, the scope and intensity of the 9/11 attacks dramatically reshaped U.S. understanding of and response to terrorism both in the short and long term.

The shift in America's response has deeply impacted the American political debate and way of life. How a nation responds to such a terrorist attack offers insight to its unique worldview. This outlook is shaped by numerous factors including political infrastructure, culture, and history.

A. HISTORICAL SURVEY

1. The Nixon Administration

The Nixon administration was confronted with international terrorism when Black September killed 11 Israeli athletes in the 1972 Munich Olympics. That day, Americans faced issues that had largely not been a part of the American culture. The impact of that day, primarily a direct result of ABC's television coverage, was significant. Consequently, a survey of America's experience with terrorist attacks begins with the Nixon administration.

According to documents made public, the Nixon administration established a terrorism taskforce.[9] The documents reflect concern regarding potential biological terrorism; however, for various reasons—the Vietnam war, Watergate, and Nixon's resignation from office—the taskforce died a natural death.

9. *See* Frank Bass & Randy Herschaft, *Nixon-Era Terrorism Task Force Envisioned Today's Threats,* Gaffney Ledger, January 24, 2005, *available at* https://www.gaffneyledger.com/articles/nixon-era-terrorism-task-force-envisioned-todays-threats/ (last visited February 15, 2024).

2. The Ford Administration

In response to the Church Committee, which investigated alleged Central Intelligence Agency (CIA) abuses, particularly in Latin America, the Ford administration issued Executive Order 12333[10] outlawing the assassination of leaders of a sovereign state: "No person employed by or acting on behalf of the U.S. government shall engage in, or conspire to engage in, assassination. . . . No agency of the intelligence community shall participate in or request any person to undertake activities forbidden by this order."[11]

The order, reissued by subsequent administrations, was the Ford administration's principal contribution to counterterrorism. It significantly curtailed counterterrorism options available to decision makers.

3. The Carter Administration

Jimmy Carter was, in large part, elected as a response to the Nixon legacy, particularly Watergate. The Carter administration's primary foreign policy focus was human rights. While a laudable aim, the policy's impact on America's national security must be addressed in the context of our survey. In November 1979, 51 Americans were taken hostage in Iran. The administration's operational effort ended when a rescue mission was aborted; eight servicemen were killed. From a counterterrorism perspective, the failed mission should have sent red lights flashing. An elite special forces unit was unable to move beyond the staging area in the Iranian desert because of a sand storm, poor planning, and incompetent command. Certainly, terrorists took note of America's inability to respond while Americans were held hostage.

4. The Reagan Administration

Ronald Reagan's counterterrorism policy sounded firm and decisive: "Let terrorists beware that when the rules of international behavior are violated, our policy will be one of swift and effective retribution."[12] However, reality was very different from stated policy. In what are considered the first suicide bombings conducted by terrorists, hundreds of U.S. Marines were killed in Beirut in two separate attacks. In response, President Reagan ordered the withdrawal of the Marines from Beirut. According to terrorists and students of terrorism alike, this decision may be the seminal event in the history of modern terrorism. Terrorist leaders realized, and no doubt internalized, a wide gulf between America's stated policy and reality. The deterrence threat may have died before it was born.

Similarly, following the brutal murder of Navy SEAL Robert Stethem by Hezbollah terrorists in Beirut during a plane hijacking, the Reagan administration's

---

10. *See* Exec. Order No. 12333, 3 C.F.R. 200, 46 Fed. Reg. 59941, December 4, 1981, *available at* http://www.archives.gov/federal-register/codification/executive-order/12333.html (last visited January 7, 2011).

11. *Id.*

12. Laura K. Donohue, *In the Name of National Security: U.S. Counterterrorist Measures, 1960-2000,* 13 Terrorism and Political Violence 15, Fall 2001.

primary efforts were to negotiate an end to the hijacking. Though television showed terrorists throwing Stethem, still barely alive, onto the airport tarmac after shooting him in the head, the American response—bluster aside—was one of weakness.

President Reagan responded forcefully to the killing of American servicemen in a Berlin disco by attacking Libyan targets, including a presidential palace, allegedly killing one child of the Libyan dictator Mu'amar Qaddafi. However, the attack appears to have been retaliatory in both nature and scope and thus in violation of international law, which does not allow for acts of reprisal.

Furthermore, in a part of the world Americans would become all too acquainted with, the United States was actively encouraging, if not aiding, the Mujahideen in Afghanistan. The Mujahideen was engaged in pitched battle with the Soviet Union following the Red Army's invasion of Afghanistan, thereby facilitating the ascendency of Osama bin Laden, who fought with the Mujahideen. America's singular focus on the Soviet Union, in the context of the Cold War, prevented the Reagan administration from correctly identifying the next threat to world order and stability—terrorism.

5. The First Bush Administration

The first Bush administration's response to the 1988 Pan Am 103 terrorist attack, which claimed 270 innocent lives (189 Americans), was to apply the criminal law paradigm initiating legal proceedings against Libyan agents responsible for the attack. One could argue that the administration was hamstrung because the attack occurred over Scottish territory; nevertheless, Americans flying in an American commercial airliner were the intended target. Not only did the administration choose not to respond operationally against Libya, but its policy response was limited to initiating traditional criminal law procedure.

What paradigm applies to terrorism? Is it criminal law, traditional warfare whereby prisoners of war (POW) status is granted to enemy combatants, or a new paradigm recognizing that terrorism and counterterrorism are neither criminal acts nor acts of war? This issue is discussed in Chapter 9.

Issues to Consider

1. Has the historical lack of a coherent U.S. policy given an unintended green light to terrorists?
2. What explains the lack of congressional involvement in the development of a U.S. counterterrorism policy?
3. Should American decision makers adopt a "walk softly and carry a big stick" (President Theodore Roosevelt) policy rather than bluster?
4. What can be learned from U.S. involvement in Afghanistan and Iraq? How should the legislature respond?

6. The Clinton Administration

The first significant U.S. legislation against terrorism was the 1996 Antiterrorism and Effective Death Penalty Act.[13] President Clinton had previously submitted antiterrorism legislation, which had been bogged down in Congress; however, after the World Trade Center bombing in 1993 and the Oklahoma City bombing in 1995, Congress and the administration agreed on counterterrorism legislation.

The Act established a list of designated foreign terrorist organizations (FTOs) and made it illegal for a person in the United States, or subject to the jurisdiction of the United States, to provide funds or other material to any group on the list. Representatives and members of a designated FTO, if they were not citizens, could be denied visas or otherwise excluded from the United States. Finally, the Act required American financial institutions to block funds of designated FTOs and their agents, and to report this action to the Office of Foreign Assets Control in the Department of the Treasury.[14]

Against the backdrop of the first World Trade Center bombing, which killed six people, the Subcommittee on International Operations of the House Foreign Affairs Committee held a hearing on July 13, 1993.[15] One of its primary purposes was for the Clinton administration to articulate its counterterrorism strategy. During the course of the hearings Assistant Secretary of State Timothy Wirth set forth that policy:

> The Clinton administration is committed to exerting strong and steady leadership in a rapidly-changing world. History has taught us the United States and all nations can meet that challenge by maintaining a commitment to democratic institutions and to the rule of law. Promoting democratic governments and institutions are full—that are fully accountable to their citizens is our most basic tool for advancing free markets and our long-term national security, and addressing the great and complex global issues of our time. Democracy does not sponsor terrorism. It is no accident that states that do—Iraq, Iran, Libya, Cuba—are also among the most repressive for their own citizens.
>
> Mr. Chairman, let me assure you the Clinton administration will remain vigilant in countering whatever threats may be posed by international terrorists to United States interests. Working in close consultation with the Congress, successive administrations have developed a set of principles which continue to guide us as we counter the threat posed by terrorists. These include making no concessions to terrorists, continuing to apply increasing pressure to state sponsors of terrorism, forcefully applying the rule of law to international terrorists, and helping other governments improve their capabilities to counter the threats posed by international terrorists.[16]

---

13. *See* Antiterrorism and Effective Death Penalty Act of 1996, Pub. L. No. 104-132, 110 Stat. 1214 (1996).

14. *Id.* at §219(a)(2)(C).

15. *Hearings and Markup of H. Res. 118, To Condemn the Release by the Government of Malta of Convicted Terrorist Mohammed Ali Rezaq: Before the Subcomm. on International Security, International Organizations and Human Rights of the H. Comm. on Foreign Affairs,* 103rd Cong. (1993).

16. *Id.* at 84.

The policy expounded by Wirth was strong on rhetoric but weak both on concrete operational counterterrorism, and practical legal and policy initiatives that would have taken the fight to the terrorists. A common recurrence—as evidenced in President Reagan's response to the bombing of the Marine barracks—in American counterterrorism strategy is rhetoric not matched by sustained action:

> Another major element of our counter-terrorism policy is a firm response. When President Clinton ordered the cruise missile strike against the headquarters of Iraq's intelligence service, he delivered a firm, proportional and necessary response to the continuing threat against the United States posed by Iraq, as shown by the outrageous Iraqi attempt against the life of former President Bush.
>
> The strike demonstrates that the Clinton administration will respond vigorously, decisively and effectively to the terrorist threat around the world.[17]

To describe this response as "firm" is inaccurate. The administration ordered the raid to be carried out in the middle of the night in order to minimize collateral damage in accordance with international law principles. Nevertheless, from a policy perspective, a nighttime bombing of a largely empty military building by the world's only superpower in response to an attempted assassination of a former president raises acute questions.

From a policy standpoint, the issue is effectiveness. If indeed Iraqi military intelligence played a significant role in the failed assassination attempt, then decision makers must ask whether an attack on the building at night serves the intended purpose of deterrence or even of "message sending." A non-response is arguably more effective because the other side is left guessing when, or if, a response will occur. A weak response—such as the bombing of the building at night—may backfire, Wirth's assessment notwithstanding.

B. POST-9/11

1. Introduction

Since 8:43 A.M. on 9/11, the United States has been playing catch-up, trying to make up for lost time by attempting to level the playing field with terrorists. In American history there is a tendency to go engage in a panic response when attacked.[18] For example, in response to the attack on Pearl Harbor, 120,000 Japanese-Americans were interned without due process. The Supreme Court upheld President Roosevelt's decision, holding it bore a direct relationship to the prevention of espionage and sabotage and was "in accordance with congressional authority."[19]

In an atmosphere of "bringing terrorists to justice" (Former President George W. Bush's frequent phrase), a skewed moral compass is a real possibility,

---

17. *Id.*

18. *See, e.g.,* The Prize Cases, 67 U.S. 635 (1862); Korematsu v. United States, 323 U.S. 214 (1944).

19. *Korematsu* at 218.

threatening the foundation of liberal democratic society and placing traditional values in, at least, temporary abeyance.

Issues to Consider

1. What is the short- and long-term effect of ineffective responses?
2. Does the U.S. leadership sufficiently differentiate between real enemies and perceived enemies?
3. Did U.S. decision makers protect the rights of real enemies and protect perceived enemies from the anger of citizens?
4. Were leaders able to restrain their worst instincts and develop a sound policy based on fundamental principles of the rule of law?
5. What is the impact of playing catch up?

2. The Bush Administration Response—Military Commissions, PATRIOT Act, National Security Strategy Document

President George W. Bush's response can best be understood by examining three documents: the PATRTIOT Act, overwhelmingly ratified by Congress on October 25, 2001;[20] the Presidential Order establishing military commissions (November 2001); and the National Security Strategy document establishing the Bush preemption doctrine (NSSD, October 2002). The timeline is significant: while the first two documents were drafted in the immediate aftermath of the attack, the NSSD was signed by the President a year later.

Post-9/11 American policy must be examined from both a domestic and a foreign perspective. The PATRIOT Act is the legislative response to an attack on American soil articulating tools and measures that Congress provided the administration to defend America; the Presidential Order established a quasi-judicial process devoid of independent judicial review for detainees suspected of involvement in terrorism in Iraq, Afghanistan, and elsewhere, be they foreigners or immigrants living in America, including those living legally in the United States;[21] the NSSD reflects the administration's post-9/11 counterterrorism policy of aggressively taking the fight to the terrorists.

3. The USA PATRIOT Act

The PATRIOT Act has been much discussed, debated, criticized, and misunderstood. Critics of the Bush administration argued that the act reflected disdain for basic civil liberties. Supporters of the administration upheld it as the

20. Uniting and Strengthening America by Providing Appropriate Tools Required to Intercept and Obstruct Terrorism (USA PATRIOT Act) Act of 2001, Pub. L. No. 107-56, 115 Stat. 272 (2001) [hereinafter PATRIOT Act].

21. Military Order of November 13, 2001, Detention, Treatment, and Trial of Certain Non-Citizens in the War Against Terrorism, 66 F.R. 57833 (November 13, 2001) [hereinafter Military Order Terrorism].

appropriate legislative response to an attack on America. Sections 203, 206, 213, 215, 218, and 411 are of particular relevance to this chapter.

To summarize, section 203 allows information from grand juries to be shared with the CIA without prior approval of a judge.[22] Section 206 grants roving surveillance authority after requiring a court order approving an electronic surveillance to direct any person to furnish necessary information, facilities, or technical assistance in circumstances where the court finds that the actions of the surveillance target may have the effect of thwarting the identification of a specified person.[23] Section 213, also known as the "sneak and peek" exception to the "knock and announce" rule, states that notification of searches can be delayed if the notice would seriously jeopardize the investigation. Section 215 authorizes the government to seize any tangible items sought for an investigation to protect against international terrorism or clandestine intelligence activities.[24] Items may include records from banks, credit bureaus, telephone companies, hospitals, or libraries. Section 218 amends the Foreign Intelligence Surveillance Act (FISA) to require that an application for an electronic surveillance order or search warrant certify that a *significant* purpose (formerly "the sole or main purpose") of the surveillance is to obtain foreign intelligence information.[25]

Section 411 of the Patriot Act addresses the issue of the definition of terrorist activity:

> Includes within the definition of "terrorist activity" the use of any weapon or dangerous device.
>
> Redefines "engage in terrorist activity" to mean, in an individual capacity or as a member of an organization, to: (1) commit or to incite to commit, under circumstances indicating an intention to cause death or serious bodily injury, a terrorist activity; (2) prepare or plan a terrorist activity; (3) gather information on potential targets for terrorist activity; (4) solicit funds or other things of value for a terrorist activity or a terrorist organization (with an exception for lack of knowledge); (5) solicit any individual to engage in prohibited conduct or for terrorist organization membership (with an exception for lack of knowledge); or (6) commit an act that the actor knows, or reasonably should know, affords material support, including a safe house, transportation, communications, funds, transfer of funds or other material financial benefit, false documentation or identification, weapons (including chemical, biological, or radiological weapons), explosives, or training for the commission of a terrorist activity; to any individual who the actor knows or reasonably should know has committed or plans to commit a terrorist activity; or to a terrorist organization (with an exception for lack of knowledge).
>
> Defines "terrorist organization" as a group: (1) designated under the immigration and nationality act or by the secretary of state; or (2) a group of two or more individuals, whether related or not, which engages in terrorist-related activities.

---

22. PATRIOT Act of 2001 §203, Pub. L. No. 107-56, 115 Stat. 272 (2001).

23. *Id.* §206; *see* Foreign Intelligence Surveillance Act of 1978, 50 U.S.C. §1805(c)(2)(B) [hereinafter FISA].

24. PATRIOT Act at §215.

25. PATRIOT Act at §218; FISA §1805(c)(2)(B).

Provides for the retroactive application of amendments under this act. Stipulates that an alien shall not be considered inadmissible or deportable because of a relationship to an organization that was not designated as a terrorist organization prior to enactment of this act. States that the amendments under this section shall apply to all aliens in exclusion or deportation proceedings on or after the date of enactment of this act.

Directs the secretary of state to notify specified congressional leaders seven days prior to designating an organization as a terrorist organization.[26]

Issues to Consider

1. Do the provisions of the PATRIOT Act provide the U.S. government with tools previously unavailable?
2. Do the provisions reflect overreaching actions reminiscent of the internment of Japanese-Americans in WWII?
3. Does the Act reflect balancing legitimate national security concerns and individual rights?
4. Has the PATRIOT Act substantially contributed to a safer America?
5. Have the rights of immigrants been substantially and unconstitutionally restricted?
6. Could the administration have implemented active domestic counterterrorism without the PATRIOT Act?
7. What are the ramifications of "sneak and peak"?

Steven Schulhofer[27] has written about the necessity of the PATRIOT Act, questioning whether its provisions fundamentally changed the ability of American law enforcement to conduct counterterrorism within the parameters of the Constitution. According to Schulhofer, the pre-9/11 regime of constitutional and statutory limits on surveillance and intelligence gathering was a complex mixture of stringent restraints, permissive powers, and awkward compromises. The PATRIOT Act shifted this balance in the direction of greatly expanded investigative power—especially by increasing opportunities to conduct e-mail and Internet searches—to authorize clandestine physical searches, to benefit from flexible FISA standards, and to apply these new powers to investigate crimes entirely unrelated to terrorism.

An important Fourth Amendment safeguard is the requirement of immediate notification when a search is conducted. Officers executing a warrant must knock and announce their presence before entering, except when doing so would expose them to danger or risk destruction of the evidence sought. Similarly, the officers must give a copy of the warrant to the occupant or leave it at the premises if he or she is not present, again with a narrow exception for situations where such notice would endanger lives or seriously impede an

26. PATRIOT Act at §411.

27. Stephen Schulhofer, *The Enemy Within: Intelligence Gathering, Law Enforcement, and Civil Liberties in the Wake of September 11* (2002).

investigation. These notice provisions serve to ensure that the target of the search will know that it occurred and have an opportunity to ensure that the particularity limitations of the warrant were respected.[28]

Schulhofer argues that until 9/11, exceptions to these notice requirements were governed by judicial decisions that examined, on a case-by-case basis, the need for conducting a clandestine search (a so-called "sneak and peek") without immediate notification. The "Patriot Act adds to federal law a provision that for the first time gives statutory authorization for clandestine intrusions and defines in broad terms the grounds that can justify delay in notifying the target that her home was searched."[29] Schulhofer has further written that:

> [a] reasonable argument can be made that the case law on clandestine searches needed to be clarified by legislation. A reasonable argument can likewise be made that the broad sneak-and-peek authority codified in the Patriot Act is preferable to the more restrictive view endorsed in some of the cases. Arguments can fairly be made in the other direction as well. But however that debate might best be resolved, this problem has nothing to do with the fight against terrorism. For international terrorism cases, authority to conduct clandestine searches already existed — in much broader terms—under FISA. The new authority conferred by the Patriot Act is simply not needed for such cases, nor is it limited to terrorism cases; it is available in *any* criminal investigation. And because the new sneak-and-peek authority is exempted from the Patriot Act's sunset provision, it will remain in effect indefinitely. There was no justification for adding this issue to an already large emergency agenda after September 11 and for using the momentum of that occasion to obtain endorsement for the justice department's preferred approach to an unrelated problem.[30]

Issues to Consider

1. What is the danger to democratic society when the executive is granted broad powers?
2. How should the effectiveness of new policies be measured, and by whom?
3. What should be the role of Congress in the aftermath of an attack?
4. When should the scope of searches be extended?
5. When should clandestine physical searches be allowed?
6. What is the significance of expanding the definition of terrorist activity?
7. Does national security justify expanded intrusions on an individual's privacy?

The USA PATRIOT Act was originally scheduled to sunset in 2005. However, Congress has consistently reauthorized its provisions, including those that most substantially impose on personal liberty by facilitating invasion of privacy.

28. *Id.* At 43.
29. *Id.*
30. *Id.*

C. THE PRESIDENTIAL ORDER

The 2001 Presidential Order[31] was based on the presidential order issued by President Roosevelt following the arrest of German saboteurs caught in New Jersey and Florida. In *Ex parte Quirin,*[32] the U.S. Supreme Court upheld presidential authority to establish military tribunals; as a result, the saboteurs, including an American citizen, were executed. President Bush's order, which established military commissions for the purpose of trying non-American citizens alleged to be supporting, aiding, and abetting al Qaeda worldwide, was criticized in the United States and abroad. Critics[33] repeatedly commented on serious violations of due process both in the order and the subsequently issued military instructions.[34]

Initial criticism focused on a number of issues, including:

1. Failure to consult with Congress before issuing the order;
2. The fact that the Authorization to Use Military Force ratified by Congress does not provide for the establishment of the Commission;
3. Lack of an independent appeals process;
4. A detainee's inability to challenge the cause for detention;
5. A reduced evidentiary standard allowing the introduction of any evidence found to be of "probative value to a reasonable person."[35]

In retrospect, the decision to hold detainees in Guantanamo Bay seems to have been based on two primary considerations: a desire to detain the individuals geographically distant from the combat zone and not to detain them in the United States, where the argument could be made that they must be granted full constitutional rights.

1. Congressional Hearings

Hearings held before the Senate Judiciary and Armed Services Committees in December 2001[36] brought to focus many of the criticisms leveled against the Military Commissions. Members of the committees (Senators Leahy, Kennedy, and Levin, among others) and expert witnesses (Professors Tribe, Katyal, and Sunstein) roundly criticized the Bush administration, emphasizing its failure to consult with Congress prior to issuing the order and questioning the order's constitutionality. Administration witnesses—Deputy Secretary of Defense Wolfowitz, Attorney General Ashcroft, and Department of Defense General Counsel Haynes—were adamant that President Bush was constitutionally

---

31. Military Order Terrorism, *supra* note 14.
32. Ex parte Quirin, 317 U.S. 1, 24 (1942).
33. *See* Ronald Dworkin, *Terror & the Attack on Civil Liberties,* The New York Review of Books, Nov. 6, 2003, at 37-38; *see also* Neal K. Katyal & Laurence H. Tribe, *Waging War, Deciding Guilt: Trying the Military Tribunals,* 111 Yale L.J., 2002, at 1259, 1277.
34. Katyal & Tribe, *supra* note 33, at 1277; Department of Defense, Military Commission Order No. 1: Procedures for Trials by Military Commissions of Certain Non-United States Citizens in the War Against Terrorism (Mar. 21, 2002, [hereinafter Military Commission Order, Procedures].
35. *See* Dworkin, *supra* note 33; *see also* Katyal & Tribe, *supra* note 33, at 1266-67, 1277.
36. *See* Testimony before the Senate Armed Services Committee on Military Commissions (December 13, 2001).

authorized to issue the order without consulting with Congress based on the "authorization for use of military force."[37] Senators Warner and Sessions argued that the order is an inherent presidential wartime power.

2. Department of Defense Instructions

In the months following the administration's testimony before the Senate, the Department of Defense issued a series of instructions,[38] intended to serve as rules for the commissions. Unlike the unilateral manner in which the administration issued the Presidential Order, the Department of Defense published the instructions to invite public response prior to their implementation. Many human rights organizations responded, overwhelmingly negatively.

3. Results

Since their establishment, the commissions have tried only three suspected terrorists.[39] The process has been continuously stalled both because of intervention by American courts and also because the commissions have been confronted with "avoidable issues." Had the administration consulted with Congress and, no less important, with constitutional and international law experts rather than relying solely on problematic precedent (*Quirin,* whose relevance is doubtful in that WWII was a declared war unlike the present conflict), the Bush administration might have avoided questionable legal advice. Administration advisors (lawyers and non-lawyers alike) whose rush to action was, in the short term, arguably understandable ill-served the President and the nation. The failure to consider that detainees might demand self-representation before an independent judiciary with clear rules of evidence, for example, illustrates a rushed internal process.

4. Combatant Status Review Tribunals

As a result of the Supreme Court's holding in *Rasul v. Bush,*[40] the administration was forced to establish "combatant status review tribunals" to determine both the status of the detainees and whether their continued detention was, based on available intelligence information, warranted. According to the Court's decisions in both *Rasul* and *Hamdi,* a detainee must be afforded notice and opportunity to contest the determination that he is an enemy combatant. According to the Department of Defense's combatant status review tribunal summary, between July 30, 2004 and February 10, 2009, in 581 hearings, 539

37. *Id.*
38. Military Commission Order, Procedures, *supra* note 28.
39. Ali H. Soufan, *Tribunal and Error,* N.Y. Times, February 11, 2010.
40. Rasul v. Bush, 542 U.S. 466 (2004); Hamdi v. Rumsfeld, 542 U.S. 507 (2004).

detainees were deemed enemy combatants and 39 were deemed not to be enemy combatants.[41]

D. THE NATIONAL SECURITY STRATEGY DOCUMENT

The following clauses of 2001 and 2002 NSSDs clearly articulate President Bush's proactive operational counterterrorism policies:

> 1) America will hold to account nations that are compromised by terror, including those who harbor terrorists—because the allies of terror are the enemies of civilization . . . must not allow the terrorists to develop new home bases. Together, we will seek to deny them sanctuary at every turn.[42]
>
> 2) [America] will cooperate with other nations to deny, contain, and curtail our enemies' efforts to acquire dangerous technologies. And, as a matter of common sense and self-defense, America will act against such emerging threats before they are fully formed. . . . In the new world we have entered, the only path to peace and security is the path of action.[43]
>
> 3) We make no distinction between terrorists and those who knowingly harbor or provide aid to them.[44]
>
> 4) We will not hesitate to act alone, if necessary, to exercise our right to self defense by acting preemptively against such terrorists, to prevent them from doing harm against our people and our country.[45]
>
> 5) For centuries, international law recognized that nations need not suffer an attack before they can lawfully take action to defend themselves against forces that present an imminent danger of attack. Legal scholars and international jurists conditioned the legitimacy of preemption on the existence of an imminent threat—most often a visible mobilization of armies, navies, and air forces preparing to attack. We must adapt the concept of imminent threat to the capabilities and objectives of today's adversaries. . . . The United States has long maintained the option of preemptive actions to counter a sufficient threat to our national security. . . . To forestall or prevent such hostile acts by our adversaries, the United States will, if necessary, act preemptively. . . . The United States cannot remain idle while dangers gather.[46]

---

41. Combatant Status Review Tribunal Summary, *available at* https://web.archive.org/web/20071204143115/http://www.dod.mil/pubs/foi/detainees/csrt_arb/index.html (last visited February 15, 2024).

42. *The National Security Strategy of the United States of America*, The White House, (September 17, 2002, *available at* https://georgewbush-whitehouse.archives.gov/nsc/nssall.html (last visited DATE) [hereinafter National Security Strategy].

43. *Id.*

44. *U.S. National Security Strategy: Strengthen Alliances to Defeat Global Terrorism and Work to Prevent Attacks Against Us and Our Friends*, U.S. Dept of State, *available at* https://2001-2009.state.gov/r/pa/ei/wh/15423.htm (last visited May 16, 2023).

45. *Id.*

46. *See generally* National Security Strategy, *supra* note 271; *U.S. National Security Strategy: Prevent Our Enemies From Threatening Us, Our Allies, and Our Friends with Weapons of Mass Destruction*, U.S. Dep't of State, *available at* https://2001-2009.state.gov/r/pa/ei/wh/15425.htm (last visited May 16, 2023).

Issues to Consider

1. Do the provisions of the NSSD mean that the United States is undertaking a policy of violating another nation's sovereignty? Does this document violate Article 51 of the U.N. Charter?
2. Does this document introduce a new concept of anticipatory self-defense? According to this document, when may the U.S. attack another sovereign state who willingly or potentially unwillingly harbors a terrorist organization or individual terrorist? Has preemption been extended further than internationally envisioned?
3. Do the 2002 and 2010 documents reflect a balanced and circumspect response to an attack, or do they reflect an approach potentially throwing world order into chaos?
4. Is the language of the 2002 and 2010 documents specific or deliberately vague in order to leave maximum maneuverability and discretion to the executive?
5. How much potential harm must be envisioned before the government decides to act? How much is reasonable?
6. To what extent were the 2002 and 2010 NSSDs created to exhibit America's strength? Who pays the price?
7. Are both documents an accurate reflection of the attitudes of the majority of American people at the time of their enactments?
8. Is the 2002 NSSD preemptive or reactive? The 2010 NSSD?
9. Do both documents grant overbroad powers resulting in overbroad responses? Is one of the documents symbolically focused on reigning in overbroad powers from a previously overly reactive response?

E. PRESIDENT OBAMA

During the 2008 Presidential campaign, President Obama (then the Democratic nominee) promised, if elected, counterterrorism policies distinct from President Bush's, including closing Guantanamo Bay and not bringing suspected terrorists before Military Commissions. To that end, in January, 2009, President Obama created three White House Task Forces mandated to carry out the following: identify a proper forum for trying suspected terrorists; articulate a lawful interrogation regime; and close Guantanamo Bay. The task forces reflected Obama's stated policy of reversing Bush-era counterterrorism measures. In addition, President Obama sought to strike a different tone: more cooperative, less confrontational, more encompassing, and less unilateral than that of his predecessor. President Obama's National Security Strategy (below) sought to articulate that shift in policy—both with respect to perception and application. However, policy implemented by President Obama was not dissimilar from President Bush's; terrorists and terrorist infrastructure in Pakistan, Afghanistan, and Yemen were aggressively attacked by U.S. drones, resulting in loss of life among intended targets and innocent civilians alike. In addition, President Obama had identified a number of High-Value Detainees who were subject to indefinite detention; furthermore, the Administration's policy on trying 9/11 suspects in U.S. courts was reversed, resulting in Khalid Sheikh Mohammed—a prime 9/11 architect—and four co-conspirators being tried before a Military Commission at Guantanamo Bay.[47] The Administration placed the blame on Congress and gave assurance to Obama's promise that Guantanamo Bay would be closed after the trials.[48] While attempts were made during Obama's terms in office, Guantanamo Bay has remained open.

President Obama's 2011 White Paper: Lawfulness of a Lethal Operation Directed Against a U.S. Citizen Who Is a Senior Operational Leader of Al-Qa'ida or an Associated Force was released to the public in a redacted document. The White Paper's purpose

> sets forth a legal framework for considering the circumstances in which the U.S. government could use lethal force in a foreign country outside the area of active hostilities against a U.S. citizen who is a senior operational leader of al-Qa'ida or an associated force of al-Qa'ida—that is, an al-Qa'ida leader actively engaged in planning operations to kill Americans.[49]

The DOJ was widely criticized since it drastically broadened the definition of a legitimate target: "[T]he condition that an operational leader present an 'imminent' threat of violent attack against the United States does not require the United States to have clear evidence that a specific attack on U.S. persons and interests will take place in the immediate future."[50] Obama's drone policy will be further discussed in Chapter 6.

F. PRESIDENT TRUMP

The Trump Administration picked up where Obama's had left off in the battles against ISIS and al Qaeda. The Administration also focused on Iran's sponsorship of terrorism and the affiliated proxy groups such as Hezbollah. While the sanctions and attack operations had some success, the president's "Muslim ban" and unwillingness to condemn domestic terrorism committed by white supremacists and far-right extremists contradicted the Administration's stated goals of preventing terrorism through work within communities.[51] Obama had previously made efforts to increase transparency regarding drone strikes; however, these efforts were reversed after President Trump signed Executive Order 13862, which removes transparency of civilian

---

47. Jason Ryan & Huma Khan, *In Reversal, Obama Orders Guantanamo Military Trial for 9/11 Mastermind Khalid Sheikh Mohammed*, ABC News, April 4, 2011, 9:46 AM, *available at* https://abcnews.go.com/Politics/911-mastermind-khalid-sheikh-mohammed-military-commission/story?id=13291750 (last visited February 15, 2024).

48. *Id.*

49. *Department of Justice White Paper*, Dep't of Justice, November 8, 2011, *available at* https://www.justice.gov/sites/default/files/oip/legacy/2014/07/23/dept-white-paper.pdf (last visited February 15, 2024).

50. Amos N. Guiora, *The Legal and Ethical Limits of Technological Warfare: Introduction*, 2013 Utah L. Rev. 1215 (2013).

51. Matthew Alcoke, *The Evolving and Persistent Terrorism Threat to the Homeland*, in Counterterrorism Under the Trump Administration: A Fractured Response to a Diversified Threat 61, 65 (Matthew Levitt ed., 2020), https://www.washingtoninstitute.org/media/4151?disposition=inline.

deaths from the public.[52] The Administration's counterterrorism budget cuts resulted in a failure to effectively address the increasing threats of terrorism in Africa. Furthermore, inconsistencies impaired U.S. efforts to work "'by, with, and through' allies in Syria."[53]

G. PRESIDENT BIDEN

Almost 20 years after the military mission in Afghanistan, President Biden pulled troops out of Afghanistan. Biden argued that the mission should have been "narrowly focused on counterterrorism—not counterinsurgency or nation building."[54] The Administration's intent is to change the focus to "threats we face today" in Somalia, al Qaeda in the Arabian Peninsula, al-Nusra in Syria, and ISIS affiliates in African and Asian countries.[55] The Administration's counterterrorism efforts also adjust the focus to internal threats. Unlike his predecessor, Biden announced in 2021 a national strategy to address domestic terrorism "driven by hate, bigotry, and other forms of extremism."[56] The Administration's strategic goals include four pillars: understand and share domestic terrorism related information; prevent domestic terrorism recruitment and mobilization to violence; disrupt and deter domestic terrorism activity; and confront long-term contributors to domestic terrorism. Biden's National Strategic approach "honors and protects both America's security and America's cherished civil rights and civil liberties."[57]

III. ISRAEL

Over the years, Israel has often been criticized for its operational counterterrorism policies and measures. This casebook does not seek to address the political and legal issues related to the occupation, the result of the 1967 Six-Day War. Similarly, the casebook does not address the security ramifications of the Oslo Peace Process, including the Israeli disengagement from the Gaza Strip

---

52. *U.S. Halts Reporting of Civilian Deaths by Drone Outside War Zones,* Reuters, (March 6, 2019, 2:18 PM, *available at* https://www.reuters.com/article/us-usa-trump-drones/u-s-halts-reporting-of-civilian-deaths-by-drone-outside-war-zones-idUSKCN1QN2PD (last visited February 15, 2024).

53. Matthew Levitt, *Introduction: In Search of a Strategy to Contend with a Diversified International Terrorist Threat,* in Counterterrorism Under the Trump Administration: A Fractured Response to a Diversified Threat 61, 65 (Matthew Levitt ed., 2020), *available at* https://www.washingtoninstitute.org/media/4151?disposition=inline.

54. *Remarks by President Biden on Afghanistan,* The White House, August 16, 2021, 4:02 PM, *available at* https://www.whitehouse.gov/briefing-room/speeches-remarks/2021/08/16/remarks-by-president-biden-on-afghanistan/ (last visited February 15, 2024).

55. *Id.*

56. *Statement by President Joseeph R. Biden, Jr. on the National Strategy for Countering Domestic Terrorism,* The White House, June 15, 2021, *available at* https://www.whitehouse.gov/briefing-room/statements-releases/2021/06/15/statement-by-president-joseph-r-biden-jr-on-the-national-strategy-for-countering-domestic-terrorism/ (last visited February 15, 2024).

57. National Strategy for Countering Domestic Terrorism, Nat'l Sec. Council, June 2021, *available at* https://www.whitehouse.gov/wp-content/uploads/2021/06/National-Strategy-for-Countering-Domestic-Terrorism.pdf (last visited February 15, 2024).

or the designations of areas, "A, B, and C" in the West Bank. Furthermore, the casebook does not address the implications-consequences of Israeli elections and the establishment (2023) of a far-right government.

Rather, the focus is solely on legal and policy responses to terrorism from a historical perspective to provide the reader as broad an overview as possible, devoid of particular nuance relevant to different Israeli governments. Given the literal "revolving door" of governments, reflecting a never-ending cycle of elections, this approach will strike the most reasonable (and feasible) discussion of Israel counterterrorism law and policy.

A. INTRODUCTION

Israel has been under attack literally from the moment of statehood (May 1948). A series of wars—1948, 1956, 1967, 1973, 1982, and 2006—between Israel and its neighbors, state and non-state alike, will not be discussed in this book. Rather, the focus, in the context of counterterrorism, will be Israeli measures relevant exclusively to the West Bank and the Gaza Strip. Accordingly, Israel's conflict with Hezbollah (southern Lebanon) will not be addressed. In focusing on the West Bank and Gaza Strip, note is taken of the changing nature of terrorist tactics and strategy; the constant tension between proactive and reactive measures reflects the reality of addressing the legal and policy aspects of operational counterterrorism. Because successive Israeli governments articulate distinct approaches—albeit largely applying similar measures—the discussion and questions below are intended to provide an overview. In broad strokes, Israeli counterterrorism measures in the West Bank and Gaza Strip became a focus for government and the Israel Defense Forces in response to the Palestinian *intifada* (1987-1994). In the subsequent years these measures have become an important, sometimes dominant, aspect of Israeli politics, culture, and society. The wax and wane reflect the intensity of attacks, whether in Israel proper or against the IDF and/or Israelis living in the West Bank and Gaza Strip.[58]

Issues to Consider

1. What is the meaning of significant terror attack?
2. Should a state respond to all terror attacks in a similar fashion?
3. In terms of policy effectiveness, what should be the benchmark for deciding when and how a state should respond?
4. How attuned should a state be to the court of international opinion when deciding on a particular course of action?

58. The consequence of Israel's disengagement from the Gaza Strip (2005) is that Israelis no longer live there and with rare exceptions the IDF does not enter with ground forces, rather attacking Hamas targets from the air.

It has been Israel's policy since 1967 to respond to terrorism with a combination of measures—some intended to punish the individual terrorist, others aimed at deterring those who might be contemplating an act of terrorism. Israeli methods have included targeted killing of a terrorist under the principle of aggressive self-defense; demolishing the home of a terrorist; imposing a curfew on neighborhoods and towns, either in response to intelligence information indicating a potential terrorist attack or in response to an actual attack; deportation of terrorists; placing terrorists in administrative detention when criminal evidence was unavailable or concern for sources prevented the information from being presented to a court of law; and trying terrorists in a court of law. These measures have been based on Israeli law, international law, or regulations inherited from the British mandate.

As all actions undertaken by the executive in Israel are reviewable by the judiciary—the Supreme Court sitting as the High Court of Justice—the Israel Defense Forces (the executive in the occupied territories) must always be conscious of the possibility that the Court will intervene, including ordering the military not to embark on a particular course of action regardless of its operational efficacy.[59]

B. POST-2000 POLICY

Since 2000, Israel has significantly changed operational counterterrorism tactics and strategy in response both to suicide bombings and the firing of thousands of Kassam missiles from Gaza into southern Israel. Rather than relying on measures considered appropriate and effective between 1967 and 2000, the IDF has implemented a far more aggressive policy reflecting a situation defined as "armed conflict short of war." This is in direct contrast to stone throwing, Molotov cocktails, stabbings, and massive demonstrations that—in large part—previously characterized Palestinian terrorism. Measures applied in response to the *intifada* have given way to more aggressive operational counterterrorism decision making, reflecting recognition that the change in Palestinian measures dictated a fundamental change.

C. SUICIDE BOMBERS

The fundamental change in Israeli counterterrorism policy is a response to the suicide bomber threat. A successful suicide bombing is the work of a well-orchestrated, difficult-to-penetrate, highly disciplined, financially solvent terror organization—not the act of a lone individual. To that end, a successful suicide bombing requires four distinct actors: the bomber, the leader, the logistician, and the financier. Operational counterterrorism decision makers, tasked with preventing suicide bombers, need to determine both which of these four distinct categories is a legitimate actor and when is the state justified to engage

59. It is unclear as of this writing how, and whether, the newly established Israeli government (Prime Minister Netanyahu) will make fundamental changes impacting both the Supreme Court and the IDF (in the West Bank).

them. Suicide bombings are a reality faced by numerous countries including the United States, Russia, Israel, Iraq, Afghanistan, Spain, England, Indonesia, and Saudi Arabia. While suicide bombers do not threaten the existence of these nations, they affect the daily lives of millions of innocent civilians.

D. THE SECURITY FENCE

The approximately 385-mile security fence Israel has erected on the Palestinian side of the Green Line has been described by Israel as a self-defense measure responding to Palestinian terrorism.[60] Different chapters of this casebook address various aspects of the fence including international law, operational counterterrorism, and judicial review. Nevertheless, the decision to build the fence is first and foremost a matter of policy; accordingly, it must be addressed in this chapter.

According to the Israeli government, the primary impetus for the construction of the fence was to prevent infiltration into Israel by Palestinian terrorists. Though the fence has been heavily criticized domestically and internationally, both legally and politically, Israel has responded to such criticism by pointing to statistics indicating that the fence has been most effective in fulfilling its primary purpose as defined by the government: protecting innocent Israeli civilians.

In deciding to erect the security barrier, the government argued it was balancing legitimate national security concerns with the equally legitimate rights of residents of the Palestinian Authority (PA) on whose land the fence would be built. In arguing that the fence was constructed on the Palestinian side of the West Bank solely for strategic and topographic reasons, the state denied the fence was an illegal grab of Palestinian land.[61] While upholding the fence's legality, the Israeli High Court of Justice wrote that it "affects the fabric of Palestinian life" by separating farmers from their land, children from their schools, and friends from neighbors, thereby causing great difficulties for Palestinians to move freely within the PA's area.[62] Accordingly, the Court ordered the state to re-contour the fence in order to minimize the damage to individual Palestinians.

The fence, then, is a manifestation of active self-defense. Israel decided to construct the fence because of a belief—ultimately shown to have statistical validity—that the measure would prove effective in preventing infiltration of suicide bombers into Israel.

International law requires the nation-state to minimize collateral damage and seek alternatives; conversely, the state's fundamental obligation is to protect its citizens. Israel's operational response to suicide bombing was two-fold: targeted killing (see Chapter 6) and the fence. As demonstrated by

60. *See Israel's Security Fence, available at* http://www.jewishvirtuallibrary.org/jsource/Peace/fence.html (last visited October 6, 2010).

61. HCJ 2056/04, Beit Sourik Village Council v. The Government of Israel & Commander of the IDF Forces in the West Bank [2004]

62. *Id.* at ¶¶ 82-85.

the significant reduction in the number of suicide bombings, the twin-edged policy has proven statistically effective. That said, criticism has been consistent and severe; the negative impact on Palestinian landowners whose land was used (though compensation was offered) for the fence has, as the Court stated, negatively impacted the civilian population.

E. OPERATION CAST LEAD

In January 2006—once Israel disengaged from the Gaza Strip (August 2005)—Hamas assumed administrative control of Gaza after winning Palestinian legislative elections. In response, Israel closed off all access to Gaza; in addition, Egypt closed the Rafah Border Crossing. The blockade allowed Israel to control the flow of goods and services, including power and water, into Gaza. Palestinians sought to bypass the blockade by digging tunnels between Gaza and Egypt; the tunnels, in addition to transporting food and supplies, were a primary means for smuggling Kassam missiles into Gaza.

Between disengagement and December 2008, Hamas fired approximately 10,000 Kassam missiles into southern Israel, thereby placing 750,000 Israelis who live in a 45-kilometer radius of the Gaza Strip in daily threat of direct attack. According to the United Nations, these attacks killed four Israeli civilians and injured an additional seventy-five. In June, 2008, Egypt helped broker a six-month ceasefire between Israel and Hamas. According to the agreement, Hamas would end its rocket and mortar attacks, and Israel would ease restrictions on goods coming into Gaza and halt military raids in Gaza.

However, in November 2008, less than four months after the ceasefire began, the IDF entered the Gaza strip killing several Hamas terrorists. Hamas responded by firing rockets into southern Israel; Israel claimed the incursion was not a violation of the ceasefire but rather a legitimate act to eliminate an immediate threat. Fawzi Barhoum, a Hamas spokesman, stated that "[t]he Israelis began this tension and they must pay an expensive price."[63]

On December 27, 2008, in response to an increase in the number and frequency of rocket attacks into Israel, the IDF launched Operation Cast Lead targeting both Hamas infrastructure and those responsible for firing the Kassam missiles.

Israel defined four distinct categories as legitimate targets:

1. Those responsible for smuggling missiles from Egypt through the tunnels between Gaza and Egypt;
2. Those responsible for making Kassam missiles in Gaza;
3. Those responsible for firing Kassam missiles; and
4. Passive supporters who knowingly and repeatedly facilitated firing of the Kassam missiles.

Unlike the person-specific counterterrorism policy that had been Israel's *modus operandi,* Operation Cast Lead unilaterally expanded the categories of legitimate targets and re-articulated proportionality in the context of

63. Rory McCarthy, *Gaza Truce Broken as Israeli Raid Kills Six Hamas Gunmen,* Guardian, November 5, 2008, *available at* http://www.guardian.co.uk/world/2008/nov/05/israelandthepalestinians (last visited February 21, 2010).

operational counterterrorism. The operation began with a series of airstrikes simultaneously hitting 100 preplanned targets. Over the following weeks, Israel continued airstrikes in Gaza, in addition to naval operations and a ground invasion. According to human rights NGOs, between 1300-1400 people were killed during the attacks; reports estimate 330 were Palestinian combatants.[64] The operation continued until January 18, 2009, when both parties declared a ceasefire.

In subsequent years, reflecting various responses to Palestinian terrorism, Israel has conducted a variety of operations, suggesting different policy approaches. Regardless of the specifics of the action—proactive or reactive—the core principles (and measures) have not fundamentally changed, reflecting the tension between targeting specific targets and reducing collateral damage and the unintended consequences of injuring, if not killing, the innocent Palestinian population. The measures, in the past years, have primarily focused on the following:

1. Targeted killing of identified targets;
2. Arrests (in the West Bank) of suspected terrorists;
3. On-the-ground engagement with suspected terrorists in the West Bank;
4. Demolition (rarely applied) of terrorist homes;

Issues to Consider

1. To what extent should counterterrorism measures be constant as compared to "fixed?"
2. What are the risks of responding to different threats with different, changing policies?
3. What are the operational cost-benefits of a limited counterterrorism policy?
4. How is effectiveness to be measured when analyzing decades-long counterterrorism?

IV. RUSSIA

A. INTRODUCTION

Russia has faced terrorism similar to that faced by Israel. Fighting terrorism committed by ethnic Chechens consumed most of Russia's counterterrorism resources for two decades following the collapse of the Soviet Union. Today,

64. B'Tselem, *B'Tselem's Investigation of Fatalities in Operation Cast Lead, available at* http://www.btselem.org/Download/20090909_Cast_Lead_Fatalities_Eng.pdf; *Rights Group Names 1,417 Gaza War Dead,* Washington Times, Mar. 19, 2009, *available at* http://www.webcitation.org/5niC4Iiub (last visited February 15, 2024); United Nations Offices for the Coordination of Humanitarian Affairs, *Field Update on Gaza from the Humanitarian Coordinator, available at* https://www.un.org/unispal/document/auto-insert-202962/ (last visited February 15, 2024).

much of Russia's counterterrorism efforts focus on suppressing dissent within the Russian population using harsh criminal charges and sentences.

The people of Chechnya attempted to declare independence in 1991 like the people of many other regions which had been part of the USSR. Chechens held a presidential election which was declared illegal by the new Russian Federation,[65] which did not recognize Chechnya's independence. Tensions between the Russian government and the self-declared independent Chechnya escalated in the First Chechen War from 1994-1996.[66] The war—which ended in Russian defeat—obliterated the capital, Grozny, and caused as many as 100,000 civilian deaths.[67] The Russian withdrawal attracted Islamic veterans of Russia's conflict in Afghanistan,[68] and the republic struggled with widespread lawlessness.[69]

In 1999, President Aslan Maskhadov of Chechnya announced that the republic would begin implementing Shariah law.[70] That same year, about 2,000 rebels from Chechnya entered the neighboring republic of Dagestan to establish an independent Islamic state,[71] and multiple apartment buildings that were bombed in Moscow and Volgodonsk were blamed on Chechen terrorists.[72] Recently appointed Prime Minister Vladimir Putin ordered the Russian military to intervene in Chechnya, which was the start of the Second Chechen War.[73] Though reliable figures are hard to come by, nearly 400,000 civilians may have been killed in this second war.[74] Though the war ended in 2009[75] and Chechen terrorism is no longer a major threat, the Chechen republic is governed repressively, and accounts of horrific human rights violations are frequent.[76]

---

65. *Soviet Union: Human Rights Developments*, Hum. Rts. Watch, *available at* http://www.hrw.org/reports/1992/WR92/HSW-05.htm#P328_99935 (last visited January 25, 2023).

66. *Chechnya Profile - Timeline*, BBC News, January 17, 2018, *available at* https://www.bbc.com/news/world-europe-18190473 (last visited February 15, 2024).

67. Andrew Higgins, *The War That Continues to Shape Russia, 25 Years Later, available at* https://www.nytimes.com/2019/12/10/world/europe/photos-chechen-war-russia.html (last visited February 1, 2023).

68. G.D. Bakshi, *The War in Chechnya: A Military Analysis*, 24 Strategic Analysis 5 (2000), *available at* https://ciaotest.cc.columbia.edu/olj/sa/sa_aug00bag01.html.

69. Higgins, *supra* note 67.

70. BBC News, *supra* note 66.

71. Mikhail Alexseev, *The Current Crisis in Dagestan and Chechnya: Will the Federation Emerge Intact?*, Wilson Ctr., November 18, 1999, *available at* https://www.wilsoncenter.org/article/the-current-crisis-dagestan-and-chechnya-will-the-federation-emerge-intact (last visited February 15, 2024).

72. *Id.* Some believe that the apartment bombings were orchestrated by the Russian government as a pretext to invade Chechnya. For information on this theory, see Mike Eckel, *Two Decades On, Smoldering Questions about the Russian President's Vault to Power*, RFE/RL, August 7, 2019, *available at* https://www.rferl.org/a/putin-russia-president-1999-chechnya-apartment-bombings/30097551.html (last visited February 15, 2024).

73. Eckel, *supra* note 72.

74. Academica Press, *Chronicles of the First and Second Chechen Wars, available at* https://www.academicapress.com/node/415 (last visited February 2, 2023).

75. Michael Schwirtz, *Russia Ends Operations in Chechnya*, N.Y. Times, Apr. 16, 2009, *available at* https://www.nytimes.com/2009/04/17/world/europe/17chechnya.html (last visited February 15, 2024).

76. *See, e.g.*, Press Release, U.S. Dep't State, Continuing Human Rights Concerns Regarding the Russian Federation's Republic of Chechnya, January 27, 2022, *available at* https://www.state.gov/continuing-human-rights-concerns-regarding-the-russian-federations-republic-of-chechnya/(last visited February 15, 2024); U.S. Mission to OSCE, Statement on Ongoing Human Rights Abuses and Violations in Chechnya, January 17, 2019, *available at* https://osce.usmission.gov/on-ongoing-human-rights-abuses-and-violations-in-chechnya/ (last visited February 15, 2024).

B. RUSSIAN POLICY—DETERRENCE AND TOUGHNESS

Toughness is of paramount importance for the Russian authorities; popular opposition to attacks against civilian targets suggests ready support for uncompromising retaliation. In response to the Chechen attack on the Moscow theater (discussed in Chapter 3), Putin apparently sanctioned use of an unspecified debilitating gas to neutralize explosive-laden terrorists.[77] Russian leadership considered both the potential for negative public reaction to any concession to the terrorists and the possibility that a harsh and swift response might deter similar acts in the future.[78]

Russia's counterterrorism legislation and policy are telling: politicians and leaders unequivocally and candidly define Russia's counterterrorism policy as active and firm. The government has clearly articulated that it intends to pursue an aggressive counterterrorism strategy, combined with maximum implementation of existing legislation granting the executive broad authority.

C. RUSSIAN LEGISLATION

Articles 205-207 and 277 of the Criminal Code of the Russian Federation address terrorism-related crimes. Article 205 defines terrorism as "the perpetration of an explosion, arson, or any other action endangering the lives of people, causing sizable property damage, or entailing other socially dangerous consequences, if these actions have been committed for the purpose of violating public security, frightening the population, or exerting influence on decision-making by governmental bodies." Violating this statute is punishable by imprisonment for five to ten years, and the length of incarceration is greater if the act is committed as part of a conspiracy, repeatedly, or with the use of firearms. The statute also grants amnesty to a person who is involved in planning an act of terrorism if the person warns the authorities and thereby helps prevent the act from being carried out.[79]

The Law on Counteraction against Terrorism, passed in 2006 and still in force, defines terrorism differently. It says terrorism is "the ideology of violence and the practice of influencing the adoption of a decision by public authorities, local self-government bodies or international organizations connected with frightening the population and (or) other forms of unlawful violent actions." The law also differentiates between a "terrorist act" and "terrorist activity." The former includes causing an explosion or arson to frighten the population and which poses danger to life or which could cause ecological catastrophe, "as well as other especially grave consequences," if the

77. *See* Matt Bivens, *Chechnya War Making Not Breaking Terrorism,* The Moscow Times, Nov. 1, 2002, at 2557.

78. Andrei Shoumikhin, *Deterring Terrorism: Russian Views,* National Institute for Public Policy, Feb. 2004, at 1.

79. *See* Russ. Federation Fed. Law No. 63-FZ, June 13, 1996, translation *available at* https://www.wto.org/english/thewto_e/acc_e/rus_e/wtaccrus48_leg_6.pdf (last visited January 19, 2023); *see also* Ugolovnyi Kodeks [UK][*Criminal Code*] arts. 205-08, 277, 360 (Russ.) (translated into English by William E. Butler & Maryann E. Gashi-Butler, *Criminal Code of the Russian Federation,* 3rd ed.).

purpose is to unlawfully influence government leaders or international organizations. The latter includes "arranging, planning, preparing, financing and implementing an act of terrorism," as well as establishing an unlawful armed group, popularizing terrorist ideas, or disseminating information urging terrorist activities or justifying such activity.[80]

Notably absent from the criminal code and the 2006 law is a definition of "terrorist." The laws instead attempt to define terrorism and terrorism-related activities, and define them broadly. They include the organization, planning, preparation, and implementation of terrorist acts. The significance of such a definition is that any individual involved in any stage—no matter its significance or ultimate contribution—of a particular terrorist action may be convicted of the crime of terrorism.

The broadness of this legislation is susceptible to abuse. Examples of ways that Russian authorities have used their broad authority to silence government critics (which they label as terrorists) will be discussed in Chapter 6.

Issues to Consider

1. Is a broad definition of terrorist activity conducive to fighting terrorism?
2. Is a broad definition conducive to balancing legitimate national security concerns and the rights of the individual?

V. INDIA

A. BACKGROUND

India is one of the world's most terrorism-afflicted countries. In 2008, in a pivotal moment called "26/11," terrorists attacked a variety of locations in Mumbai, killing at least 183 people, including 22 foreigners and 14 members of the police and security forces. In addition, over 300 individuals were injured.

Over the years India has faced complicated terrorist threats from multilateral sources.[81] Israel's threat comes from Palestinian terrorism; Russia's from Chechen terrorism; Spain's, until March 2004, was Basque terrorism. But the threats India faces come in many forms—ethnic separatists, nationalists, and the disenfranchised.[82] India's challenge in developing coherent legal and policy responses is to counter one threat without inviting criticism from another

80. Federal Law on Counteraction against Terrorism 2006, No. 35-FZ, art. 3, *available at* https://rm.coe.int/ct-legislation-russian-federation/16806415f5 (last visited February 15, 2024).

81. *The Current Crisis in South Asia: Hearing Before the Subcomm. On the Middle East and S. Asia of the H. Comm. On Int'l Relations*, 107th Cong., 2002, at 10 (statement of Michael Krepon, Founding President, The Henry L. Stimson Center).

82. *See* Law Commission of India, 173rd Report on Prevention of Terrorism Bill, 2000 §II 1.5-9 (2000), *reprinted in* L.K. Thakur, *Essentials of Pota and Other Human Rights Laws* 58-60 (2002) (citing over 2000 militant-related deaths in the northeast region of India during the late 1990s).

group, which may conclude that a particular policy or legislation unfairly impinges on their rights.

B. LEGISLATION

1. Terrorism and Disruptive Activities Act

In 1985 the government approved the Terrorism and Disruptive Activities (Prevention) Act (TADA) (amended 1987).[83] TADA came into law partly in response to the 1984 assassination of Prime Minister Indira Gandhi by militant Sikh extremists. Rajiv Gandhi, Indira's son and successor as prime minister, supported the legislation because various militant groups in India's east, north, and south were engaging in ongoing guerrilla attacks against the state. TADA's provisions expanded the central government's powers with respect to individuals whom the statute classified as terrorists. For example, at a judge's discretion, trials of accused terrorists could be held *in camera*. Moreover, Section 21 of the Act presumed that suspected terrorists were guilty until proven innocent. In addition, the state could arrest anyone upon mere suspicion of terrorist activity and hold the person without bail.

While the Act was created to enable the government to counter terrorism, the legislation died a natural death in 1995 when public pressure forced Parliament not to reenact the Act at its two-year renewal date. Consistent internal and international criticism accused the government of using the legislation as a means to target minorities and political opponents. Although TADA died a "legislative death," its shadow continues to loom for two reasons. First, even though TADA is no longer in effect, the state retains the power to charge suspected persons retroactively for crimes committed during the period of its enactment. Second, the Indian Supreme Court, in 1994, legitimized the statute by deeming constitutional one of its central provisions, allowing courts to admit into evidence uncorroborated witness statements gathered by the police. Observers wondered whether the executive branch would push for legislation further enhancing the powers of the police; in the years that followed, these concerns were justified.[84]

2. Prevention of Terrorism Act

The December 13, 2001 attack on the Indian parliament carried out by five Muslim terrorists resulted in legislating the Prevention of Terrorism Act (POTA). According to Human Rights Watch, POTA was a source of great concern:

> POTA creates an overly broad definition of terrorism, prevention of terrorism act while expanding the state's investigative and procedural powers. Suspects can be detained for up to three months without charge, and up to three months more with the permission of a special judge. Its close resemblance to TADA foreshadowed a return to widespread and systematic curtailment of civil

---

83. Terrorist and Disruptive Activities Prevention Act, No. 28 of 1987 (India) [hereinafter TADA].

84. Jayanth K. Krishnan, *India's "Patriot Act": POTA and the Impact on Civil Liberties in the World's Largest Democracy,* 22 Law & Ineq. J., 2004, at 265, 267-269.

> liberties. Under TADA, tens of thousands of politically motivated detentions, acts of torture, and other human rights violations were committed against Muslims, Sikhs, Dalits (so-called untouchables), trade union activists, and political opponents in the late 1980s and early 1990s. In the face of mounting opposition to the act, India's government acknowledged these abuses and consequently let TADA lapse in 1995.
>
> Indian and international human rights groups, journalists, opposition parties, and minority rights groups have unequivocally condemned POTA. Numerous political parties have alleged the misuse of POTA against political opponents in states such as Uttar, Pradesh, and Jammu and Kashmir. Since it was first introduced, the government has added some safeguards to protect due process rights but POTA's critics stress that the safeguards do not go far enough and that existing laws are sufficient with respect to the threat of terrorism. India's national human rights commission has stated that "existing laws are sufficient to deal with any eventuality, including terrorism, and there is no need for a draconian POTA."
>
> Since its passage, POTA has been used against political opponents, religious minorities, Dalits, tribals and even children. In February 2003 alone, over three hundred people were arrested under the act.
>
> On February 19, 2003, the Gujarat government charged 131 Muslims under POTA for allegedly attacking Hindus. Human rights watch investigations revealed that attacks against Muslims were carried out with extensive state participation and support and planned months in advance of the Godhra attack. The Hindu nationalist Bharatiya Janata party that heads the state government has not charged any Hindus under POTA for violence against Muslims.[85]

On September 17, 2004, the new Indian government of Prime Minister Manmohan Singh announced that it would honor an election pledge to repeal POTA and amend existing laws targeting terrorist activity. The new government acknowledged that certain provisions of POTA allowed for widespread abuse, such as dispensing with the presumption of innocence, the compulsory denial of bail, and the admissibility of confessions despite the rampant use of torture and coercion by police and security forces.

Issues to Consider

1. How did POTA define terrorism? Is the definition too broad, curtailing civil liberties?
2. Was the bill aimed at one particular ethnic group, or was it all-encompassing, reflecting India's ethnic and religious diversity?
3. Did the legislation enable the Indian government to arrest with minimal standards?
4. Were the rights of detainees adequately protected?
5. Would special POTA courts fully protect the rights of the accused?

85. In the Name of Counter-Terrorism: Human Rights Abuses Worldwide: A Human Rights Watch Briefing Paper for the 59th Session of the United Nations Commission on Human Rights, March 25, 2003, *available at* http://www.hrw.org/en/reports/2003/03/25/name-counter-terrorism-human-rights-abuses-worldwide (last visited December 27, 2023).

6. Would special POTA courts raise concerns similar to those raised with respect to the military commissions and the rights guaranteed to the detainees at Guantanamo?
7. How did the legislation affect civil liberties and civil rights in India?
8. Can terrorism be deterred by a counterterrorism policy that is largely legislation-oriented?

Minister of Home Affairs Advani pointed out during the debate on POTA that the Supreme Court recommended to the police how to conduct investigations. According to Advani, these recommendations were incorporated into the new bill. For example, under POTA, defendants could invoke the right to silence while police had to provide warnings that anything defendants said in the course of the interrogation could be used against them in court.[86] Moreover, POTA explicitly barred the police from using coercion in order to obtain a statement from an individual.[87] The state could punish any police official found abusing this authority with a fine and up to two years' incarceration. POTA also assured defendants a statutory right to appeal a criminal conviction to a state high court.[88] For these reasons, both Advani and Prime Minister Vajpayee promised POTA could effectively combat terrorism while protecting defendants' rights to due process and a fair trial.

Some parliamentarians (members of the opposition who argued against the bill's passage) charged that the Bhartiya Janta Party (BJP) was using POTA as a means of pandering to its Hindu fundamentalist constituency. Others suggested that POTA was not so much an antiterrorism measure but rather a "terrorist law [that would be] . . . used to terrorize minorities." Still others worried that the BJP would employ POTA as a tool to harass or threaten political enemies who disagreed with government policy. These dissenting voices failed to carry the day,[89] though ultimately—only two years later—the Act was repealed.

3. India's Current Antiterrorism Laws (Post-2008)

In response to the November 2008 Mumbai attacks, the Indian government proposed a new agency, the National Investigative Agency, to create a national-level capability to investigate and potentially prosecute similar acts. Also, in response to the Mumbai attacks, the Indian government amended existing laws to strengthen security and law enforcement agencies in fighting terrorism. Two themes that have framed the public debate with respect to the

86. *Id.* at art. 32(2).
87. V. Venkatesan, *POTA Prospects,* 19 Frontline, March 30-April 12, 2002, *available at* https://frontline.thehindu.com/the-nation/article30244424.ece (last visited February 15, 2024).
88. The Prevention of Terrorism Act, 2002, Act No. 15 of 2002, art. 34, *available at* http://www.satporg/satporgtp/countries/india/document/actandordinances/POTA.htm (last visited Oct. 1, 2010) [hereinafter Prevention of Terrorism Act].
89. Krishnan, *supra* note 84, at 271-73.

new legislation are states' rights versus federal power and civil liberties versus stronger law enforcement powers.

Issues to Consider

1. What is an appropriate legislative response to an act of terrorism?
2. What powers should the legislature grant the executive in times of crisis?
3. Does an attack—regardless of the cost of human life—justify legislation limiting civil and political rights?
4. What are the lessons learned from TADA and POTA?
5. How should the effectiveness of such legislation be weighed and determined?
6. What limits should be placed on the security forces in response to successful terrorist acts?

VI. SPAIN

On March 11, 2004, 198 Spaniards were killed and more than 1400 wounded in Madrid when 10 bombs exploded in commuter trains, 3 days prior to national elections. According to most commentators, the objective of the attacks was both to influence the election and to force Spain to withdraw its military forces that were part of the coalition fighting the regime of Saddam Hussein in Iraq. Following the election, won by the Socialist Party's Luis Rodriguez Zapatero, Spain withdrew from Iraq in spite of strong international political pressure to remain there.

In the following months, Spanish authorities arrested 62 people in connection with the bombing and more than 30 individuals involved in planning additional attacks. According to Spanish sources, some of those arrested had connections to international terrorism, suggesting that not only is Spain a target of international terrorism, but it has, furthermore, become an "entry point to Europe" for terrorists.[90]

Though Islamic fundamentalists carried out the attack, Spaniards have encountered domestic terrorism for years. The Euskadi Ta Askatasuna (Basque Homeland and Freedom, ETA) had waged a decades-long campaign against the Spanish government in seeking to establish an independent Basque state. The Basque nationalists have killed hundreds, intimidated thousands, and forced thousands of Spaniards to live under the threat of violence. Spain's counterterrorism legislation and policy have been, over the years, tailored to the threat posed by ETA (domestic terrorism) rather than to an international/domestic threat.

---

90. Renwick McLean, *Spain Arrested More than 130 Suspects in Islamic Terrorism in '04*, N.Y. Times, Jan. 6, 2005, at A6.

A. SPANISH DOMESTIC LEGISLATION

Chapter VIII of the Spanish Criminal Code (article 571) defines terrorism as "belonging, acting in the service of or collaborating with armed groups, organizations or groups whose object is to subvert the constitutional order or seriously alter public peace."[91] According to this legislation, mere support—either direct or indirect—of terrorism may lead to prosecution under the law. The low threshold required for liability under the law is reminiscent of the "material support" clause of the PATRIOT Act.[92]

The Spanish model serves as a point of discussion for an additional issue: whether the legislative response to domestic/international terrorism should differ from exclusively domestic terrorism. Over the years, Spain has been criticized for domestic legislation regarding ETA that has violated human rights.[93] Terrorists in Spain are tried before the Audiencia Nacional (National High Court), created in 1977 with jurisdiction over "crimes committed by persons belonging to armed groups or related to terrorist or rebel elements when the commission of the crime contributes to its activity, and by those who in some way cooperate or collaborate in the acts of these groups or individuals."[94] Since Spain does not have a special antiterrorism law, terrorists are brought to trial in accordance with Spain's Criminal Code.[95]

While Article 55 (2) of the Spanish constitution guarantees criminal process, fundamental rights may be suspended in terror cases.[96] Furthermore, according to the Law of Political Parties (Party Act) introduced in 2001, a party that supports terrorism may be outlawed.[97]

Issues to Consider

1. Until recently, Spain had been confronted only with domestic terrorism. How does the introduction of international terrorism affect policy and legislation?
2. Is legislation oriented towards domestic terrorism applicable for combating international terrorism?
3. Are Spanish efforts of countering Basque (i.e., domestic) terrorism relevant to countering al Qaeda (i.e., international) terrorism?

---

91. Judith Sunderland, Human Rights Watch, *Setting an Example? Counter-Terrorism Measures in Spain*, 2005, *available at* http://hrw.org/reports/2005/spain0105/ [hereinafter HRW *Counter-Terrorism in Spain*] (last visited July 24, 2007).

92. PATRIOT Act, *supra* note 15, at §805.

93. *See* Tracy Wilkinson, *Spain Could Do Better on Terror Suspects, Group Says; Human Rights Watch Asserts, Among Other Things, That Detainees Need Greater Legal Access*, L.A. Times, January 27, 2005, at A6.

94. HRW *Counter-Terrorism in Spain*, *supra* note 91.

95. The primary distinction between the treatment of terrorists and that of criminal defendants is that, whereas a non-terrorist must be brought before a judge within 72 hours, a suspected terrorist may be held for up to five days without seeing a judge (an additional 48 hours).

96. Constitución [C.E.] art. 55(2) (Spain).

97. *Id.*

4. Is criminal legislation appropriate for countering terrorism?
5. The Spanish response to the train station bombings has been widely criticized for reflecting weakness, if not capitulation; how does such criticism affect policy?

B. SPANISH RESPONSE TO TERRORISM

1. 9/11

According to a Human Rights Watch report at a hearing on human rights in the European Union, Spain after 9/11 applied its existing strict counterterrorism regime to the investigation, apprehension, and detention of suspected al Qaeda operatives. The climate created by the international campaign against terrorism provided the Spanish authorities with a further pretext to crack-down on Basque separatists and supporters of the pro-independence movement. Spanish authorities were also quick to issue public statements equating stricter controls on immigration with the war against terrorism, contributing to a climate of fear and suspicion toward migrants, asylum seekers, and refugees.

The Party Act adopted in June 2002 enables the state to declare a political party illegal if it fails to respect democratic principles and values. With two exceptions, the legislation is aimed at the Basque nationalist party Batasuna and will not be further addressed.

According to the Party Act, "the government will be able to block financial accounts and operations when it considers that such a step might prevent terrorist activities. The bill authorizes the administration to act not only against terrorist groups, but also against those who support or help them."[98] On June 27, 2002, the Spanish Congress of Deputies passed the LSSICE "Internet Law" which "obliges ISPs to retain traffic logs of their customers for at least one year. An opposition amendment bars police or intelligence officials from using such data without court permission."[99]

2. March 2004

The Spanish response to the train bombings must be considered from three different perspectives: criminal law, judicial rulings, and policy regarding withdrawal of Spanish forces from Iraq.

98. Rachel Ehrenfeld, *Financing Osama,* FrontPageMagazine.com, February 25, 2005 (stating that "Article 9 of the New Party Act, Organic Law 6/2002 of June 27, 2002 stipulates that a political party will be declared illegal if it systematically harms fundamental rights and freedoms by promoting, justifying or exonerating attacks against the right to life and the integrity of the individual, if it foments, facilitates or legitimizes violence, or complements and supports the actions of terrorist organizations").

99. Reporters Without Borders, *The Internet Under Surveillance* 103, 2003, *available at* http://www.rsf.org/IMG/pdf/doc-2236.pdf (last visited February 15, 2024).

Spain did not enact special or emergency legislation in response to the death of almost 200 innocent civilians. There are a number of possible reasons for the non-response, in and of itself a response: (1) existing legislation was deemed sufficient; (2) Spain did not want to be perceived as pursuing Islamic terrorists; or (3) Spanish authorities believed the criminal law paradigm appropriate to countering terrorism and therefore special legislation was seen as superfluous.

In sum, rather than implementing numerous measures intended to grant the law enforcement community additional powers or undertaking vigorous policy initiatives, the Spanish government adopted, in response both to 9/11 and March 2004, a largely passive approach.

In its response to a major terrorist attack on its own soil, Spain differs dramatically from the other surveyed nations whose legislative models have been aggressive. The inconsistency in Spanish policy between domestic and international terrorism is palpable. Spain has responded to long-standing, domestic-based terrorism with resolve politically, legislatively, and operationally, whereas its response to international-based—albeit domestically executed—terrorism has introduced a profoundly different model, one diametrically opposed to the model it previously implemented.

Issues to Consider

1. What national interests are served by seeking to allay the aggressor as Spain did when the government decided to withdraw forces from Iraq?
2. Does allaying the aggressor encourage additional attacks or serve as positive reinforcement for terrorists?
3. Should counterterrorism policy be primarily domestic driven, or are international geopolitical ramifications legitimate considerations?
4. What are the fundamental distinctions between exclusively domestic terrorism and internal/external terrorism, and how do those distinctions affect legal and policy considerations?

VII. CHINA

A. BACKGROUND

China contains over 50 recognized nationalities and ethnic groups; the majority are Han Chinese. The northwest province of Xinjiang—bordering Mongolia, Russia, Afghanistan, Kazakhstan, Kyrgyzstan, Pakistan, and India—is unique in its cultural background and challenges. The province is a mix of Han Chinese and Uyghur ethnic groups, which has led to extraordinary tensions and outbreaks of violence including terrorist attacks. Since 1949, periodic unrest in Xinjiang has resulted, in part, from Islamic and Uyghur nationalist movements. Recently, the violence has been influenced by extremism facilitated by external funding and training, particularly Pakistani.

B. STRIKE HARD

The standard Chinese response to the violence described in Chapter 3 has been the "Strike Hard" campaigns. The aim of these periodic campaigns is to reduce crime dramatically, negate potential terrorist attacks, and restore social order. The campaigns use intelligence information against suspected criminals via swift and severe tactics that process people quickly through the judicial system and punish them harshly. These campaigns serve as reminders of the control that the government exercises over social, judicial, economic, and political aspects of daily life, particularly when public order is affected. To that end, religious- and nationalist-based unrest in Xinjiang has powerful implications both locally and more broadly: the former because of the recurring violence between Uyghurs and Hans; the latter because other ethnic minorities may feel emboldened.

For those reasons, the campaigns consistently focus their efforts on particular categories of crimes, especially those deemed to pose threats to public order and state security, including potential acts of terrorism. The policy represents aggressive counterterrorism intended to directly strike at religious and nationalist forces perceived as possible sources of unrest.

The government originally launched the "Strike Hard" campaign in 1996 to combat the rising national crime rate. In most of China, "Strike Hard" was used to combat crime and drug use. In Xinjiang it was implemented to prevent attacks by proactively eliminating terrorist groups and by punishing individuals involved with suspected terrorist organizations, clearly intending to have a deterrent effect. The campaign included increased surveillance, pressure to report suspected separatists, and expedited judicial procedures and executions.

China labeled the East Turkestan Movement a separatist group, based on religious extremism, and convinced the United States and the United Nations to classify the group as terrorists. Suspected separatists accused of participating in protests, bombings, and assassinations were detained. In February 1997, an incident that began as a demonstration against Strike Hard turned into a riot with clashes between police and civilians. This was followed by further arrests after three bombs simultaneously exploded on buses in Urumqi.

In 2007, the Chinese police raided a suspected training camp of the East Turkestan Islamic Movement near the border between Afghanistan and Pakistan. Eighteen suspects were killed, and seventeen were captured.

Issues to Consider

1. What are the costs and benefits of aggressive counterterrorism?
2. What are the policy implications of identifying a particular ethnic group as endangering state security?
3. What are the limits of deterrence as a policy?
4. When does aggressive counterterrorism have negative repercussions?
5. How important is the court of international opinion?

6. How legitimate is it for a domestic policy to be predicated on an external development?
7. What is the relationship between religious extremism and national separatism?

VIII. COLOMBIA

The National Front of Colombia was a group of conservative and liberal politicians who sought to reduce the violence spreading across the country in the 1950s and 1960s. They excluded certain dissidents and other political forces from joining the National Front organization. As a result of this exclusion, several groups, including the Fuerzas Armadas Revolucionarias de Colombia (FARC), created their own paramilitary groups to combat the National Front. By 1974, FARC had become the largest guerrilla group, in addition to the M-19 and the National Liberation Army (ELN). Therefore, the creation of the National Front indirectly contributed to the emergence of these guerrilla groups.

During the 1970s and 1980s, Colombia became a predominant source of illegal drugs through both production and worldwide trafficking. Guerrilla groups, including ELN and FARC, became actively involved in the drug trade during the 1980s because it provided a major revenue source. As a result of the influx of significant financial resources, both FARC and ELN extended their influence to regions throughout the country through incursions to urban areas, where previously they had been relatively inactive.

FARC committed armed assaults, assassinations, bombings, hijackings, and kidnappings, as well as drug-related crimes. For example, in 1998, FARC and ELN conducted over 40 attacks countrywide over a two-day period. The attacks were aimed at an extraordinarily wide range of targets including government, military, oil facilities, and private citizens, thereby creating a viable threat to national stability and control. The scope of the attacks suggested both significant motivation and resources, not to mention operational capabilities that extended beyond mere region-specific terrorism. The attacks—and threats—were aimed at government institutions across the country. The attacks killed over 275 and caused an unknown number of wounded. In addition, 30 soldiers and policemen were missing and presumed kidnapped.

Individuals assumed to have either financial resources or to be in positions of political influence were subject to kidnapping for purposes of ransom. Kidnapping victims included the brother of Colombia's president, Americans, diplomatic officials, and peasants who could be convinced to aid FARC or whose families had the money or influence needed by FARC. Kidnapping poses extraordinary challenges to government counterterrorism policy because of the vulnerability of families from whom ransom is demanded. Rather than enabling the government to articulate, establish, and implement a cohesive counterterrorism policy, kidnapping—because of family pressure—limits government ability to impose policy in an unencumbered manner.

As a result of this increase in the range, power, and influence of terrorist organizations, the government embarked on a policy largely predicated on attempting to negotiate with terrorists. To that end, in 1998 former President Pastrana gave FARC 51,000 square kilometers in the south-central part of Colombia, which FARC used to increase production of illegal drugs, transport military equipment, and negotiate kidnapping ransoms. President Uribe continued to conduct negotiations with terrorist organizations while security forces simultaneously engaged guerilla groups. As a result of this two-headed—and arguably contradictory—approach, the United Self-Defense Forces of Colombia and M-19 were partially demobilized.

The Executive and Legislative branches have both struggled to develop a consistent, effective counterterrorism policy that would have long-term impact. Perhaps, as a result, policy has often been limited to short-term responses instead of long-term strategies. Complicating implementation of more comprehensive strategies has been a reality not faced by the other nations surveyed: a ubiquitous, powerful, and ruthless illegal drug industry and its relationship with various guerilla groups. To that end, illegal drugs have made it difficult to combat paramilitary groups and outside threats, especially as they often overlap and cooperate.

Issues to Consider

1. Given Colombia's unique challenges—the combination of terrorist organizations and the drug trade—is creating a consistent counterterrorism policy realistic?
2. Do the twin realities—drugs and terrorist organizations—lend themselves to violations of human rights akin to Russia's conduct in Chechnya?
3. Would China's aggressive ("Strike Hard") counterterrorism policy be viable in Colombia?
4. Is Colombia's negotiation policy reflective of Spain's largely non-responsive policy?
5. How does the availability of significant financial resources affect a government's policy?
6. Given the complexity of the historic challenges facing Colombian governments, how is effectiveness best measured?

CHAPTER 5

JUDICIAL REVIEW

I. INTRODUCTION

A critical component of counterterrorism is the role of a nation's judiciary. An unfettered executive, unrestrained by courts and legislatures, is detrimental to liberal democracies attempting to balance national security and individual rights. In examining the role of the judiciary in each of the surveyed nations, an understanding that different regimes have differing systems is incumbent. Nevertheless, there is a common thread through this chapter: an examination of the willingness of a nation's judiciary to actively review and, if need be, criticize and intervene in the decisions and actions of the executive branch.

Clearly, executives would prefer to conduct their business without judicial interference; however, what separates liberal democratic regimes from dictatorships is the executive's accountability for its decisions. Whether and how the courts review executive decisions during armed conflict is the principal issue to be analyzed.

Issues to Consider

1. How much should a judiciary defer to the executive?
2. How much deference should courts ascribe to "national security?"
3. Is judicial review appropriate in times of armed conflict?
4. How much compromising of individual rights should courts tolerate?
5. When should courts intervene?
6. Are courts equipped to intervene and review decisions related to warfare when only the commanders are responsible for the lives of their soldiers?

The seminal court case that articulated the scope of executive power in the United States is based on notice given by the United Steelworkers of America of an impending nationwide strike. Hours before the strike was to begin, President Truman issued Executive Order 10340, directing the Secretary of Commerce to take possession of and operate most of the nation's steel mills. In *Youngstown Sheet & Tube Co. v. Sawyer,* the Supreme Court held that the President did not have the authority to issue such an order. While the executive argued that the "President had 'inherent power' to do what he had done supported by the Constitution, by historical precedent, and by court decisions,"[1] the Supreme Court disagreed. The Court held that "the President's power, if any, to issue the order must stem either from an act of Congress or from the Constitution itself."[2]

Even though the majority held the President did not have the power to issue such an order, the lasting significance of the case is Justice Jackson's concurrence. Justice Jackson analyzed the limits of the President's powers in three different situations.

1. When the President acts pursuant to an express or implied authorization of Congress, his authority is at its maximum, for it includes all that he possesses in his own right plus all that Congress can delegate. In these circumstances, and in these only, may he be said (for what it may be worth), to personify the federal sovereignty. If his act is held unconstitutional under these circumstances, it usually means that the Federal government as an undivided whole lacks power. The strongest of presumptions and the widest latitude of judicial interpretation would support a seizure executed by the President pursuant to an Act of Congress, and the burden of persuasion would rest heavily upon any who might attack it.
2. When the President acts in absence of either a congressional grant or denial of authority, he can only rely upon his own independent powers, but there is a zone of twilight in which he and Congress may have concurrent authority, or in which its distribution is uncertain. Therefore, congressional inertia, indifference or quiescence may sometimes, at least as a practical matter, enable, if not invite, measures on independent presidential responsibility. In this area, any actual test of power is likely to depend on the imperatives of events and contemporary imponderables rather than on abstract theories of law.
3. When the President takes measures incompatible with the expressed or implied will of Congress, his power is at its lowest ebb, for then he can rely only upon his own constitutional powers minus any constitutional powers of Congress over the matter. Courts can sustain exclusive Presidential control in such a case only be disabling the Congress from acting upon the subject. Presidential claim to a power at once so conclusive and preclusive must be scrutinized with caution, for what is at stake is the equilibrium established by our constitutional system.[3]

As a point of reference, one could argue that the judicial activism advocated both intellectually and in practice by the retired President of the Israel

---

1. Youngstown Sheet & Tube Co. v. Sawyer, 343 U.S. 579, 584 (1952).
2. *Id.* at 585.
3. *Id.* at 635-638.

Supreme Court, Aharon Barak, represents one end of the judicial review scale, and the position suggested by late Chief Justice Rehnquist represents, if not the extreme other end, then at least an opposing view. The positions of the Russian, Indian, Spanish, Chinese, and Colombian courts will be examined in the context of the debate between Barak and Rehnquist.

Retired President Barak propounded and implemented judicial activism in his decisions over 15 years.[4] Important for our purposes here are Barak's opinions addressing Israel's counterterrorism efforts. Barak articulated his thesis in "A Judge on Judging";[5] Rehnquist in his book *All the Laws But One.*[6] The American experience regarding judicial intervention in counterterrorism is recent, but judicial review of executive decisions during time of war is not. An attempt will be made to compare approaches while examining holdings in *Padilla v. Rumsfeld,*[7] *Hamdi v. Rumsfeld,*[8] *Rasul v. Bush,*[9] and *Boumedienne v. Bush.*[10]

An overriding theme this chapter seeks to address is the proper role of the judiciary in counterterrorism. The word "proper" elicits much debate and little consensus. Some propose that the executive should be allowed to make critical command decisions while enclosed in a bubble. Others insist that such an approach is inherently dangerous. Succinctly put, the primary question becomes whether a supreme court should interfere or intervene in the executive's wartime decision making or whether the executive should be granted unfettered discretion.

Differences between the seven nations, with respect to the level of judicial review of executive decisions, are best viewed within the following spectrum:

High Involvement ←		--------------------------------		→ Low Involvement		
Israel	India	Spain	Colombia	Russia	United States	China

Because of the unique nature of the subject, this chapter is organized differently. Prior to a discussion of the seven surveyed nations, Barak's and Rehnquist's opinions are reviewed to illustrate diametrically contrasting perspectives.

A. PRESIDENT BARAK

1. Role of the Court

President Barak's seminal article in the Harvard Law Review, written while sitting as President of the Israel Supreme Court, is a compelling discussion of

4. President Barak retired from the Israel Supreme Court in the fall of 2006.
5. Aharon Barak, *A Judge on Judging: The Role of a Supreme Court in a Democracy,* 116 Harv. L. Rev. 16 (2002).
6. William H. Rehnquist, *All the Laws But One: Civil Liberties in Wartime* 225 (1998).
7. Padilla v. Rumsfeld, 352 F.3d 695 (2d Cir. 2003). 542 U.S. 426 (2004).
8. Hamdi v. Rumsfeld, 542 U.S. 507 (2004).
9. Rasul v. Bush, 542 U.S. 466 (2004).
10. Boumedienne v. Bush, 553 U.S. 723 (2008).

judicial activism in armed conflict.[11] It advocates active judicial review against the background of Israel's ongoing struggle with Palestinian terrorism. President Barak's article is a message to the executive that the judiciary will be watching, monitoring, and—if need be—intervening in executive decisions pertaining to armed conflict.

In the article, President Barak discusses the challenges that terrorism presents for democratic countries, arguing that not all effective means are legal.[12] While terrorists adhere to no rules, "a democracy must fight with one hand tied behind its back."[13] Even though a democracy has to fight in this manner, President Barak argues that it still has the upper hand, since it preserves the rule of law and respects individual liberties. President Barak argues that these two factors strengthen democracies in fighting terrorism. A democracy is not unlimited or unencumbered in its fight to protect its territory; unlike terrorists, its citizens have rules and laws that must be abided. It is precisely those rules that separate liberal democracies from terrorists. Protecting democracy from "the means the state wants to use to fight terrorism" is necessary in order to preserve democracy.[14]

Should a state resort to illegal means to fight terrorism or disregard its own rule of law, then terrorism has won. A democracy that compromises its values and standards in order to fight terrorists allows the terrorists to undermine the very core of the democracy. Laws are most important in times of war. They were created and developed "precisely so that they will be consulted and obeyed, not ignored" during times of crisis.[15]

According to President Barak, there is a basic tension between components of democracy. Citizens, through their elected representatives, may expect the government to take all steps necessary in fighting terrorism, regardless of their effect on human rights. However, the human rights component of democracy "may encourage protecting the rights of every individual, including the terrorists, even at the cost of undermining the fight against terrorism."[16] Therefore, the executive of a democracy must balance between these fundamentally competing interests so as to protect the rule of law, the essence of democracy. As President Barak wrote, "Terrorism does not justify the neglect of accepted legal norms."[17] The role of the court is to "ensure the constitutionality and legality of the fight,"[18] regardless of whether the decisions of the court are popular with the executive or with the public. The independence of the court enables the justices to protect individual rights, regardless of what the public demands.

The role of a justice in protecting democracy and individual human rights is "a much more formidable duty in times of war and terrorism than in times of peace and security."[19] It is during times of war and terrorism that citizens often

---

11. Barak, *supra* note 5.
12. *Id.* at 157.
13. *Id.* at 148.
14. *Id.* at 149.
15. *Id.* at 151.
16. *Id.* at 148.
17. *Id.* at 151.
18. *Id.*
19. *Id.* at 149.

think that compromising rights and protections in order to help maintain security is permissible. However, justices cannot compromise citizens' rights, either during war time or peacetime. Justices cannot have different procedures or standards for wartime without eroding peacetime protections as well. Judicial decisions during times of crisis "remain with the democracy when the threat of terrorism passes . . . entrenched in the case law of the court as a magnet for the development of new and problematic laws."[20]

It is much easier for the executive to change directions or policy, or for the legislature to revoke, amend, or pass new laws to amend existing legislation, than for the judiciary to reverse itself. Mistakes made by the judiciary live on even after they have been overruled. The logic, reasoning, and basis for a decision are recorded in judicial history to be used in the future for other cases, whereas overturned executive or legislative actions are generally ignored.[21]

2. President Barak's Theory

President Barak argues that the Israeli Supreme Court's willingness to review executive actions is not improper interference.[22] He sees a crucial distinction between intervening in military considerations and intervening in matters regarding equality of treatment that may arise from military actions.[23] President Barak sees the role of the Supreme Court not as ruling on the efficiency of security measures for fighting terrorism, but rather as ensuring that the military acts "within the framework of the 'zone of reasonableness'" with regard to its actions and measures.[24]

President Barak believes the judiciary must ensure that executive actions harmonize with principles of democracy; accordingly, they must be evaluated in real time. "The protection of human rights would be bankrupt if, during armed conflict, the courts—consciously or unconsciously—decided to review the executive branch's behavior only after the period of emergency has ended."[25] If a court postpones reviewing executive actions until the period of emergency or time of crisis has passed, then any ruling issued by the court would not contribute to the rule of law. Rights must be protected when the executive seeks to impinge upon them.

Courts must balance between the national security interests personified by executive actions and the harm that any action may cause to the rights of individuals. To perform this balancing act, courts must review the actions of the executive at the time that they are taking place. In other words, nations must impose their own limits. "Judicial review of the legality of the war on terrorism may make this war harder in the short term, but it also fortifies and strengthens the people in the long term."[26]

---

20. *Id.*
21. *Id.*
22. *Id.* at 151.
23. *Id.* Barak in discussing the gas mask case from the Gulf War said that the Court was addressing specifically the equality of the distribution of the gas masks, not whether or not the masks should be distributed.
24. *Id.* at 157.
25. *Id.* at 156.
26. *Id.* at 158.

President Barak's theory of "self-imposed restraints" is not an abstraction. It reflects the activist approach adopted by Israel's High Court of Justice (HCJ). HCJ intervention—what others would define as interference—will be examined later in this chapter by analyzing a number of seminal decisions handed down over the past few years.

B. CHIEF JUSTICE REHNQUIST

Whereas President Barak strongly believes in the responsibility of the Supreme Court to review actions of the executive in a timely fashion, the late Chief Justice Rehnquist's perspective was markedly different. Chief Justice Rehnquist advocated a hands-off approach in contrast to President Barak's very hands-on theory. In those rare instances where the judiciary did review the legality of executive actions related to armed conflict, Chief Justice Rehnquist believed the examination should wait until the time of crisis passed.

Chief Justice Rehnquist neither propounded *inter arma silent leges* (in times of war laws are silent), nor did he believe that the law plays the same role in war as in peace. Unlike President Barak, who forcefully argues the judiciary should interpret the laws in the same manner regardless of whether or not it is a time of war, Chief Justice Rehnquist stated that the laws "will speak with a somewhat different voice" during a time of war.[27]

Distinct from the direction taken by the Israeli High Court under President Barak, the U.S. Supreme Court historically has not interpreted laws uniformly in war and in peace. Chief Justice Rehnquist pointed out that the Supreme Court traditionally gave the executive branch more leeway during war or crisis, particularly World War II.[28] Though recognizing that "the government's authority to engage in conduct that infringes civil liberty is greatest in time of declared war," Chief Justice Rehnquist argued that the judiciary should not review all executive actions, especially during a crisis.[29]

Even if a court examines the actions of the executive, the timing is critical. Courts have a general reluctance "to decide a case against the government on an issue of national security during a war."[30] While President Barak believes an essential duty of the judiciary is to treat the law equally during war and during peace, Chief Justice Rehnquist argued for recognition of "the human factor that inevitably enters into even the most careful judicial decision."[31] Therefore, he implied postponing decisions until the crisis passed. As an example, Chief Justice Rehnquist referred to *Ex parte Mitsuye Endo,* in which the Supreme Court voted to uphold civil liberties only near the end of WWII.[32] The Supreme Court decision that Japanese internment was illegal came well after martial law had already ended and American citizens were no longer

---

27. Rehnquist, *supra* note 6.
28. *Id.* at 221.
29. *Id.* at 218.
30. *Id.* at 221.
31. *Id.* at 222.
32. *Id.* at 221 (citing *Ex parte Mitsuye Endo*, 323 U.S. 283 (1944) (the Supreme Court held that power to protect the war effort from espionage and sabotage did not include the power to detain a loyal citizen)).

living in internment camps.[33] By waiting until after World War II ended to rule on *Endo,* the Supreme Court was ostensibly able to uphold civil liberties but not practically. Chief Justice Rehnquist suggested that it may "actually be desirable to avoid decision on" civil liberties during the time of war or crisis.[34]

The difference between the two approaches is palpable. President Barak advocates and practices active judicial review; the late Chief Justice Rehnquist's approach was much more restrained. They differ not only to the *extent* of judicial review regarding executive actions, but also to the *timing* when the judiciary should review. The decisions of their respective courts reflect their differing approaches.

II. UNITED STATES

A. INTRODUCTION

On November 13, 2001, President Bush issued a Presidential Order establishing military commissions for enemy combatants.[35] Over the course of the next four months, three hundred detainees were transported to Guantanamo Bay[36] for purposes of interrogation and hearings before the military commissions. According to Section Four of the Presidential Order, a detainee convicted on any charge could appeal only to the President of the United States or the Secretary of Defense.[37] The significance of this is now clear: the United States government held hundreds of detainees in Guantanamo Bay while denying them independent judicial review of their status and a determination whether they were a present and continuing danger to the national security of the United States. While it is true that the Supreme Court of the United States does not function as a High Court of Justice (unlike the Israel Supreme Court), the question is whether Chief Justice Rehnquist's philosophy influenced the executive's decisions.[38] When the Chief Justice writes "there remains a sense that

---

33. *Id.* at 221.

34. *Id.* at 222.

35. *Detention, Treatment, and Trial of Certain Non-Citizens in the War Against Terrorism,* 66 Fed. Reg. 57833 (Nov. 16, 2001) [hereinafter *Trial of Certain Non-Citizens*].

36. On January 7, 2002, there were 346 detainees in U.S. custody but the United States refused to comment on the number to be held at Guantanamo Bay. By March 1, 2002, there were 300 known detainees in Guantanamo Bay. Jim Garamone, *Tension Eases at Guantanamo Holding Facility,* Am. Forces Info. Serv., March 1, 2002, *available at* http://www.defenselink.mil/news/Mar2002/ n03012002_200203012.html (last visited July 22, 2007).

37. *Trial of Certain Non-Citizens, supra* note 35 ("submission of the record of the trial, including any conviction or sentence, for review and final decision by" the President or the "Secretary of Defense if so designated by me for that purpose"). *See also* §7(b)(2) ("the individual shall not be privileged to seek any remedy or maintain any proceeding, directly or indirectly, or to have any such remedy or proceeding sought on the individual's behalf, in (i) any court of the United States, or any State thereof, (ii) any court of any foreign nation, or (iii) any international tribunal").

38. According to unconfirmed media reports, President Barak implored the Justices of the U.S. Supreme Court, in particular Chief Justice Rehnquist, to adopt a philosophy of judicial activism. According to these reports, Barak argued that judicial acquiescence in misbegotten executive decisions is more harmful than problematic legislation, for legislation can be more easily repealed than the Court could reverse itself.

there is some truth to the maxim *inter arma silent leges* at least in the purely descriptive sense,"[39] the executive is granted broad leeway.

Issues to Consider

1. Are U.S. policy interests advanced by Chief Justice Rehnquist's philosophy of deference to the executive branch during armed conflict?
2. Does the U.S. administration adopt the posture of an "unfettered executive" because it understands that the judicial oversight will be lax at best?
3. Given that the Chief Justice's position had been clearly stated and that Congress was not consulted regarding the establishment of the military commissions, had the concept of checks and balances been seriously weakened?

B. PADILLA v. RUMSFELD

José Padilla sought *habeas corpus* relief against Secretary of Defense Donald Rumsfeld after being detained as an unlawful combatant. While the Supreme Court eventually reversed and remanded the case solely on jurisdictional grounds, the Court of Appeals (see below) analyzed whether the President had the authority to designate someone within the United States an enemy combatant.

Padilla v. Rumsfeld

352 F.3d 695 (2d Cir. 2003)

We agree that great deference is afforded the President's exercise of his authority as Commander-in-Chief. We also agree that whether a state of armed conflict exists against an enemy to which the laws of war apply is a political question for the President, not the courts. Because we have no authority to do so, we do not address the government's underlying assumption that an undeclared war exists between al Qaeda and the United States. We have no quarrel with the former chief of the Justice Department's Criminal Division, who said:

> For [al Qaeda] chose not to violate the law but to attack the law and its institutions directly. Their proclaimed goal, however unrealistic, was to destroy the United States. They used powerful weapons of destructive force and openly declared their willingness to employ even more powerful weapons of mass destruction if they could lay hold of them. They were as serious a threat to the national security of the United States as one could envision.

However, it is a different proposition entirely to argue that the President even in times of grave national security threats or war, whether declared or undeclared, can lay claim to any of the powers, express or implied, allocated

39. Rehnquist, *supra* note 6, at 221.

to Congress. The deference due to the Executive in its exercise of its war powers therefore only starts the inquiry; it does not end it. Where the exercise of Commander-in-Chief powers, no matter how well intentioned, is challenged on the ground that it collides with the powers assigned by the Constitution to Congress, a fundamental role exists for the courts. To be sure, when Congress and the President act together in the conduct of war, "it is not for any court to sit in review of the wisdom of their action or substitute its judgment for theirs." But when the Executive acts, even in the conduct of war, in the face of apparent congressional disapproval, challenges to his authority must be examined and resolved by the Article III courts.

These separation of powers concerns are heightened when the Commander-in-Chief's powers are exercised in the domestic sphere. The Supreme Court has long counseled that while the Executive should be "indulge[d] the widest latitude of interpretation to sustain his exclusive function to command the instruments of national force, at least when turned against the outside world for the security of our society," he enjoys "no such indulgence" when "it is turned inward." This is because "the federal power over external affairs [is] in origin and essential character different from that over internal affairs," and "congressional legislation which is to be made effective through negotiation and inquiry within the international field must often accord to the President a degree of discretion and freedom from statutory restriction which would not be admissible were domestic affairs alone involved." But, "Congress, not the Executive, should control utilization of the war power as an instrument of domestic policy." Thus, we do not concern ourselves with the Executive's inherent wartime power, generally, to detain enemy combatants on the battlefield. Rather, we are called on to decide whether the Constitution gives the President the power to detain an American citizen seized in this country until the war with al Qaeda ends.

The government contends that the Constitution authorizes the President to detain Padilla as an enemy combatant as an exercise of inherent executive authority. Padilla contends that, in the absence of express congressional authorization, the President, by his June 9 Order denominating Padilla an enemy combatant, has engaged in the "lawmaking" function entrusted by the Constitution to Congress in violation of the separation of powers. In response, no argument is made that the Constitution expressly grants the President the power to name United States citizens as enemy combatants and order their detention. Rather, the government contends that the Commander-in-Chief Clause implicitly grants the President the power to detain enemy combatants domestically during times of national security crises such as the current conflict with al Qaeda.

C. HAMDI v. RUMSFELD

Hamdi was an American citizen captured in Afghanistan during a time of active military hostilities[40] and transferred to Guantanamo Bay. When it was discovered that Hamdi may not have renounced his American citizenship, he

40. Hamdi v. Rumsfeld, 316 F.3d 450, 460 (4th Cir. 2003), *rev'd*, 542 U.S. 507 (2004).

was transferred to the Norfolk Naval Station Brig.[41] On his behalf, a petition for writ of *habeas corpus* was filed, challenging the legality of the government's decision to detain him on U.S. soil as an enemy combatant. Furthermore, Hamdi demanded that he be provided the opportunity to challenge the government's decision to so define him.[42]

In writing the majority opinion, Justice O'Connor reviewed both international law and constitutional dilemmas. Justice O'Connor's analysis underscores the significantly different approaches of the U.S. Supreme Court and the Israeli High Court. Even when similar conclusions are reached, Justice O'Connor commented that the Constitution "assuredly envisions a role for all three branches when individual liberties are at stake."[43] The real issue, of course, is the particular role of the judiciary: when and how should the judiciary be involved?

In *Hamdi,* the government argued for strong separation of powers in which the judiciary would have very limited ability to review executive actions.[44] Furthermore, the government posited that, should the judiciary review the executive, it must do so based on a very deferential standard of review. The government's arguments reflected the view that the Supreme Court should interpret laws differently in times of war and in times of peace.

Justice O'Connor's opinion highlights the tension between national security considerations and individual civil rights. In balancing the state's and petitioner's concerns, the judiciary weighs "'the private interest that will be affected by the official action' against the government's asserted interest, 'including the function involved' and the burdens the government would face in providing greater process."[45] Justice O'Connor's opinion analyzes, step by step, the balancing between national security and "the most elemental of liberty interests—the interest in being free from physical detention by one's own government."[46]

Hamdi v. Rumsfeld

542 U.S. 507, 527-530 (2004)

The government's second argument requires closer consideration. This is the argument that further factual exploration is unwarranted and inappropriate in light of the extraordinary constitutional interests at stake. Under the government's most extreme rendition of this argument, "[r]espect for separation of powers and the limited institutional capabilities of courts in matters of military decision-making in connection with an ongoing conflict" ought to eliminate entirely any individual process, restricting the courts to investigating only whether legal authorization exists for the broader detention scheme. At most, the government argues, courts should review its determination that

41. *Id.*
42. *Id.*
43. Hamdi v. Rumsfeld, 542 U.S. 507, 536 (2004).
44. *Id.* at 527.
45. *Id.* at 529.
46. *Id.*

a citizen is an enemy combatant under a very deferential "some evidence" standard. Under this review, a court would assume the accuracy of the government's articulated basis for Hamdi's detention, as set forth in the Mobbs Declaration, and assess only whether that articulated basis was a legitimate one.

In response, Hamdi emphasizes that this Court consistently has recognized that an individual challenging his detention may not be held at the will of the Executive without recourse to some proceeding before a neutral tribunal to determine whether the Executive's asserted justifications for that detention have basis in fact and warrant in law. He argues that the Fourth Circuit inappropriately "ceded power to the Executive during wartime to define the conduct for which a citizen may be detained, judge whether that citizen has engaged in the proscribed conduct, and imprison that citizen indefinitely," and that due process demands that he receive a hearing in which he may challenge the Mobbs Declaration and adduce his own counter evidence. The District Court, agreeing with Hamdi, apparently believed that the appropriate process would approach the process that accompanies a criminal trial. It therefore disapproved of the hearsay nature of the Mobbs Declaration and anticipated quite extensive discovery of various military affairs. Anything less, it concluded, would not be "meaningful judicial review."

Both of these positions highlight legitimate concerns. And both emphasize the tension that often exists between the autonomy that the government asserts is necessary in order to pursue effectively a particular goal and the process that a citizen contends he is due before he is deprived of a constitutional right. The ordinary mechanism that we use for balancing such serious competing interests, and for determining the procedures that are necessary to ensure that a citizen is not "deprived of life, liberty, or property, without due process of law," U.S. Const., Amdt. 5, is the test that we articulated in Mathews v. Eldridge, 424 U.S. 319, 47 L. Ed. 2d 18, 96 S. Ct. 893 (1976). *Mathews* dictates that the process due in any given instance is determined by weighing "the private interest that will be affected by the official action" against the government's asserted interest, "including the function involved" and the burdens the government would face in providing greater process. The *Mathews* calculus then contemplates a judicious balancing of these concerns, through an analysis of "the risk of an erroneous deprivation" of the private interest if the process were reduced and the "probable value, if any, of additional or substitute safeguards." We take each of these steps in turn.

It is beyond question that substantial interests lie on both sides of the scale in this case. Hamdi's "private interest . . . affected by the official action" is the most elemental of liberty interests—the interest in being free from physical detention by one's own government. "In our society liberty is the norm," and detention without trial "is the carefully limited exception." "We have always been careful not to 'minimize the importance and fundamental nature' of the individual's right to liberty," and we will not do so today.

As previously discussed, the U.S. Supreme Court has historically been very accommodating to the executive. Indeed, Rehnquist's philosophy clearly

Issues to Consider

1. Should a court write deferentially when holding against the executive?
2. In the context of national security, are the tone and style of judicial review as important as content?
3. Should the administration have considered judicial activism prior to establishing Guantanamo and its attendant rules?
4. Did the American judicial history of a lack of judicial activism in the context of national security give the administration a false sense of security?

supports such an approach. In *Hamdi,* Justice O'Connor's tone and style reveal a similar viewpoint, though the decision itself reflects evolution and, potentially, movement towards a more active Court. Justice Stevens' opinion in *Rasul* (see below) is similarly reflective of a more vigorous judiciary. Perhaps the reality of Guantanamo Bay and the treatment of detainees convinced the Court that there was no alternative but to restrain the administration.

D. RASUL v. BUSH

In *Rasul v. Bush,* the Supreme Court addressed the following question concerning judicial review: "(w)hether United States' courts lack jurisdiction to consider challenges to the legality of the detention of foreign nationals captured abroad in connection with hostilities and incarcerated at the Guantanamo Bay Naval Base, Cuba."[47] The petitioners were two Australians and twelve Kuwaitis who had been captured in Afghanistan during hostilities with the Taliban and held in military custody at Guantanamo Bay.[48]

In his majority opinion, Justice Stevens held that "what is presently at stake is only whether the federal courts have jurisdiction to determine the legality of the Executive's potentially indefinite detention of individuals."[49] Even though the Court ultimately held against the executive in *Rasul,* it did so narrowly.

Justice Stevens' opinion begins with a brief description of the September 11th attacks on the United States.[50] By including details about the attacks and the damage caused by them, Justice Stevens subtly acknowledges the executive's national security concerns. Unlike Justice O'Connor's direct acknowledgement of the concerns and arguments of the executive, Justice Stevens implies the strength of the executive's argument, stating that the President acted pursuant to congressional authorization.[51]

Justice Stevens explicitly states that the judiciary has the jurisdiction to decide the legality of executive actions. In reaching this decision, Stevens

47. Rasul v. Bush, *supra* note 9, at 470.
48. *Id.*
49. *Id.* at 485.
50. *Id.* at 470.
51. *Id.*

focuses on why the judiciary has jurisdiction without giving undue emphasis to the arguments of the government. His opinion shows more deference to the executive than what President Barak would have given, yet much less than Justice O'Connor did in *Hamdi.* The tone of Justice Stevens' opinion shows that the Court seems to be moving away from strict interpretation of Chief Justice Rehnquist's philosophy. However, the timing of *Rasul* clearly reflects the late Chief Justice's views on when judicial review should occur.

As discussed earlier, Chief Justice Rehnquist believed that there were times when it was better for the Court to wait to review executive actions. In reference to *Endo,* Rehnquist wrote that it may "actually be desirable to avoid decision on" civil liberties during the war or time of crisis.[52] Rehnquist's views are, perhaps, best revealed by cases not brought before the Court. Though hundreds of detainees have been held at Guantanamo Bay since the opening of its detention camp, the Supreme Court has heard very few cases. Chief Justice Rehnquist "believed that the court should reserve its time and effort for cases of national importance that absolutely require its attention."[53]

Unlike the U.S. Supreme Court, which deliberated Guantanamo Bay cases three years after the military commissions were implemented, the Israeli HCJ heard *Marab* while the Israeli Defense Forces were continuing to detain Palestinian terrorists and heard *Physicians for Human Rights* while the conflict was ongoing. Solutions needed to be developed and implemented by the IDF while the Court heard arguments. The U.S. Supreme Court, as highlighted in both *Rasul* and *Hamdi,* demonstrates reluctance to respond in real time and directly reflects Chief Justice Rehnquist's philosophical approach that certain cases should not be heard during times of crisis. Real-time decisions of the Court in response to ongoing executive action are the essence of robust judicial activism when the executive is engaged in operational counterterrorism.

E. HAMDAN v. RUMSFELD

In *Hamdan v. Rumsfeld,* the Supreme Court signaled to the Bush administration that military procedures[54] were inadequate and demanded a reformulation.[55] Specifically, in discussing the current procedural deficiencies, the Court wrote:

> The commission's procedures . . . provide . . . that an accused and his civilian counsel may be excluded from . . . ever learning what evidence was presented during any part of the proceeding . . . the presiding officer decides to "close."

52. Rehnquist, *supra* note 6, at 222.

53. Charles Lane, *The Rehnquist Legacy: 33 Years Turning Back the Court,* Wash. Post, September 5, 2005, at A8.

54. Hearings in the United States Senate, Committee on the Judiciary showed the various interpretations of the impact of the *Hamdan* decision, and the response appropriate from the U.S. Senate. *See House Armed Services Committee Hearing on Standards of Military Commissions and Tribunals,* July 26, 2006, *available at* https://www.globalsecurity.org/security/library/congress/2006_h/060726-scharf.pdf (last visited December 23, 2023).

55. The Court signaled this by stating that the Authorization for the Use of Military Force was not a blank check for the Administration to set up military commissions however they saw fit, but rather, the AUMF was more like the "lowest ebb" of power, akin to *Youngstown Sheet & Tubing Co. v. Sawyer,* requiring further Congressional approval for such commissions.

> Grounds for closure include the protection of classified information, the physical safety of participants and witnesses, the protection of intelligence and law enforcement sources, methods, or activities, and "other national security interests." Appointed military defense counsel must be privy to these closed sessions, but may, at the presiding officer's discretion, be forbidden to reveal to the client what took place therein. . . . Moreover, the accused and his civilian counsel may be denied access to classified and other "protected information," so long as the presiding officer concludes that the evidence is "probative."[56]

In further analyzing these deficiencies, the Court held that

> even assuming that Hamdan is a dangerous individual who would cause great harm or death to innocent civilians given the opportunity, the Executive nevertheless must comply with the prevailing rule of law in undertaking to try him and subject him to criminal punishment.[57]

In response to *Hamdan,* the United States Congress passed the Military Commissions Act of 2006[58] which expressly eliminated court jurisdiction over all pending and future *habeas* causes of action. While this congressional action addressed some of the Court's concerns in *Hamdan,* it failed to formulate proper interrogation standards. Furthermore, rather than specifically articulating permissible interrogation methods, the Military Commissions Act granted the Executive authority to interpret the scope and application of Common Article III of the Geneva Convention. The Act's lack of clarity invited continued violations of detainee rights, resulting in the Court's revisiting the issue in *Boumediene v. Bush.*[59]

F. BOUMEDIENE v. BUSH

In *Boumediene v. Bush,* the Supreme Court held in a 5-4 opinion that non-citizens designated as enemy combatants and detained at Guantanamo Bay have the constitutional privilege of *habeas corpus.*[60] The court also found that §7 of the Military Commissions Act (MCA), which limited judicial review of executive determinations of the petitioners' enemy combatant status, did not provide an adequate *habeas* substitute and unconstitutionally suspended the writ of *habeas.* The petitioners argued they possessed a constitutional right to *habeas* review and that the MCA violated the Suspension Clause, which prohibits suspension of the writ of *habeas corpus* except during cases of rebellion or invasion when public safety may require it. The government did not claim MCA was a suspension of writ, but instead argued that non-citizens designated as enemy combatants and detained outside the *de jure* territory of the U.S. do not have constitutional rights, and therefore stripping the courts of jurisdiction to hear their *habeas* claims did not violate the Suspension Clause.

The Court noted that the writ was one of the few Constitutional protections of individual liberty prior to the Bill of Rights. The Court also viewed the

56. *Hamdan v. Rumsfeld,* 548 U.S. 557, 734 (2006).
57. *Id.* at 737.
58. 120 Stat. 2600 (Oct. 17, 2006).
59. 553 U.S. 723 (2008).
60. *Id.* at 732.

Suspension Clause under the separation of powers doctrine, and concluded it provides the judiciary with a "time-tested device, the writ, to maintain the delicate balance of governance" among the branches and to prevent "cyclical abuses" made by the legislative or executive branches.[61] The Court determined the Suspension Clause has full effect at Guantanamo, rejecting the government's argument regarding the petitioners' constitutional rights because the U.S. did not assert legal sovereignty over Guantanamo. The Court held that accepting such an argument would create separation of powers problems by allowing the political branches to govern without restraint.

The Court found three factors in assessing the reach of the Suspension Clause: (1) citizenship and status of the detainee and the adequacy of the status determination process; (2) the nature of the site where the person is seized and detained; and (3) the practical obstacles inherent to resolving the prisoner's entitlement to the writ. In applying those principles to the facts at hand, the Court noted that the detainees have been held by executive order for the duration of a conflict already one of the longest in American history, and although Guantanamo is not technically a part of the U.S., it is under the complete and total control of the U.S. government.[62]

After holding, the detainees were entitled to *habeas corpus* review, and the Court next addressed whether MCA's jurisdiction stripping was permissible under the Suspension Clause. Because the MCA did not purport to be a formal suspension of the writ, the issue was whether or not Congress provided an adequate substitute for *habeas corpus*. The Court held that by enacting the MCA, Congress clearly intended to create a much more limited procedure than traditional *habeas corpus* review. Although the Court did not want to offer a "comprehensive summary of the requisites for an adequate substitute for habeas corpus," the Court did outline some necessary requirements.[63] "The prisoner is entitled to a meaningful opportunity to demonstrate that he is being held pursuant to 'the erroneous application or interpretation' of relevant law."[64] In addition,

> the habeas court must have the power to order the conditional release of an individual unlawfully detained—though release need not be the exclusive remedy and is not the appropriate one in every case in which the writ is granted.[65]

The Court also stated that depending on the circumstances, additional *habeas* protections may be required. Some additional rights detainees should be granted include the ability to find and present evidence, assistance of counsel, access to government records, information regarding allegations relied upon by the government in the detention, and the ability to confront witnesses, thereby limiting the use of hearsay evidence.

The Court stated that there was significant risk of error in the tribunal's finding of fact, and this risk was too serious to ignore, considering that the

---

61. *Id.* at 744.
62. *Id.* at 770.
63. *Id.* at 777.
64. *Id.*
65. *Id.*

error may result in detention for the duration of hostilities that may last more than a generation. The Court held that the MCA failed to provide an adequate substitute for *habeas* and as such the writ was unconstitutionally suspended. Therefore, all detainees in Guantanamo have a right to a *habeas corpus* review in federal district courts.

The initial case in which a Circuit court applied the *Boumediene* decision was *Al-Bihani v. Obama.*[66] In that case, the defendant was a Yemeni citizen held in Guantanamo since 2002. The two issues the court addressed were whether or not the President can lawfully detain pursuant to an act of Congress, and what procedure is due to detainees challenging their detention in *habeas* proceedings. The defendant based his argument on principles of international law, arguing that relying on "support" of al Qaeda as a basis for detention violates international law. According to Al-Bihani, an individual not belonging to a recognized state's military is a civilian who must commit direct hostile acts before they can be lawfully detained. Al-Bihani further argued that the conflict for which he was detained, between the U.S. and Taliban-controlled Afghanistan, officially ended when the Taliban lost control over Afghanistan, and therefore he should be released, absent a determination of future threat.

The Court rejected the argument that the U.S. should be bound by international law, stating "international laws of war as a whole have not been implemented domestically by Congress and are therefore not a source of authority for U.S. courts."[67] The Court went on to say: "we have no occasion here to quibble over the intricate application of vague treaty provisions and amorphous customary principles."[68] The Court wrote:

> any person subject to a military commission trial is also subject to detention, and that category of persons includes those who are part of forces associated with Al Qaeda or the Taliban or those who purposefully and materially support such forces in hostilities against U.S. Coalition partners.[69]

The Court summarily rejected the defendant's claims that procedures used in his habeas proceedings were inadequate, and therefore the petition for a writ of *habeas corpus* was denied.

Padilla v. Rumsfeld Jennifer K. Elsea & Michael John Garcia, Judicial Activity Concerning Enemy Combatant Detainees: Major Court Rulings

Congressional Research Service Report for Congress, Apr. 1, 2010[70]

Recent District Court Rulings Concerning Scope of Executive Detention Authority

In the aftermath of the Supreme Court's decision in *Boumediene,* federal *habeas* courts reviewing claims raised by Guantanamo detainees have reached

66. 590 F.3d 866 (2010).
67. *Id.* at 871.
68. *Id.*
69. *Id.* at 872.
70. *Available at* https://apps.dtic.mil/sti/tr/pdf/ADA518967.pdf (last visited February 16, 2024).

differing conclusions regarding the scope of the Executive's detention authority under the AUMF and the law of war. Judge Richard J. Leon, the first district court judge to rule on this issue post-*Boumediene,* applied the standard employed by the Department of Defense (DOD) in 2004 CSRT proceedings, which authorized the detention of those who were "part of or supporting Taliban or al Qaeda forces, or associated forces that are engaged in hostilities against the United States or its coalition partners . . . [including] any person who has committed a belligerent act or has directly supported hostilities in aid of enemy armed force." More recent rulings by district courts have taken a more limited view of the Executive's detention authority. A few district court judges have held that the Executive has authority to detain persons who were "part of" or "substantially supported" Al Qaeda, the Taliban, or associated forces, so long as those terms are understood to include only those persons who were members of the enemy organizations' *armed forces* at the time of capture. Other judges have held that the Executive has authority under the AUMF and the law of war to detain persons who were "part of" the Taliban, Al Qaeda, or associated forces, but lacks authority to detain nonmembers who provide "support" to such organizations (though such support may be considered when determining whether a detainee was "part of" one of these groups). As discussed *supra,* in *Al-Bihani v. Obama* a three-judge D.C. Circuit panel endorsed the definitional standard used by Judge Leon to assess the Executive's detention authority. It is possible that this issue will be the subject of further litigation, either before the circuit court sitting *en banc* or the Supreme Court.

Several (though not all) district court judges have concluded that an individual's continuing threat to U.S. security is not a relevant consideration in determining whether he may be lawfully detained under the AUMF1. At least one district court judge has expressly held that "the President is authorized to detain [a properly designated enemy belligerent] for the duration of the conflict in Afghanistan, even if [he] poses no threat of returning to the field of battle." However, this conclusion has not been endorsed by every district court judge who has considered the issue.

Al Maqaleh v. Gates, 604 F. Supp. 2d 205 (D.D.C. 2009)

In April 2009, District Court Judge John D. Bates held in *Al Maqaleh v. Gates* that *habeas* may extend to non-Afghan detainees currently held by the United States at the Bagram Theater Internment Facility in Afghanistan, when those detainees had been captured outside of Afghanistan but were transferred to Bagram for long-term detention as enemy combatants. Judge Bates held that the circumstances surrounding detention of the petitioners in *Al Maqaleh* were "virtually identical to the detainees in *Boumediene*—they are [non-U.S.] citizens who were . . . apprehended in foreign lands far from the United States and brought to yet another country for detention." Applying *Boumediene* as relevant to a determination of the extraterritorial scope of the writ of *habeas corpus,* Judge Bates concluded that the writ extended to three of the four petitioners at issue in *Al Maqaleh,* who were not Afghan citizens.

In May 2010, the D.C. Circuit Court, in *Al-Maqaleh v. Gates,* overturned Judge Bates' decision holding that detainees held in an "active theater of war in a territory under neither the *de facto* nor *de jure* sovereignty of the United States and within the territory of another *de jure* sovereign" are not entitled to *habeas corpus*.[71]

Issues to Consider

1. What are the ramifications of denying detainees the right to *habeas corpus?*
2. What are the dangers of indefinite detention?
3. How does *Al-Maqaleh* impact *Boumediene*?
4. What is the most effective argument for granting detainees *habeas* rights?
5. Does the D.C. Circuit Court decision reflect policy articulated by President Bush in the immediate aftermath of 9/11?
6. Is the D.C. Circuit Court decision in accordance with the principles proposed by the late Chief Justice Rehnquist with respect to the role of courts in times of armed conflict?

III. ISRAEL

In developing and implementing a counterterrorism strategy, Israel's policy and decision makers are confronted by the doors of the High Court of Justice that are literally and figuratively open 24/7 to hear petitions of aggrieved Palestinians, or those acting on their behalf. A junior military commander's decision to conduct a particular operation, a senior officer's order that a particular geographic area be declared a closed military zone, and a non-commissioned officer's decision not to allow someone to pass through a checkpoint can all be petitioned in real time to the High Court. The U.S. standard of standing and justiciability are irrelevant; anyone may petition the High Court on behalf of a potentially aggrieved party.

The principle of judicial activism in Israel is examined here by analyzing three petitions filed with the High Court of Justice. The three cases are representative and indicative of the interplay between the executive (which in the West Bank is the IDF); the aggrieved (either a Palestinian who directly petitions or a human rights group petitioning on his behalf); and the Court.

These petitions were filed at the height of Palestinian terrorism and Israeli counterterrorism. The HCJ hearings do not take place in a vacuum; while the Court adjudicates, the IDF is either planning or engaged in military operations against Palestinian terrorists, who similarly are planning their next attack. The decisions have been chosen because they represent three distinct issues brought before the Court.

71. 605 F.3d 84, 97-98 (D.C. Cir. 2010).

Issues to Consider

1. What is the legal and policy significance of the phrase "democracies fight terrorism with one arm tied behind their back"?
2. What is the meaning of Barak's argument that the Court's expertise lies in humanitarian law and not in military combat?
3. What is the significance of judicial intervention when the issue is presented in real time rather than deferring until the conflict ends?
4. What does the phrase "if executive acts within the 'zone of reasonableness' then there is no basis for intervention" mean?
5. What does the phrase "security considerations are not magic words" mean?

A. MARAB v. IDF COMMANDER IN THE WEST BANK

With the advent of the military operation "Ebb and Flow," the IDF arrested thousands of Palestinians suspected of involvement in terrorism. The operation was a response to a terrorist act that resulted in the deaths of 30 Israelis, many of them elderly, celebrating the Passover meal. The military operation had not been planned thoroughly in advance, and critical non-combat issues were addressed on the fly. As a result, important issues were not considered and left to individual initiative.

One issue not properly planned for was where to detain thousands of Palestinians arrested during the operation. As the detention process developed, initial screening of detainees was conducted at brigade headquarters—a process requiring a significant amount of time, sometimes in questionable conditions.

According to Military Order 378, as amended in 1997, a detainee may be held for eight days before seeing a judge. When the IDF realized the number of detainees who needed to be processed would result in the Order's violation, the military commander signed Order 1500.[72] According to this Order, detainees could be held up to 18 days before seeing a military judge.

A petition was filed against this Order by Iad Ashak Mahmud Marab, a detainee.[73] In the petition and oral arguments, counsel argued the Order leads to detention without judicial review and to prolonged mass detention rather than individual review. Counsel claimed the Order was neither preventive nor administrative and violated the principles of proportionality and due process.[74]

The state responded to the petition by arguing that the standard detention law was not suitable for combat situations and that screening of detainees is a time-consuming process. The state argued that keeping detainees from

72. *See* B'tselem, *Operation Defensive Shield: Soldiers' Testimonies, Palestinian Testimonies* 16, *available at* www.btselem.org/Download/200207_Defensive_Shield_Eng.pdf (last visited October 8, 2010).

73. HCJ 3239/02, Marab v. IDF Commander in the West Bank (2002).

74. *Id.* at ¶¶8-10.

meeting with counsel prevents the passing of messages that endanger soldiers. The state also argued that the detentions were individualized rather than collective, and they were unique in the context of the special circumstances of armed conflict. In essence, the state argued that its standards were proportional and reasonable.

The Court held that the Order was illegal, ruling that holding individuals for 12 or 18 days without bringing them before a judge conflicted with "fundamentals of both international and Israeli law."[75] The Court also held that judicial review is not separate from detention, but rather is "an integral part of the detention process" and as such cannot legally be separated.[76] The Court's insistence that judicial review is integral to executive detentions reflects President Barak's belief that the judiciary *can* and *must* review executive actions *in real time.*

Marab v. IDF Commander in the West Bank

HCJ 3239/02 (2002)

Against this normative background, which demands prompt judicial review of detention orders, the question again arises whether the arrangement established in Order 1500, under which a person may be detained for a period of 18 days without having been brought before a judge, is legal. Similarly, is the arrangement established in Order 1505 legal? This arrangement—which was unaffected by Order 1512 or Order 1518—provided that a person may be detained for a period of 12 days without having being brought before a judge. In answering these questions, the special circumstances of the detention must be taken into account. "Regular" police detention is not the same as detention carried out "during warfare in the area," Order 1500, or "during anti-terrorism operations," Order 1505. It should not be demanded that the initial investigation be performed under conditions of warfare, nor should it be demanded that a judge accompany the fighting forces. We accept that there is room to postpone the beginning of the investigation, and naturally also the judicial intervention. These may be postponed until after detainees are taken out of the battlefield to a place where the initial investigation and judicial intervention can be carried out properly. Thus, the issue at hand rests upon the question: where a detainee is in a detention facility which allows for carrying out the initial investigation, what is the timeframe available to investigators for carrying out the initial investigation without judicial intervention?

In this regard, the respondents claim before us that it was necessary to allow the investigating officials 18 days and after Order 1505, 12 days to carry out "initial screening activities, before the detainee's case is brought before the examination of a judge." This was due to the large number of persons being investigated, and constraints on the number of professional investigators. In their response, the respondents emphasized that "during the warfare operations, thousands of people were apprehended by the IDF forces, under

75. *Id.* at ¶32.
76. *Id.*

circumstances which raised the suspicion that they were involved in terrorist activities and warfare. The object of Order 1500 was to allow the 'screening' and identification of unlawful combatants who were involved in terrorist activities. This activity was necessary due to the fact that the terrorists had been carrying out their activities in Palestinian populations centers, without bearing any symbols that would identify them as members of combating forces and distinguish them from the civilian population, in utter violation of the laws of warfare." See para. 51 of the response brief from May 15, 2002. The respondents added that it is pointless to bring detainees before a judge, when they have not yet been identified, and the investigative material against them has not yet undergone the necessary processing. This initial investigation, performed prior to bringing the detainee before the judge, is difficult and often demands considerable time. This is due, among other reasons, to "the lack of cooperation on the part of those being investigated and their attempts to hide their identities, their hostility towards the investigating authorities due to nationalistic and ideological views, the inability to predetermine the time and place of the detentions, the fact that most of the investigations are based on confidential intelligence information which cannot be revealed to the person being investigated, and the difficulty of reaching potential witnesses." See para. 62 of the response brief from June 11, 2002.

The respondents thus claim that the investigating authorities must be allowed the time necessary for the completion of the initial investigation. This will, of course, not exceed a period of 18 days, under Order 1500, or 12 days, under Order 1505, as it was amended in Orders 1512 and 1518. In this timeframe, all those detainees against whom there is insufficient evidence will be released. Only those detainees, whose initial investigation has been completed, such that the investigation is ready for judicial examination, will remain in detention.

In our opinion, this approach is in conflict with the fundamentals of both international and Israeli law. This approach is not based on the presumption that investigating authorities should be provided with the minimal time necessary for the completion of the investigation, and that only when such time has passed is there room for judicial review. The accepted approach is that judicial review is an integral part of the detention process. Judicial review is not "external" to the detention. It is an inseparable part of the development of the detention itself. At the basis of this approach lies a constitutional perspective which considers judicial review of detention proceedings essential for the protection of individual liberty. Thus, the detainee need not "appeal" his detention before a judge. Appearing before a judge is an "internal" part of the dentition process. The judge does not ask himself whether a reasonable police officer would have been permitted to carry out the detention. The judge asks himself whether, in his opinion, there are sufficient investigative materials to support the continuation of the detention

Thus, we hold the 18-day detention period without judicial oversight under Order 1500, and the 12-day detention period without judicial oversight under Orders 1505, 1512, and 1518, to be null and void. They will be substituted by a different period, to be set by the respondents. To this end, the respondents should be allowed to consider the matter. Therefore, we hold that this declaration of nullification will be effective six months from the date at which this judgment is given. Compare Tzemach, at 284. We have considered respondents' request to present us with classified information. We are of the opinion that such is neither appropriate nor desirable. We hope that the half-year suspension will allow for the reorganization required by both international and internal law.

Issues to Consider

1. Under what circumstances must detainees be afforded the opportunity to voice complaints before the detaining authority?
2. Detention must not be arbitrary; rather, an evidentiary basis should indicate that a particular detainee endangers or may endanger security. How is this possible during operational counterterrorism?
3. In special circumstances, is detention without judicial intervention acceptable? How much time is reasonable for judicial review of the detention process?
4. What is the significance from the perspective of the military commander of such a decision?
5. Is this judicial intervention or judicial interference?
6. Should the Court take into account operational requirements?
7. Should the Court be concerned with how such a decision affects military planning?
8. Is the Court's expertise truly only limited to humanitarian law issues, as Barak writes in the article quoted earlier?
9. Is the decision of the Court in line with Barak's theory that democracies fight terrorism with one armed tied behind their back?
10. In a time of combat, when terrorists fight with both hands in front of them, is such judicial activism responsible and reasonable?

B. PHYSICIANS FOR HUMAN RIGHTS v. COMMANDER OF THE IDF FORCES IN THE GAZA STRIP[77]

This case illustrates the Israel Supreme Court's immediate response to petitions filed during combat regarding the IDF's responsibility to honor international humanitarian law obligations. In response to widespread smuggling of arms and ammunition through an intricate series of tunnels dug between Egypt and the city of Rafah (located in the southern part of the Gaza Strip), the IDF conducted a military operation intended to locate and destroy the tunnels in an effort to weaken terrorist infrastructure.

During the course of the fighting, civilians were injured and the water supply was affected. In addition, complaints were lodged that the IDF was not allowing basic supplies, such as medication, to enter the city. A petition was filed by Physicians for Human Rights, Association for Civil Rights in Israel,

77. HCJ 4764/04, Physicians for Human Rights v. Commander of the IDF Forces in the Gaza Strip.

The Center for the Defense of the Individual, and B'Tselem, asking the Court to order the IDF to enable critical humanitarian supplies to be received by the local population and to ensure that the water supply be adequate.[78] Similar to *Marab,* the Court heard the case during the course of the armed conflict. The petition was filed on a Thursday, and the hearing held the next day. A senior IDF Commander was present in the courtroom to respond directly to the Court's questions.

Whether the Court should directly intervene in IDF combat operations while IDF soldiers are at risk must be weighed against the danger to a civilian population similarly at risk—this is the essence of robust judicial activism in times of armed conflict. This dilemma served as the centerpiece of the petition in oral arguments before the Court.

According to the state, the Court should exercise judicial restraint. The state declared the operation's goals were to prevent additional arms smuggling and to destroy terrorist infrastructure. The state also argued that humanitarian measures were taken within the confines of a military operation; furthermore, according to the State, the IDF was attempting to minimize danger to innocent civilians, while Palestinian terrorists were using civilians as "human shields."[79]

Issues to Consider

1. Are protections of civilians absolute?
2. How must a military balance between a legitimate combat operation and the obligation to ensure the safety and welfare of civilians?
3. What is the obligation of a military commander to a civilian population during the course of operational counterterrorism?

What does the High Court of Justice review in the context of combat while attempting to balance national security and individual rights? The Court states it will not rule on the manner in which combat is conducted because that is the responsibility of military commanders when "soldiers' lives are in danger."[80] The decision of whether or not to take military action is not a judicial question. Rather, the sole question before the court is whether the operation meets international humanitarian legal obligations as the Court assumes the operations are a military necessity.[81]

Physicians for Human Rights v. Commander of the IDF Forces in the Gaza Strip

HCJ 4764/04 (2004)

In general, the judicial review of this Court is exercised ex post facto. A petition is submitted against an action that has already been taken. Occasionally,

78. *Id.* at ¶7.
79. *Id.* at ¶9.
80. *Id.* at ¶16.
81. *Id.* at ¶17.

a significant period of time can elapse between the time the action is taken and before that action is examined by this Court. This, however, is not the case here. Petitioners have not requested that we examine the legal import of military operations that have already concluded. The purpose of this petition is to direct the present actions of the military. This is ex ante judicial review, exercised while military operations are currently underway. This imposes certain constraints on the Court. Of course, petitions that look towards the future are not novel to us. For example, in HCJ 5100/94 Public Committee Against Torture in Israel v. The State of Israel, we examined the legality of guidelines that allowed for the imposition of moderate physical pressure on suspects of an investigation. The purpose of our review there was not to examine actions that had been taken in the past, but to review investigations that were underway at that time. Even so, the current petition is unique in that it asks us to review military operations while they are underway and while IDF soldiers are subject to the dangers inherent to combat. As such, it is appropriate to emphasize that:

> Clearly this Court will take no position regarding the manner in which combat is being conducted. As long as soldiers' lives are in danger, these decisions will be made by the commanders. In the case before us, it was not claimed that the arrangement at which we arrived endangered the lives of soldiers.

The same applies here: humanitarian concerns have been resolved, without endangering the lives of soldiers or the military operations. Subject to this caveat, the situation before us is no different than other situations where this Court has reviewed the legality of military operations.

We do not review the wisdom of the decision to take military action. We review the legality of the military operations. As such, we presume that the operations in Rafah are necessary from a military standpoint. The question before us is only whether these military operations adhere to domestic and international law. The fact that operations are necessary from a military standpoint does not automatically mean that they fulfill legal requirements. Of course, with regard to issues of military concern, we do not stand in the stead of the military commander, and we do not substitute our discretion for his own. That is his expertise. We examine the legal import of his decisions. That is our expertise.

The Future

According to the humanitarian principles of international law, military activities require the following: First, that the rules of conduct be taught to, and that they be internalized by, all combat soldiers, from the Chief of General Staff down to new recruits. See Physicians for Human Rights, at 5. Second, that procedures be drawn up that allow implementation of these rules, and which allow them to be put into practice during combat. An examination of the conduct of the army while fighting in Rafah, as detailed in the petition before us—and we have nothing other than what has been presented to us—indicates significant progress compared to the situation two years ago. See Barake; Physicians for Human Rights and other decisions. This is the case regarding the implementation of the duty to ensure water, medical equipment, medicines, food, evacuation of the wounded, and the burial of the dead. This is also the case regarding the preparation of the army, and the design of procedures that allow humanitarian obligations to be satisfied. The establishment of the Humanitarian Hotline and the District Coordination Office, as well as the assignment of a liaison officer of the Coordination Office to every battalion, greatly aided the implementation of humanitarian principles.

In the framework of our discussion regarding the internalization of humanitarian laws, we emphasize that it is the duty of the military commander not only to prevent the army from harming the lives and dignity of the local residents (the "negative" duty: see supra para. 11). He also has a "positive" duty (para. 11). He must protect the lives and dignity of the local residents. For example, regarding the burial of local residents, the military commander was satisfied that the corpses were transferred to A-Najar Hospital. But this was not enough. He is obligated to do his utmost to ensure that the bodies be brought to a dignified burial according to local custom. He must make prior arrangements in order to ensure there are sufficient supplies of food and water. Damage to the water supply is something that can be anticipated from the outset, and if it cannot be avoided, a solution to this problem must be prearranged. Supplies of medicines, medical equipment and food should also be prepared in advance. Harm to local residents is expected and if, despite every effort to limit this, in the end there will be casualties among residents, this must be prepared for from the outset. Respondent should not rely solely on international and Israeli aid organizations to solve these problems, though their aid is important. The recognition that the basic duty belongs to the military commander must be internalized, and it is his job to adopt different measures from the outset so that he can fulfill his duty on the battlefield.

Additional measures should be adopted so that the established institutional arrangements will be more effective. We were informed that those who called the Humanitarian Hotline had to wait many hours. Col. Mordechai noted several times that some issues should have been referred to him, and not to the Humanitarian Hotline. The lack of information led, on several occasions, to inefficiency in aid efforts by third parties. Thus, for example, a vehicle of Petitioner 1 laden with medical equipment and medicines waited at Erez Crossing while the entrance point was Karni Crossing. However, at Karni Crossing their entrance was again denied, since Israeli doctors were among the passengers in the vehicle, and the army was only prepared to allow the entry of non-Israeli doctors. These issues and others need to be addressed. It is possible that the Humanitarian Hotline needs to be expanded, and there needs to be more effective communication between it and the District Coordination Office and the Coordination Office's liaison officers placed with the combat battalions. It is possible that there is a need, with regard to international and Israeli organizations whose humanitarian involvement is anticipated, to bypass the Humanitarian Hotline and facilitate direct contact with the DCO. It is possible that there is a need to take other measures. This matter is for the respondent to address; it must learn from the events of the day.

With the conclusion of the arguments in the petition, we ordered that the military staff in the area ensure that they solve not only the problems raised by petitioners, but also anticipate new problems that, in the nature of things, will arise in the future. For this reason it has been decided that Col. Mordechai will appoint a senior officer who will remain in direct contact with petitioners. This is the least that should have been done at the time the events were unfolding. The main thing is that it must be done now in order to learn lessons from the episode.

In granting a majority of the petitioners' requests, the Court held all soldiers must learn and internalize rules of conduct, regardless of their rank.[82] The Court also required that "procedures be drawn up that allow implementation of these rules, and which allow them to be put into practice during combat." The Court confirms that the military commander has a duty to prevent his troops from "harming lives and dignity of the local residents."[83]

The above decisions illustrate the unique role of the Israeli HCJ in the context of counterterrorism. Petitions are filed and the Court hears the petitioner almost immediately. In its decisions, the Court adopts a very proactive approach reflecting Barak's jurisprudential philosophy as articulated in the Harvard Law Review article. Does this approach guarantee that the state adopts a balanced approach to counterterrorism by enforcing self-imposed restraints, or does the Court unnecessarily limit command decision making by placing itself in the shoes of the commander?

Physicians for Human Rights illustrates Barak's view that real time review is imperative. Barak ordered supplies be brought into the city even though the crisis was ongoing and soldiers were still at risk. The decision both to hear the case and order supplies into Rafah while IDF soldiers were involved in combat reflects a belief that laws should be applied equally in times of war and peace. In this case, the Court demonstrates not only its willingness to review executive actions but also the importance of timing. Timing was literally a matter of life and death as the water supply and humanitarian supplies were crucial to the survival of those living in Rafah.

C. BEIT SOURIK VILLAGE COUNCIL v. THE GOVERNMENT OF ISRAEL AND THE COMMANDER OF THE IDF FORCES IN THE WEST BANK[84]

In developing a counterterrorism strategy, Israel implemented a number of different policies. One that has drawn much attention is the construction of the security fence between Israel and the West Bank.

The government of Israel decided to build the fence as a means to prevent the infiltration of Palestinian terrorists into Israel. The fence has proven successful; according to available statistics, there has been a 90 percent reduction in Palestinian terrorist attacks where the fence has been constructed. The government constructed the fence on the Palestinian side of the Green Line rather than on the Israeli side. According to the government, this was done for strategic and topographical reasons, not because the fence is

---

82. *Id.* at ¶66.

83. *Id.*

84. HCJ 2056/04, Beit Sourik Village Council v. The Government of Israel and Commander of the IDF Forces in the West Bank [2004] [hereinafter *Beit Sourik*].

a political fence intended to mark the future boundaries between Israel and a future Palestinian state.[85]

In the petition filed, petitioners from the West Bank village of Beit Sourik argued that the fence prevents access to their land, impacts their ability to move freely without excessive bureaucracy, makes use of local water wells almost impossible, greatly hinders access to water for crops, uproots olive trees, injures the livelihood of farmers, does not benefit the local population, and that the real purpose of the fence is annexation of the land for the benefit of the IDF and the Jewish population. Furthermore, the petitioners argued that due process had been violated since military orders regarding the construction of the fence had not been published, denying those injured the right to appeal the decision.

The state in its response to the petition argued that affected landowners were both offered compensation and entitled to appeal to the West Bank military commander against the order to use their land for the fence. Additionally, the state argued the primary purpose of the fence was self-defense, intended to protect Israeli citizens against Palestinian terrorists who could easily infiltrate Israel proper.[86] The state further argued that the measure was a proportional, security-based decision not intended to annex Palestinian lands for political purposes. The state insisted that commanders had balanced national security and individual rights, concluding that the fence reflected a proportional balance.[87] The state did not deny that injury had been incurred by Palestinians, but argued that an effort had been made to minimize the damage.

Issues to Consider

1. How should commanders balance military necessity (self-defense) and individual rights?
2. What are legitimate security considerations?
3. How is the Court to determine if the means are proportional?
4. What is the proper scope of intervention?
5. How much should the Court press on commanders to find alternatives?

Consider what the court wrote regarding the extent and scope of judicial review and proportionality.

Beit Sourik Village Council v. The Government of Israel and Commander of the IDF Forces in the West Bank

HCJ 2056/04

Before we examine the proportionality of the route of the separation fence, it is appropriate that we define the character of our examination. Our point of departure is the assumption, which petitioners did not manage to negate,

85. *Id.* at ¶¶12-15.

86. Israel proper refers to lands not captured in the 1967 Six-Day War (the West Bank, Gaza Strip, Golan Heights, Sinai Peninsula, and East Jerusalem including the Old City of Jerusalem).

87. *Beit Sourik, supra* note 84, at ¶13.

that the government decision to construct the separation fence is motivated by security, and not a political, considerations. As such, we work under the assumption—which the petitioners also did not succeed in negating—that the considerations of the military commander based the route of the fence on military considerations that, to the best of his knowledge, are capable of realizing this security objective. In addition, we assume—and this issue was not even disputed in the case before us—that the military commander is of the opinion that the injury to local inhabitants is proportionate. On the basis of this factual foundation, there are two questions before us. The first question is whether the route of the separation fence, as determined by the military commander, is well-founded from a military standpoint. Is there another route for the separation fence which better achieves the security objective? This constitutes a central component of proportionality. If the chosen route is not well-founded from the military standpoint, then there is no rational connection between the objective which the fence is intended to achieve and the chosen route (the first subtest); if there is a route which better achieves the objective, we must examine whether this alternative route inflicts a lesser injury (the second subtest). The second question is whether the route of the fence is proportionate. Both these questions are important for the examination of proportionality. However, they also raise separate problems regarding the scope of judicial review. My colleague Justice M. Cheshin has correctly noted:

> Different subjects require, in and of themselves, different methods of intervention. Indeed, acts of state and acts of war do not change their character just because they are subject to the review of the judiciary, and the character of the acts, according to the nature of things, imprints its mark on the methods of intervention.

. . . Our answer is that there relationship between the injury to the local inhabitants and the security benefit from the construction of the separation fence along the route, as determined by the military commander, is not proportionate. The route undermines the delicate balance between the obligation of the military commander to preserve security and his obligation to provide for the needs of the local inhabitants. This approach is based on the fact that the route which the military commander established for the security fence—which separates the local inhabitants from their agricultural lands—injures the local inhabitants in a severe and acute way, while violating their rights under humanitarian international law. Here are the facts: more than 13,000 farmers (falahin) are cut off from thousands of dunams of their land and from tens of thousands of trees which are their livelihood, and which are located on the other side of the separation fence. No attempt was made to seek out and provide them with substitute land, despite our oft repeated proposals on that matter. The separation is not hermetic: the military commander announced that two gates will be constructed, from each of the two villages, to its lands, with a system of licensing. This state of affairs injures the farmers severely, as access to their lands (early in the morning, in the afternoon, and in the evening), will be subject to restrictions inherent to a system of licensing. Such a system will result in long lines for the passage of the farmers themselves; it will make the passage of vehicles (which themselves require licensing and examination) difficult, and will distance the farmer from his lands (since only two daytime gates are planned for the entire length of this segment of the route). As a result, the life of the farmer will change completely in comparison to his previous life. The route of the separation fence severely violates their right of property and their freedom of movement. Their livelihood is severely impaired. The difficult reality of life from which they have suffered (due, for example, to high unemployment in that area) will only become more severe.

These injuries are not proportionate. They can be substantially decreased by an alternate route, either the route presented by the experts of the Council for Peace and Security, or another route set out by the military commander. Such an alternate route exists. It is not a figment of the imagination. It was presented before us. It is based on military control of Jebel Muktam, without "pulling" the separation fence to that mountain. Indeed, one must not forget that, even after the construction of the separation fence, the military commander will continue to control the area east of it. In the opinion of the military commander—which we assume to be correct, as the basis of our review—he will provide less security in that area. However, the security advantage reaped from the route as determined by the military commander, in comparison to the proposed route, does not stand in any reasonable proportion to the injury to the local inhabitants caused by this route. Indeed, the real question in the "relative" examination of the third proportionality subtest is not the choice between constructing a separation fence which brings security but injures the local inhabitants, or not constructing a separation fence, and not injuring the local inhabitants. The real question is whether the security benefit reaped by the acceptance of the military commander's position (that the separation fence should surround Jebel Muktam) is proportionate to the additional injury resulting from his position (with the fence separating local inhabitants from their lands). Our answer to this question is that the military commander's choice of the route of the separation fence is disproportionate. The gap between the security provided by the military commander's approach and the security provided by the alternate route is minute, as compared to the large difference between a fence that separates the local inhabitants from their lands, and a fence which does not separate the two (or which creates a separation which is smaller and possible to live with). Indeed, we accept that security needs are likely to necessitate an injury to the lands of the local inhabitants and to their ability to use them. International humanitarian law on one hand, however, and the basic principles of Israeli administrative law on the other, require making every possible effort to ensure that injury will be proportionate. Where construction of the separation fence demands that inhabitants be separated from their lands, access to these lands must be ensured, in order to minimize the damage to the extent possible.

We have reached the conclusion that the route of the separation fence, which separates the villages of Beit Likia and Beit Anan from the lands which provide the villagers with their livelihood, is not proportionate. This determination affects order Tav/103/03, which applies directly to the territory of the mountain itself, and leads to its annulment. This detention also affects order Tav/104/03 which applies to the route west of it, which turns in towards the village of Beit Likia, in order to reach the mountain. The same goes for the western part of order Tav/84/03, which descends from the mountain in a southeasterly direction. The eastern part of the latter order was not a matter of significant dispute between the parties, but as a result of the annulment of the aforementioned orders, it should be examined anew.

In deciding whether the fence properly balanced security and liberty interests, the Court developed a three-pronged proportionality test for determining legality of state action. According to the Court, the objective must be related to the means (a rational means test), the means used must injure the individual to the least extent possible (least injurious test), and the means used must be of proper proportion to the benefit gained (proportionality test). According to the Court, the state failed to meet this test. Therefore, while holding that the fence is legal, the Court ordered the government to take the necessary steps to reduce the effect on Palestinian lives by re-contouring the fence.

Subsequently, an additional petition was filed to the HCJ regarding the fence's effect on the residents of the town of Bil'in.[88] The petitioners argued that the fence directly impacts construction of housing projects, access to agricultural lands, and therefore villagers' livelihoods; in addition, the petitioners argued that construction of the security fence on Palestinian lands violates public international law. The military commander (respondent) argued the fence, as contoured, is necessary from a security perspective for the purpose of protecting citizens of the State of Israel.

The Court held that security considerations were within the purview of the military commander; however, in applying a proportionality test, the Court concluded that the military commander did not sufficiently examine alternatives that would have enabled meeting legitimate security requirements while minimizing harm to the daily life of village residents.

Issues to Consider

1. How does the Court determine whether alternatives have been sufficiently examined?
2. What is the significance of the Court's holding that the commander did not satisfactorily assess harm to Palestinian residents of the village?
3. To whom—according to the Court—does the military commander owe a duty?
4. Is the Court stepping into the military commander's shoes?

IV. RUSSIA

Russia is, in many ways, an emerging democracy. Institutions that were in place during the Soviet period are no longer relevant; the former USSR has

88. HCJ 8414/05, Yassin v. Israel and Military Commander in the West Bank [2005].

been replaced by a number of new nations stretching from Europe to Asia. How the Russian judiciary reacts to counterterrorism is the focal point of this section; to that end, reviewing how the courts function is useful.

RUSSIA

Jurist Legal News and Research[89]

I. Law, Courts & Judgments

The Russian judiciary is divided into three branches: The courts of general jurisdiction (including military courts); subordinated to the Supreme Court; the arbitration (commercial) court system under the High Court of Arbitration; and the Constitutional Court (as well as constitutional courts in a number of administrative entities of the Russian Federation). Civil and criminal cases are tried in courts of primary jurisdiction, courts of appeals, and higher courts. The general court system's lowest level is the municipal court, which serves each city or rural district and hears more than 90 percent of all civil and criminal cases. The next level of courts of general jurisdiction is the regional courts. At the highest level is the Supreme Court. Decisions of the lower trial courts can be appealed only to the immediately superior court unless a constitutional issue is involved. The arbitration court system consists of city or regional courts as well as appellate circuit courts subordinated to the High Court of Arbitration. Arbitration courts hear cases involving business disputes between legal entities and between legal entities and the state.

Russia's judiciary and justice system are weak. Numerous matters that are dealt with by administrative authority in European countries remain subject to political influence in Russia. The Constitutional Court was reconvened in March 1995 following its suspension by President Yeltsin in October 1993. The 1993 constitution empowers the court to arbitrate disputes between the executive and legislative branches and between Moscow and the regional and local governments. The court also is authorized to rule on violations of constitutional rights, to examine appeals from various bodies, and to participate in impeachment proceedings against the president. The July 1994 Law on the Constitutional Court prohibits the court from examining cases on its own initiative and limits the scope of issues the court can hear.

In the past few years, the Russian government has begun to reform the criminal justice system and judicial institutions, including the reintroduction of jury trials in certain criminal cases. Despite these efforts, judges are only beginning to assert their constitutionally mandated independence from other branches of government.

The Duma passed a Criminal Procedure Code and other judicial reforms during its 2001 session. These reforms help make the Russian judicial system more compatible with its Western counterparts and are seen by most as an accomplishment in human rights. The reforms have reintroduced jury trials in certain criminal cases and created a more adversarial system of criminal trials that protect the

89. *Available at* https://2009-2017.state.gov/outofdate/bgn/russia/20735.htm (last visited February 16, 2024).

rights of defendants more adequately. In 2002, the introduction of the new code led to significant reductions in time spent in detention for new detainees, and the number of suspects placed in pretrial detention declined by 30%.

In order to analyze judicial review, we must understand what the relevant court believes it is reviewing and how the conflict is defined:

> The Constitutional Court of the Russian Federation in its review of Presidential decrees that authorized the use of military force in Chechnya, while never directly referring to hostilities there as a "non-international armed conflict," none-the-less cited Additional Protocol II as a source of law that should have been applied by parties to the conflict. The Court did not analyze the Protocol, nor did it consider it as applicable law in the judicial review of decrees.[90]

This signifies that the Constitutional Court believes the conflict is not criminal in nature, but rather, that it is a non-international armed conflict. From the perspective of the state, measures available to handle the conflict are very different than if the conflict were defined as criminal. However, Russia continues to use its criminal laws and codes with respect to detained suspected terrorists. The significance of this decision affects the rights and obligations of the state, soldiers, and individuals with whom the state is engaged in combat. How the Constitutional Court applies this definition to the conflict and how the state responds to the Court's decisions are critical aspects of operational counterterrorism.

In an emerging democracy, the relationship between the executive and the nascent judiciary is vital; a democracy cannot fully function unless the executive truly respects the judiciary. The two excerpts below offer insight into what the future might hold.

> The Constitutional Court of the Russian Federation was established in 1991 in the wake of the collapse of the Soviet Union. The sources of its authority were the Constitution, which, with its patchwork of amendments, hardly resembled the original text of 1978, and the Law on the Constitutional Court of the Russian Socialist Federal Republic of 1991. The Court decided its first case in January 1992. It failed to stay clear of the power struggle between the president and the Parliament that reached its violent climax in the fall of 1993, and was suspended until February 1995.
>
> Currently, the Constitutional Court derives its powers from the Constitution of 1993 and the Federal Constitution Law on the Constitutional Court of the Russian Federation of 1994 (hereafter the Law on the Constitutional Court). It is part of the three-tiered judicial system. But unlike the Supreme Court and the Higher Court of Arbitration that sit at the apex of the pyramids of, respectively, courts of general jurisdiction and courts of arbitration, the Constitutional Court does not rest on a foundation of lower courts. . . .
>
> The first category of cases involves legislative acts passed by public authorities, whether federal or regional, and only public authorities may petition the Court. These cases need not arise from any ongoing dispute. A party with due authority may request an abstract review of a statute.

---

90. Bakhtiyar Tuzmukhamedov, *Chechnya and the Laws of War*, Crimes of War Project, (1999).

When confronted with such petitions, the Court shall rule on the constitutionality of federal laws and normative acts issued by the president, or by either chamber of Parliament, or by the Russian government. It may also rule on the constitutionality of constitutions, charters and laws of the component entities of the Russian Federation, as well as on treaties concluded by those entities with the federal authorities and between those entities. Finally, the Court may decide on the conformity with the Constitution of international treaties that have not yet come into force.

The second category comprises cases about jurisdictional disputes between federal authorities, or between federal and regional authorities, or between regional authorities.

The third category consists of cases in which the Constitutional Court is petitioned by private persons or by courts requesting a constitutional review of a law that has been applied or ought to be applied in a particular case.

It is only natural to expect the supreme judicial body of constitutional review to interpret the Constitution; however, unlike the U.S. Supreme Court, the Russian Constitutional Court may deal with it as an abstract question.[91]

The following publicly stated view provides insight into President Putin's position regarding the role and importance of the Court:

> In assessing the ten-year-long history of the Constitutional Court, Vladimir Putin said "all the Constitutional Court's powers proved necessary." The President explained that the Court protected the constitution, defended people's rights and freedom, and was active in creating and strengthening the legal foundation of the state. Turning to specific features of the legal institution, the President demonstrated that the Constitutional Court, on the one hand, "does not supplant other bodies of power or interfere with their jurisdiction," while, on the other, "it is not dependent on the bodies of power and may influence their activities by its decisions." In this sense, the Constitutional Court "is a higher level of authority, just as an organ of constitutional justice should be."
>
> The Russian president noted that these days, the Constitutional Court enjoys the reputation of a most important and authoritative body. In his view, the fact that representatives of practically all the world courts have come to Moscow, points to the high international prestige of the Constitutional Court of Russia.
>
> When commenting on the quality of the Constitutional Court judges in terms of their responsibility at work, Vladimir Putin stressed that their activities "call for a profound legal knowledge, professional dignity, and occasionally civic courage."
>
> "At the same time," said the President, "the line of development of this most important institution was not a straight one." He admitted that there were repeated attempts to use the court as an arena of political struggle but it was "the principle of independence and non-interference in politics" that won the day.
>
> "Today, this principle is accepted and supported by society and the authorities," said the President proudly. Moreover, "it has been confirmed by the world practice of constitutional justice."[92]

91. 94 Am. Soc'y Int'l L. Proc. 166 – ASIL.

92. Russian President Offers his Evaluation of the Russian Constitutional Court, November 1, 2001, *available at* http://www.cdi.org/russia/johnson/5521-7.cfm (last visited November 28, 2006).

Issues to Consider

1. What is the significance of the Court's definition of the conflict in understanding judicial review?
2. How independent can a Court be in an emerging democracy?
3. How attentive must the executive be to the judiciary?
4. What is the proper role of the judiciary in a non-international armed conflict?

A. CONSTITUTIONALITY OF THE CHECHEN SITUATION

The Russian government's actions in the Chechen conflict were addressed by the Constitutional Court in the Judgment of the Constitutional Court of the Russian Federation of 31 July 1995 on the Constitutionality of the Presidential Decrees and Resolutions of the Federal Government Concerning the Situation in Chechnya. The first excerpt below discusses the impact of the majority opinion in the case. Given the extraordinary nature of this opinion, lengthy quotes directly from the dissenting opinions are also provided.

Paola Gaeta, The Armed Conflict of Chechnya Before the Russian Constitutional Court

7 E.J.I.L. 563 (1996)[93]

The constitutionality of four decrees of the central government in the prosecution of the Chechen conflict was challenged in the Russian Constitutional Court by a group of deputies of the State Duma and the Federal Council of the Russian Federation (hereinafter RF). Among other things, the applicants argued that two of the decrees at issue, namely those providing for the dispatch of armed forces on the territory of the Chechen Republic, had resulted in a violation of international treaties to which the Russian Federation was a party, and of Article 15, paragraph 4, of the Constitution, by virtue of which both general and conventional international law shall be part of the Russian legal system.

It is not unusual for domestic courts to be called upon to settle cases relating to armed conflict taking place within the territory of a sovereign state. Nevertheless, this decision can be regarded as unique in national case-law, since the Russian Constitutional Court was asked to pronounce upon the lawfulness under international law of *coercive measures by a State against a segment of its own population seeking to secede from the state.* In fact, this could well be the first time a national court has been called upon to scrutinise compliance by a state's armed forces with international rules

93. *Available at* http://www.ejil.org/pdfs/7/4/1393.pdf/ (last visited February 16, 2024).

concerning the protection of civilians and the conduct of hostilities during an armed conflict. . . .

. . . [T]he applicants argued that two decrees of the central authorities were unconstitutional, contending that *they had resulted* in a violation of Article 15 of the Russian Constitution, under which all international law is part of the Russian domestic legal system. The Court had thus been asked, *inter alia,* to verify whether the military action of the Russian armed forces in Chechnya resulted in, or gave rise to, breaches of international humanitarian law.

The Court refrained from dealing with this matter. It stated that an examination of the actions of the Russian armed forces from the point of view of compliance with international law: may not be a subject for consideration by the Constitutional Court of the Russian Federation and ought to be performed by other competent organs.

The Court consequently scrutinised the constitutionality of the decrees by only taking into account their *normative* content and not their *actual* application. The Court found that only one of the challenged acts did not conform to the Russian Constitution, while the other was to be considered in accordance with the Constitution.

Although the Court deemed it inappropriate to pronounce on the question of whether the decrees, as applied by the Russian military authorities, were in conflict with Article 15 of the Constitution, nonetheless it was not unresponsive to the issue of actual compliance with international humanitarian law raised by the applicants.

The Court determined that at the international level the provisions of Protocol II were binding on both parties to the armed conflict and that the actions of the Russian armed forces in the conduct of the Chechen conflict violated Russia's international obligations under Additional Protocol II to the 1949 Geneva Conventions. Nonetheless, the Court sought to excuse this non-compliance because Protocol II had not been incorporated into the Russian legal system. . . .

. . . Another point which deserves to be highlighted is that the Court clearly spelled out that the provisions of Protocol II are binding upon *both* parties to the armed conflict, *i.e.* that the Protocol confers rights and imposes duties also on insurgents. . . .

It is important to [sic] emphasize the determination by the Court that the Russian Parliament had failed to pass legislation to implement Protocol n, and that this failure was one of the grounds—probably even the primary ground—for non-compliance by Russian military authorities with the rules embodied in the Protocol. It is probably true that the enactment of *ad hoc* legislation to implement Protocol II was necessary even if Article 15, paragraph 4, of the Russian Constitution provides that international treaties are part of the Russian domestic legal system: indeed Protocol II [sic] cannot be considered as self-executing in all its provisions. . . .

[The Court's] decision must be commended for the strongly internationalist outlook it reflects. The Court has given pride of place to international law, by taking into account international rules and principles in assessing the constitutionality of the challenged decrees. This approach clearly demonstrates that the Court is fully aware of the close interplay between constitutional and international law. . . [Even] the highest bodies of the Russian Federation must comply not only with constitutional provisions, but also with international rules whenever such rules impinge upon the conduct of State organs at home or abroad. Under the principle of the rule of law laid down in the Russian Constitution, the Court emphasized that 'the bodies of power in their activities are bound both by internal and international law.

This laudable approach has manifested itself not only in the various points made by the Court on international law relating directly to the Chechen conflict, but also in two more specific respects. First, the Court has expressly directed the Russian Parliament to implement Protocol II, thus showing how much importance it attaches to actual compliance with that treaty. Secondly, the Court underscored that according to the Russian Constitution and the U.N. Covenant on Civil and Political Rights "victims of any violations, crimes and abuses of power shall be granted efficient remedies in law and compensation for damages caused." In this way the Court has established the applicability of these human rights instruments to remedy at least the most blatant violations of international humanitarian law.

This decision thus clearly demonstrates that the Russian Constitutional Court has become an important institution promoting compliance with international law in the Russian legal system.

In an opinion such as the one described above, the Constitutional Court must define the limits of the phrase "all means at the disposal." The justices' responsibility and the decision's significance are particularly crucial because this was the first case in which important questions were brought before the newly established Court. Determining the limits of state power is the essence of judicial review; doing so while the armed conflict is underway is more reflective of the Israeli model than of the late Chief Justice Rehnquist's approach.

A state's obligation to respect international law must be met even if the other side fails to do so. The failure of the Chechens to conduct themselves in accordance with relevant Geneva Convention requirements cannot be used by the Russian government as justification for not respecting those obligations themselves; this point is of major significance in this opinion. By determining that failure to comply with Geneva Convention provisions cannot be brought before the Court, the judges are clearly expressing the limits of the scope of their judicial review.

The Court ultimately holds that use of the Russian armed forces in the Chechen conflict is a matter to be decided by the legislature rather than by the judiciary. The decision reflects a self-imposed limit on judicial review. Nevertheless, the Constitutional Court directly addressed many of the most important operational questions related to counterterrorism. Furthermore, the Court articulated the position that in the context of separation of powers, the legislature is charged with establishing the guidelines for the conduct of the conflict.

Now consider some of the dissenting opinions in the case.

Judgment of the Constitutional Court of the Russian Federation of 31 July 1995 on the Constitutionality of the Presidential Decrees and Resolutions of the Federal Government Concerning the Situation in Chechnya

Translation by Federal News Service Group[94]

Summary of the Dissenting Opinions of Six Judges of the Constitutional Court of the Russian Federation

[R]egarding the examination of the constitutionality of: decree No. 2137 of the President of the Russian Federation of 30 November 1994 on measures to restore constitutional legality and law and order in the territory of the Chechen Republic; decree No. 2166 of the President of the Russian Federation of 9 December 1994 on measures to halt the activities of illegal armed formations in the territory of the Chechen Republic and in the zone of the Ossetian-Ingush conflict; order No. 1360 of the Government of the Russian Federation of 9 December 1994 on ensuring the state security and territorial integrity of the Russian Federation, the rule of law, the rights and freedoms of citizens and the disarming of illegal armed formations in the territory of the Chechen Republic and adjacent areas of northern Caucasus; and decree No. 1883 of the President of the Russian Federation of 2 November 1993 on the fundamental provisions of military doctrine of the Russian Federation.

Dissenting Opinion of Judge Vitruk

In 1991-94 in the Chechen Republic, which, under Article 65 of the Constitution of the Russian Federation, forms part of the Russian Federation, there did in fact arise an extraordinary situation requiring the central authority to take practical steps, not excluding the use of force, to restore constitutional order in the territory of the Chechen Republic. However, any action by federal authorities must be taken on the basis of and in conformity with the Constitution and the federal laws.

The executive authorities' texts under consideration *viz* decree Nos. 2137 and 2166 and order No. 1360, as well as decree No. 2169 of December 11 on measures to ensure the rule of law, law and order and public safety in the territory of the Chechen Republic form a whole. It is therefore impossible to assess the constitutionality of any one of these texts in isolation.

If the objectives set out in the preambles of the texts are examined independently of the measures they involve, they can be seen to be in conformity with the Constitution of the Russian Federation. They are designed in particular to restore constitutional legality (decree No. 2137), ensure national security, safeguard the rights and freedoms of citizens (decree No. 2166) etc. On the other hand, the measures for which the texts provide in order to attain those goals are a violation of the terms of the Constitution. Their purpose was to establish a special regime that was neither a state of emergency nor a state of war. This regime, which was described by the representative of the

94. *Available at* https://www.venice.coe.int/webforms/documents/default.aspx?pdffile=CDL-INF(1996)001-e (last visited March 6, 2024).

President and the Government as a regime for re-establishing the foundations of the constitutional system, constitutional legality and the legal order in the territory of the federal component concerned and which is known in world as "federal intervention," had no basis in Russian constitutional law when the texts in question were issued.

The special regime should have been preceded by the adoption of a federal law on the subject, particularly as regards the use of the armed forces to resolve a constitutional crisis and the curtailment of the rights and freedoms of citizens.

The regime established in the territory of the Chechen Republic has at least two main features. First, it relies heavily on the armed forces of the Ministry of the Interior and the special units of the Federal Security Service and other services, to resolve the conflict between the authorities of the Chechen Republic and the federal authority; this led to a military conflict of a domestic nature. Secondly, it entails a substantial limitation of the rights and freedoms of citizens.

Neither the Constitution nor legislation makes any provision for the special regime established by the presidential and governmental texts, and they lay down no procedural arrangements for establishing such a regime. The references by the representative of the President and the government to the provisions of the laws on security, on defence, on the internal troops of the Ministry of the Interior of the Russian Federation, on the police and on judicial information in the Russian Federation are not legally correct, because these laws do not regulate relations in the situation existing in the territory of a federal component that has declared its sovereignty and its withdrawal from the federation.

The reference to the "Fundamental provisions of military doctrine of the Russian Federation," approved by presidential decree No. 1833, in so far as they provide for the possibility of using the armed forces to resolve domestic conflicts is not correct either, as these provisions are contrary to the Constitution of the Russian Federation and to Article 10 (2) and (3) of the law on defence act. Article 90 (3) of the Constitution stipulates that presidential decrees and orders may not be contrary to the Constitution's terms.

By promulgating decree Nos. 2137, 2166 and 2169, the President exceeded his powers under Articles 83-90 of the Constitution. The President is not free to act as he chooses, because he is required to comply with the Constitution and with federal laws (Article 90 (3) of the Constitution). The President must also observe a principle applicable to all state officials, *viz.* they may do only whatever is provided for by law. (Article 80 (2)) of the Constitution is perfectly clear on this point: the President of the Russian Federation shall adopt measures to protect the country's sovereignty, independence and territorial integrity in accordance with the procedure established by the Constitution of the Russian Federation. . . .

The recognition of the existence of presidential powers not enumerated in Articles 83-90, i.e., implicit powers, denotes an illegitimate enlargement of the presidential powers, to the detriment of the powers of the Federal Parliament and the Government. The self-executing nature of the Constitution, as provided for in Article 15 (1) of the Constitution, does not admit of any arbitrary interpretation of these provisions, as that would lead to a violation of other constitutional principles and norms. . . .

The presidential decrees under consideration are in contradiction with the hierarchy of constitutional principles, where absolute priority is given to respect for human rights and fundamental freedoms (Art. 2 of the Constitution). According to Article 18 of the Constitution, human rights and freedoms are self-executing. Unfortunately, the orientation of the presidential decrees and governmental orders towards the use of all the means at the State's disposal, without the provision of any safeguards against abuse of such means, together with the absence of any machinery for preventing violations of the rights and freedoms of the peaceable population, has resulted in grave violations of the rights and freedoms of Russian citizens.

From the foregoing I draw the following conclusion. Presidential decree Nos. 2137 and 2166 and governmental order No. 1360 are not in conformity with the Constitution of the Russian Federation, as they violate the constitutional principle of respect for human rights and freedoms laid down in Articles 2, 6 (2), 17 (1) and (2), 18 and 55 of the Constitution, as well as being inconsistent with the Constitution's demarcation of powers, because the promulgation of these texts exceeds the powers of the President and the Government as defined in the Constitution.

Moreover, the procedure employed for the enactment and bringing into force of presidential decree No. 2137 of 30 November 1994 is unconstitutional. Although the decree affects constitutional rights and freedoms, it was not officially published, which is a breach of Article 15 (3) of the Constitution. Furthermore, the procedure for examining the constitutionality of the decree was not completed in accordance with Article 43 (2) of the federal law on the Constitutional Court of the Russian Federation, on the ground that the effects of the decree had ceased to exist by the time the matter was referred to the Court. The governmental order of 9 December 1994 is not in conformity with the Constitution of the Russian Federation as regards the procedure used for its adoption, as it was not adopted by the Government as a collegiate body. . . .

Issues to Consider

1. What issues are the minority opinions focusing on?
2. What is the significance of these issues in the context of the Chechen conflict?
3. What are the limits of judicial intervention?
4. In an emerging democracy, should the judiciary hesitate in criticizing the executive?
5. How are rights of those opposing the State to be determined and defined?

In the majority opinion, the Constitutional Court was sparing in its criticism of the executive branch. The minority opinion is highly critical of the executive branch, far more so than the U.S. Supreme Court usually is when criticizing the executive branch and perhaps more so than the Israeli judiciary is. The minority opinions address the most critical aspects of counterterrorism: balancing equally legitimate considerations, defining the conflict, determining the respective parties' rights and obligations, and confronting the executive with the consequences of failing to satisfactorily address these issues—severe human rights violations.

B. REGISTRATION

According to press accounts and reports submitted by various human rights groups, the Russian government and certain cities practice "propiska," which literally means "the record of place of residence." In practice it is a system that allows local authorities to deny freedom of movement to certain ethnic groups by requiring a residence permit that restricts both an individual's right to choose his place of residence and to travel within the country.

The practice has been widely implemented against Chechens residing in Moscow. In 1996, the matter was first brought before the Constitutional Court, which ruled that the practice violates the Russian Constitution and is therefore unconstitutional.[95] Though the mayor of Moscow, Yuri Luzhkov, declared he would disregard the Court's ruling, the decision reflects the judiciary's determination to actively review executive counterterrorism measures.

In ruling on the propiska in Moscow, the Constitutional Court held that "in the course of guaranteeing constitutional rights, the legislator must adhere to the demands of Art. 55.2 of the Constitution, which says that no laws denying or belittling human and civil rights and liberties may be issued in the Russian Federation."[96]

The Court also held the following:

> [A]ccording to Art. 114 of the Constitution, the federal government ensures the implementation in the Russian Federation of a uniform financial, credit, and monetary policy [and] implements measures to ensure legality and the rights and freedoms of citizens." Regions may not introduce local taxes that violate federal legislation. Under federal law, people should be required to pay only a small, symbolic fee when registering with local authorities as new residents. Instead, the regions were imposing fees of a confiscatory nature. The amount of the registration fees was disproportionate to citizens' real income. In the face of such burdens, the right to freedom of movement and choosing one's place of residence had become a hollow declaration.[97]

The Court went on to hold:

> Furthermore, the fact that the fees applied only to the new residents of a particular region constituted real discrimination against citizens based on social origins. Article 19.2 of the Constitution guarantees "the equality of rights and liberties regardless of gender, race, nationality, language, origin, property or employment status, residence, attitude toward religion, convictions,

---

95. Noah Rubins, *Recent Development: The Demise and Resurrection of the Propiska: Freedom of Movement in the Russian Federation,* 39 Harv. Int'l L. J. 545 (1998).

96. Konstantin Katanian, *Freedom of Movement in the Russian Federation Today, The Propiska and the Constitutional Court,* 7 East European Const. Rev. 2 (1998).

97. *Id.*

> membership of public associations, or any other circumstance." In addition, the article categorically forbids "any restrictions on the rights of citizens based on social, racial, national, linguistic, or religious grounds."[98]

In attempting to limit freedom movement of ethnic groups, the local government was acting in violation of the Russian Constitution. The mayor's refusal to respect the holding and his continuation of the policy present a major challenge to the Court and the national executive alike.

C. EVOLUTION OF RUSSIA'S COURTS

The Russian judicial system does not rely on precedents in reaching decisions. However, the Russian Constitutional Court appears to be forging in the direction of using precedents. In January 2010, the Constitutional Court declared that Russia's Higher Arbitrage Court has the right to set precedents that lower arbitrage courts must follow.[99] This decision reflects precedent that might, eventually, extend to the entire Russian legal system. The Constitutional Court also called for an amendment to the legal code in order to ensure compliance with this new decision. "The adoption of a precedent-based legal system would have enormous consequences for Russia. Among the most obvious would be a more level legal field for the courts, prosecutors, and defendants across the entire country and a requirement for better trained and informed lawyers and judges to handle individual cases."[100]

V. INDIA

A. INTRODUCTION

Given the threats faced by the Indian government, the role of the Indian Supreme Court as a possible "restrainer"[101] presents a great challenge in the context of judicial activism. In considering the Court's role, an important detail to recall is that India, similar to Israel, was under British rule prior to attaining independence. Just as the Israeli High Court of Justice is rooted in the British *order nisi*, the Indian Public Interest Litigation (PIL) mechanism is similarly based.

Public Interest Litigation is intended to provide the citizen with means to seek redress from the Court regarding a government decision or action.[102] Redress may be sought either directly by the affected individual or on the

---

98. *Id.*

99. Paul Goble, *Some Russian Courts Told to Use Precedents to Decide Cases,* Window One Eurasia, January 22, 2010, available at https://windowoneurasia.blogspot.com/2010_01_22_archive.html (last visited February 16, 2024).

100. *Id.*

101. The phrase is intended in the context of President Barak's concept of "self-imposed restraints."

102. Public Interest Litigation was an attempt to guarantee fundamental rights and the assurances of the Constitution to all people in reality, not just on paper. Ashok H. Desai & S. Muralidhar, *Public Interest Litigation: Potential and Problems* 159, *in* Supreme But Not Infallible—Essays in Honour of the Supreme Court of India (B.N. Kirpal et al. eds, 2000).

individual's behalf. The petition requests that the government desist from a particular activity; the purpose may be defined as "correcting a wrong."

Issues to Consider

1. The Israeli High Court of Justice has been accused of interfering (rather than intervening) with the executive; does PIL unnecessarily restrict the Indian executive attempting to respond to complex and varied threats?
2. Why should "standing" requirements be loosely applied in PIL?
3. What does it mean in the context of counterterrorism to "correct a wrong?"

Jurisdiction of the Supreme Court

Supreme Court of India[103]

The Supreme Court has original, appellate and advisory jurisdiction. Its exclusive original jurisdiction extends to any dispute between the Government of India and one or more States or between the Government of India and any State or States on one side and one or more States on the other or between two or more States, if and insofar as the dispute involves any question (whether of law or of fact) on which the existence or extent of a legal right depends. In addition, Article 32 of the Constitution gives an extensive original jurisdiction to the Supreme Court in regard to enforcement of Fundamental Rights. It is empowered to issue directions, orders or writs, including writs in the nature of habeas corpus, mandamus, prohibition, quo warranto and certiorari to enforce them. The Supreme Court has been conferred with power to direct transfer of any civil or criminal case from one State High Court to another State High Court or from a Court subordinate to another State High Court. The Supreme Court, if satisfied that cases involving the same or substantially the same questions of law are pending before it and one or more High Courts or before two or more High Courts and that such questions are substantial questions of general importance, may withdraw a case or cases pending before the High Court or High Courts and dispose of all such cases itself. Under the Arbitration and Conciliation Act, 1996, International Commercial Arbitration can also be initiated in the Supreme Court.

Issues to Consider

1. Does effective judicial review require timeliness?
2. What is the significance of judicial backlog?

103. *Available at* https://main.sci.gov.in/jurisdiction#:~:text=Its%20exclusive%20original%20jurisdiction%20extends,any%20question%20(whether%20of%20law (last visited February 16, 2024).

3. If the Court's legitimacy is challenged, what restraints may it impose on the executive?
4. Is effective judicial review possible when a nation like India faces multiple external and internal threats?
5. What are the limits of restraints that a Court should self-impose?
6. Does the executive naturally take advantage of judicial backlog?

While PIL seeks to provide an aggrieved citizen with speedy recourse to government imposition on civil and political rights, the lack of immediacy caused by backlog directly affects the impact of judicial review. India's judicial review model reflects a combination of Barak's and Rehnquist's competing philosophies. PIL is similar in purpose to the HCJ; however, the objective reality of judicial backlog lends itself to the Rehnquist model, for PIL is largely predicated on accessibility and judicial independence. Unwarranted delay in scheduling hearings or rendering decisions suggests—whether intentionally or unintentionally—an approach advocated by Rehnquist and by the U.S. Supreme Court in *Endo.*

B. JUDICIAL REVIEW—PUBLIC SAFETY ACT

> The Jammu and Kashmir Public Safety Act of 1978 is the main law relating to preventive detention in Jammu and Kashmir and permits administrative detention without trial for a period of up to one year if a person is to be prevented from acting in a manner deemed "prejudicial to the maintenance of public order" or up to two years if their actions are likely to be "prejudicial to the security of the State." The detention orders of the APHC leadership brought under the PSA cited grounds of activities being anti-national, subversive or prejudicial to the security of the state.[104]

The 1978 Act contributed to serious human rights violations. As previously discussed, an unfettered executive unrestrained by an acquiescent judiciary is more prone to violate civil and political rights. In examining Indian judicial activism, the critical query is whether the Court is sufficiently vigilant with respect to the executive's decisions. While PIL seeks to provide the citizen with protection—similar to the Israeli High Court of Justice—the question is whether the Court actually does so.

India: Punitive Use of Preventive Detention Legislation in Jammu and Kashmir

Amnesty International, May 16, 2000[105]

The state government's disregard for court orders quashing detention orders or granting bail is particularly disconcerting as courts are the only resort for

104. *India: Abuse of the Public Safety Act in Jammu and Kashmir,* Amnesty International, April 5, 2000, *available at* https://www.amnesty.org/en/documents/asa20/013/2000/en/ (last visited March 6, 2024).

105. *Available at* https://www.amnesty.org/en/wp-content/uploads/2021/06/asa200102000en.pdf (last visited March 6, 2024).

anyone seeking legal redress. The function of the judiciary to uphold and protect human rights is undermined in this process. The pattern that has emerged is one of harassment, intimidation and deliberate disregard for the civil and political rights of those who are critical of the government. The government uses preventive detention legislation to silence critics and punish dissent.

. . .

Arbitrary detention in Jammu and Kashmir has a long history. The findings of the Basic Rights Protection Committee under its chairman Justice Farooqi in 1994 are still valid today. It noted the arbitrary detention of people even after their release ordered by designated courts and said that fresh detention orders were served on people immediately after they were shown to have been set free either on court orders or after completing their term of detention. It observed that young men were picked up and held in detention centres "for weeks, months and sometimes even for years before detention orders under the Public Safety Act are served on them; they are booked under the Terrorist and Disruptive Activities (Prevention) Act [TADA] even as they may not be applicable on facts." It said that of a total of 865 of detainees then in Kot Balwal Jail, 560 detainees had "neither been served detention orders under PSA nor booked under TADA."

Similarly, a Jammu and Kashmir High Court judge ruling on a public interest petition alleging torture and arbitrary detention, noted in October 1994: "The Police agencies and the administration appear to have thrown to winds the rule of law. All sorts of illegalities are being committed by them and even criminals and terrorists may be ashamed of them. The High Court is replete with such complaints . . . many of which stand substantiated. Hundreds of cases have been brought to my notice where the detenues are in illegal detention. Despite the strong directions of this court they are not be[ing] released. . . . Scores of cases are pending wherein the detenues have been allegedly done away with after arrest. For years the detenues are languishing in jails/Sub-Jails and interrogation centres without any legal authority. In short, there is a total break down of law and order machinery . . . even this court has been made helpless by the so-called law-enforcing agencies. Nobody bothers to obey orders of this court. . . ."

. . .

When the phased elections in Jammu and Kashmir were almost over, the arrest and detention of almost the entire top leadership of the APHC began. Among the 25 APHC leaders arrested were all the members of the APHC Executive Committee, the highest policy making body of the APHC, except its former chairman, Mirvaiz Moulvi Umar Farooq, who plays an important spiritual role in the state. They were arrested in small groups between 26 August and early November and held in different police stations where criminal complaints were lodged against them; most were transferred from police station to police station or to jails which made it difficult for their families to trace them. At this stage, lawyers had no access to them. Detention orders under the Public Safety Act were served on most of the detainees around 25 September 1999 by the Jammu and Kashmir government, in most cases ordering detention for a period of one or two months.

The detention orders of the APHC leaders stated that since they were likely to obtain bail in connection with these criminal complaints brought against them, and as "you will not refrain from continuing such illegal anti-national and subversive activities in future . . . which are prejudicial to the security of the state . . . as such in order to deter you from continuing such activities your detention under the provisions of the PSA has become imperative."

. . .

Several of the detainees completed their detention period under the PSA on 24 October but were not released. An order from the Government of Jammu and Kashmir merely directed that the detention period in the detention order be omitted; the detention orders remained in force. On 18 November 1999, after several of the detainees in Jodhpur Jail had been presented to the Advisory Board (for composition and functions of the Advisory Board see chapter 4.1), the Home Department of the Government of Jammu and Kashmir confirmed their detention under the PSA and extended the period of their detention to 24 months from the date of arrest, without giving any reason for this extension.

Petitions challenging the detention of the APHC leaders were filed in the Jammu and Kashmir High Court in the first week of October; they challenge their detention on three sets of grounds and aim at the quashing of the detention orders:

- the detention orders suffer from *procedural flaws* as the order of detention and grounds of detention were not communicated to the detainees within the required period; the time of serving the detention order and the grounds of detention were not recorded; supporting material was not given either to the detainees or the detaining authority thus failing to give the detainees the opportunity to make adequate representation to the government; and detainees were not informed if the government approved the detention order within the statutory period;
- and *substantive flaws* as they failed to establish grounds for detention under the PSA; the petitions argue that the orders provided no evidence that the detainee would act in a manner prejudicial to the security of the state in future and that the activities alleged did not fall within the purview of section 8 of the PSA;
- *detention of the APHC leaders in Jodhpur* is unlawful; the detention orders stated that the detainees be lodged in Central Jail Srinagar. The petition also argues that the state legislature cannot make laws with application outside the state, hence the amendment made to section 10 PSA is unconstitutional. . . .

Hearings of the petitions in the Jammu and Kashmir High Court started in December 1999. In February 2000 Amnesty International was informed that the Government of Jammu and Kashmir applied for the petitions to be transferred to the bench of the High Court in Jammu. Amnesty International is not aware of the reasons given for the request of transfer, and a transfer, if granted, may delay further hearings. Meanwhile, the petitions came up for a hearing on 14 March 2000 in the Srinagar bench of the Jammu and Kashmir High Court; the Advocate General sought adjournment till 18 April which was granted by the High Court.

. . .

Noor Mohammad Kalwal, a member of the Jammu and Kashmir Liberation Front (JKLF) was arrested by the Central Reserve Police Force (CRPF) on 8 September 1991; several months later, during which time it is not known if he was charged with any criminal offence, on 27 February 1992, he was served a PSA detention order for one year and lodged in Udhampur subjail. After the expiry of the detention period, he was neither released nor charged with any offence nor produced in any court. On 26 February 1993, he was transferred to the Joint Interrogation Centre at Kot Balwal, Jammu. A petition (387/93) challenging his continued detention was filed but despite his being transferred to subjail Rangreth in Srinagar so he could be produced in court in Srinagar, he was not actually brought before the High Court.

In early 1994, a complaint was brought against Kalwal on two counts under TADA, on both of which the Additional Designated Court, Srinagar granted him bail. When Kalwal was not released, the Designated Court directed police authorities, including the Director General of Police (DIG) to bring the detainee to court. The authorities failed to respond at the first date of hearing in February 1994. On 8 June 1994, police authorities and the Counter Intelligence Kashmir (CIK) moved an application in the court for a new date as, due to non-availability of police escort, the detainee had not been brought to court. On the new date set by the High Court, 14 June 1994, police authorities did not appear nor was the detainee brought to court. The Additional Judge of the Designated Court, Srinagar stated: "It is quite strange that the law executing authorities are not giving due regard to the orders passed by the Court for which the authorities are meant.... In this case, not to speak of the execution of the orders by superior officer of the rank of DIG, he has not even cared to send a few lines to this court in respect of compliance with the orders of this court."

It is not known to Amnesty International what happened to Noor Mohammad Kalwal between June 1994 and early 1996 except that he was not released. He was detained under a new PSA detention order (DMS/PSA/415/96) of 26 February 1996 for one year. A petition (107/97) challenging this new detention order was filed in the Jammu and Kashmir High Court which quashed it on 10 November 1997 and ordered his release. He was not released. Instead he was arrested on a charge under TADA which referred to an FIR (No 128/92) registered in 1992 relating to his alleged unlawful possession of a revolver claimed to have been recovered from him at the time of his arrest in 1992—when he had already been in detention for several months, having been arrested in September 1991. The designated TADA court granted bail to Noor Mohammad Kalwal on 17 July 1999. At the time of the bail petition hearing, the prosecution showed the presiding judge a letter from Counter Intelligence Kashmir (CIK) which stated that the detainee should not be released; but in case of release, the CIK should be notified immediately. The prosecution also reportedly showed a letter from CIK to Central Jail Srinagar instructing jail authorities to inform CIK of any imminent releases.

As Noor Mohammad Kalwal was about to be released from Central Jail Srinagar, he was re-arrested at the jail gate by CIK. Two days later he was transferred to Khanyar police station. He was then served another PSA one-year detention order (DMS/BSA/58 dated 30 July 1999, signed by the District

Magistrate Srinagar), alleging that he was an "active, dedicated and staunch member of the JKLF," had been involved in crimes including firing on security forces which resulted in the death of a child and activities prejudicial to the security of the state. Noor Mohammad Kalwal has since then been held in Central Jail Srinagar. He was reportedly shifted to Udhampur Jail on 8 February 2000.

. . .

The PSA has been challenged in court mainly on the two grounds given below; neither of these challenges have so far been decided.

The definitions used in the Act including terms in the notion 'acting in a manner prejudicial to the security of the state or the maintenance of public order' are too vague and imprecise to be legally relevant. Kashmir lawyer Syed Tassaduq Hussain in 1999 raised this point in a Social Action Litigation (No.677/99); this petition was admitted in the Jammu and Kashmir High Court but may be sent to a larger bench which could delay the hearing.

The same petition also argues that sections 10 and 11 of the PSA which permit the transfer of a detainee to jails outside the state wrongly ascribes to legislators in the state the power to enact laws having extra-territorial effect. The right to transfer detainees to jails outside the state had already been challenged in the early 1990s by Justice Farooqi. This petition had apparently been transferred to a full bench but had then never been heard and decided. More recently lawyers have also pointed out that all legal changes effected during President's rule in the state (1990 to 1996), including amendments to the PSA, lapsed a year after the elected government took office, unless confirmed by the state legislative assembly. To Amnesty International's knowledge, President's Act No 3 of 1992 has not been confirmed by the Jammu and Kashmir Legislative Assembly and would appear to be void since October 1997.

The transfer of detainees to distant jails had earlier been stopped on the consideration for the dignity of the detainee. In November 1995, the Jammu and Kashmir High Court had directed that no detainee should be transferred to jails outside the sate in response to a public interest litigation initiated by Jalil Andrabi. He had argued inter alia that detainees have the right to a life with human dignity, to contact family and friends, wear their own clothes and consult and be defended by a lawyer of their own choice. Such conditions are only fulfilled if detainees are held close to their homes.

. . .

[S]ome detention orders have been quashed, usually on formal grounds. The following case shows how thoroughly the legal requirements of the PSA are sometimes ignored revealing the intention of the detaining authorities to stifle dissent at any cost. Javed Ahmed Kathwari (21) described as a member of the Hizbul Mujahideen which advocates the accession of Kashmir to Pakistan, was arrested by the CIK Srinagar on 8 January 1995 under TADA in connection with FIR 1/1994 filed in police station CIK, Srinagar, according to which he had been found with arms and ammunition and was alleged to have murdered Sohan Lal Mahra of Gogjibagh in September 1993. As the state anticipated that he would be released on bail, a PSA detention order (DMS/PSA/137/95) for 24 months was issued by the District Magistrate Srinagar on 5 July 1995. He was directed to be detained in subjail Gupkar, Srinagar, as his activities were declared to be "highly prejudicial to the security of the state." The grounds for his detention included that "there is every likelihood that you may get released on bail which will defeat the purpose to deter you from continuing your subversive activities."

Contrary to the magistrate's order, Kathwari was transferred to Sangroor jail outside the state, then to Kot Balwal jail in Jammu. In September 1995, Vijay Kumar Mehra, son of the alleged victim of the detainee, submitted an affidavit in the High Court at Srinagar stating that his father had died a natural death in Amritsar in 1965, i.e. seven years before Kathwari was born.

The expectation that this disclosure would lead to the immediate quashing of the charge and the detention order proved premature. A petition challenging the detention order filed in September 1995 alleged that most of the legal requirements of the PSA had been ignored: the detainee had not been given a detention order, had not been informed of the grounds of detention, or shown relevant material, had not been informed of his right to make representation against his detention, nor had the case been referred to an Advisory Board in the stipulated time, nor had the government confirmed the detention order upon obtaining the opinion of the Advisory Board. Moreover, the detainee had not applied for bail so that the very basis of the detention order was non-existent. On 6 February 1996, the High Court quashed the PSA detention order ordering Kathwari's release while noting that the state "did not care to respond [to the petitioner's arguments] after having been duly served" notice. It had "not followed due course of law in depriving the petitioner of his liberty, guaranteed to him under the constitution." It is not known to Amnesty International if Javed Ahmed Kathwari was in fact released.

In other cases, too, detention orders were issued when the persons concerned were already in detention on a criminal charge in connection with which they had not sought release on bail. In November 1998, the Jammu and Kashmir High Court at Jammu quashed a PSA detention order against Altaf Ahmed Wani issued on 1 October 1997 for a period of 24 months while he was already in detention on the basis of an FIR (65/1997) of 17 August 1997. Justice Sharma said that the detaining authorities had not considered if the detainee had or was likely to move a bail application and as such the detention order lacked any basis.

Only in very rare cases have detainees been awarded compensation for illegal detention when their detention orders were quashed. In August 1997, the Jammu and Kashmir High Court quashed 12 detention orders, ordered the release of those who were detained under these orders and ordered the state to pay Rs. 10,000 to each of the detainees. They were also advised that they could sue the state for damages in a civil court.

4.4. Disregard of the Jammu and Kashmir Government for Court Orders

The quashing of a detention order and a court direction to release a detainee does not necessarily mean that the detainee will in fact be released. Amnesty International is aware of many instances in which court directives have been ignored by state authorities. The pattern of arbitrary detention described in this report, in which detention periods under the PSA are alternated with detention under strings of FIRs in cases for which the accused often obtained bail without ever being released, indicates the intent of the authorities to detain activists critical of the government irrespective of whether courts consider detention legal or not.

The practice of not releasing detainees who completed their detention, whether preventive detention or detention following conviction and sentence, is not new. The Jammu and Kashmir Bar Association on 7 October 1993 filed a petition in the Jammu and Kashmir High Court in which it brought several human rights matters to the attention of the High Court, including inadequate provision of food, drinking water and medical attention in the Joint Interrogation Centres (JIC) Hariniwas and Rangreth in Srinagar. It also said: "there are also a lot of people unlawfully detained at JIC Rangreth, where period of detention has expired and instead of being released, they have been held up for no fault of theirs. People against whom detention orders have been passed by various authorities are also not being shifted to their places of lodgement without any justification. Similarly persons whose interrogation is complete and investigation reports are ready, are also neither being released from JIC Hariniwas nor are they shifted to judicial lockup. The condition of all the detenues lodged at Hariniwas is critical for each one of them is treated inhumanely." It asked the High Court to ensure the release of all detainees languishing in the two joint interrogation centres without any legal justification.

The above highlights the overwhelming problem faced by the Indian Courts engaged in judicial review of the executive during armed conflict. Much like the Israeli model, the model the judiciary is determined to develop is meant to enable immediate judicial review based on accessibility and independence. Dissimilar from the American model, which articulates restraint with respect to *when* to intervene, the Indian model seeks to restrain or, at least, to actively review, the executive's actions in real time.

That model, however, is hampered by logistic realities that prevent timely implementation of decisions. Effective judicial review of the executive requires decisions that both mandate restraint and require the state's ability and willingness to ensure enforcement. Enforcement of PIL decisions would not only guarantee their relevance but also signal executive respect of the judiciary.

Issues to Consider

1. What are the consequences of an executive that ignores decisions of the judiciary?
2. What judicial measures can be taken to avoid limitless detention of individuals?
3. Can the judiciary compel the release of individuals that the executive refuses to release or to bring before a court?

VI. SPAIN

Spain steadfastly defines terrorism as a criminal act and therefore applies the traditional criminal law paradigm to counterterrorism. Since Spain considers terrorism a criminal act, judicial review of counterterrorism measures must be considered in that vein.

Issues to Consider

1. Does application of the traditional criminal law paradigm to counterterrorism suggest limited judicial review?
2. What are the operational limits of using a traditional criminal law paradigm for counterterrorism?
3. What are the benefits of using a traditional criminal law paradigm for pursuing terrorists?
4. What are the similarities and differences between terrorists and criminals?
5. Should there be different measures for terrorists pre-arrest and post-arrest?
6. Should there be special courts and judges that specialize in terrorism cases?

As discussed in Chapter 3, the primary counterterrorism method adopted by the Spanish government in response to the Madrid train bombing is the incommunicado detention of suspected terrorists.

Counter-Terrorism Legislation and Practice: A Survey of Selected Countries

Secretary of State, United Kingdom (Oct. 2005)[106]

Spain

94. In terrorist cases, the judge may order that suspects be held incommunicado if they have grounds to believe that knowledge of the suspect's detention would prejudice the investigation. This involves a limitation of detainees' rights in two ways: relatives may not be informed of the detention, and legal assistance is provided by a duty solicitor, not a lawyer of their own choice. All other rights, including habeas corpus, continue to apply. The initial incommunicado order is valid for 72 hours following arrest. It can be prolonged for a further two days upon the authority of the investigating magistrate. After this period the investigating magistrate must decide whether to commence criminal proceedings.

106. Dep't of State, *Counter-Terrorism Legislation and Practice: A Survey of Selected Countries*, 2005, *available at* http://image.guardian.co.uk/sys-files/Politics/documents/2005/10/12/foreignterrorlaw1.pdf (last visited March 6, 2024).

If so, the investigative magistrate may order preventive detention, at which point the suspect is transferred from police custody to judicial custody (prison). At this point, he may extend the incommunicado period by five days, exceptionally followed by a final period of three days. Thus, it is possible for a person against whom criminal proceedings have begun to be held incommunicado for up to 13 days

95. While the detainee is held incommunicado in police custody, he may be questioned in the presence of the duty solicitor (not a lawyer of his own choosing), who is called in immediately on arrest. The lawyer may advise their client on procedural matters, but may not consult privately with the suspect. A forensic doctor examines the detainee to ensure that they are not physically mistreated and sends a report to the judge. Within the incommunicado period of detention, the suspect is transferred to the judge at the National High Court who has three days in which to hold a judicial interrogation. If the judge thinks there is a case for prosecution, criminal proceedings begin and the suspect is transferred to judicial custody; if not, the detainee is released. The judge must issue a reasoned judgement justifying his decision to begin criminal proceedings and any extension of the incommunicado period. Once in judicial custody, the detainee has the right to be seen by a second court-appointed forensic doctor and continued legal assistance. He may only have access to a lawyer of his own choosing once the incommunicado period has ended.

96. When a person has been charged and held in judicial custody, the period of preventative detention may last two years if the penalty for the offence is imprisonment of three years or more. Where circumstances exist that mean that the matter may not be tried within two years, the court may order one extension of up to a further two years. If the defendant is convicted and the sentence is under appeal, the period of custody may be extended for up to half of the sentence imposed. In practice, therefore, investigating magistrates have up to four years during which they can keep a terrorist suspect in detention and prepare the case for trial, although the defendant must be tried within the four year period.

A. SPANISH JUDICIAL SYSTEM

In Spain, the National High Court hears terrorism cases as part of its criminal docket, but the Constitutional Court can return a case to the court where it was originally adjudicated, should the Constitutional Court determine that constitutional rights were violated during the course of the proceedings. The National High Court is composed of six investigating judges who examine the cases assigned, gather evidence, and evaluate whether or not the case should be brought to trial, but the Court does not actually try the cases.[107] At the time, the most prominent judge in the National High Court was Judge Baltasar

107. *Profile: Judge Baltasar Garzon*, BBC, September 26, 2005, *available at* https://www.bbc.com/news/world-europe-16591284 (last visited February 16, 2024).

Garzon. Judge Garzon indicted Osama bin Laden in 2003[108] and investigates suspected terrorist organizations and activities, including suspected al Qaeda cells, in Spain.[109]

According to Spanish law, judicial review is limited to a determination of whether or not there is sufficient basis for continuing the detention of a suspected terrorist. In the event that the judge concludes there is insufficient evidence, the detainee is released. However, should the judge determine otherwise, the detainee will be remanded for further detention. As indicated above, if the detainee has been placed in incommunicado detention, he may not see an attorney of his choosing; rather the attorney is essentially court-appointed. As the judiciary is integrally involved in the decision to hold an individual in incommunicado detention, the concept of judicial review is inherently different than the judicial activism of the other surveyed nations.

Issues to Consider

1. What is the role of the Spanish judiciary in determining the legality of an incommunicado detention?
2. Whose role is it to oppose the imposition of an incommunicado detention?
3. Is incommunicado detention reflective of unfettered prosecutorial discretion without significant judicial review?
4. What standards and criteria are relevant for determining the appropriateness of an incommunicado detention?
5. What branch of government should determine the criteria?
6. What is the proper mechanism for judicial review in such circumstances?

B. MADRID TRAIN BOMBINGS

In the aftermath of the bombing of the Madrid train stations, the Spanish authorities responded by arresting a number of suspects. The following Human Rights Watch report addresses the issue of incommunicado arrests and how the Spanish legal system interprets the significance of this measure.

Limitations on Challenging the Lawfulness of the Detention

Human Rights Watch, Jan. 2005[110]

As of the end of 2004, eighteen people were in jail in Spain in connection with 11-M and forty-one people had been arrested and subsequently released

108. *Id.*

109. *Judge "Knew Madrid Bombs Not ETA,"*, BBC News, July 15, 2004, *available at* http://news.bbc.co.uk/1/hi/world/europe/3897741.stm (last visited October 8, 2010).

110. *Available at* https://www.hrw.org/reports/2005/spain0105/7.htm (last visited February 16, 2024).

after varying amounts of time in police custody and prison. The vast majority of the forty-one are on provisional release. A few were simply questioned and released without charge. Rabei Osman el Sayed, an Egyptian who was arrested in Milan on June 7 was extradited to Spain on December 7. He is suspected of masterminding the March 11 attacks. Of the eighteen in pre-trial detention, nine are Moroccans and five are Spaniards, while the remaining four are Syrian, Lebanese, Algerian and Egyptian, respectively; Moroccans account for twenty-two of those detained and subsequently released, while seven Spaniards fall into this category. The twelve Spaniards who have been detained are all suspected of involvement in the theft and/or sale of the explosives used the attacks, or the sale of drugs whose profits were used to finance the attacks.

The detainee, his or her spouse or companion, relatives, and, in the case of minors and incapacitated persons, their legal guardians; the Public Prosecutor; the Defensor del Pueblo; and the competent instructing judge on his own initiative may all file a writ of habeas corpus. The examining magistrate of the district where the detainee is being held is competent to review the petition, except in cases of detention of suspected members of armed groups or terrorists, whose writs of habeas corpus must be reviewed by the Central Instructing Judge, in other words, the same examining magistrate of the Audiencia Nacional who may have ordered the detention in the first place. By contrast, appeals against orders remanding a detainee into pre-trial detention issued by Audiencia Nacional magistrates are reviewed in the first instance by the same examining magistrate but in the second instance by a panel of three judges.

While the letter of the habeas corpus law in Spain appears to be in conformity with international standards, the interpretation of the law among legal professionals is so narrow as to render it effectively meaningless. In conversations with Human Rights Watch, the attorney general and high-level representatives of the Ministry of Justice argued that habeas corpus was irrelevant in cases of incommunicado detention because this is a situation in which the arrest and period of detention are under judicial supervision and therefore a priori legal. The criminal defense lawyers consulted similarly stated that they did not consider filing a writ of habeas corpus on behalf of their clients because the detention had been ordered and supervised by a competent judge. One of the 11-M legal aid attorneys said, "Habeas corpus is hardly ever used in Spain. It's absurd . . . it only serves to place [the detainee] at the disposal of the judge, and in this case it didn't make sense, all of the time frames were respected."

Human Rights Watch is particularly concerned that the Ombuds Institution (Defensor del Pueblo), though empowered by law to file writs of habeas corpus, does not see it as a useful or even appropriate tool. María Luisa Cava de Llano, First Adjunct of the Defensor del Pueblo, explained that "it is not common because illegal detentions don't happen. In the last four years, we have not submitted any nor have we been asked to do so." When asked if they ever ex officio go to places of detention to verify the conditions or situation of an incommunicado detainee, she said, "It is not our job to disrupt the work of the National Police; in principal we have no reason to believe that a person in incommunicado detention will be mistreated. Our national police and civil guard enjoy prestige among the public and their work is good until it is proven otherwise. Our assumption is that there will not be problems."

Even if there were a broader interpretation of the law and a greater willingness to use this legal tool, there are several practical impediments to incommunicado detainees enjoying the right to habeas corpus. First, they are not informed of this right. The right to challenge the lawfulness of the detention through a writ of habeas corpus is not among the rights that police are obligated to read to detainees at the time of arrest and before the official statement is recorded. It is a fair assumption that many detainees are not aware of this right or of the procedure for exercising it, particularly given that lawyers appear not to regard it as an important right.

Second, the fact that incommunicado detainees do not have the right to notify a person of their choice about the arrest or the place of detention clearly undermines the ability of third parties to file a writ of habeas corpus on their behalf. The CPT, while recognizing that it may be necessary in exceptional cases to deny notification of a third party for brief period of time, has stated that "to deny for up to five days the exercise of [this] right . . . is not justifiable." The CPT takes the position that "a period of a maximum of 48 hours would strike a better balance between the requirements of investigations and the interests of detained persons."

Finally, as detailed above, in most cases the detainee does not see a lawyer until the legally permissible period of incommunicado detention in police custody is almost over. Given that it is the lawyer who is in the best position to counsel the detainee about his various options, including that of filing a writ of habeas corpus, this delay has a direct impact on the detainee's ability to exercise this fundamental right. The European Court of Human Rights has held that "where a detained person has to wait for a period to challenge the lawfulness of his custody, there may be a breach of Article 5(4)." The Court considered that a period of seven days "sits ill with the notion of 'speedily'" under that article. The Human Rights Committee concluded that Article 9(4) of the ICCPR had been breached in a case where the applicant had the theoretical right to file a writ of habeas corpus but had been denied access to counsel throughout his detention.

Many human rights groups, including Amnesty International, have called for Spain to desist from applying incommunicado detention to suspected terrorists.

VII. CHINA

China's counterterrorism strategy is more centralized than almost any other country. The decision of when to arrest, interrogate, and try suspected terrorists largely comes from the central government. The constitution, on its face, provides for an open, fair, and independent judicial system. The reality, however, is vastly different.

China's constitution provides for the creation of several courts: local courts, special courts, and the Supreme Court. Local courts consist of tribunals in counties and administrative districts of cities and are responsible for criminal, civil, and administrative cases. The special courts control military, maritime, and railway cases. The Supreme People's Court is the highest court and has jurisdiction over all of the lower courts. The Supreme People's Court has first hearing rights to criminal and civil cases of national importance and must approve all death penalty cases. The constitution provides for open trials in all cases, except those involving state secrets, privacy, or juveniles.

While seeming to be a transparent court system, the 2008 U.S. Department of State Human Rights report suggested otherwise:

> in practice the judiciary was not independent. It received policy guidance from both the government and the [Chinese Communist Party (CCP)], whose leaders used a variety of means to direct courts on verdicts and sentences, particularly in politically sensitive cases. At both the central and local levels, the government and CCP frequently interfered in the judicial system and dictated court decisions. Trial judges decide individual cases under the direction of the adjudication committee in each court. In addition the CCP's law and politics committee, which includes representatives of the police, security services, procuratorate, and courts, had the authority to review and influence court operations at all levels of the judiciary; in some cases the committee altered decisions.[111]

Issues to Consider

1. Is judicial review possible in what is largely a centralized governmental system?
2. How does the court carve a niche for itself enabling judicial review?
3. What are the conditions necessary for creating judicial review?
4. What are the practical implications of a regime free of judicial review?
5. How is judicial review to be developed in a largely centralized government structure?
6. How are individual rights protected if there is no judicial review of the executive?

VIII. COLOMBIA

A. INTRODUCTION

Colombia is faced with several challenges in developing counterterrorism strategies, much less in developing a process and mechanism for active judicial review of the executive. The judicial system faces threats from paramilitaries, interference from the executive, and a corrupt political and criminal system. Historically, the Colombian courts have been viewed as weak with very little oversight power over the executive. In 2006, Colombia's Constitutional Court

111. Bureau of Democracy, Human Rights, and Labor, *2008 Human Rights Report: China*, Department of State, February 25, 2009, *available at* https://2009-2017.state.gov/j/drl/rls/hrrpt/2008/eap/119037.htm (last visited February 16, 2024).

made clarifications to the Justice and Peace Law; paramilitaries who wished to receive reduced sentences must give full and truthful confessions and were penalized for hiding the truth.

B. INVESTIGATION BY THE SUPREME COURT INTO CONGRESS' LINKS TO PARAMILITARIES

According to the Colombian Constitution, members of Congress should be investigated and tried only by the Supreme Court. In 2005, the Supreme Court's criminal chamber launched investigations of members of the Colombian Congress for links to paramilitaries. Previously, reports of cooperation between paramilitary and public officials were received, but no claims were investigated. The Attorney-General has investigated over 2,100 institutions.[112] These prosecutions confirm the extent of infiltration by paramilitary groups in Colombia. However, Human Rights Watch has reported that the executive branch has taken steps to undermine the investigation, including replacing justices on the Court and proposing constitutional amendments that would remove jurisdiction from the Court.

BREAKING THE GRIP? OBSTACLES TO JUSTICE FOR PARAMILITARY MAFIAS IN COLOMBIA

Human Rights Watch (2008)[113]

On September 26, 2007, the Supreme Court indicted Sen. Mario Uribe for conspiring with paramilitaries. The decision was of great significance because of the high profile of Sen. Uribe. Mario Uribe is a second cousin of President Álvaro Uribe and they have a close and longstanding political alliance. The two of them co-founded a branch of the Liberal Party called Sector Democrático in the 1980s. They both ran for Congress in 1986, with Álvaro becoming senator and Mario becoming a representative. When Álvaro Uribe became governor of Antioquia in 1994, Mario was elected to the Senate. Mario's political movement, Colombia Democrática, strongly supported Alvaro's bid for the presidency in 2002. Later, Mario Uribe was a leading proponent of two of Alvaro Uribe's most controversial initiatives in the Congress: the Alternative Penalties Law (a predecessor to the Justice and Peace Law) and the amendment to the Colombian Constitution that allowed Álvaro Uribe's reelection as president in 2006.

Sen. Uribe resigned his Senate seat shortly after the indictment, and so the investigation was transferred to the Office of the Attorney General, where it was assigned to prosecutor Ramiro Marín. On April 21, 2008, Marín ordered Mario Uribe's arrest. Uribe found out about the arrest warrant and fled to the

112. Sarah Kinosian, *11,179 Colombian Politicians, Officials, Businessmen Involved in Parapolitics: Report*, Colombia Reports, June 7, 2012, *available at* https://colombiareports.com/11179-colombian-politicians-officials-businessmen-involved-in-parapolitics-scandal-report/#https://colombiareports.com/component/tag/justice-and-peace-law.html (last visited February 16, 2024).

113. *Available at* https://www.hrw.org/report/2008/10/16/breaking-grip/obstacles-justice-paramilitary-mafias-colombia (last visited February 16, 2024).

embassy of Costa Rica, where he sought political asylum. The asylum request was denied and on April 22 Mario Uribe was arrested. Human Rights Watch reviewed the prosecutorial resolution ordering Mario Uribe's arrest. The decision was based primarily on the following pieces of evidence, mentioned in the resolution:

First, Salvatore Mancuso testified, first in his Justice and Peace confession and then again before the Supreme Court, that he had met with Mario Uribe on two occasions. During one of those meetings, Mancuso said, Mario Uribe and Eleonora Pineda (a former hairdresser who was running for a seat as a representative in the same region as Mario Uribe, with the backing of the AUC) visited Mancuso in a rural area in the paramilitary-controlled municipality of Tierralta, Córdoba, where Mancuso was hiding due to the criminal convictions and charges pending against him. In his first statement Mancuso said he was not certain of the exact date or order of the meetings; however he later said that the first meeting definitely happened before the 2002 congressional elections. Mancuso said that the meeting had two goals: first, to formalize in front of him a political agreement between Uribe and Pineda by which the two of them would help each other get votes in some areas of Córdoba. According to Mancuso, Sen. Uribe had to have known that Pineda was a candidate of the paramilitaries, as that was why the two of them had gone to Tierralta to visit him. Mancuso added that at the meeting Sen. Uribe committed himself to support the paramilitaries' efforts to initiate negotiations with the government. Mancuso said that the other meeting happened when Sen. Uribe once again went to Tierralta to meet with Carlos Castaño; according to Mancuso, because Castaño was busy at the time, he asked Mancuso to meet with Sen. Uribe to once again discuss the negotiations with the government. Sen. Uribe claimed that there was only one meeting and that it was not planned: he said that Eleonora had invited him to lunch with some friends in her house, but she surprised him by instead taking him to Mancuso's ranch. Uribe said that the meeting happened after the 2002 elections. Eleonora Pineda also said the meeting happened after the elections, in 2002, and that she did not initially explain to Mario Uribe that they were going to meet with Mancuso—though she said she did explain it to him as they were on their way. Also, Pineda noted that when they were on their way to meet with Mancuso, at one point she asked Mario Uribe to leave all his escorts and other companions behind for the last stretch of the road trip.

The prosecutor chose to believe Mancuso's version of events over the versions given by Uribe and Pineda. He pointed out that Pineda was close to Mario Uribe, who the prosecutor notes allowed her to join his political movement, even though he obviously knew of her relationship with the paramilitaries. Indeed, starting in 2002 Pineda and Rocio Arias, another congresswoman, were the two most active and open defenders of the paramilitaries' positions in Congress; they have both pled guilty to conspiring with paramilitaries. Yet Mario Uribe, who was the leader of the Colombia Democrática party, allowed both of them to remain within the ranks of the party until February of 2006, when it was reported in the Colombian media that US officials had warned that party leaders who kept politicians linked to paramilitaries in their ranks might have their US visas revoked.

Another factor that might affect Pineda's testimony is fear. On October 5, 2007, shortly after Pineda pled guilty, one of her brothers was killed in the state of Córdoba; according to news reports, members of the military shot him, claiming he was a member of an armed group and had opened fire on them. Pineda's lawyer asserted that her brother's killing was meant to silence Pineda. Also, the prosecutor points out that there is another important piece of evidence against Mario Uribe that tips the scale in favor of Mancuso's version of events: the unusual and very high spike in votes for Mario Uribe in the 2002 elections. Specifically, Sen. Uribe went from getting 3,985 votes in the 1998 elections to nearly triple that amount—11,136 votes—in the 2002 elections. That's the time when, if Mancuso's version is correct, he presumably would have benefited from the votes that Eleonora Pineda, with paramilitary backing, could have brought him. By the 2006 elections, when he had expelled Eleonora from the party, his votes once again dropped to 3,233.

According to the prosecutor's analysis, the unusual voting patterns are particularly noticeable in the municipalities, such as Montelíbano, Sahagún, and Planeta Rica, where Mancuso had supposedly ordered that people vote for Pineda and Uribe. The prosecutor explains that the paramilitaries apparently divided up the municipalities, ordering that some vote for Uribe and others for another candidate—Miguel de la Espriella—who was also elected to the Senate. Mancuso stated that de la Espriella had been upset with Mancuso for offering some share of his votes to Mario Uribe, but Mancuso calmed him down by assuring him that he would be elected anyway. The prosecutor notes that De la Espriella lost votes in some municipalities in 2002 compared to the 1998 elections—and argues that Mario Uribe got those votes instead.

The prosecutor did not accept Mario Uribe's argument that the spike in votes for him was due to his association with the presidential candidate, Alvaro Uribe, because that argument would not explain the 2006 drop in votes (when Alvaro Uribe was once again running for president, with even higher popularity in the polls). In addition to the allegations about Uribe's dealings with Mancuso in connection with the 2002 elections, the charges against Sen. Uribe are based on allegations that Sen. Uribe sought to work with the paramilitaries to pressure landowners to sell or give him cheap land in 1998. The allegations are based on the testimony of witness Jairo Castillo Peralta, also known as "Pitirri." Castillo is a former paramilitary who operated in the state of Sucre. After leaving the paramilitaries' ranks in the late 1990s, he began providing testimony to prosecutors in several cases. He now has political asylum in Canada and has continued testifying before the Colombian Supreme Court and prosecutors in the parapolitics cases.

Castillo has testified that in 1998 he participated in a meeting with Mario Uribe and landowners, including Olegario Otero Bula, in Sahagun, Cordoba. According to Castillo's testimony, Mario Uribe was seeking "cheap land," and Castillo was ordered to look for such land, determine what people in the region were making payments to the paramilitaries, and seek out the ones—such as Mrs. Luz Marina Zapa—who had not been "paying their quota." . . .

A few months after his arrest, Mario Uribe was once again set free. Deputy Attorney General Guillermo Mendoza Diago granted an appeal Uribe made from the resolution ordering his arrest. In his decision reviewing the arrest order, Mendoza Diago goes over the evidence against Sen. Uribe and reaches the opposite conclusion from that reached by the prosecutor. . . . Based on this analysis, Mendoza Diago concluded that the evidence against Mario Uribe was insufficient to justify his detention and ordered his release.

Issues to Consider

1. What are the obstacles to creating a culture of judicial review?
2. What is the impact of semi-governmental organizations or paramilitaries on exercising restraint of the executive?
3. How does judicial review address questions of corruption?
4. What are the circumstances—political, social, and cultural—facilitating judicial reviews of the executive?
5. If judicial review is not fully developed, how are restraints imposed on the executive?

IX. CONCLUSION

While it is too early to comment on the U.S. Supreme Court under Justice Roberts, perhaps *Hamdan v. Rumsfeld* and *Boumediene v. Bush* indicate a move toward the Barak model. The Barak model—as articulated in both scholarly writings and court holdings—represents judicial review at its most extreme. Russian judicial review is in its infancy; among the most important questions are whether the executive branch intends to respect judicial decisions and, if not, what enforcement methods and sanctions the court might have. The cases presented highlight the tension regarding the Chechen conflict. India has introduced Public Interest Litigation as a means of providing the aggrieved individual recourse against the executive. However, the backlog of cases severely hampers the timeliness—and therefore effectiveness—of Indian judicial review. Spain's judicial review is limited to the traditional criminal law paradigm and, in particular, whether or not incommunicado detentions are lawful. In clear contrast to the other surveyed countries, China has very little judicial review, clearly reflecting the power of the central government. Colombia's judicial review is largely restrained both by historical, institutionalized corruption and by the powerful presence of semi-governmental organizations, particularly paramilitaries.

CHAPTER 6

OPERATIONAL COUNTERTERRORISM METHODS

I. INTRODUCTION

Understanding operational decision making requires examining the dilemmas facing the decision maker. While the decision to engage—whether detaining, minimizing the threat, or killing the suspected terrorist—is the essence of operational counterterrorism, the process is complex, requiring careful analysis of distinct factors and considerations.

The discussion below considers decision making based on the nation-state's respect for the rule of law and the recognition that the executive branch is subject to review, whether by the nation's judiciary or the legislative branch. Furthermore, in an age of increasing international jurisdiction, the conduct of military commanders is subject to greater scrutiny.

The discussion below applies to interaction between the nation and non-state actors, distinct from domestic terrorism. In addition to domestic and international terrorism (the primary focus of this book), attention must be paid to crossover terrorism, which reflects a confluence between the two more traditional forms of terrorism. The 2013 Boston Marathon attack is but one example of crossover: the two terrorists were radicalized and trained outside the U.S., but committed their act of terrorism in the U.S.

Examples of domestic terrorism include attacks that occur exclusively within a nation's borders, devoid of outside influence and participants. Such instances are discussed throughout this book. International terrorism, distinct from domestic, indicates cross-border issues—raising questions of sovereignty, international law, nation-states supporting terrorism, and geopolitics.

The state/non-state terrorism-counterterrorism paradigm is subject to principles of international law and domestic law and, in some instances, to an examination of the limits of power through the lens of morality. That is in addition to, and distinct from, an analysis consistent with legal principles discussed throughout this book.

Operational decision making is affected—whether positively or negatively is a matter of interpretation—by the power, range, and speed of social media. Events that in years past would have gone unreported and unrecorded go "viral" at a pace posing significant challenges to nation-state decision makers seeking to control the narrative. The court of public opinion is particularly important, both domestically and internationally, as it can directly impact reactions, with a focus on unintended consequences and their ramifications. The discussion below applies both to operational engagement in response to an imminent threat and to a planned attack, in accordance with targeted killing (primarily Israel) or drone policy (primarily the U.S.).

Operational counterterrorism conducted in accordance with the rule of law/limits on state power requires decision makers to narrowly define both the term "legitimate target" and to subsequently determine when that individual is a legitimate target. While the UN Charter seeks to articulate relations between nation-states, the principle of self-defense (Article 51 of the Charter) has been expanded—by analogy—to the interaction between nation-states and non-state actors.

In the same way that Article 51 is applied to counterterrorism, Article 2 (4), which limits the nation-state's use of force, is similarly relevant to the state/non-state paradigm. Accordingly, the limits which govern traditional war—when conducted in accordance with accepted laws of war—are relevant to lawful operational counterterrorism from the perspective of the nation-state and its decision-making process, which reflect self-imposed limits on its power. The principle of distinction is a critical component of self-defense as a mechanism for limiting the use of force.

The identification of an individual as suspected of involvement in terrorism is no more than that and must not be understood as "tagging" that person as terrorist, much less a legitimate target. This reality is relevant to decisions whether to detain, interrogate, or prosecute the individual, or to operationally engage with the intent to kill the individual. The determination, as discussed elsewhere in this book, reflects a combination of intelligence gathering and analysis. From a commander's perspective, when faced with the dilemma of whether to detain or engage the suspected individual, the primary obligation is to minimize the loss of innocent life (collateral damage), in addition to international law principles of proportionality, military necessity, and exhaustion of other alternatives.

The decision to engage rather than detain must reflect an assessment, in accordance with self-defense, that the identified target poses an imminent threat and that alternatives are not reasonably available from an operational perspective. Imminence, as in the traditional criminal law definition, is dependent on circumstances, conditions, and judgement, and must be viewed through the lens of subjective, rather than objective, analysis.

An overly broad definition of imminence can result in unwarranted and unjustified use of force; an unduly limited definition can result in an unnecessary self-restraint and the loss of innocent lives that may have otherwise been preventable. The balance necessary between respecting national security and individual rights demands understanding that both are equally legitimate.

Non-state actors are not subject to international laws, treaties, or conventions. Accordingly, limits on the use of force are self-imposed and self-governed, not subject to external review and judgement, unless captured and subsequently interrogated and prosecuted by the nation-state with whom they are engaged in conflict. The question of whether terrorism is understood to be a traditional crime or viewed through a separate lens is addressed elsewhere in this book. The same goes with determining what rights, privileges, and protections are to be extended to a suspected terrorist in accordance with relevant domestic law.

While operational decision making is integral to understanding counterterrorism, it is—notwithstanding its importance—but one aspect of the broader issues discussed in this book. The decision whether or not to engage a suspected terrorist reflects the sum total of an accumulation of different factors, conditions, and circumstances that merge in a critical moment when the commander faces a "go/no go" decision vector. To ensure the decision is in accordance with standards of legality, morality, and effectiveness examined throughout this book, the commander needs to carefully assess as many variables as possible prior to making the final decision. Among the primary challenges, of which there are many, are the limited window of opportunity in which to decide and act, and, in most cases, the lack of information available. More than that: the information made available to the commander may reflect a problematic combination of misinformation and disinformation, in addition to information that has been vetted and deemed reliable by the intelligence community. Discerning, or delineating, the interaction between the three is challenging, requiring distinct skill sets including information management, teamwork, and decision making, with recognition that the ultimate assessment may be incorrect and the consequences tragic.

That is a reality commanders face in the state/non-state paradigm, distinct from the state/state conflict whereby soldiers wear readily identifiable uniforms and unit insignia. That is not the case with terrorists who easily blend into the civilian population, since their attire is not distinguishable from innocent members of their community. That complicated reality must not prevent a commander from engagement. It must, however, deter engagement. Therein lies the great tension in operational counterterrorism at its most critical juncture. That dilemma and its various iterations—including the process by which decisions are made—are at the core of this book, as they reflect the essence of effective counterterrorism when conducted in accordance with the rule of law.

Issues to Consider

1. At whom are counterterrorist measures aimed: the specific terrorist, his or her family, or the community at large?
2. What does deterrence mean, and how is it to be implemented?
3. What is collective punishment, and how does it differ from individual punishment?
4. Should counterterrorism measures be considered from both legal and policy perspectives?

II. THE UNITED STATES

A. INTRODUCTION

Since 9/11, the United States has been catching up in the field of counterterrorism. This is most readily apparent in the development and implementation of operational counterterrorism measures. Has the United States clearly articulated a policy that shows foresight, clear principles, and a willingness to alter plans according to lessons learned? Did the Bush and Obama administrations keep their eye on the ball with respect to immediate and potential threats? Have the Trump and Biden administrations done so?

In addition, did the Bush administration's response, which included a clear desire to pin the attack on Saddam Hussein, result in critical missteps in the development of an operational counterterrorism policy? By emphasizing a non-existent link between Iraq and bin Laden, did the Bush administration prevent the military from exclusively focusing its efforts and resources on directly engaging al Qaeda? These questions serve as backdrops to a discussion of the United States' post-9/11 operational counterterrorism policies.

B. POST-9/11

America's counterterrorism policy in the immediate aftermath of 9/11 is best analyzed by examining two distinct responses: a broad, generalized response illustrated by Operation Enduring Freedom (OEF), and a specific response reflected by drone attacks, initially implemented by President Bush and subsequently widely applied by President Obama.

On October 7, 2001, the United States attacked Afghanistan in a determined effort to root out bin Laden from the caves where al Qaeda was allegedly hiding.[1]

> Operation Enduring Freedom commenced on Oct. 7, 2001. Early combat operations included a mix of air strikes from land-based B-1, B-2 and B-52 bombers; carrier-based F-14 and F/A-18 fighters; and Tomahawk cruise missiles launched from both U.S. and British ships and submarines.
>
> The initial military objectives of Operation Enduring Freedom, as articulated by President George W. Bush in his Sept. 20th Address to a Joint Session of Congress and his Oct. 7th address to country, include the destruction of terrorist training camps and infrastructure within Afghanistan, the capture of al Qaeda leaders, and the cessation of terrorist activities in Afghanistan.
>
> Secretary of Defense Donald Rumsfeld stated in an Oct. 7th DoD News Briefing that U.S. objectives were to make clear to Taliban leaders that the

---

1. *Afghanistan Wakes After Night of Intense Bombings,* CNN.com, October 7, 2001, *available at* https://edition.cnn.com/2001/US/10/07/gen.america.under.attack/ (last visited December 23, 2023); *Bin Laden Says He Wasn't Behind Attacks,* CNN.com, September 17, 2001, *available at* https://edition.cnn.com/2001/US/09/16/inv.binladen.denial/ (last visited December 23, 2023); Carl Nolte, *Afghanistan's Ancient Defense; Like Generations Past, Taliban Fighters Finding Refuge Underground,* S.F. Chron., November 7, 2001, at A3.

> harboring of terrorists is unacceptable, to acquire intelligence on al Qaeda and Taliban resources, to develop relations with groups opposed to the Taliban, to prevent the use of Afghanistan as a safe haven for terrorists, and to destroy the Taliban military allowing opposition forces to succeed in their struggle. Finally, military force would help facilitate the delivering of humanitarian supplies to the Afghan people.
>
> The British had also defined the goals of their involvement (termed Operation Veritas) in "Her Majesty's Government's Campaign Objectives," dated Oct. 16th. The short term goals of the military action included the capture of Osama bin Laden and other al Qaeda leaders, the prevention of further attacks by al Qaeda, the end of Afghanistan's harboring of terrorists, their training camps and infrastructure, and the removal of Mullah Omar and the Taliban Regime. Long term goals include the end of terrorism, the deterrence of state sponsorship of terrorism, and the reintegration of Afghanistan into the international community.[2]

According to former President Bush, the American campaign was not directed at the citizens of Afghanistan, but rather against the terrorist infrastructure. While the extent of al Qaeda's relationship with the ruling Taliban government prior to September 2001 is a matter of dispute, bin Laden had clearly established northern Afghanistan as a base of operations after the Sudanese government expelled him. Formed in 1994, the Taliban government established control over a chaotic Afghanistan when Kabul was captured from the mujahedeen in 1996. However, only three countries—Pakistan, the United Arab Emirates, and Saudi Arabia—recognized the Taliban government. Mullah Omar, the head of the Taliban government, requested that bin Laden keep a low profile in Afghanistan. While bin Laden promised to accede to this request, evidence clearly suggests that Afghanistan served as al Qaeda's operational headquarters for the planning and execution of 9/11.

During the initial military operation which lasted 78 days, the U.S.–led coalition forced al Qaeda to go on the run, initially to western Pakistan (reportedly with the active facilitation of the Pakistani intelligence agency, ISI) and increasingly to Yemen. The coalition also killed approximately 1000 Afghan civilians and dropped 24,000 bombs within the first year. The stated goal of the operation, according to then Secretary of Defense Donald Rumsfeld and President Bush, was to "make clear to the Taliban leaders and their supporters that harboring terrorists is unacceptable and carries a price."[3] The articles below reflect the inherent difficulty in operational decision making, particularly when the mission is broadly and vaguely stated.

---

2. *Operation Enduring Freedom–Afghanistan,* Global Security.org, *available at* http://www.globalsecurity.org/military/ops/enduring-freedom.htm (last visited Oct. 8, 2010).

3. *Rumsfeld and Myers Briefing on Enduring Freedom,* News Transcript, October 7, 2001, *available at* https://avalon.law.yale.edu/sept11/dod_brief22.asp (last visited December 23, 2023); *U.S. Rapidly Checking Off Anti-Terrorism Goals List, Taliban,* Los Angeles Times, November 25, 2001, *available at* https://www.latimes.com/archives/la-xpm-2001-nov-25-mn-7954-story.html (last visited February 16, 2024).

THE TERROR TIMELINE

Paul Thompson, September 7, 2004[4]

Early October 2001: US Launches Attacks on Afghanistan from Pakistani Bases

The US begins using the Shahbaz air force base and other bases in Pakistan in their attacks against Afghanistan. However, because of public Pakistani opposition to US support, the two governments claim the US is there for purely logistical and defensive purposes. Even six months later, the US refuses to confirm it is using the base for offensive operations. Such bases in Pakistan become a link in a chain of US military outposts in Central Asia. Other countries also falsely maintain that such bases are not being used for military operations in Afghanistan despite clear evidence to the contrary.

October 2001: US Military Downplays Importance of Targeting bin Laden

On October 8, 2001, Gen. Tommy Franks, Central Command commander in chief, says of the war in Afghanistan, "We have not said that Osama bin Laden is a target of this effort. What we are about is the destruction of the al-Qaeda network, as well as the . . . Taliban that provide harbor to bin Laden and al-Qaeda." Later in the month, Defense Secretary Donald Rumsfeld makes similar comments, "My attitude is that if [bin Laden] were gone tomorrow, the same problem would exist. He's got a whole bunch of lieutenants who have been trained and they've got bank accounts all over some 50 or 60 countries. Would you want to stop him? Sure. Do we want to stop the rest of his lieutenants? You bet. But I don't get up in the morning and say that is the end; the goal and the endpoint of this thing. I think that would be a big mistake." One military expert will later note, "There appears to be a real disconnect between what the US military was engaged in trying to do during the battle for Tora Bora—which was to destroy al-Qaeda and the Taliban—and the earlier rhetoric of President Bush, which had focused on getting bin Laden."

Early October 2001: General Franks Disregards Advice to Open Second Front in Afghanistan

The Washington Post reports in late 2004 that, shortly after Richard Myers officially becomes Joint Chiefs of Staff Chairman on October 1, 2001, he raises doubts about the military plan to topple the Taliban in Afghanistan. General Tommy Franks, the chief of US Central Command, plans a single thrust towards the capital, Kabul, from the north. Myers urges Franks to open a southern front. A brigade of the Army's 10th Mountain Division in Uzbekistan and two Marine Expeditionary Forces in the Arabian Sea are prepared and in position for the role. However, Franks does not position a blocking force to meet any retreating forces. The Washington Post reports, "Some Bush

4. Paul Thompson, The Terror Timeline: Year by Year, Day by Day, Minute by Minute: A Comprehensive Chronicle of the Road to 9/11 and America's Response, (ReganBooks, 1st ed., 2004).

administration officials now acknowledge privately they consider that a costly mistake." Franks later claims that it would have taken too much time to put a force into position and would have antagonized the country's Pashtun majority. Most of al-Qaeda and the Taliban's leaders are eventually able to escape the country. "A high-ranking war planner [later] likened the result to throwing a rock at a nest of bees, then trying to chase them down, one by one, with a net."

Early October-Mid-November, 2001: Air Force Is Repeatedly Denied Permission to Bomb Top al-Qaeda and Taliban Leaders

In mid-November 2001, the Washington Post will report that senior Air Force officials are upset they have missed opportunities to hit top al-Qaeda and Taliban leaders since the start of the bombing of Afghanistan. According to these officials, the Air Force believes it has the leaders in its crosshairs as many as ten times, but they are unable to receive a timely clearance to fire. Cumbersome approval procedures, a concern not to kill civilians, and a power play between the Defense Department and the CIA contribute to the delays. One anonymous Air Force official later says, "We knew we had some of the big boys. The process is so slow that by the time we got the clearances, and everybody had put in their 2 cents, we called it off." The main problem is that commanders in the region have to ask for permission from General Tommy Franks, based in Central Command headquarters in Tampa, Florida, or even Defense Secretary Rumsfeld and other higher-ups. Air Force generals complain to Franks about the delay problem, but never receive a response. For example, at one point in October, a Taliban military convoy is moving north to reinforce front line positions. Targeters consider it an easy mark of clear military value. But permission from Central Command is denied on the suspicion that the target is so obvious that "it might be a trick." In another example, a target is positively identified by real-time imagery from a Predator drone, but Central Command overrides the decision to strike, saying they want a second source of data. An anonymous official calls this request for independent verification of Predator imagery "kind of ridiculous." The London Times paraphrase officials who claim that, "Attempts to limit collateral damage [serve] merely to prolong the war, and force the Pentagon to insert commandos on the ground to hunt down the same targets." By the end of the war, only one top al-Qaeda leader, Mohammed Atef, is killed in a bombing raid (see November 15, 2001), and no top Taliban leaders are killed.

Furthermore, in analyzing the operational considerations and policy calculations of the Bush administration's decision to attack Afghanistan, uncertainty arises as to whether OEF was a war or a large-sized counterterrorism operation. According to international law, war can be fought only between nation-states. In determining the status of OEF, President Bush's speech before the Congress on September 20, 2001 is instructive:

> The leadership of al Qaeda has great influence in Afghanistan and supports the Taliban regime in controlling most of that country. In Afghanistan, we see al Qaeda's vision for the world.

> Afghanistan's people have been brutalized—many are starving and many have fled. Women are not allowed to attend school. You can be jailed for owning a television. Religion can be practiced only as their leaders dictate. A man can be jailed in Afghanistan if his beard is not long enough.
>
> The United States respects the people of Afghanistan—after all, we are currently its largest source of humanitarian aid—but we condemn the Taliban regime. It is not only repressing its own people, it is threatening people everywhere by sponsoring and sheltering and supplying terrorists. By aiding and abetting murder, the Taliban regime is committing murder.
>
> And tonight, the United States of America makes the following demands on the Taliban: Deliver to United States authorities all the leaders of al Qaeda who hide in your land. Release all foreign nationals, including American citizens, you have unjustly imprisoned. Protect foreign journalists, diplomats and aid workers in your country. Close immediately and permanently every terrorist training camp in Afghanistan, and hand over every terrorist, and every person in their support structure, to appropriate authorities. Give the United States full access to terrorist training camps, so we can make sure they are no longer operating.
>
> These demands are not open to negotiation or discussion. The Taliban must act, and act immediately. They will hand over the terrorists, or they will share in their fate.[5]

OEF was defined as an "operation" rather than as a war. While the classification may have been political—not declaring war against a state (Afghanistan) whose ruling regime (the Taliban) was not recognized universally and therefore considered illegitimate—from the perspective of international law, the United States was not at war with Afghanistan. As discussed in Chapter 4, the Israel Supreme Court sitting as the High Court of Justice defined the conflict with the Palestinians as "armed conflict short of war." Should the United States have adopted a similar definition, or a variation on that theme, with respect to the American attack on Afghanistan? Do the measures implemented more closely resemble operational counterterrorism than war in the classical sense? According to the Israel's HCJ analysis, actions of the coalition forces in Afghanistan would be considered operational counterterrorism, though—unconventionally—an entire terrorist network located in a sovereign nation was deemed a legitimate target.

Issues to Consider

1. Are large-scale attacks effective?
2. Is individual-specific counterterrorism preferred to group-particular actions?
3. What is the fallout effect from operations such as Operation Enduring Freedom in the context of winning hearts and minds?
4. Does a policy such as OEF suggest actions inconsistent with the principles of a liberal democratic society as articulated by President Aharon Barak in Chapter 5?

5. *Address to a Joint Session of Congress and the American People,* President Bush, Sept. 20, 2001, *available at* https://georgewbush-whitehouse.archives.gov/news/releases/2001/09/20010920-8.html (last visited Dec. 30, 2023).

C. U.S. TARGETED KILLING

1. The Drone Policy

Though Executive Order 12333 forbids American intelligence organizations from assassinating foreign political leaders, the Bush administration actively engaged in drone attacks, and the Obama administration implemented a similar policy in Afghanistan, Pakistan, and Yemen against identified targets, primarily members of the Taliban and al Qaeda.

Following the attack on the USS *Cole* in Yemen on October 12, 2000, which resulted in the deaths of 17 American sailors, the United States conducted a targeted killing of those responsible for the attack. According to media reports, six members of al Qaeda were killed, including one American citizen.[6] When analyzing targeted killings, one must note that, according to international law, acts of retaliation are illegal. A country may only perform targeted killings if there is reliable, corroborated intelligence information that the action will prevent a future terror attack. With respect to the American drone attacks, media reports have never clearly indicated whether those killed intended to carry out additional attacks or if the targeted killing was solely a response to their role in the *Cole* bombing.

KENNETH ANDERSON, TARGETED KILLING IN U.S. COUNTERTERRORISM STRATEGY AND LAW

Brookings Institute Working Paper, May 11, 2009[7]

It is a slight exaggeration to say that Barack Obama is the first president in American history to have run in part on a political platform of targeted killings—but not much of one. "The Bush administration has not acted aggressively enough to go after al Qaeda's leadership," he said. "I would be clear that if Pakistan cannot or will not take out al Qaeda leadership when we have actionable intelligence about their whereabouts, we will act to protect the American people. There can be no safe haven for al Qaeda terrorists who killed thousands of Americans and threaten our homeland today."

Obama did not take long, on assuming office, to begin keeping his promise. On January 23, 2009 a mere three days into his presidency, strikes by Predator drones in the tribal areas of Pakistan destroyed two compounds and killed numerous people, reportedly including a high-value target. Strikes continued, even expanded, over the successive months, and administration officials made clear that they had no plans to curtail them—even as they reined in coercive interrogations and announced the closure of Guantánamo Bay.

Obama was right as a candidate and is correct as president to insist on the propriety of targeted killings—that is, the targeting of a specific individual to be killed, increasingly often by means of high technology, remote-controlled Predator drone aircraft wielding missiles from a stand-off position. The strategic

6. Doyle McManus, *A U.S. License to Kill; a New Policy Permits the C.I.A. to Assassinate Terrorists, and Officials Say a Yemen Hit Went Perfectly. Others Worry about Next Time,* L.A. Times, January 11, 2003, at A1.

7. *Available at* https://www.brookings.edu/articles/targeted-killing-in-u-s-counterterrorism-strategy-and-law/ (last visited February 16, 2024).

logic that presses toward targeted stand-off killing as a necessary, available and technologically advancing part of counterterrorism is overpowering. So too is the moral and humanitarian logic behind its use. Just as crucial programs of Predator-centered targeted killing are underway now in Afghanistan and, with increasing international controversy, Pakistan, over the long term these programs of stand-off targeted killing will be an essential element in United States counterterrorism into the future—and with targets having little or nothing to do with today's iteration of the war on terror.

American domestic law—the law codifying the existence of the CIA and defining its functions—has long accepted implicitly at least some uses of force, including targeted killing, as self-defense toward ends of vital national security that do not necessarily fall within the strict terms of armed conflict in the sense meant by the Geneva Conventions and other international treaties on the conduct of armed conflict.

Targeted killing and the drone policy significantly differ from OEF; coalition air attacks in Afghanistan were intended to destroy the al Qaeda infrastructure, while targeted killings and the drone policy reflect attempts to neutralize a specific terrorist identified as presenting a threat. Drone attacks—according to numerous reports—have resulted in significant collateral damage resulting from a combination of faulty intelligence, lack of clearly developed guidelines and criteria defining when the policy can be implemented, and an articulated desire to aggressively engage identified targets.

2. Effectiveness

Governments that fail to determine the effectiveness of a particular course of action will ultimately fail in developing a viable policy. The issue of how to measure effectiveness of a particular policy has been addressed by Edward H. Kaplan, Alex Mintz, Shaul Mishal, and Claudio Samban in an empirical study.[8]

Issues to Consider

1. Should liberal democracies implement policies that may be borderline illegal?
2. Are deliberately murky goals and policies advantageous?
3. In developing operational counterterrorism, what is the distinction between a non-state actor and a state actor who provides safe haven to the non-state actor?
4. What are the limits of state power in the context of counterterrorism?
5. Is the twin policy approach adopted by the U.S. reflective of a balance between national security and individual rights?
6. Is balancing relevant when taking the fight to the terrorists?

8. Edward H. Kaplan, *What Happened to Suicide Bombings in Israel? Insights from a Terror Stock Model,* 28 Studies in Conflict and Terrorism 225 (2005).

If effectiveness is measured as mere response, then any action is effective. However, if policies are intended to meet a well-defined goal, then effectiveness can be determined by analyzing whether the particular goal was achieved. Governments, however, are hesitant to articulate a clearly defined terrorist policy, preferring to address the issue in generalities and clichés.

III. ISRAEL

A. INTRODUCTION

Over the years, various Israeli governments have tried different policies in response to Palestinian terrorism. The policies below reflect an understanding and recognition that defeating terrorism is not possible, and that the focus rather is double-edged: attacking specific targets (imminent threats) and minimizing longer-term threats, while acknowledging (stated or otherwise) that there is no "victory" in operational counterterrorism. When examining Israeli counterterrorism policy, one must recall that deterrence serves as a primary purpose under the "umbrella" of an aggressive application of self-defense. The deterrence argument is intended to serve a two-fold purpose: immediate (tactical) and long-term (strategic). That philosophical, jurisprudential, and operational approach serves as the basis for the discussion below; the two measures analyzed must be understood in that context. Analyzing the two measures in particular—and counterterrorism in general—requires recognizing that "trial and error" is inherent to operational decision making, both tactically and strategically.

While the Oslo Agreement (1994) called for security cooperation between Israel and the Palestinian Authority—initially in the West Bank and the Gaza Strip, and later only in the West Bank after Israeli disengagement from the Gaza Strip—the discussion below focuses exclusively on Israeli counterterrorism decision making. This reflects the operational, on-the-ground reality that, notwithstanding the Agreement, Israel has conducted counterterrorism independent of any significant strategic cooperation or engagement with the Palestinian Authority. That is not to gainsay the fact that in specific instances there was cooperation to address a particular issue-crisis,[9] but this cooperation does not reflect a long-term strategic perspective. The security cooperation is directly impacted by the relationship between Israeli national leaders and PA leadership, which also reflects political realities and considerations on both sides. For that reason, the discussion below focuses exclusively on Israeli policy and its implementation.

In examining operational counterterrorism decision making, we must recall that some measures are reactive, whereas others are proactive. In either paradigm, regardless of the actual measures, aggressive self-defense is the

9. I address this in an article based on my experience negotiating the implementation of the Oslo Agreement in the Gaza Strip. Amos N. Guiora, *Negotiating Implementation of a Peace Agreement: Lessons Learned from Five Years at the Negotiating Table*, 11 Cardozo J. Conflict Resol. 411 (2010), https://static1.squarespace.com/static/60a5863870f56068b0f097cd/t/60a69a8fa7a01358d9fc7828/1621531280065/411-436.pdf (last visited February 16, 2024).

Israeli model, but that principle is subject to judicial review by the Israeli Supreme Court, sitting as the High Court of Justice. The role of the judiciary in restraining policy—and in policy implementation—while being subject to public criticism reflects a reality impacting command decision making.

The discussion below is intended to highlight the interaction between terrorism, counterterrorism, the rule of law, and the limits of power. The two examples below highlight the complexity of the confluence between the four disparate elements. Additional examples could have been incorporated reflecting responses to different iterations of Palestinian terrorism:

1) In response to the outbreak of the Intifada (1987-1993), administrative detentions and house demolitions were widely used.

2) Following a series of terrorist attacks carried out by Hamas in late 1992, 415 Palestinians were deported to Lebanon where they had to remain for two years.

3) In response to suicide bombings, targeted killings were implemented, and the security fence between Israel and the West Bank was constructed.

To deter and prevent family members from aiding those involved in significant terrorist activity, the policy of assigned residence was established and implemented for a limited time. The section below analyzes whether the assigned residence policy respects lawful self-defense.

B. ASSIGNED RESIDENCE

Israel made the decision to implement an assigned residence policy when the intelligence community recognized that family members were actively participating in the terrorist activities of their siblings, spouses, and sons. Unlike deportation, which involves deporting an individual from the West Bank or the Gaza Strip to a foreign nation, assigned residence is the removal of an individual from one area to another area (in the cases to date, the assignment was from the Gaza Strip to the West Bank).

The policy's goal was to weaken the base of support and assistance provided to terrorists by their family members. Previously, person-specific counterterrorism was largely, but not exclusively, directed against the particular terrorist (for example, targeted killing, administrative detention, deportation, or incarceration). In contrast, the assigned residence policy represented an administrative sanction directed at specific family members.

The High Court of Justice in *Ajuri v. IDF Commander in West Bank* articulated a two-part test regarding assigning residence. The criteria for implementing the policy were the "serious security threat presented by the individual to be assigned" and the significant assistance provided to the terrorist by that individual.[10]

A particular family member would have his residence assigned if intelligence indicated that his sibling or other family members could not conduct terrorism without that individual's aid, and if the person to be assigned

---

10. HCJ 7019/02, Ajuri v. IDF Commander in West Bank [Isr.].

presented a threat to state security separate from his family member. The possibility that an individual assigned from the West Bank would become dominant in Gaza-based terrorist groups was deemed unlikely, as the person assigned would lack a power base in the new location.

Issues to Consider

1. What is the "human cost" of assigning the residence of an individual?
2. How far can operational counterterrorism be taken?
3. Is the practice of separating family members a reasonable policy?
4. From the perspective of deterrence, is this a viable policy?
5. If this is deportation without being called deportation, is the policy a violation of international law?

The Israeli government announced the policy with great fanfare, declaring that it struck at the core of the terrorists' support network.

> One of the measures upon which the Ministerial Committee for National Security decided—all of which within the framework of the Attorney-General's opinion—was assigning the place of residence of family members of suicide bombers or the perpetrators of serious attacks and those sending them from Judaea and Samaria to the Gaza Strip, provided that these family members were themselves involved in the terrorist activity. This measure was adopted because, according to the evaluation of the professionals involved (the army, the General Security Service, the Institute for Intelligence and Special Tasks (the Mossad), and the police), these additional measures might make a significant contribution to the struggle against the wave of terror, resulting in the saving of human life. This contribution is two-fold: first, it can prevent a family member involved in terrorist activity from perpetrating his scheme (the preventative effect); second, it may deter other terrorists who are instructed to act as human bombs or to carry out other terror attacks from perpetrating their schemes (the deterrent effect).[11]

The government further argued that the policy was less harsh than deportation because the individual would still be residing in the territory of the Palestinian Authority. After only 15 instances, however, the government stopped the policy as quickly as it was implemented. The policy was so short-lived that it would be empirically and intuitively impossible to discern any possible effect. Nevertheless, the underpinnings of the policy are highly relevant to a study of operational counterterrorism because the policy targets the terrorists' immediate support system.

Even though the policy is no longer in place, it merits closer examination.

1. Ajuri v. IDF Commander in West Bank

The assigned residence policy, argued before the High Court of Justice, was initially implemented against three individuals: the brother and sister of one

---

11. *Id.*

terrorist and the sibling of a second. Kipah Mahmad Ahmed Ajuri and Abed Amasser Mustafa Ahmed Asida,[12] and Amtassar Muhammed Ahmed Ajuri filed the petitions[13] after a Military Appeals Board upheld the military commander's order to assign the residence of all three. According to the Military Appeals Board, Kipah Ajuri acted as a lookout when terrorists moved explosives while his sister, Amtassar, sewed suicide belts. Abed Asida, according to the Appeals Board, provided his terrorist brother food and clothing, and drove him in his car without knowing of his activities. The petitioners argued that the West Bank and Gaza Strip are separate entities and therefore assigned residence was tantamount to deportation, a violation of Article 49 of the Fourth Geneva Convention.[14] The state based its argument regarding the policy's legality on Article 78 of the Fourth Geneva Convention, which enables an occupying power to assign the residence of an individual for imperative security reasons.

> **Article 78**
> If the Occupying Power considers it necessary, for imperative reasons of security, to take safety measures concerning protected persons, it may, at the most, subject them to assigned residence or to internment. Decisions regarding such assigned residence or internment shall be made according to a regular procedure to be prescribed by the Occupying Power in accordance with the provisions of the present Convention. This procedure shall include the right of appeal for the parties concerned. Appeals shall be decided with the least possible delay. In the event of the decision being upheld, it shall be subject to periodical review, if possible, every six months, by a competent body set up by the said Power. Protected persons made subject to assigned residence and thus required to leave their homes shall enjoy the full benefit of Article 39 of the present Convention.[15]

The High Court of Justice reversed the decision with respect to Asida's petition, holding that while the petitioner provided assistance to his brother, those actions alone did not satisfy the second part of the test because they did not endanger state security.

> With regard to the first level, it is accepted by all the parties before us—and this is also our opinion—that an essential condition for being able to assign the place of residence of a person under art. 78 of the Fourth Geneva Convention is that the person himself constitutes a danger, and that assigning his place of residence will aid in averting that danger. It follows that the basis for exercising the discretion for assigning residence is the consideration of preventing a danger presented by a person whose place of residence is being assigned. The place of residence of an innocent person who does not himself present a danger may not be assigned, merely because assigning his place of

12. HCJ 7015/02, Asida v. IDF Commander in West Bank, IDF Commander in Gaza Strip and Bridget Kessler. (Bridget Kessler's daughter was killed in a suicide bombing in Jerusalem. Mrs. Kessler asked and was granted permission by President Barak to address the court.)

13. *Id.*

14. Geneva Convention relative to the Protection of Civilian Persons in Time of War, Aug. 12, 1949, Art. 49, 75 U.N.T.S. 287.

15. Geneva Convention Relative to the Protection of Civilian Persons in Time of War, Aug. 12, 1949, Art. 78, 75 U.N.T.S. 287.

> residence will deter others. Likewise, one may not assign the place of residence of a person who is not innocent and did carry out acts that harmed security, when in the circumstances of the case he no longer presents any danger. Therefore, if someone carried out terrorist acts, and assigning his residence will reducc the danger that he presents, it is possible to assign his place of residence. One may not assign the place of residence of an innocent family member who did not collaborate with anyone, or of a family member who is not innocent but does not present a danger to the area. This is the case even if assigning the place of residence of a family member may deter other terrorists from carrying out acts of terror. This conclusion is required by the outlook of the Fourth Geneva Convention that regards the measures of internment and assigned residence as the most severe and serious measures that an occupying power may adopt against protected residents.[16]

The commander is obligated to implement the assigned residence policy with a balanced approach that reflects reasonableness and proportionality. Of the three petitioners, intelligence identified Amtassar Ajuri as the most dangerous. When implementing a counterterrorism strategy, the commander had to decide not only which individual posed the greatest threat to state security, but also whether or not the High Court of Justice (in the context of judicial review) would uphold the decision. The severity of the threat posed by Amtassar Ajuri is clear from the Court's recounting of her activities:

> Amtassar Muhammed Ahmed Ajuri (an unmarried woman aged 34) is the sister of the terrorist Ahmed Ali Ajuri. Much terrorist activity is attributed to the brother, Ahmed Ali Ajuri, including sending suicide bombers with explosive belts, and responsibility, inter alia, for the terrorist attack at the Central Bus Station in Tel-Aviv in which five people were killed and many others were injured. The Appeals Board (chaired by Col. Gordon), in its decision of 12 August 2002, held—suicide bombers with explosive belts—on the basis of privileged material presented to it and responsibility, inter alia, for the terrorist attack at the Central Buyon the basis of testimonies of members of the General Security Service that the petitioner directly and substantially aided the unlawful activity of her brother, which was intended to harm innocent citizens. The Board determined that there was more than a basis for the conclusion that the petitioner knew about the forbidden activity of her brother—including his being wanted by the Israeli security forces and that she knew that her brother was wounded when he was engaged in preparing explosives, and prima facie she also knew that her brother was armed and had hidden in the family apartment an assault rifle. It was also held that the petitioner aided her brother by sewing an explosive belt. The Board pointed out that, on the basis of privileged evidence, which it found "reliable and up-to-date," it transpired that the petitioner indeed aided her brother in his unlawful activity. It held that this was a case of "direct and material aid in the preparation of an explosive belt, and the grave significance and implications of this aid were without doubt clear and known [to the petitioner]." Admittedly, the petitioner testified before the Board that she was not involved in anything and did not aid her brother, but the Board rejected this testimony as unreliable. It pointed out that "we found

16. *Ajuri, supra* note 10.

her disingenuous and evasive story totally unreasonable throughout her testimony before us, and it was clear that she wished to distance herself in any way possible from the activity of her brother . . . her disingenuous story left us with a clear impression of someone who has something to hide and this impression combines with the clear and unambiguous information that arises from the privileged material about her involvement in preparing an explosive belt." For these reasons, the appeal of the petitioner to the Appeals Board was denied. It should also be pointed out that in the Respondent's reply in the proceeding before us—which was supported by an affidavit—it was stated that "the petitioner aided her brother in the terrorist activity and, inter alia, sewed for his purposes explosive belts"—explosive belts, and not merely one explosive belt.[17]

Issues to Consider

1. Is assigned residence a form of self-defense?
2. Is the distinction between deportation and assigned residence a fine line?
3. Is the sanction a significant contribution to the commanders' toolbox?
4. Was the threat presented by the Ajuri siblings responded to in a proportional manner?
5. Why did the High Court of Justice develop a two-part test in determining the policy's legality?
6. What is the appropriate, proportional relationship between a particular counterterrorism measure and the severity of the offense?
7. What is the cost of declaring a policy and then quickly abandoning it?

C. TARGETED KILLING

Targeted killing reflects a deliberate decision to order the death of a particular terrorist. Significantly, an individual will be targeted only if: (1) he presents a serious threat to public order and safety based on criminal evidence, or (2) reliable, corroborated intelligence clearly implicates him.[18] Intelligence information is corroborated when it is confirmed by at least two separate, unrelated sources. In addition, for a targeted killing to be lawful, no reasonable alternative to eliminating the threat (such as detention) can be operationally viable.

According to international law, every effort must be made to ensure that collateral damage is limited to a minimum. Accordingly, when military commanders plan a targeted killing, they must do their best to avoid injury and damage to innocent civilians.[19]

---

17. *Id.*

18. Amos N. Guiora, *Targeted Killing as Active Self-Defense,* 36 Case W. Res. J. Int'l L. 319, 322 (2004).

19. Protocol Additional to the Geneva Conventions of Aug. 12, 1949, and Relating to the Protection of Victims of International Armed Conflicts, June 8, 1977, 1125 U.N.T.S. 3, art. 57.

According to a report in the Jerusalem Post, the IDF has expanded "the list of criteria that need to be met before staging a targeted interception . . . the 'ticking bomb' now refers not only to those on their way to an attack, but those planning and training for one."[20] In September 2004, an Israel Air Force helicopter attacked terrorists training at a base in Syria. Though the attack was not aimed at a specific terrorist engaged either in planning or executing a specific attack, the raid can be considered an expansion of the targeted killing policy. The attack on the training base, which followed a double suicide bombing in Beer Sheba (a city in southern Israel), was aimed at terrorists in training, without specific knowledge regarding their particular intentions.

1. Israel's Legal Arguments for Targeted Killing

Israel's targeted killing policy was articulated in its response to a petition against the practice filed with the Israel Supreme Court sitting as the High Court of Justice. In *Public Committee Against Torture, Committee for Clean Environment and Human Rights v. The State of Israel,*[21] the state argued that the petition should be denied for the following reasons: (1) The present conflict between Israel and Palestinian terror organizations is defined as "armed conflict short of war."[22] (2) According to the law of armed conflict, terrorists taking part in attacks against civilian or public targets are illegal combatants, not civilians, and are therefore legitimate targets. "Acts of terrorism against a country by non-state sponsored organizations or individuals need to be considered more than just criminal acts. Instead, they should be considered acts of war against the victim nation."[23] In *Israel v. Marwan Barghouti,* the Tel Aviv district court ruled that "terrorists who attack civilians are not 'lawful combatants' entitled to POW status in light of their unlawful activities. . . . Unlawful combatants who attack civilians are not entitled to this status." (3) The principle of proportionality must be respected when implementing targeted killing. (4) Targeted killing is used only when the targeted terrorist cannot be arrested

20. Arieh O'Sullivan, *The Army Redefines the "Ticking Bomb,"* The Jerusalem Post, September 13, 2004, at 2.

21. The opinion, written by retired President Aharon Barak, articulates the limits of operational counterterrorism by holding that the targeted killing of known terrorists is legal if done in accordance with international law. This means that the decision and order for a terrorist's targeted killing must be rooted in the principles of proportionality, collateral damage, and alternatives. The decision, the last in Barak's corpus of rulings on fighting terrorism, is the final piece in a puzzle of judicially mandated rules for how an army should conduct operational counterterrorism. Rather than engaging in broad, academic discourse, the ruling establishes clear criteria: a checklist of how the state is to make operational considerations. Harming civilians that "take direct part in hostilities," as defined in the decision, "even if the result is death, is permitted, on the condition that there is no other means which harms them less, and on the condition that innocent civilians nearby are not harmed. Harm to the latter must be proportional. That proportionality is determined according to a values-based test, intended to balance between the military advantage and the civilian damage." HCJ 769/02, Public Committee Against Torture v. The State of Israel.

22. *Id.* (This characterization had been previously accepted and adopted by the Supreme Court in a number of decisions.)

23. Frank A. Biggio, *Neutralizing the Threat: Reconsidering Existing Doctrines in the Emerging War on Terrorism,* 34 Case W. Res. J. Int'l L. 1, 4 (2002).

using reasonable means, and it must be in accordance with international principles requiring exhaustion of all reasonable alternatives.

The state also argued that legal scholars who examined the *jus ad bellum* dimensions of terrorism would agree on at least four principles: (1) if it (a state) has suffered an armed attack by terrorist actors, a state is entitled to defend itself forcibly; (2) a victim state's forcible self-defense measures should be timely; (3) a victim state's forcible self-defense measures should be proportionate; and (4) a victim state's forcible self-defense measures should be discriminate and taken against targets responsible in some way for the armed attack.

2. Who Are Legitimate Targets?

Determining whether suicide bombers and others involved in terrorist infrastructure are legitimate targets, even though they are not "soldiers" in the traditional sense of the word, is essential to analyzing whether operation counterterrorism is lawful. Presently, terrorists who take a direct role are viewed as combatants (albeit illegal combatants not entitled, inter alia, to POW status) and therefore legitimate targets. Furthermore, a legitimate target is not limited to the potential suicide bomber who, according to corroborated and reliable intelligence, is on his way to carry out a suicide bombing. Rather, a legitimate target is identified as any person who plays a significant role in the suicide bomber infrastructure—that is, "doers" who execute attacks, and "senders" who orchestrate them. In addition, both those responsible for the logistics of an attack and those financing terrorist attacks are increasingly considered legitimate targets, though the question of "when" remains unresolved.

Issues to Consider

1. In determining counterterrorism policy, what weight should the state give to the possibility of collateral damage?
2. Should the possibility that innocent civilians will be killed prevent the state from implementing a particular aggressive policy?
3. What should the chain of command be for implementing a targeted killing, and what should the test be for determining necessity?
4. What criteria/guidelines should be established before implementing the policy of targeted killing?
5. Does the principle that combatants die on the battlefield apply also to terrorists killed in a targeted killing?

3. Policy Concerns

To examine counterterrorism is to not only argue the law (particularly in an area considered "gray" by most international law experts), but also to analyze the decision-making process. Accordingly, determining effectiveness of the targeted killing policy is essential.

Israel considers its policy effective for the following reasons: (1) terrorists understand that Israel has been able to penetrate informants in small cells;

(2) terrorists have had to change their living and sleeping habits on a regular basis; and (3) a significant number of terrorists have been killed.

At the same time, Israel's policy of targeted killings has been highly criticized. Professor Michael Scharf suggests four arguments for why the targeted killings "may still be misguided"[24] even though the policy is legal: (1) instances of collateral damage; (2) instances of mistaken identity; (3) cascading threats to the world order; and (4) strengthening enemy morale via martyrdom.[25]

Issues to Consider

1. If effectiveness is an elusive term, is arguing "self-defense" sufficient to justify the killing of an individual suspected of involvement in a future terrorist act?
2. In deciding to order the killing of an individual suspected of involvement in a future terrorist act, what criteria should be used for determining operational success?
3. What criteria should be applied in determining when to perform a targeted killing?
4. What is the significance of "freezing" and then "unfreezing" a particular policy?
5. What process is appropriate for the decision to perform a targeted killing, and what should be considered before authorizing a specific action?

Notwithstanding criticism of the policy, particularly in the "court of international public opinion," Israeli decision makers, regardless of their political affiliation, have implemented targeted killings. The policy is understood to be a particularly effective form of operational counterterrorism that meets the test of lawful self-defense as upheld by the Supreme Court (above), despite the inherent controversy and complexity. The legality—in accordance with self-defense—is predicated on the targeted individual posing an imminent threat in accordance with available intelligence information. Arguably the standard represents a "slippery slope," thereby imposing on decision makers—in the context of the rule of law—the requirement to rigorously review/analyze the intelligence information. Conversely, "over-thinking" can have negative repercussions, as the terrorist attack that arguably could otherwise have been prevented were targeted killing implemented could be successful.

From the perspectives of national leadership and the public alike, such an occurrence would be viewed, understandably, as a failure with potentially significant consequences. However, while Israel applies a self-defense model more aggressive than other countries, it is not intended as a "carte blanche" allowing an unrestrained use of force, as that would violate both the Supreme Court decision and international law.

24. Michael P. Scharf, *In the Cross Hairs of a Scary Idea,* Wash. Post, April 25, 2004, at B1.
25. *Id.*

IV. RUSSIA

A. INTRODUCTION

Russia's operational counterterrorism methods are best described as unapologetically hardline. In the 1990s and early 2000s, in response to Chechen terrorism, the government's stated goal was the elimination of Chechen leaders and terrorists. After several apartment buildings were bombed in Moscow in 1999, then acting President Vladimir Putin threatened them this way: "We will pursue the terrorists everywhere. You will forgive me, but if we catch them on the toilet, we will wipe them out in the outhouse."[26]

The threat of terrorism since that time has receded significantly. In its 2021 report on terrorism in Russia, the U.S. Department of State reported that the country experienced no terrorist attacks that year.[27] Russian state media reported that the government had prevented 65 "terrorism-related crimes" and "eliminated" 23 "bandits" as a result of its use of "forceful and preventative measures."[28] It also shut down 62 international terrorist cells, prevented 926 people involved in terrorist activities from entering the country, and froze over 100 million rubles in assets of people believed to have ties to extremism.[29] It carried out 327 counterterrorism exercises and 323,000 preventative efforts designed to promote intolerance toward terrorism among 15 million youth.[30]

Despite these statistics, the U.S. Department of State continues to warn its citizens of the threat of terrorism in Russia. The Department's travel advisory dated February 13, 2023 warns American citizens not to travel to Russia due to concerns of terrorism, civil unrest, kidnapping and hostage-taking, and wrongful detention. However, it lists the North Caucasus region (which encompasses Chechnya) as the only area of the country to avoid specifically because of the threat of terrorism. The U.S government strongly discourages its citizens from traveling to this region and outright prohibits its employees from traveling there. The advisory warns that terrorist attacks may occur anywhere within Russia, however, and not just the North Caucasus.[31]

The 2006 Law on Counteraction against Terrorism (discussed in Chapter 4) created the National Antiterrorism Committee to coordinate the counterterrorism efforts of the nation's seventeen security agencies, with the Federal Security Service (FSB) on top.[32] These agencies conduct legitimate

---

26. Robyn Dixon, *Chechen War Propels Putin to Front Ranks*, L.A. Times, January 1, 2000, *available at* https://www.latimes.com/archives/la-xpm-2000-jan-01-mn-49592-story.html (last visited February 16, 2024).

27. *Country Reports on Terrorism 2021: Russia*, U.S. Dep't of State, *available at* https://www.state.gov/reports/country-reports-on-terrorism-2021/russia (last visited March 29, 2023).

28. *Russia Suffered No Terrorist Attacks in 2021 — Russian Counterterrorism Agency*, TASS, December 14, 2021, *available at* https://tass.com/society/1375297 (last visited February 16, 2024).

29. *Id.*

30. *Id.*

31. *Russia Travel Advisory*, United States Department of State—Bureau of Consular Affairs, February 13, 2023, *available at* https://travel.state.gov/content/travel/en/traveladvisories/traveladvisories/russia-travel-advisory.html (last visited February 16, 2024).

32. Joshua Sinai, *The Terrorist Threats against Russia and Its Counterterrorism Response Measures*, 14 Connections 95, 99 (2015).

counterterrorism activities, with particular attention still paid to the North Caucasus region.[33] Russia's counterterrorism efforts are, however, criticized as being highly counterproductive. Instead of focusing on the root causes of radical ideology that lead to terrorism, Russia responds to terrorist threats with disproportionate military force. Russia's counterterrorism strategy

> is almost entirely based on physically liquidating extremists. Russian authorities do not try to win hearts and minds or engage in efforts at deradicalization or social reintegration. Russian security forces in the North Caucasus frequently apply the principle of collective retribution—often imprisoning, threatening, and sometimes even killing relatives of suspected militants. While sometimes effective at the tactical level, strategically this approach only engenders a perpetual cycle of radicalization.
>
> Russian counterterrorism operations also pay little regard to civilian or "collateral" casualties. The botched raids of the Dubrovka Theater in Moscow or the tragic attempt to free hostages in Beslan demonstrate a shocking disregard for human life. Even worse, . . . Russian authorities often use the pretext of fighting extremism to crack down on dissidents.[34]

Three laws passed in 2021 particularly furthered the government's ability to use allegations of extremism or terrorism to chill speech and to silence political opponents and unfavored or unpopular groups. The United States Department of State describes those laws and their effect this way:

> Under the coordination of the National Antiterrorism Committee, the Federal Security Service (the FSB) — with aid from the Ministry of Internal Affairs (the MVD) and Rosgvardiya (the National Guard of Russia), when appropriate—perform counterterrorism functions. Russia has continued to use its counterterrorism and anti-extremism legislation as a tool to stifle political opposition, independent media, and certain religious organizations, including Jehovah's Witnesses,[35] to criminalize the exercise of freedoms of religion or belief, expression, and association.
>
> In 2021, Russia continued to use terrorism as a pretext to stifle internal dissent. The State Duma (Parliament) adopted three bills meant to silence individuals who provide any dissent toward the government and prevent them from participating in public life. These bills target Russians who support civil

---

33. *Country Reports on Terrorism 2020: Russia*, U.S. Dep't of State, *available at* https://www.state.gov/reports/country-reports-on-terrorism-2020/russia/ (last visited February 15, 2023).

34. *Russia's Counterproductive Counterterrorism: Hearing Before the Comm'n on Sec. & Cooperation in Europe*, 116 Cong. (2019) (statement of Dr. Michael Carpenter), *available at* https://www.congress.gov/event/116th-congress/house-event/LC64162/text (last visited February 22, 2024).

35. The State Department reports that religious groups classified as "terrorist" or "extremist" "without any credible evidence of violent actions or intentions [include] two foreign-based Church of Scientology organizations, four Protestant groups from Latvia and Ukraine, a regional branch of Falun Gong and seven Falun Gong-associated NGOs, Jehovah's Witnesses, the Fayzrakhmani Islamic community, Tablighi Jamaat, followers of the Muslim theologian Said Nursi, and Hizb ut-Tahrir. These designations effectively banned their worship and activities, and members were subject to prolonged imprisonment, harsh detention conditions, house arrest and house raids, discrimination, harassment, and criminal investigation for participating in the activities of a banned organization." *2022 Country Reports on Human Rights Practices: Russia*, U.S. Dep't of State, *available at* https://www.state.gov/reports/2022-country-reports-on-human-rights-practices/russia/ (last visited March 30, 2023).

society and religious organizations that have been declared "extremist" or "terrorist" under the law that designates organizations as "undesirable."

Those bills are the following:

- Adopted on June 4, Bill No.1165649-7 bans leaders, staff, and supporters of organizations labeled as "extremist" from running for parliamentary elections. The bill gives Russian authorities the power to label any political group or entity as "extremist."
- Adopted on June 9, Bill No.1165650-7 amends the law on "undesirable" organizations and prohibits Russian citizens from participating in activities of these organizations. It also imposes stricter measures on finances for organizations that operate with Russian bank accounts and those that receive money from persons who have been labeled as foreign agents.
- Adopted on July 1, Bill No.1165661-7 simplifies the process for charging and convicting those who have been designated as affiliates of "undesirable" organizations.[36]

The language of these laws is vague and thus encompasses any number of organizations. The laws empower the government to exercise immense control over elections and to regulate organizations that citizens may want to associate with, whether political, religious, or otherwise. The result of these laws is a society where not only is the citizenry's ability to petition the government, protest, or express dissent severely diminished, but doing so often leads to punishment.

B. SILENCING POLITICAL OPPONENTS

As noted above, Russian authorities do conduct legitimate counterterrorism operations. However, a primary facet of modern Russian counterterrorism is different from traditional counterterrorism as described in this book, and different from how counterterrorism is normally conceptualized. Unlike the other nations covered by this book, Russian authorities use far-fetched, exaggerated, or false charges of terrorism against groups and people that the government disfavors and wants to silence and oppress. Though this approach may meet a technical definition of counterterrorism, the dubiousness of the allegations in these instances calls for an examination into the accuracy of labeling such operations as "counterterrorism." Despite these concerns, the following material will attempt to demonstrate how Russian authorities approach counterterrorism in these kinds of situations.

Alexei Navalny, perhaps the most well-known Kremlin critic, began expressing his opposition to the Russian government by blogging in the early 2000s about corruption within state-owned corporations.[37] In 2011, he led

---

36. U.S. Dep't of State, *supra* note 35.

37. Paul LeBlanc, *'We Don't Realize How Strong We Actually Are': How Alexey Navalny Became Russia's Opposition Leader*, CNN, August 8, 2022, 11:52 AM, *available at* https://www.cnn.com/2022/04/22/world/who-is-alexey-navalny/index.html (last visited February 16, 2024).

protests in response to allegations of fraud in the country's parliamentary elections, during which he was arrested and sentenced to 15 days in jail.[38] In 2013, Navalny was found guilty of embezzlement in a trial widely viewed as being politically motivated.[39] However, he was freed the day after receiving his five-year prison sentence, and was allowed to continue pursuing candidacy for mayor of Moscow while appealing his conviction.[40] Navalny did not win the election, but received 27% of the vote.[41] The European Court of Human Rights ruled in 2016 that Navalny's right to a fair trial was violated,[42] and the Russian Supreme Court ordered a retrial.[43] Navalny was convicted again in 2017, which barred him from running for president in 2018 as he had intended.[44]

In August 2020, Navalny became severely ill while on a flight from Tomsk, Russia to Moscow.[45] The plane made an emergency landing, and Navalny was flown to Berlin for treatment.[46] He recovered after spending more than two weeks in a medically-induced coma.[47] German officials determined Navalny was poisoned with a Soviet-era nerve agent called Novichok, and the UN concluded the poisoning was an attempted assassination by the Russian government.[48] Russia has denied responsibility for Navalny's illness,[49] though Russia is the only nation known to have ever used Novichok.[50]

Russian police arrested Navalny at the airport when he returned to Russia from Germany in January 2021 for failing to appear at a parole hearing that occurred while he was receiving treatment.[51] The arrest provoked international

---

38. Ellen Barry, *Rally Defying Putin's Party Draws Tens of Thousands*, N.Y. Times, December 10, 2011, *available at* https://www.nytimes.com/2011/12/11/world/europe/thousands-protest-in-moscow-russia-in-defiance-of-putin.html (last visited February 16, 2024).

39. Miriam Elder, *Russia: Alexei Navalny Found Guilty of Embezzlement*, Guardian, July 18, 2013, 4:58 AM, *available at* https://www.theguardian.com/world/2013/jul/18/alexei-navalny-found-guilty-embezzlement (last visited February 16, 2024).

40. Miriam Elder, *Russian Opposition Leader Alexei Navalny Released from Custody*, Guardian, July 19, 2013, 8:28 AM, *available at* https://www.theguardian.com/world/2013/jul/19/alexei-navalny-released-custody-russia (last visited February 16, 2024).

41. Nataliya Vasilyeva & Vladimir Isachenkov, *Court Bars Russian Opposition Leader from Presidential Race*, Associated Press, February 8, 2017, *available at* https://apnews.com/article/moscow-russia-ap-top-news-elections-international-news-aa48d14a47f040278d0c9cbf5108efee (last visited February 16, 2024).

42. *European Court Rules Russia Violated Navalny's Right to Fair Trial*, Radio Free Europe/Radio Liberty, February 23, 2016, 1:52 PM, *available at* https://www.rferl.org/a/russia-european-court-navalny-rights-violated/27569325.html (last visited February 16, 2024).

43. Vasilyeva et al., *supra* note 41.

44. *Id.*

45. *Putin's Poisons: 2020 Attack on Aleksey Navalny*, U.S. Embassy Tbilisi, April 18, 2022, *available at* https://ge.usembassy.gov/putins-poisons-2020-attack-on-aleksey-navalny/ (last visited February 16, 2024).

46. *Id.*

47. Colin Dwyer, *Vladimir Putin Shrugs Off Alexei Navalny's Poisoning: 'Who Needs Him?'*, NPR, December 17, 2020, 10:20 AM, *available at* https://www.npr.org/2020/12/17/947460586/putin-shrugs-off-navalny-poisoning (last visited February 16, 2024).

48. *Russia Responsible for Navalny Poisoning, Rights Experts Say*, UN News, March 1, 2021, *available at* https://news.un.org/en/story/2021/03/1086012 (last visited February 16, 2024).

49. U.S. Embassy Tbilisi, *supra* note 45.

50. *Id.*

51. Andrew Roth & Luke Harding, *Alexei Navalny Detained at Airport on Return to Russia*, Guardian, January 17, 2021, 1:06 PM, *available at* https://www.theguardian.com/world/2021/jan/17/alexei-navalny-detained-at-airport-on-return-to-russia (last visited February 16, 2024).

condemnation and outrage.[52] Navalny was sentenced to two and a half years for the alleged parole violations, and in 2022 was convicted and sentenced to nine more years on fraud charges he insisted were fabricated.[53] While in prison, Navalny was presented with additional charges of "propagating extremism, calling for terrorism, financing extremist activity, and rehabilitating Nazism" because of content on a YouTube channel started by his associates after he was incarcerated.[54] His Anti-Corruption Foundation, which investigated corruption within the Russian government, was labeled an extremist organization in 2021 and banned from the country.[55] Navalny himself was labeled a "terrorist" and "extremist" by the government that same year as he remained in prison.[56]

While preparing for trial on the extremism charges in April 2023, Navalny learned about new terrorism charges against him.[57] The charges sought to retroactively criminalize activities of the Anti-Corruption Foundation and were related to the bombing death of a Russian military blogger that same month.[58] The suspect in the bombing was reported to be a supporter of Navalny, a fact Russian authorities used to tie Navalny to the crime.[59] In August 2023, a Russian Court concluded Navalny had financed and incited "extremist activities" and sentenced him to 19 years.[60] On February 16, 2024, the Russian prison service announced that Navalny had died at the age of 47 from "sudden death syndrome."[61] Due to the past assassination attempt, Western leaders and those in Navalny's circle are holding Vladimir Putin directly responsible for Navalny's death.[62]

---

52. Eva Hartog, *Russian Opposition Leader Navalny Arrested upon Arrival in Moscow*, Politico, January 17, 2021), *available at* https://www.politico.eu/article/russian-opposition-leader-alexei-navalny-arrested-upon-arrival-in-moscow/ (last visited February 16, 2024).

53. Camille Gijs, *Alexei Navalny Given 9-Year Jail Term after Being Found Guilty on Fraud Charges*, Politico, March 22, 2022, *available at* https://www.politico.eu/article/russia-court-alexei-navalny-guilty-fraud-charges/ (last visited February 16, 2024).

54. *Russia: Alexey Navalny Faces 'Terrorism' Charges; 30 Years' Jail*, Al Jazeera English, October 20, 2022, *available at* https://www.aljazeera.com/news/2022/10/20/russian-opposition-figure-alexei-navalny-says-faces-new-charges (last visited February 16, 2024).

55. Lucia Binding, *Putin Critic Navalny Says Russia Investigating Him on 'Absurd' Terrorism Charges - and Could Jail Him for Decades*, Sky News, April 26, 2023, 10:42 AM, *available at* https://news.sky.com/story/putin-critic-navalny-says-russia-investigating-him-on-absurd-terrorism-charges-and-could-jail-him-for-decades-12866645 (last visited February 16, 2024).

56. Uliana Pavlova, *Alexei Navalny: Jailed Kremlin Critic 'Reclassified from Flight Risk to Terrorist,'* Sky News, October 11, 2021, 2:55 PM, *available at* https://news.sky.com/story/alexei-navalny-jailed-kremlin-critic-reclassified-from-flight-risk-to-terrorist-12431436 (last visited February 16, 2024).

57. *Jailed Kremlin Foe Navalny Says He May Face Life Sentence*, AP News, April 26, 2023, *available at* https://apnews.com/article/russia-navalny-extremism-trial-corruption-b4300cf7a3769779d30e550eccc9bbae (last visited February 16, 2024).

58. *Id.*

59. *Id.*

60. *Russian Appeals Court Upholds Opposition Leader Alexei Navalny's 19-year Prison Term*, James Doubek, NPR, September 26, 2023 *available at* https://www.npr.org/2023/09/26/1201839908/alexei-navalny-russia-putin-prison-sentence-upheld-appeal (last visited February 16, 2024).

61. Lucy Papachristou, *What We Know About Alexei Navalny's Death in Arctic Prison*, Reuters, (February 19, 2024) https://www.reuters.com/world/europe/alexei-navalnys-death-what-do-we-know-2024-02-18/.

62. Andrew Roth, *Western Leaders Point Finger at Putin After Alexei Navalny's Death in Jail*, The Guardian (February 16, 2024) https://www.theguardian.com/world/2024/feb/16/russian-activist-and-putin-critic-alexei-navalny-dies-in-prison.

The severity of accusations of extremism or terrorism makes them effective tools of political oppression. As in Navalny's case, the government can use such accusations to shut down organizations that it dislikes and to imprison opposition leaders. Charges of extremism and terrorism in these circumstances are based on the premise that challenging the status quo of Russian politics and government through organized protest and distribution of information—especially information that exposes corruption or paints the government negatively—are a threat to the nation. Similar tactics are being employed to crush dissent related to Russia's 2022 invasion of Ukraine.

C. PUNISHING CRITICS OF WAR IN UKRAINE

Shortly after Russia invaded Ukraine in February 2022, the Russian parliament passed laws designed to limit criticism of the invasion. The laws banned describing the invasion as a "war" or "invasion," disseminating "deliberate false information about the use of Russian Armed Forces," calling for the military to stop fighting, and supporting the sanctions levied against Russia by other nations.[63] Depending on the charge, persons convicted could face up to 15 years in prison.[64] While these charges are not directly tied to terrorism, allegations that a person has committed one of these crimes tends to lead to charges of extremism or terrorism as well.

In late 2022, 19-year-old Olesya Krivtsova posted a story on Instagram criticizing Russia's war in Ukraine.[65] Fellow students at her university in Arkhangelsk reported the Instagram story and screenshots of anti-war messages Krivtsova had written in a thread on the messaging app Telegram to authorities, who arrested her.[66] Krivtsova, who had participated in other anti-war activities previously, was not only charged with discrediting the Russian army but was also added to the country's list of terrorists and extremists.[67] The designation barred her from spending more than $145 a month, using the internet, or talking on the phone.[68] Facing up to ten years in prison, Krivtsova fled Russia for Lithuania in March 2023.[69]

Krivtsova is one of dozens of Russians charged with justifying, promoting, or inciting terrorism in relation to protesting the country's invasion of Ukraine.[70] The dramatic response to Krivtsova's social media posts demonstrates Russian authorities' willingness to clamp down on criticism by even

63. *Russia Criminalizes Independent War Reporting, Anti-War Protests*, Human Rights Watch, last updated March 23, 2022, *available at* https://www.hrw.org/news/2022/03/07/russia-criminalizes-independent-war-reporting-anti-war-protests (last visited February 16, 2024).

64. *Id.*

65. Mary Ilyushina, *After Classmates Snitch, Russia Charges 19-Year-Old War Critic as Terrorist*, Wash. Post, January 19, 2023, 10:55 AM, *available at* https://www.washingtonpost.com/world/2023/01/19/arkhangelsk-student-war-critic-arrested/ (last visited February 16, 2024).

66. *Id.*

67. *Id.*

68. *Id.*

69. Valerie Hopkins, *She Posted Online About the War in Ukraine. Then She Faced a Prison Term.*, N.Y. Times, March 22, 2023, *available at* https://www.nytimes.com/2023/03/22/world/europe/russia-ukraine-social-media-crackdown.html (last visited February 16, 2024).

70. *Id.*

ordinary citizens who do not possess particular influence. Such a response severely inhibits the willingness of other citizens to speak out against the government's actions in Ukraine. Otherwise, they too may face allegations of extremism and terrorism and be given long prison sentences.

Issues to Consider

1. Does the marked decline of traditional terrorist activity in Russia justify the use of collective retribution or the reduction of civil liberties enjoyed by Russian citizens?
2. Rather than emphasizing "liquidating" extremists, what investments could the Russian government make in its citizens or its cities that might help reduce extremist activity even in the most volatile areas?
3. Alexei Navalny knew that he would likely face arrest and incarceration upon his return to Russia after receiving medical treatment in Germany. What might have led him to choose to return to Russia anyway?
4. Navalny returned to Russia despite the risk of prosecution, while Olesya Krivtsova fled Russia while being prosecuted. Can you understand the motivations behind their different choices? Given the risks they each faced, what would you do?

V. INDIA

A. INTRODUCTION

India's development of an operational counterterrorism policy is based on threats that are more complicated than those faced by the other surveyed nations. In the aftermath of 9/11, the United States is principally focused on Islamic terrorism; Israel's counterterrorism efforts are almost exclusively directed at Palestinian terrorism; Russia is primarily concerned with Chechnya; Spain in the aftermath of the Madrid train station bombing is primarily concerned with al Qaeda and its local progeny; China is primarily concerned with a Uyghur threat that the government believes must be quashed to deter possible separatist ambitions among other ethnic groups; and Colombia faces several internal threats (distinct in their complications from India's internal threats). The Indian government must navigate three distinct threats: domestic religious tensions involving Hindus, Sikhs, and Muslims; Kashmiri-based terrorism with Pakistani backing; and an external threat posed by Pakistan, with whom India has gone to war thrice in the past 50 years. Not by chance did former U.S. President Bill Clinton argue that South Asia is "perhaps the most dangerous place in the world today."[71]

---

71. Terence Hunt, *Security Fears Force Change in Clinton Bangladesh Visit,* Cleveland Plain Dealer, Mar. 20, 2000, at 4A.

India's operational counterterrorism methods must take into consideration a number of geopolitical realities in the post-9/11 world: (1) America's view of Pakistan as a lynchpin in the effort to track down bin Laden and other al Qaeda operatives; (2) India's increasingly important role as a major player in the high-tech field; and (3) the importance India places on truly being a member of the global village, implying that power has its limits.

B. TERROR THREATS FACED

While the principal terrorist threat faced by India has historically been based in Kashmir, major terrorist attacks have occurred primarily—but not exclusively—in Mumbai. Nevertheless, the primary focus of the Indian military in developing and implementing an operational counterterrorism strategy is predicated on responding to events in Kashmir. What is important to note, as has been previously discussed, is that Kashmiri terrorism is not local or indigenous based; rather, according to most reports, Kashmiri terrorists are supported by Pakistan and interlinked with Islamic radical terrorism.

Bruce Reidel, Terrorism in India and the Global Jihad

The Brookings Institution, Nov. 30, 2008[72]

The attacks on multiple targets in downtown Mumbai in late November 2008 is only the latest in a long series of horrific terrorist operations in India. Terrorism in India is a complex phenomenon with numerous perpetrators. The most dangerous terrorist menace comes from groups with intimate connections to the global jihadist network centered around Usama bin Laden and al Qaeda and its allies in the Pakistani jihadist culture. While it is too soon to draw firm conclusions about responsibility for the attacks in Mumbai in November 2008, the odds are good that the terrorists and the masterminds behind their plot are connected into the global jihad.

. . . [T]he most dangerous terror menace comes from Kashmiri groups based in Pakistan with long and intimate connections to al Qaeda and bin Laden. The group which has been linked by initial Indian assessments of the Mumbai attack, Lashkar-e Tayiba (literally the army of the pure or righteous), was founded in Afghanistan and Pakistan in the late 1980s and early 1990s by a group of Kashmiri activists with the assistance of the Pakistani intelligence service, the Inter Services Intelligence Directorate or ISI. Usama bin Laden was an early supporter of the group and provided some of the initial funding for its start. The ISI was an enthusiastic supporter of the Kashmiri insurgency and wanted to use asymmetric warfare, i.e. terrorism to undermine Indian control of Kashmir.

The Mumbai attacks displayed a level of sophisticated planning that marks another milestone in the global jihad. Multiple targets within an urban

---

72. *Available at* https://www.brookings.edu/articles/terrorism-in-india-and-the-global-jihad/ (last visited February 16, 2024).

environment, trained and armed killers intent on operating in small teams or alone targeting Americans, Brits, Israelis as well as Indians, careful casing of the targets ahead of the attack and the use of small boats to get close in to the targets are signs of the continuing evolution of terrorist planners. Hotels have long been a favorite target of al Qaeda and its allies from the multiple hotel bombings in Amman by al Qaeda's Iraq franchise in November 2005 to the attack on the Serena Hotel in Kabul this January and the bombing of the Marriott hotel in Islamabad in September.

Issues to Consider

1. When facing multiple threats, is it possible to develop a counterterrorism strategy that balances rights without violating domestic laws?
2. Should India's counterterrorism methods be restricted to the person-specific approach adopted by Israel or the two-tiered policy adopted by the U.S. and Russia?
3. Are the limits on individual freedom that India's legislation imposes an adequate substitute for operational counterterrorism?
4. In weighing options and their effectiveness, is an aggressive, operational policy (U.S., Russia) more effective than a legislative policy (India)?
5. What is the operational significance of legislation that imposes limits on individual liberty?
6. Given India's geopolitical reality, is operational counterterrorism as exercised by the U.S., Israel, and Russia a viable option?
7. What is the flexibility (or lack thereof) in developing a counterterrorism policy when a bordering sovereign nation supports a particular terrorist group?
8. What military options does India have given that Pakistan supports Kashmir terror while proclaiming to be America's ally?

C. THE DILEMMA

Eben Kaplan & Jayshree Bajoria, Counterterrorism in India

Council on Foreign Relations, Nov. 27, 2008[73]

. . . Experts say the government's response to terrorist attacks have been episodic; soon after an attack the government appears to take short-term measures. "India lacks a coherent strategic response to terrorism; there is no doctrine (BusinessWeek), and most of our responses are kneejerk," says retired Major General Sheru Thapliyal, who works at the Center for Land Warfare Studies in New Delhi.

Indian security officials usually focus their investigations on the country's Muslim minority following such attacks. India is home to 150 million

73. *Available at* https://www.cfr.org/backgrounder/counterterrorism-india (last visited February 16, 2024).

Muslims, the second largest Muslim population in the world. But a large percentage of them feel disadvantaged and discriminated against by the government and the security forces. . . .

India's counterterrorism measures have often been the subject of appeals by human rights organizations. Deol says Indian officials have a higher tolerance for collateral damage than counterterrorism authorities in many other nations. In an example of such tactics, he says, "Agencies and arms of the state have been accused of turning a blind eye in order to run rival gangs that would be tasked with killing other insurgents, but would also kill innocent people." . . .

Issues to Consider

1. Do the human rights abuses alluded to above reflect an official policy or rather a frustration felt by the military and security services whose freedom of action is limited by India's geopolitical realities?
2. What significance should be attached to a counter-infiltration policy rather than counterterrorism operations?
3. If the U.S., Israel, and Russia have clearly articulated operational counterterrorism policies, how would India's policy be defined?
4. If India were to attack terror camps inside Pakistan, would that be akin to the U.S.'s targeted killing in Pakistan? Or would it be construed as a violation of Pakistani sovereignty and therefore an act of war?
5. For India to conduct truly effective operational counterterrorism, is attacking targets inside Pakistan a requirement?
6. If the overwhelming threat India faces is Pakistani-driven, then what internal measures—other than legislation—can India develop?

VI. SPAIN

A. INTRODUCTION

The Spanish government has neither developed nor implemented policy similar to the other surveyed nations. While it is true that in the aftermath of the Madrid train bombings, eight al Qaeda operatives were killed by Spanish forces and others were arrested, the response to the bombing was limited from an operational perspective.

The initial response was the decision by the newly-elected socialist government of Jose Luis Rodriguez Zapatero to withdraw Spanish forces from Iraq despite strong American opposition to the decision. The decision, which according to many American commentators was capitulatory,[74] seemingly reflected a victory for the terrorist.

74. Leslie Crawford, *Baptism of Ire,* Financial Times Weekend Magazine, July 17, 2004; Marlise Simons, *Spain's New Premier Orders Pullout in Iraq,* Chi. Trib., April 19, 2004. *See Iraq: Spanish Troop Withdrawal a "Blow" to Coalition,* GlobalSecurity.org, April 23, 2004, *available at* http://www.globalsecurity.org/wmd/library/news/iraq/2004/04/wwwh40423.htm (last visited July 21, 2010).

Issues to Consider

1. Does the fact that Spain has not been the target of an act of Islamic-based terrorist attack since the train station bombings suggest that the decision to withdraw from Iraq was effective?
2. Though Prime Minister Zapatero had promised the electorate during the campaign to withdraw from Iraq, should the bombings have outweighed the promise?
3. After a reported attempt to assassinate the first President Bush, then President Clinton ordered the nighttime bombing of the Iraqi Intelligence headquarters, an act heavily criticized for being too tepid. What is more effective: a response that causes minimal injury and damage to property, or a conscious decision not to engage terrorists in operational counterterrorism?
4. President Reagan ordered the "strategic re-deployment" of American marines from Lebanon in the aftermath of the 1983 attack on barracks that killed 243 marines. According to some students of terrorism, this was a watershed event because terrorists concluded that the United States was a "paper tiger." Could the Spanish decision have a similar long-term effect?

B. COUNTERTERRORISM POLICIES COMPARED

The second response to the bombing was the attempted arrest of suspected al Qaeda terrorists. Nevertheless, unlike the other surveyed nations that actively, if not aggressively, seek to engage or eliminate terrorists, the Spanish operational counterterrorism policy appears to be predicated on non-engagement. Jonathon Schell's article below discusses the difference between the American and Spanish responses to attacks on their respective soil:

> From the start, the countries' responses differed. In Spain, the attack upon civilians in four Madrid railway stations—killing 191 and wounding some 2,000 people—prompted immediate, huge public demonstrations. Viewed from the United States, where no such response occurred after 9/11, the response at first seemed puzzling: Why demonstrations? Did Spaniards imagine that marches with placards would reach the hearts of people who carry out massacres? On second thought, the logic of the act became apparent: Terrorism is an attack upon civilians, not soldiers; it is meant to strike fear into other civilians. It made sense, then, for civilians, not soldiers, to respond with a clear message: We are not intimidated. Since intimidation is the purpose, the demonstration scored an immediate victory over terrorism. At a stroke, it removed the point of the attack.
>
> Meanwhile, Spanish authorities have been relentless in pursuit of the terrorists. Seventy-nine people are under active suspicion, and of these, 24 are in jail. A Pakistani cell has allegedly been broken up. The Spanish police had also been busy arresting other terrorist suspects—57 are now in prison, awaiting charges—and, according to the police, foiling other possible attacks.
>
> All of this, of course, has differed greatly from the US reaction to 9/11. In the United States, no nationwide public demonstrations occurred; the government took the lead. And it went to war, first in Afghanistan, then in Iraq. The

> president not only launched the two wars, but set forth a rationale for others. Identifying an "axis of evil" of three governments—Iraq, Iran, and North Korea—that supported terrorists and sought weapons of mass destruction, President Bush has, so far, overthrown only the first of the three.[75]

When analyzing counterterrorism methods developed and implemented by the surveyed nations, Spain clearly stands at an extreme end of the spectrum. The Spanish response has been limited to arrests, an action more reflective of a traditional criminal law paradigm rather than a military or counterterrorist paradigm.

C. CRIMINAL LAW PARADIGM

The following excerpt from a Washington Post report highlights the effect of implementing a criminal law paradigm instead of an operational counterterrorism approach:

> In Madrid, Spanish police arrested more than two dozen people for playing a role in the March 11, 2004, commuter-train explosions that killed 191 people and wounded more than 1,800. Seven other suspects were killed a few weeks later after police surrounded them in a suburb of the capital. Many of those detained were Moroccan immigrants who had lived in Madrid for several years and had records for petty crime, but were not veterans of al Qaeda training camps or considered terrorist threats.
>
> Since then, Spanish investigators have identified two al Qaeda veterans who they think may have helped orchestrate the bombings but whose exact roles remain a mystery. One of them, Amer Azizi, is a Moroccan national who provided military training at camps in Afghanistan and who is also a suspect in the May 16, 2003, suicide bombings in Casablanca, according to Spanish court records.
>
> Another is Mustafa Setmarian Nasar, a native of Syria with Spanish citizenship who is a leading ideologue in radical Islamic circles. The U.S. Justice Department has posted a $5 million reward for Nasar's capture, accusing him of training extremists to concoct chemical weapons.[76]

Issues to Consider

1. Is capitulation in the face of terrorism a valid domestic policy in the present age?
2. Are there long-term policy benefits to a nonaggressive form of counterterrorism?
3. Is the application of the criminal law paradigm appropriate in response to terror attacks such as the train bombing?
4. Does the policy adopted and implemented by Spain encourage additional attacks?
5. Does such a response reflect the globalization of counterterrorism?

---

75. Jonathan Schell, *The Atlantic Divide over Fighting Terrorism,* Yale Global, March 16, 2005, *available at* https://archive-yaleglobal.yale.edu/content/atlantic-divide-over-fighting-terrorism (last visited Dec. 31, 2023).

76. Craig Whitlock, *Terror Probe Find "the Hands, but Not the Brains," Attackers Often Caught as Masterminds Flee,* Wash. Post Foreign Service, July 11, 2005 at 10.

VII. CHINA

A. INTRODUCTION

China's operational counterterrorism efforts in Xinjiang largely focus on a strategy of capturing or killing leaders responsible for the 2009 Urumqi riots—a series of violent riots over five days in the capital city of the Xinjiang Uyghur autonomous region—while addressing root causes; the primary emphasis, however, is on "striking hard" to prevent future attacks.

Operational counterterrorism in China often has two phases: an initial, immediate response to an attack either by the police or military, followed by imposition of long-term restrictions on rights and government pressure seeking to influence change from within the attacking group. In the aftermath of an attack, China imposes significant force to minimize potential violence by sending security forces to enforce restrictions, including curfew, intended to ensure public order. The second phase includes limiting information sources, restricting movement within a particular region, and expediting trials for those who allegedly violated the law.

Issues to Consider

1. How are limits of a harsh policy defined (if at all), and how is effectiveness defined?
2. What are the dangers of a counterterrorism policy devoid of restraints?
3. Is the court of international opinion a relevant consideration?
4. How—if at all—are proportionality and balance applied in the Chinese paradigm?

B. 2009 XINJIANG RIOTS

The initial response to the riots in Urumqi was to send police to the area to quell the disturbances; it was reported that police opened fire indiscriminately on protesters. In addition, Urumqi was locked down; as a result, a communications blackout was imposed, text messages were banned, and the internet was shut down for what authorities described as measures essential for regional security.

In the immediate aftermath of the riots, Chinese leaders stated that they would administer severe punishments to people involved in the rioting, warning that those guilty of murder would be executed. Within the week, Chinese officials stated that they had arrested over 1,000 people; a month later it was unclear how many had been released from prison. Shortly thereafter, China re-implemented the "Strike Hard" campaign in Xinjiang; officials claimed they would "root out places where criminals breed, and change the face of public security situation in these areas."[77] In the six months following the

77. *Xinjiang Police to "Strike Hard,"* BBC NEWS, November 3 2009, *available at* http://news.bbc.co.uk/2/hi/asia-pacific/8339367.stm (last visited February 6, 2009).

riots, China proceeded to implement additional measures to prevent terrorism in the region; however, in the coming months, texting was allowed and internet access gradually restored.

Martin Wayne wrote that China's brutal tactics have worked to turn the society of Xinjiang against the government, marking the approach as remarkably ineffective.[78]

Issues to Consider

1. What is the price of harsh measures?
2. How is the effectiveness of a carrot-and-stick approach measured?
3. Is the Chinese policy reflective of tactics (short-term) or strategy (long-term)?
4. How—if at all—are human rights preserved in such a model?
5. What is the impact of limiting communication methods?
6. What are the dangers of the Chinese counterterrorism policy?

VIII. COLOMBIA

A. INTRODUCTION

In the 1960s and 1970s, Marxist guerilla groups—M-19, Revolutionary Armed Forces of Colombia (FARC), and the National Liberation Army (ELN)—engaged in attacks plunging Colombia into instability and violence. By the 1980s, Colombia was a major center for drug production and trafficking. In the 1990s, numerous right-wing paramilitary groups formed, which presented an additional threat to the government.

In response to guerilla violence and drug trafficking, President Ayala (1978-1982) imposed a security statute curtailing individual rights, enabling suspected terrorists to be tried in military courts, and restricting news coverage. While Ayala earned praise for his successful resolution of a 1980 attack on the Dominican Republic's embassy by M-19, the following year the four primary guerilla organizations increased their attacks on banks and military bases and stepped up their kidnappings (including the kidnapping and death in a failed rescue attempt of Ayala's daughter).

The consequence was a sense that political change was not possible through traditional means, which directly contributed to an increase in the size of paramilitary groups. Accordingly, Colombian decision makers confront three distinct challenges and threats to public order: drug cartels, guerilla groups, and paramilitary organizations. Complicating the dilemma is the groups' representation of both the political right (paramilitaries) and left (guerilla groups) alike, combined with the extraordinary violence of the drug cartels. In response to this unique threat—reflecting enormous financial stakes and extraordinary violence—different governments have sought alternative

78. Martin Wayne, China's War on Terrorism 141-142 (2008).

methods, including direct negotiation with paramilitaries, to resolve the seemingly irresolvable.

The three-pronged threat is based on violence motivated by a powerful combination of economic and political forces facilitated by corruption. This complex, multi-dimensional threat is akin to India's challenges—with one significant distinction: the multiple threats India faces are largely externally oriented, whereas the numerous threats posed to Colombia are exclusively domestic. In addition—and fundamentally distinguishable from the other surveyed countries—Colombia's counterterrorism efforts are significantly impacted by the enormous financial resources available to the drug cartels and the inevitable resulting corruption.

B. BOJAYÁ MASSACRE

One of the realities of the numerous threats faced by the Colombian government is the violence between competing groups. In 2002, in the town of Bojayá in the Chocó region, 119 innocent civilians seeking shelter in a church were killed during a clash between FARC guerillas and paramilitaries. According to various reports, the Colombian military had received previous warning regarding the presence of paramilitaries in the region; however, it failed to take proactive measures to protect the civilian population. Whether this was a result of military incompetence or corruption is unclear.

After the Bojayá Massacre, the Colombian government was pressured in the court of international opinion by the United Nations and other nation-states. Newly-elected President Uribe was called to show a strong response both to terror organizations and to paramilitaries who had attacked innocent civilians while passive military forces failed to intervene. Furthermore, human rights organizations, which had been very critical of the military and government, called on the government to prosecute both the perpetrators of the crime and the security forces that had enabled the massacre to occur. In addition, the United States has consistently demanded that the Colombian government proactively engage both the terror organizations and paramilitaries, often in exchange for additional funding from the United States.

To that end, in the aftermath of the massacre, the government changed its strategy by pursuing a security policy aimed at strengthening the state's military capacity with the intent to gain control over the country. Simultaneously to this change in policy, the government launched peace talks with terrorist groups, reflecting—in many ways—government action devoid of strategic policy and seemingly lurching from event to event.

C. NEGOTIATION

Colombia has a long history of negotiation with terrorism-related groups. While this has been considered a positive act, negotiations often fail as terrorist organizations continue to successfully target innocent civilians. The willingness to negotiate creates the potential for a vicious cycle: the government engages in negotiation with a terrorist group only when it becomes powerful enough to pose a threat, at which point the government will seek to negotiate an amnesty agreement freeing the group from responsibility for acts previously committed.

Nevertheless, as a result of negotiations, a number of groups have dissolved. In the late 1980s, the 19th of April Movement (M-19) gave up its weapons, members were pardoned, and the group transitioned into a political party. However, several factions of M-19 refused to become part of the new political party and continued to participate in killings, kidnappings, and bombings. This reality seems to strengthen the argument that negotiation may have an impact in the short term, but questionable long-term effectiveness.

D. FALSE POSITIVES

An additional operational counterterrorism concern is referred to as "false positives." The military created a rewards system for soldiers to receive vacation or other benefits depending on the number of guerrillas killed. However, this policy ultimately failed because soldiers would attempt to earn rewards without actually proving that a person killed was a member of a terrorist organization. In one instance, victims were lured with false job offers to an area near the Venezuelan border, where they were murdered and presented to the army as paramilitaries killed in combat with the soldiers.

Issues to Consider

1. How do Colombia's complex internal threats present an objective barrier to developing coherent and consistent counterterrorism policies?
2. What does the range of counterterrorism policies, from negotiation to false positives, indicate regarding government decision making?
3. What is the impact of economic factors in developing a counterterrorism policy?
4. Does the range of threats suggest that a strategic policy cannot be articulated and implemented?
5. What is the significance of the court of international opinion?

CHAPTER 7

INTELLIGENCE GATHERING AND PROCESSING

I. INTRODUCTION

Intelligence is one of the most important counterterrorism tools. Some argue intelligence is *the* most critical issue; without it, operational counterterrorism would literally be "groping in the dark." This chapter focuses on how nations gather, analyze, and utilize intelligence information.

Intelligence is defined as the collection and analysis of information necessary to implement operational counterterrorism. Critical to understanding the significance of intelligence is understanding how governments translate this information into operational measures. Without intelligence information, governments would be unable to "connect the dots" in the best case; in the worst case, governments would be unable to even identify the "dots."

Issues to Consider

1. How does intelligence gathering keep pace with rapidly developing communication technology?
2. Must we distinguish between foreign intelligence and domestic law enforcement?
3. Should the standard for issuing a search warrant be lessened for purposes of intelligence gathering?
4. What are the limits of surveillance?
5. Are reasonable expectations of privacy extended to the Internet?

Intelligence gathering must be specifically tailored to how terrorists and their supporters communicate. Over reliance on one form of intelligence limits the ability to gather intelligence information and makes the state more vulnerable if that means of intelligence is cut off. Reliance on outdated and obsolete methods places governments at a distinct disadvantage. Conversely, unduly infringing on citizens' rights may violate domestic laws specifically legislated to protect against government intrusion. The debate about means is not conducted in a vacuum. Former President Bush criticized the debate over the legality of the administration's wiretapping policy, claiming the enemy listens to the discussion.

II. DEFINING TERMS

Intelligence is gathered primarily from four sources:

(1) human sources (HUMINT) (gathered directly from personal contacts)
(2) signal intelligence (SIGINT) (intercepted communications)
(3) open source information (OSINT) (analysis of publicly available information)
(4) imaging intelligence (IMINT) (gathered through imagery and collateral materials)

Intelligence is defined as information concerning an enemy or possible enemy.[1] Determining if the information is "actionable" for operational purposes requires that the information meets a four-part test: the intelligence must be **reliable, viable, relevant,** and **corroborated.**

Test Prong	Definition/Use
Reliable	Past experiences show the source to be a dependable provider of correct information; requires discerning whether the information is useful and accurate; demands analysis by the case officer whether the source has an agenda.
Viable	Is it possible that an attack could occur in accordance with the source's information?
Relevant	The information has bearing on upcoming events; consider the time-sensitivity and timeliness of the information.
Corroborated	Another source confirms the information in whole or part.

The intelligence community is—in large part—divided into two distinct categories: gathering and analysis. The former gathers the information from the sources listed above, while the latter analyzes and translates the information for different audiences, including operators and decision makers.

Intelligence information is the basis for a wide range of counterterrorism measures and sanctions, including detention for interrogation, administrative detention, house demolition, assigned residence, drone attacks, and targeted

1. Merriam Webster Dictionary, *available at* http://www.merriam-webster.com/dictionary/intelligence (last visited March 22, 2010).

killing. Without intelligence premised on the four-part test above, counterterrorism efforts are nothing more than a "crapshoot" with all the risks the term implies.

While intelligence is at the core of operational counterterrorism, decision makers must develop effective filters before acting on the information or else run the risk of violating civil and political rights. In the detention paradigm, decision makers must consider the following:

Factors to Consider when Balancing Source and Detainee Concerns:

Source	Detainee
• Who is the source? • Does the source have an agenda? • Who is the target of the source's information? • What are the risks to the source if the targeted individual is detained? • What are the risks to the source if the intelligence is made public?	• What is the purpose of the potential detention? • What are the risks/cost-benefits if detention is delayed? • What is the nature of the suspicious activity? • What information can the detainee provide? • What is the detention policy? • What are review standards, and is detention subject to independent judicial review?

III. SOCIAL MEDIA

The rise of social media around the globe has created more methods of communication and a new need for surveillance. As social media has become more popular over the years, the sharing of propaganda has also increased—from videos of ISIS beheadings to secret chat rooms used to plan an insurrection in Washington D.C. on January 6, 2021. Tweets and posts can incite violence and provide inspiration for future attacks.

Social media provides mass amounts of information across Facebook, X (formerly known as Twitter), Instagram, TikTok, etc. Monitoring, gathering, and taking down information can be complicated because platforms are owned by private corporations, and technology is evolving much faster than legislative attempts at regulation. Issues of free speech also arise with regulations and attempts to identify and prevent legitimate threats.

The internet has also enhanced the ability for cyberterrorism as well as recruiting efforts by terrorist organizations. Acts of terrorism can be planned and implemented between individuals in different countries without them ever having to leave their homes. States must continually adapt to the new internet platforms if they are to have effective intelligence gathering and processing. States also need to learn the coded language used on the websites and chatrooms and quickly sort through mass amounts of data to find legitimate threats.

Prevention of both attacks and the spread of terrorist propaganda is not the only function of gathering and processing information from social media; identifying and finding terrorists after an attack that have used social media can also provide aid and spread alerts and warnings to civilians of any danger. Terrorists have also used social media to claim credit for implementing or inspiring various attacks—this is something ISIS has done many times.

Some states have adapted faster than others in gathering and processing intelligence from social media, but the challenges continue to grow. Online bot accounts often spread misinformation online, affecting the reliability of information. With the wide availability of social media, almost every individual is able to create an account (or various accounts) that do not always contain accurate personal information. The platforms themselves—especially Twitter and Facebook—have struggled with the regulation of bots, misinformation, and hacking.

Issues to Consider

1. Are social media posts intelligence?
2. Are "unverified" online sources reliable?
3. How should bots be dealt with?
4. Do individuals have a right to privacy when using direct social media messaging?
5. How should the dark web be monitored?
6. Are current surveillance technologies capable of effectively monitoring social media?
7. Is there a concern for intelligence gatherers and analysts about information overload?

IV. UNITED STATES

In the aftermath of 9/11, the primary question was how the United States could not have known of al Qaeda's plans, given that US intelligence agencies had state-of-the-art technology enabling them to intercept conversations worldwide. Despite the available technology, al Qaeda operatives were able to enter the United States, live in the country legally, enroll in and attend flight schools, and implement a well-synchronized terror attack involving 19 terrorists. The plan was not detected even throughout the summer of 2001, when U.S. intelligence agencies consistently heard chatter regarding a possible terror attack.

A. THE 9/11 COMMISSION

The 9/11 Commission was established primarily to investigate how the intelligence community failed to prevent 9/11.[2] The commission's mandate was

2. *National Commission on Terrorist Attacks Upon the United States, available at* http://www.9-11commission.gov/ (last visited December 24, 2023) [hereafter The 9/11 Commission Report].

to provide a "full and complete accounting" of the attacks of 9/11, and to recommend how to prevent such attacks in the future.[3]

Testimony of Stephen J. Schulhofer Before the 9/11 Commission on Domestic Intelligence-Gathering

December 8, 2003[4]

An effective intelligence process requires that information be gathered, translated (when necessary), pooled by the relevant agencies, analyzed and then delivered to those in a position to investigate further or take quick preventive action. Legal rules are largely irrelevant at the stages where our past and current problems have been greatest—translation, analysis, and delivery. Law has posed significant obstacles to the pooling of intelligence, but the obstacles of agency culture, resources, and lines of communication have mattered and still matter much more. Even at the stage of gathering domestic intelligence, the stage where we expect law to govern, capabilities are largely determined by non-legal constraints—technical, budgetary and human resources, the training and priorities of our officers and the organization and cultures of the relevant agencies—all areas where our deficits have been, and continue to be, enormous.

In reaction to the events of September 11th, legal experts, along with most citizens, quickly concluded that we needed immediate steps to strengthen the government's intelligence-gathering authority, steps that, in the conventional cliché, would "shift the balance" between liberty and security. More than two years later, questions centered on legal authority, such as the merits of the U.S. Patriot Act, continue to dominate public discussion of the domestic intelligence function. Yet when the intelligence process suffers from major deficits in resources, personnel, organizational strength, and translation, analytic and delivery capabilities, a preoccupation with questions of legal authority can be misleading and dangerous.

The government's legal powers, prior to September 11th, were very strong, though not perfect; those imperfections bear little if any of the blame for the failure to prevent September 11th. Rather, severe human, budgetary, and organizational deficits prevented our law enforcement and intelligence agencies from using their strong legal powers effectively. And there is no reason to believe that additional legal authority, in that environment, would have been used to any greater advantage. Though many clear warning signs were in hand, our grave non-legal deficiencies—in organization, staffing levels, technical resources, and priority setting—cost us what chances we had to abort the plot.

Overall, the government currently has amply sufficient legal tools, but it remains sorely lacking in the non-legal capabilities needed to deploy those tools effectively.

---

3. *Frequently Asked Questions About the 9-11 Commission, available at* http://www.9-11commission.gov/about/faq.htm#q1 (last visited July 21, 2010).

4. *Available at* https://govinfo.library.unt.edu/911/archive/hearing6/index.htm (last visited December 24, 2023).

Many new measures, though relevant to the counterterrorism effort, are so overbroad that they sacrifice liberty and privacy needlessly and in ways that are likely to prove counterproductive, leaving us both less free and less secure.

Intelligence Gathering Authority Prior to September 11th

Before September 11th, the government possessed far-reaching intelligence-gathering authority, including the electronic surveillance powers conferred by Title III and the still-broader search and surveillance authorities available under FISA. Both statutes had been updated frequently to meet newly identified needs. In particular, FISA authority, primarily concerned with monitoring agents of foreign governments, was made available many years before 9/11 for monitoring individuals (both foreign nationals and US citizens) believed to be associated with international terrorism, even when not associated with any state actor.

Nonetheless, there were weaknesses. Several statutory surveillance authorities had failed to keep pace with new technologies, including cable providers, voice-mail systems and mobile phones. There were many gaps in our powers to trace and neutralize the sources of terrorist financing.

These legal weaknesses were no doubt worth fixing. But it is crucial for the public to understand that they did not play a significant role in our failure to foil the 9/11 attack.

Prior to 9/11, FBI agents and other officials had many items of information that, at least in retrospect, raised bright-red flags about the unfolding plot. Yet, as the Joint Inquiry documented, these alarm bells were repeatedly overlooked or ignored by those who were in a position to take action. Even in the high-risk environment that had been identified in the summer of 2001, there was little to no investigative focus on the would-be hijackers or their accomplices. There was virtually no effort to deploy readily available investigative tools to gather more information about them. Relevant intelligence obtained by CIA and FBI agents typically was not communicated promptly enough (or at all), and when communicated, such intelligence was largely ignored.[5]

According to Prof. Schulhofer, the United States' failure to prevent 9/11 was not the result of a lack of HUMINT or SIGINT. On the contrary, his testimony indicates that the intelligence community had the information necessary to obtain a clear understanding of terrorist aims prior to September 11, 2001. The shortcomings were related primarily to intelligence sharing and analysis, rather than to intelligence gathering.

Nevertheless, some officials within the executive branch blamed the U.S. legal system for hindering successful intelligence gathering. It was these hindrances, they argued, that enabled the 9/11 attacks; Attorney General

5. A full transcript of Prof. Schulhofer's Testimony before the 9/11 Commission is available at https://govinfo.library.unt.edu/911/archive/hearing6/index.htm (last visited December 23, 2023).

John Ashcroft was particularly vocal in his criticism of government-imposed restrictions.

Testimony of Attorney General John Ashcroft Before the National Commission on Terrorist Attacks upon the United States

April 13, 2004[6]

But the simple fact of September 11th is this: We did not know an attack was coming because for nearly a decade our government had blinded itself to its enemies. Our agents were isolated by government-imposed walls, handcuffed by government-imposed restrictions and starved for basic information technology.

The old national intelligence system in place on September 11th was destined to fail.

There was a covert action program to capture bin Laden for criminal prosecution, but even this program was crippled by a snarled web of requirements, restrictions and regulations that prevented decisive action by our men and women in the field. When they most needed clear, understandable guidance, and our agents and operatives were given instead the language of lawyers. Even if they could have penetrated bin Laden's training camps they would have needed a battery of attorneys to approve the capture. With unclear guidance, our covert action teams' risk of injury may have exceeded the risk to Osama bin Laden.

The single greatest structural cause for the September 11th problem was the wall that segregated or separated criminal investigators and intelligence agents. Government erected this wall, government buttressed this wall and before September 11th, government was blinded by this wall.

The basic architecture for the wall in the 1995 Guidelines was contained in a classified memorandum entitled "Instructions on Separation of Certain Foreign Counterintelligence and Criminal Investigations."[7] The memorandum ordered FBI Director Louis Freeh and others, quote, "We believe that it is prudent to establish a set of instructions that will more clearly separate the counterintelligence investigation from the more limited, but continued criminal investigations.

"These procedures," the memo went on to say, "which go beyond what is legally required, will prevent any risk of creating an unwarranted appearance that FISA is being used to avoid procedural safeguards which would apply in a criminal investigation."

This memorandum laid the foundation for a wall separating the criminal and intelligence investigations, as a matter of fact, established the wall following the 1993 World Trade Center attack, which at the time was the largest

6. *Available at* https://govinfo.library.unt.edu/911/archive/hearing10/index.htm (last visited December 24, 2023).

7. Jamie S. Gorelick Office of the Deputy Attorney General, *Instructions on Separation of Certain Foreign Counterintelligence and Criminal Investigations, available at* https://www.globalsecurity.org/security/library/report/2004/1995_gorelick_memo.pdf (last visited December 23, 2023).

international terrorism attack on American soil, the largest prior to September 11th.

The 9/11 Commission disagreed with John Ashcroft; in its final report, the Commission stated that the failure to prevent the attacks resulted primarily from the intelligence community's inability to properly understand and analyze the information it acquired.[8] The argument that constitutionally based restrictions should be loosened to enhance the U.S. intelligence gathering ability falsely assumes the law had prevented intelligence gathering.

B. PRIVACY AND THE CONSTITUTION

The development of a viable counterterrorism policy requires intelligence gathering; the question in civil democratic society is what costs are legitimate, given constitutional and legislative limits on government intrusions of personal privacy.

Nowhere has the debate addressing the commensurate means to achieve satisfactory intelligence gathering and an individual's right to privacy been as public as in the United States. The following testimony, given to the 9/11 Commission by Marc Rotenberg, executive director of the Electronic Privacy Information Center, highlights the increasingly critical role technology plays in obtaining intelligence. Rotenberg's testimony also suggests that increased technical abilities can reduce constitutionally granted protections.

> Now, the other key cornerstone to think about in assessing privacy protection in the United States is the Federal Wiretap Act. The wiretap statute was passed in 1968, following perhaps two of the most important privacy cases decided by the United States Supreme Court. One, as indicated above, concerned the use of a tape recorder in a public payphone in the streets of Los Angeles and whether that new investigative method would require the use of a warrant, which is to say judicial approval, or whether law enforcement could be free to use any new form of technology without judicial oversight to gather evidence that could be used in the criminal prosecution.
>
> And the court said quite clearly in Katz v. United States that this new type of technology needs to be subject to Fourth Amendment standards; not that it could not be used or that a prohibition should be established but rather that the traditional Fourth Amendment standards would be required for electronic surveillance. And the following year, in 1968, when the Congress passed the federal wiretap statute, based on *Katz* and the Berger v. New York opinion, it constructed an elaborate regulatory framework imposing significant oversight responsibilities on federal agencies that were using electronic surveillance authority.[9]

---

8. The 9/11 Commission Report, *supra* note 2, at 339-360.

9. From testimony provided by Marc Rotenberg to the National Commission on Terrorist Attack Upon the United States (9/11 Commission), Dec. 8, 2003. Full text available at: https://www.9-11commission.gov/archive/hearing6/9-11Commission_Hearing_2003-12-08.htm (last visited December 24, 2023).

In *Katz vs. United States,*[10] the Supreme Court overturned a Court of Appeals decision regarding the legality of government wiretaps on a pay phone used by a suspected gambler. The Supreme Court held that the individual's reasonable expectation of privacy was violated. Using a public phone booth did not constitute a waiver of the individual's right to privacy.

Katz v. United States

389 U.S. 347 (1967)

The Government contends, however, that the activities of its agents in this case should not be tested by Fourth Amendment requirements, for the surveillance technique they employed involved no physical penetration of the telephone booth from which the petitioner placed his calls. It is true that the absence of such penetration was at one time thought to foreclose further Fourth Amendment inquiry. . . . Indeed, we have expressly held that the Fourth Amendment governs not only the seizure of tangible items, but extends as well to the recording of oral statements, over-heard without any "technical trespass under . . . local property law." Once this much is acknowledged, and once it is recognized that the Fourth Amendment protects people—and not simply "areas"—against unreasonable searches and seizures, it becomes clear that the reach of that Amendment cannot turn upon the presence or absence of a physical intrusion into any given enclosure. . . .

The Government's activities in electronically listening to and recording the petitioner's words violated the privacy upon which he justifiably relied while using the telephone booth and thus constituted a "search and seizure" within the meaning of the Fourth Amendment. The fact that the electronic device employed to achieve that end did not happen to penetrate the wall of the booth can have no constitutional significance.

The question remaining for decision, then, is whether the search and seizure conducted in this case complied with constitutional standards. In that regard, the Government's position is that its agents acted in an entirely defensible manner: They did not begin their electronic surveillance until investigation of the petitioner's activities had established a strong probability that he was using the telephone in question to transmit gambling information to persons in other States, in violation of federal law. Moreover, the surveillance was limited, both in scope and in duration, to the specific purpose of establishing the contents of the petitioner's unlawful telephonic communications. The agents confined their surveillance to the brief periods during which he used the telephone booth, and they took great care to overhear only the conversations of the petitioner himself.

Accepting this account of the Government's actions as accurate, it is clear that this surveillance was so narrowly circumscribed that a duly authorized magistrate, properly notified of the need for such investigation, specifically informed of the basis on which it was to proceed, and clearly apprised of the

10. Katz v. United States, 389 U.S. 347 (1967).

precise intrusion it would entail, could constitutionally have authorized, with appropriate safeguards, the very limited search and seizure that the Government asserts in fact took place.

Searches conducted without warrants have been held unlawful "notwithstanding facts unquestionably showing probable cause," . . . for the Constitution requires "that the deliberate, impartial judgment of a judicial officer . . . be interposed between the citizen and the police. . . ."

. . . "Over and again this Court has emphasized that the mandate of the [Fourth] Amendment requires adherence to judicial processes," and that searches conducted outside the judicial process, without prior approval by judge or magistrate, are per se unreasonable under the Fourth Amendment subject only to a few specifically established and well-delineated exceptions.

The Government does not question these basic principles. Rather, it urges the creation of a new exception to cover this case. It argues that surveillance of a telephone booth should be exempted from the usual requirement of advance authorization by a magistrate upon a showing of probable cause. We cannot agree. Wherever a man may be, he is entitled to know that he will remain free from unreasonable searches and seizures.

Issues to Consider

1. How should surveillance be conducted?
2. Should the government establish different standards and controls dependent on the method of electronic intelligence gathering (e.g., wiretapping versus computer monitoring)?
3. How should democracies balance effective surveillance with minimizing intrusion?
4. How much intrusion is permissible?
5. How does the government protect the privacy rights of perceived "enemies"?
6. What limits should be set regarding electronic surveillance?
7. When does surveillance impede free speech?
8. What limits, if any, should be set on intelligence gathering?
9. Do Fourth Amendment restrictions apply to terrorism-related intelligence gathering?

C. FISA

The U.S. Congress enacted the Foreign Intelligence Surveillance Act (FISA) in 1978.[11] Its primary purpose was to "secure framework . . . [for] electronic surveillance for foreign intelligence purposes within the context of this Nation's commitment to privacy and individual rights."[12] To achieve these ends, FISA

11. Foreign Intelligence Surveillance Act Pub. L. No. 95-511, 92 Stat. 1783 (codified as amended at 50 U.S.C. §§1801-1811, 1821-1829, 1841-1846, and 1861-1862).

12. United States v. Pelton, 835 F.2d 1067, 1074 (4th Cir. 1987).

established the Foreign Intelligence Surveillance Court (FISC), a special court with exclusive jurisdiction to hear and grant foreign intelligence surveillance orders. Much like with a grand jury, the only party to FISC is the government; hearings are closed to the public and classified.

According to section 1804 of FISA, gathering foreign intelligence information from a suspected foreign agent must be a significant purpose of the surveillance.[13] Section 1804(a)(7)[14] allows the government to conduct wiretap surveillance of foreign powers or agents of a foreign power. However, section 1804(a)(7) limits surveillance: the conversations cannot involve American citizens; a significant purpose of the surveillance must be to obtain foreign intelligence information; such information cannot reasonably be obtained by normal investigative techniques; and the FISA court must issue a wiretap.[15] According to section 1802,[16] the government may order a wiretap without a warrant, provided the FISA court issues a warrant within 72 hours. Between 1978 and 2009, the government submitted 80,625,358 warrant requests; 81,425,360 were issued.[17] Since 1978, only nine warrant requests have been rejected by the FISA court.

Even though the Court grants an overwhelming number of warrant requests, the Bush administration—in the aftermath of 9/11—decided to bypass FISA and ordered warrantless wiretaps on phone conversations originating overseas. According to numerous media reports, the taps included American citizens,[18] a clear violation of FISA.

The Bush administration argued that such surveillance was not only necessary, but legal. On December 17, 2005, during his weekly radio address, President Bush defended his authorization of the NSA program.

Radio Address of President George W. Bush

The Roosevelt Room, Dec. 17, 2005[19]

In the weeks following the terrorist attacks on our nation, I authorized the National Security Agency, consistent with U.S. law and the Constitution, to intercept the international communications of people with known links to al Qaeda and related terrorist organizations. Before we intercept these

---

13. 50 U.S.C. §1801(a)(1)-(6) defines foreign power. 50 U.S.C. 1801(b)(1), (2) (defines agent of a foreign power).

14. 50 U.S.C. §1804 (2006).

15. *Id.*

16. 50 U.S.C. §1802.

17. The number discrepancy is based on modification and withdrawal of some orders. *Electronic Privacy Information Center, Foreign Intelligence Surveillance Act Orders 1979-2022 available at* https://epic.org/foreign-intelligence-surveillance-court-fisc/fisa-stats/ (last visited December 24, 2023).

18. James Bamford, *The Agency that Could be Big Brother,* N.Y. Times, Dec. 25, 2005, *available at* http://www.nytimes.com/2005/12/25/weekinreview/25bamford.html?ei=5088&en=3d099136bc2b2eac&ex=1293166800&partner=rssnyt&emc=rss&pagewanted=print (last visited July 21, 2010).

19. *Available at* https://georgewbush-whitehouse.archives.gov/news/releases/2005/12/20051217.html (last visited December 24, 2023).

communications, the government must have information that establishes a clear link to these terrorist networks.

This is a highly classified program that is crucial to our national security. Its purpose is to detect and prevent terrorist attacks against the United States, our friends and allies. Yesterday the existence of this secret program was revealed in media reports, after being improperly provided to news organizations. As a result, our enemies have learned information they should not have, and the unauthorized disclosure of this effort damages our national security and puts our citizens at risk. Revealing classified information is illegal, alerts our enemies, and endangers our country.

As the 9/11 Commission pointed out, it was clear that terrorists inside the United States were communicating with terrorists abroad before the September the 11th attacks, and the commission criticized our nation's inability to uncover links between terrorists here at home and terrorists abroad. Two of the terrorist hijackers who flew a jet into the Pentagon, Nawaf al Hamzi and Khalid al Mihdhar, communicated while they were in the United States to other members of al Qaeda who were overseas. But we didn't know they were here, until it was too late.

The authorization I gave the National Security Agency after September the 11th helped address that problem in a way that is fully consistent with my constitutional responsibilities and authorities. The activities I have authorized make it more likely that killers like these 9/11 hijackers will be identified and located in time. And the activities conducted under this authorization have helped detect and prevent possible terrorist attacks in the United States and abroad.

The activities I authorized are reviewed approximately every 45 days. Each review is based on a fresh intelligence assessment of terrorist threats to the continuity of our government and the threat of catastrophic damage to our homeland. During each assessment, previous activities under the authorization are reviewed. The review includes approval by our nation's top legal officials, including the Attorney General and the Counsel to the President. I have reauthorized this program more than 30 times since the September the 11th attacks, and I intend to do so for as long as our nation faces a continuing threat from al Qaeda and related groups.

On January 27, 2006, amid increasing controversy surrounding the NSA wiretapping program, the White House responded more directly to claims regarding its illegality. The Administration issued a document to journalists entitled *The National Security Agency Program to Detect and Prevent Terrorist Attacks: Myth vs. Reality,*[20] which addressed many of the issues that had come

20. *The National Security Agency Program to Detect and Prevent Terrorist Attacks: Myth vs. Reality,* Jan. 31, 2006, *available at* https://www.justice.gov/archive/opa/docs/nsa_myth_v_reality.pdf (last visited Decmber 23, 2023).

to the forefront of the debate surrounding the President's establishment of the NSA program.

In response to claims that Bush's authorization of the warrantless wiretaps exceeded executive powers, the White House asserted the following points:

- As Commander-in-Chief and Chief Executive, the President has legal authority under the Constitution to authorize the NSA terrorist surveillance program.
- The Constitution makes protecting our Nation from foreign attack the President's most solemn duty and provides him with the legal authority to keep America safe.
- It has long been recognized that the President has inherent authority to conduct warrantless surveillance to gather foreign intelligence even in peacetime. Every federal appellate court to rule on the question has concluded that the President has this authority and that it is consistent with the Constitution.
- Since the Civil War, wiretaps aimed at collecting foreign intelligence have been authorized by Presidents, and the authority to conduct warrantless surveillance for foreign intelligence purposes has been consistently cited and used when necessary.[21]
- The White House document also rejected assertions that the NSA program violated the Fourth Amendment: The Supreme Court has long held that the Fourth Amendment allows warrantless searches where "special needs, beyond the normal need for law enforcement," exist. Foreign intelligence collection, especially in a time of war when catastrophic attacks have already been launched inside the United States, falls within the special needs context.
- As the Foreign Intelligence Surveillance Court of Review has observed, the nature of the "emergency" posed by al Qaeda "takes the matter out of the realm of ordinary crime control."
- The program easily meets the Court's reasonableness test for whether a warrant is required. The NSA activities described by the President are narrow in scope and aim, and the government has an overwhelming interest in detecting and preventing further catastrophic attacks on American soil.[22]

Finally, the White House rejected the argument that warrantless wiretaps violated provisions of FISA:

> The NSA activities come from the very center of the Commander-in-Chief power, and it would raise serious constitutional issues if FISA were read to allow Congress to interfere with the President's well-recognized, inherent constitutional authority. FISA can and should be read to avoid this.[23]

---

21. *Id.*
22. *Id.*
23. *Id.*

Issues to Consider

1. Was bypassing the FISA court justified? Why or why not?
2. What standard did the court apply in issuing the FISA warrants?
3. How does one determine if wiretaps are effective?
4. Does the administration's bypassing of the FISA court suggest that the court will scrutinize future applications more carefully?
5. Does the administration's action suggest short-term gain at the expense of long-term benefit?

D. 9/11 AND THE SEPARATION OF VARIOUS INTELLIGENCE AGENCIES

During the 9/11 Commission hearings, the requirement that evidence from a criminal law investigation be kept separate from intelligence gathering operations was discussed at length. Many cited this so-called "wall" as the fundamental weakness in the United States' counterterrorism strategy, arguing that it clearly prevented the government from sharing information obtained in criminal investigations with information obtained through foreign intelligence gathering. The U.S. Dept. of Justice has defined this issue as the "sharing of grand jury investigations with FISA information."[24]

In response to concerns over the wall's perceived obstruction of government intelligence gathering, Congress passed the U.S. PATRIOT Act. Under Sections 202-215 of the PATRIOT Act, investigation of terrorist activities may include both electronic surveillance and search activities.[25] Former Deputy Attorney General Larry Thompson testified before the 9/11 Commission:

> Now, with the help of Congress, we in this country have made great strides toward getting more tools and resources in our efforts to combat terrorism. Many of the new resources or tools are embodied in laws, especially, as the Chairman mentioned, the Patriot Act. I'd like to just mention one provision of the Patriot Act this morning, highlight one provision that I think is extremely important, and that is section 218. Section 218 of the Patriot Act has allowed

---

24. Former U.S. Deputy Attorney General Larry Thompson stated:

> Before the Act was passed, federal law restricted prosecutors' ability to share with the intelligence community information obtained in grand jury testimony or from a criminal wiretap. Evidence about an impending terrorist threat that was presented to a grand jury, for instance, could not be shared with CIA officials. In situations where additional time spent identifying and tracking down terrorists could cost people's lives, this limitation was a significant obstacle to preventing terrorist attacks. Under the new law, law enforcement officers may now share grand jury and wiretap information regarding foreign intelligence with a wide range of federal personnel, including U.S. immigration authorities and members of the intelligence and national defense communities.

Department of Justice Leadership Address, November 8, 2001, *available at* https://www.justice.gov/archive/dag/speeches/2001/110801dagspeechtodojleadership.htm (last visited December 23, 2023).

25. The PATRIOT Act amended the Foreign Intelligence Surveillance Act.

> the FBI and the Department of Justice prosecutors to expand the nature of the investigation of terrorist activity, especially as it relates to electronic surveillance activities and search activities.
>
> As you know, section 218 provides that FISA investigations, investigations under the Foreign Intelligence Surveillance Act, can be utilized when foreign intelligence is a significant purpose of the investigation, as opposed to the old primary purpose of the investigation. This is a very important distinction and this is a very important provision.[26]

Stewart A. Baker, former general counsel for the National Security Agency, in his testimony before the 9/11 Commission, also addressed the intelligence-gathering ability of the United States and the so-called "wall" between traditional law enforcement and the intelligence community.

Testimony of Stewart A. Baker at the Public Hearing of the National Commission on Terrorist Attack upon the United States

Dec. 8, 2003[27]

I'd like to focus on a question that actually Commissioner Ben-Veniste asked or observed. That we actually had pretty good intelligence about the terrorists in the lead up to September 11. And I think that's right and what I'd like to focus on is not September, but August. Because in August the FBI learned that there were two terrorists whose names we had, who were in the country who were clearly here to kill Americans.

We had two and a half weeks to find them. They were living openly in San Diego, they were getting California IDs, they were buying stuff, engaging in financial transactions, signing rental agreements all in their own name, making reservations on the plane that they would ultimately fly into the Pentagon. We couldn't find them. That's a terrible failure. And I'd like to explore a little, from what I can gather, I'm not cleared to review any of this material anymore, but I have reviewed pretty carefully the public discussions of what happened to try to explore what went wrong there.

And I think when you look at it closely, it's really a failure of tools and a failure of rules. The tools problem is the problem we're here to talk about today. The FBI agent who discovered this and made it his mission to try to find these guys had some electronic tools, he was able to look in some databases for arrests, for certain automobile registrations. They hadn't been arrested and they hadn't been registered in any vehicles. He did not have access to a lot of government information, so that it took him about a week and a half to figure out what address one of the terrorists had put on his visa as he entered and then to check with the hotel that he put down to see if the guy ever stayed there.

---

26. National Commission on Terrorist Attacks upon the United States, Public Hearing, December 8, 2003, Larry Thompson, *available at* http://govinfo.library.unt.edu/911/archive/hearing6/9-11Commission_Hearing_2003-12-08.htm (last visited July 21, 2010).

27. *Available at* https://govinfo.library.unt.edu/911/archive/hearing6/index.htm (last visited December 24, 2023).

He didn't have a computerized access once he got legal authority to go into either of those databases. So we lost weeks there. Once more, he didn't have computerized access to any of the records that these guys were generating—not the financial records, not the travel reservation or even some of the California records. So there's clearly a failure of tools. If he could have been able to find those two guys and then check the links that they had to many of the other terrorists—there were direct shared addresses as I remember, links to the people who flew into the south tower and the north tower. We had a chance to stop this. The one chance that I can see in all of the errors that were made where we really could have prevented this if we had the tools to find these guys, and it is a scandal that we don't have them.

So we need that. We need at a minimum an ability to do those searches quickly and efficiently, not just by shoe leather and by calling people which is the method that the FBI has used for a generation. That's just to fight the last war. Obviously the next set of terrorists is not going to be so accommodating as to use their real names. We're going to need other mechanisms and I've listed in my testimony which I've provided about a dozen IT capabilities that our investigators need in order to find these folks and to respond appropriately to crises.

So clearly we need more tools. But I think when you read the story of what went wrong in those two weeks with an eye that is informed by bureaucratic realities and political realities you'll see that there's a problem with the rules as well. It's really—it's heartbreaking to read what this agent said when he asked for the authority to get the assistance of law enforcement—there are a million law enforcement agents in the country, there were three times as many FBI law enforcement agents as intelligence agents, he wanted to get help on that side of the FBI and he was told by FBI headquarters, not on your life. You cannot capitalize, cannot do that because there's a wall between law enforcement and intelligence.

And his response was to say, the American people will not understand this, someone is going to die because of this. Osama bin Laden is the principal beneficiary of the wall that we have built. How can we possibly maintain this? The answer was, we don't like it either, but that's the rule.

Now, I feel strongly about this, obviously, because I was part of building the wall. I was at NSA. I thought the wall responded to an appropriate, reasonable worry—theoretical but real—about civil liberties and privacy and that we could have a wall and still have an effective response to the national security problems that we have. We wrote rules and we thought we had done a fine job of carefully balancing all of those equities. We obviously failed. We failed terribly.

And that failure I think reflects both a desire to constantly add to the protections even against theoretical risks to privacy that we have built into our system, and at the same time, not to spend as much time worrying about whether people will actually be able to do their jobs to protect Americans. Because what finally happened in this case was the rules might just barely have been workable if it were not for the fact that there was a privacy scandal in the FISA Court in 2000 and 2001, in which the court believed it had not been properly informed about contacts across the wall when it was given FISA orders to sign. It ordered a massive review. It threw out one of the principal

FBI investigators who appeared before it and I'm guessing, though I don't know, that disciplinary action and maybe even a perjury indictment was considered for that fellow.

This was so bad that we dropped coverage on terrorism suspects in the United States in early 2001. So al Qaeda is preparing to kill thousands of Americans, we can't even keep up the wiretaps that we have authorized in the past. It's a disaster. And it's a disaster because there was such an intent focus on preventing even the most theoretical privacy abuse. That's the lesson that I would draw from September 11.

I just would say one more thing. I'm very worried that we're going back there, that what we have seen—I gave a speech once, I said, you know, we had two and a half years of serious failures. We had a major failure on September 11. We've had two and a half years to figure out what went wrong, who should be disciplined, and one person has been forced out of government, Admiral Poindexter. And the lesson that you can draw from that is, well, you can screw up pretty badly in protecting the American people, but if you get crossed wires with privacy lobby, you're gone. That is exactly the wrong message to be sending to our FBI and CIA agents.

Issues to Consider

1. What are the limits to the right to privacy?
2. To what extent should different intelligence agencies share information about U.S. citizens?
3. What measures would most effectively guarantee that law enforcement agencies do not abuse intelligence-gathering operations?
4. What constitutional protections exist to prevent undue invasion of privacy, and does 9/11 justify waiving otherwise protected rights?

E. INTELLIGENCE POST-9/11

U.S. policy makers recognize the importance of human sources "on the ground" to infiltrate terrorist organizations and provide crucial information that would otherwise be unavailable. The following excerpt illustrates how critical HUMINT can be to the neutralization of terrorist leaders.

> Gen. George Casey, the top U.S. commander in Iraq, said the hunt for al-Zarqawi[28] began two weeks ago, and his body was identified by fingerprints and facial recognition.

28. On June 7, 2006, U.S. forces in Iraq launched an air strike on a safe house some fifty-five miles north of Baghdad, where al-Zarqawi was hiding. Jordanian by birth, Abu Musab al-Zarqawi transformed himself into a nationless freelance terrorist. Tactically, geographically, and to some extent philosophically, he established a pattern of inconsistency. His flexibility made him all the more fearsome—and all the more difficult to pin down. Despite a bounty of $25 million on his head and vastly increased media attention over the past five years, hard facts about al-Zarqawi's past are few and far between. Hearsay, on the other hand, abounds. As *Foreign Policy* put it, al-Zarqawi's story has become "one of the most powerful and enduring myths of the war on terror." Lee Hudson Teslik, *Profile: Abu Musab al-Zarqawi,* Council on Foreign Relations,

Casey said an American airstrike targeted "an identified, isolated safe house."

He said tips and intelligence from senior leaders of al-Zarqawi's network led U.S. forces to al-Zarqawi as he was meeting with some of his associates. Casey also said Iraqi police were first on the scene after the airstrike. . . .

Al-Maliki said the Wednesday night airstrike by U.S. forces was based on intelligence reports provided to Iraqi security forces by area residents.

A Jordanian official said the kingdom also provided the U.S. military with information that helped track down al-Zarqawi, who claimed responsibility for a November triple suicide bombing against Amman hotels that killed 60.

The official, who spoke on condition of anonymity because he was addressing intelligence issues, would not elaborate, but Jordan is known to have agents operating in Iraq to hunt down Islamic militants. Some of the information came from Jordan's sources inside Iraq and led the U.S. military to the area of Baqouba, the official said.[29]

Issues to Consider

1. Given the importance of human sources, does the U.S. sufficiently penetrate international terror organizations?
2. Does penetration of domestic terror organizations raise constitutional concerns?
3. What should the criteria for determining source reliability be?
4. What level of source reliability justifies operational counterterrorism based on HUMINT?
5. What are the risks involved in trusting a source?
6. What, if any, constitutional guarantees exist for the potential victim of a source?
7. Should operational counterterrorism decisions be predicated only on SIGNIT, with HUMINT serving as a confirmation?

While the Bush administration suggested the 9/11 attacks could have been prevented if not for legal barriers, the findings of the 9/11 Commission suggest otherwise. Many of the provisions enacted in the PATRIOT Act regarding surveillance and intelligence-gathering powers were previously available to federal officials. According to many commentators,[30] the failure was an institutionalized and systemic inability to maximize sophisticated technology available to the intelligence community. Simply put, the United States was

---

June 8, 2006, *available at* https://www.cfr.org/backgrounder/profile-abu-musab-al-zarqawi (last visited December 25, 2023).

29. *Al Qaeda in Iraq's al-Zarqawi "Terminated,"* MSNBC, June 8, 2006, *available at* https://www.nbcnews.com/id/wbna13195017 (last visited December 24, 2023).

30. *See* Joshua Rovner & Austin Long, *Intelligence Failure and Reform: Evaluating the 9/11 Commission Report,* 14 Breakthroughs 10 (2005). *See also* The Intelligence Community and 9/11: Congressional Hearings and the Status of the Investigation 1/16/03, *available at* https://irp.fas.org/crs/RL31650.pdf (last visited December 24, 2023).

unable to make use of the intelligence it had gathered because it lacked the human capability to translate and act on it.

Given that 9/11 was predominantly an intelligence failure, the central question is whether lessons have been learned and applied. This is relevant to operational counterterrorism both in the United States and abroad. The U.S. drone policy has been characterized by significant collateral damage reflecting, in part, inaccurate intelligence information regarding the presence of innocent civilians. Similarly, the struggles of U.S. ground forces in Afghanistan could be attributed, in part, to intelligence gathering/analysis limitations in the complicated Afghan paradigm.

In regards to the attempted Christmas Day bombing (December 2009) on Northwest Airlines Flight 253, much of the blame rests squarely on the shoulders of various airport security procedures (beyond the purview of this book). However, the inability to develop a sophisticated model that would have identified the bomber as an imminent threat and to develop a tracking model that would have facilitated identifying a known threat represent an overwhelming failure of the intelligence community.

The U.S. intelligence community possesses the tools necessary to prevent terrorist attacks. There is widespread agreement that information available to the U.S., including HUMINT, SIGINT, and OSINT, was sufficient to prevent 9/11. The challenge facing decision makers is establishing protocol in the years ahead to maximize effective use of available information. The 9/11 Commission addressed many of these issues, encouraging dialogue to answer these difficult questions. But more than dialogue is required to ensure that the United States protects its borders from attacks by terrorists armed with increasing capabilities. While little doubt exists regarding the extraordinary sophistication of the U.S. with respect to signal intelligence, significant doubt remains regarding its human intelligence capabilities.

Intelligence gathering requires innovation and initiative. The constitutional limits on surveillance that *Katz*[31] articulated were not a barrier to preventing attacks. The FISA court, as demonstrated by the available statistics, has proven very receptive to government requests for warrants. As we have discussed, the state of intelligence gathering should not be limited to the viability of wiretapping and other forms of SIGINT. Well-placed human sources can provide governments with the invaluable capability of infiltrating cells, and in regards to the U.S. drone policy, can pinpoint targets while minimizing collateral damage.

V. ISRAEL

A. INTELLIGENCE SOURCES

Israel's counterterrorism intelligence gathering is primarily based on HUMINT and SIGINT.

31. 389 U.S. 347 (1967).

In Israel, intelligence gathering is largely directed at Palestinians residing in the West Bank and Gaza Strip.[32] The intelligence community in Israel considers intelligence gathering to be a vital piece in the counterterrorism puzzle; invading the privacy of Palestinian communities and other groups deemed possible "threats to national security" are considered "necessary evils," if they are considered at all.

As discussed in the previous section, much criticism was directed at the Bush administration's NSA wire-tapping program for the perception that it was an unwarranted—if not unconstitutional—measure. According to Israeli law,[33] wiretaps on phone calls originating from Israel proper must be court-ordered and subject to judicial review. However, the interception of phone conversations originating in the West Bank and Gaza Strip need not be court-ordered. In addition to significant SIGINT abilities, the Israel Security Agency (ISA) has developed a highly sophisticated, effective, and efficient network of Palestinian collaborators. The strength of the Israeli intelligence community is its ability to create and maintain significant HUMINT networks. According to a variety of sources, Palestinians provide their case officers information regarding Palestinian terrorists for any of the following reasons: (1) economic gain (information received is financially remunerated); (2) erasing a criminal record; or (3) preventing a terror attack. The network of sources has proven extremely successful in preventing terror attacks.[34] However, collaborators are at great personal risk; Palestinian terrorists killed 1,124 suspected collaborators over a six-year period.[35]

One of the most important issues in intelligence gathering is the source. The ISA depends on sources to provide information. While the case officer is responsible for analyzing the information provided, the service rendered by the informant is invaluable. The case officer determines the quality of the intelligence by assessing its reliability and accuracy. Furthermore, the case officer must be convinced that the informant is not giving grudge-based information, intended to take revenge on an innocent member of the community.

Issues to Consider

1. What reliability standards should be implemented when assessing the quality of intelligence received from informants whose lives are in constant danger as described above?
2. What are the most effective and realistic methods of corroborating the information provided by an informant?

---

32. The exceptions to this are the ISA's reported intelligence-gathering efforts against Jewish right-wing and left-wing extremists alike in new immigrant and minority communities. None of these will be addressed in this book. In addition, Israel's foreign intelligence-gathering efforts will not be discussed.

33. The Secret Monitoring Law, 5739-1979, Laws of the State of Israel, vol. 33, pp. 141-46

34. *See* Bethany M. Nikfar, *Families Divided: An Analysis of Israel's Citizenship and entry into Israel Law,* 3 Nw. U. J. Int'l Hum. Rts. 5 (2005); Gabriel Danzig, *In Defense of Collaborators,* The Jerusalem Post, August 28, 2002; Martin Peretz, *"Front Line" in The New Republic Online,* Post Date 9/1/05; Issue Date 9/5/05.

35. *Victims of Palestinian Violence and Terrorism since September 2000, available at* https://www.gov.il/en/Departments/General/victims-of-palestinian-violence-and-terrorism (last visited December 25, 2023).

3. What criteria should be established when determining the reliability of a source who has a vested interest in providing information?
4. What safeguards should be implemented for a source-focused intelligence-gathering system?
5. Can operational counterterrorism measures be based on uncorroborated intelligence information?
6. Does the fact that terrorist groups have perpetrated attacks despite infiltration by sources suggest inherent limitations of intelligence?
7. Should there be limits on the methods case officers may use in extracting information they know an informant has?

B. RELIABILITY OF SOURCES

For intelligence information to be deemed actionable, a source must be considered reliable, and the information provided must be corroborated. In developing the informant network referred to above, the ISA seeks to cross-reference information prior to recommending specific operational missions to IDF commanders.

The criteria for determining source reliability—the essence of the process—has been highly developed in Israel. Sources are classified according to a variety of indexes: quality and accuracy of information previously provided; actionability of information previously provided; whether the informant has a vendetta against the subject of the information; the uniqueness of the information provided (for instance, whether the information is commonly known); and the importance of the information.

Conducting operational counterterrorism based on single-source information creates significant risks. Therefore, prior to acting on the available information, the case officer must seek corroborating information. Uncorroborated intelligence presents a significant dilemma: if the information suggests a major terrorism attack, delay in acting may result in innocent civilian deaths. Conversely, undertaking operational counterterrorism missions against an individual falsely identified by a source results, at best, in an unjustified loss of freedom and, at worst, the death of an innocent individual.

This dilemma is at the core of intelligence gathering and operational counterterrorism decision making. The effort to corroborate intelligence information has been a mainstay in Israel's strategy; nevertheless, operational decisions have been made based on single-source information. Though Israeli domestic law does not specifically address source reliability or information corroboration, petitions have been filed before the High Court questioning the reliability of sources. The Court's concern is clear: whether or not the information available to the ISA justifies a decision to impinge on the freedom of a Palestinian in a non-criminal context.

After bombing a purported chemical-producing factory in the Sudan,[36] then President Clinton largely said "trust me" when asked to submit the

36. *See* Jules Lobel, *The Use of Force to Respond to Terrorist Attacks,* 24 Yale J. Int'l L. 537 (1999).

Issues to Consider

1. If the High Court does not directly question the source, is intelligence reliability largely a matter of "trust me"?
2. What institutional safeguards are required to protect Palestinians named by sources?
3. How—if at all—does the High Court analyze source reliability?

evidence justifying the attack. In the follow-up investigation, the intelligence that had been the basis for the President's decision to bomb was found to be incorrect. Was this the only time that executive decisions were based on faulty intelligence?

Since the answer is clearly no, the challenge facing lawyers, judges, and decision makers is how best to assess both the information and the informant in determining what institutional safeguards should be implemented to protect the potential target. In the U.S., the arguable safeguard is FISA, though the Bush administration's decision to bypass the court casts doubt on that notion. In Israel, the High Court of Justice assumes that responsibility of a safeguard.

As evidenced by the above material, intelligence failures are an inevitable aspect of counterterrorism. Unlike other nations, Israel's intelligence failures are not caused by legal restrictions or judicial intervention. Its successes, of which there are many, are directly contributable to the effective convergence of HUMINT and SIGINT.

If no legal barriers exist, how should a nation account for recorded failures? Perhaps the inherent limitations of intelligence gathering are best highlighted by the Israeli model. As discussed earlier, the ISA has penetrated many terrorist cells operating in the Palestinian territories through a well-developed source network in the West Bank and the Gaza Strip. Yet the intelligence community, in spite of the tools at its disposal, is unable to prevent every terrorist attack and has repeatedly misgauged the ability of terrorist organizations. Unlike the Bush administration, which sought to bypass existing laws, Israel's legal structure provides the intelligence community with the means necessary, but ultimately demonstrates that no counterterrorism operation, no matter how sophisticated the intelligence, can be infallible.

VI. RUSSIA

Understanding intelligence gathering in Russia requires understanding the extraordinary power of the Soviet-era KGB.

Russia: Internal Security Before 1991

RussiansAbroad.com[37]

The KGB had been an integral feature of the Soviet state since it was established by Nikita S. Khrushchev (in office 1953-64) in 1954 to replace the People's Commissariat for Internal Affairs (Narodnyy komissariat vnutrennikh del—NKVD), which during its twenty-year existence had conducted the worst of the Stalinist purges. Between 1954 and 1991, the KGB acquired vast monetary and technical resources, a corps of active personnel numbering more than 500,000, and huge archival files containing political information of the highest sensitivity. The KGB often was characterized as a state within a state. The organization was a rigidly hierarchical structure whose chairman was appointed by the Politburo, the supreme executive body of the Communist Party of the Soviet Union ("CPSU"). Key decisions were made by the KGB Collegium, a collective leadership including the agency's top leaders and selected republic and departmental chiefs. The various KGB directorates had responsibilities ranging from suppressing political dissent to guarding borders to conducting propaganda campaigns abroad. At the end of the Soviet period, the KGB had five chief directorates, three smaller directorates, and numerous administrative and technical support departments.

In contrast to the United States government, which assigns the functions of domestic counterintelligence and foreign intelligence to separate agencies, the Federal Bureau of Investigation (FBI) and the Central Intelligence Agency (CIA), respectively, the Soviet system combined these functions in a single organization. This practice grew out of the ideology of Soviet governance, which made little distinction between external and domestic political threats, claiming that the latter were always foreign inspired. According to that rationale, the same investigative techniques were appropriate for both foreign espionage agents and Soviet citizens who came under official suspicion. For example, the KGB's Seventh Chief Directorate, whose task was to provide personnel and equipment for surveillance operations, was responsible for surveillance of both foreigners and Soviet citizens.

The KGB's branches in the fourteen non-Russian republics duplicated the structure and operations of the unionwide organization centered in Moscow; KGB offices existed in every subnational jurisdiction and city of the Soviet Union. The KGB's primary internal function was surveillance of the Soviet citizenry, using a vast intelligence apparatus to ensure loyalty to the regime and to suppress all expressions of political opposition. This apparatus served as the

37. *Available at* http://www.russiansabroad.com/russian_history_364.html (last visited March 14, 2010).

eyes and ears of the party leadership, supplying information on all aspects of Soviet society to the Politburo.

A. RUSSIAN INTELLIGENCE TECHNOLOGY

The extent to which Russia utilizes SIGINT is murky, although satellite phone signals have been used to target terrorist leaders' locations. The Russian constitution and various legislations outline the parameters regarding signal intelligence.

PRIVACY INTERNATIONAL, RUSSIAN FEDERATION

Dec. 18, 2007[38]

The Constitution of the Russian Federation recognizes rights of privacy, data protection and secrecy of communications. Article 23 states, "1. Everyone shall have the right to privacy, to personal and family secrets, and to protection of one's honor and good name. 2. Everyone shall have the right to privacy of correspondence, telephone communications, mail, cables and other communications. Any restriction of this right shall be allowed only under an order of a court of law." Article 24 states, "1. It shall be forbidden to gather, store, use and disseminate information on the private life of any person without his/her consent. 2. The bodies of state authority and the bodies of local self-government and the officials thereof shall provide to each citizen access to any documents and materials directly affecting his/her rights and liberties unless otherwise stipulated under the law." Article 25 states, "The home shall be inviolable. No one shall have the right to enter the home against the will of persons residing in it except in cases stipulated by the federal law or under an order of a court of law."

In 2006, Russia adopted the Law on Personal Data, and the Law on Information, Information Technologies and Protection of Information, which replaced the 1995 Law of Information, Informatization and Protection of Information. Adoption of the Law on Personal Data fulfills Russia's obligation to transpose the Council of Europe Convention for the Protection of Individuals with regard to Automatic Processing of Personal Data into national law. The Law on Personal Data generally protects personal data from being collected and processed illegally and without consent of data subject. However, the law is still far from ideal since it gives wide exemptions to the government. The Law on Personal Data came into force in January 2007, but most of its provisions are still inactive; for example, the law provides for the creation of a data protection authority, but none is operational to date.

The 2003 Communications Law protects secrecy of communications. The tapping of telephone conversations, scrutiny of electronic communications,

---

38. *Available at* http://www.privacyinternational.org/article.shtml?cmd[347]=x-347-559497 (last visited March 14, 2010).

delay, inspection and seizure of postal mailings and documentary correspondence, receipt of information therein, and other restriction of communications secrets are allowed only with a court order except as otherwise provided by a federal law. The Law on Operational Investigation Activity that regulates surveillance methods used by secret services requires a court-issued warrant. The law was amended in December 1998 by the State Duma. Guarantees for the protection of privacy were emphasized and additional controls imposed on prosecutors. Article 5 of the Law provides that an investigative structure must secure people's privacy. The Law also provides: "If one believes that some actions of bodies conducting operational investigation have infringed on an individual's rights or freedoms, the individual has the right to appeal to a court, a prosecutor, or to a higher body that carries out investigative activities."

The law also provides: "If a person has not been proved guilty during a legally established procedure, then all materials obtained during this operational investigation must be archived for a period of one year and subsequently deleted." However this provision is virtually revoked by the following addition: ". . . unless official interests or justice require otherwise." In December 1999, the law was amended to allow surveillance by the tax police, the Ministry of Internal Affairs, Border Guards, the Kremlin Security Service, the Presidential Security Service, the parliamentary security services and the Foreign Intelligence Service. In 2001, the following provision was added to the Law: "Audio recordings and other materials resulting from interception and wiretapping of the conversation of persons being out of criminal proceedings must be deleted within six months after the wiretapping is over with an appropriate protocol. The judge must be notified three months before materials reflecting the results of operational investigations, implemented on the basis of a court warrant, are deleted." Disclosure of data that affects someone's privacy without his or her consent is legally prohibited unless otherwise stipulated by federal laws. . . .

In 2005, the government, citing concerns about terrorism, approved new regulations for interactions between communication companies and certain government agencies. The new regulations give law enforcement agencies greater access to telephone and cellular phone company clients' personal information and require providers to grant the Ministry of Internal Affairs and Federal Security Service (FSB) 24-hour remote access to their client databases. Some experts believed these new rules contradict the Constitution. Given that the authorities have had legal access to these records for 10 years, mobile operator MegaFon's press secretary suggested that the new rules change nothing, and simply make the process "more transparent."

The FSB has conducted phone tapping using the "SORM" system (or "System of Operative Investigative Activities"). In 1998, information about a new SORM-2 system that applies to the Internet was revealed. SORM-2 requires Internet Service Providers (ISPs) to install surveillance devices and high-speed links to local FSB departments, which would allow the FSB to directly access Internet users' communications, although with a warrant requirement. . . .

After the terrorist attack in Moscow of October 2002, the State Duma quickly adopted several amendments to the laws on Mass Media and Terrorism, banning any distribution of information that could impede anti-terrorist actions. In December 2004, a new concept of the "state of a terrorist emergency" was introduced in the State Duma as one counterterrorism measure. The new regime of a "state of a terrorist emergency" could seriously limit civil rights in case Russian law enforcement bodies receive information about a terrorist act prepared but failed to check this information. In the beginning of 2006, after lengthy discussions, the parliament removed the new proposal from the counterterrorism bill. However, according to the new counterterrorism law enacted in 2006, Russian secret services can easily wiretap and intercept communications during their counterterrorist operations.

B. RUSSIA AND HUMINT

Russian intelligence services have traditionally had limited success in penetrating both Chechen society and Chechen terror organizations.

While the KGB was highly regarded for its ability to infiltrate institutions perceived hostile to the Soviet Union, present Russian intelligence efforts to infiltrate Chechnya have largely failed. Commentators assign this failure to the fact that close-knit Chechen society remains a difficult breeding ground for informants. As noted above, intelligence gathering largely depends on the infiltration of sources into specifically identified communities and organizations; Russia's inability to achieve this in Chechnya has negatively affected counterterrorism strategy and tactics.

Issues to Consider

1. Does the inability to infiltrate terror organizations suggest that nations should not conduct counterterrorism?
2. What is the proper relationship between Barak's "self-imposed restraints" and the legitimate need to conduct counterterrorism when human rights abuses may be inevitable given the lack of specific intelligence information?
3. Can signal intelligence alone provide sufficient basis for counterterrorism operations?

Limited human intelligence-gathering capabilities hinder person-specific counterterrorism. In contrast to Israel's operational counterterrorism—largely dependent on human intelligence—Russia's difficulty in developing sources within Chechen terror cells limits the military's ability to conduct similar counterterrorism. Nevertheless, Russia's counterterrorism efforts have been successful against specific individuals (albeit on a limited basis). The targeted killings of Chechen Presidents Dzhokha Dudayev on April 21, 1996 and Maskhadov on March 8, 2005 were the result of traceable satellite phones rather than improved on-the-ground intelligence. These successful operations are the most notable exceptions to Russia's intelligence failures.

Arguably, the widely reported human rights abuses by Russian soldiers are a direct result of an inability to specifically identify particular targets. Unlike

Issues to Consider

1. How much intelligence should be considered sufficient for counterterrorism operations, and what criteria should be developed?
2. Given the significant number of human rights violations reported in Chechnya, should Russian decision makers establish criteria for determining when a counterterrorism operation attack may be warranted?
3. Do attacks such as Beslan warrant "an all-out effort" even if the intelligence picture is not clear?
4. Should the lack of actionable intelligence limit operational counterterrorism measures?
5. What does Russia's limited response to Beslan suggest regarding "the limits of power"?
6. Does Beslan suggest an intelligence failure?
7. How should regimes compensate for a lack of specific actionable intelligence?
8. Are closed-clan cultures penetrable?

the Israeli High Court of Justice's judicial activism, the Russian constitutional court does not act as a "restrainer" on military decision makers.

C. RUSSIAN SUCCESS

Better intelligence, exemplified by the following incident, enables the Russian forces to successfully execute pinpoint operational counterterrorism. The results are clear—legitimate targets are attacked, while human rights violations are minimized. The difference between accurate intelligence and an incomplete picture is "night and day" from both a tactical and strategic perspective.

Russian intelligence capabilities remain a mixed bag, though Russia has shown the ability to develop and utilize sources close to Chechen terrorist leaders. By using tactics similar to Israel—financial renumeration of informants—to gain information that facilitates person-specific counterterrorism, Russia has made significant strides.

Acting on a tip from within the target's own network, police killed Chechen leader Abdul-Khalim Sadulayev during a raid on a hideout in his hometown. Sadulayev had been planning a terror attack in Argun to coincide with the Group of Eight summit of leading industrialized nations in St. Petersburg.

Similarly, Shamil Basayev, the Chechen leader responsible for the Beslan school massacre, was killed by Russian security forces with the help of an informant who was paid $600,000. Although security forces were very tight-lipped about the circumstances of Basayev's death, he was clearly betrayed by one of his own men.

Issues to Consider

1. Reliable intelligence information directly contributes to successful, person-specific counterterrorism; when such intelligence does not exist, should governments refrain from acting operationally?
2. The lack of actionable intelligence has undoubtedly resulted in significant human rights abuses and minimal operational successes. What should the baseline be for determining that intelligence is actionable?

The killings of the two Chechen leaders suggest a change in the Russian authorities' ability to penetrate the closed-clan culture of Chechnya. These two attacks indicate a policy more akin to the U.S.'s and Israel's targeted killing policies, rather than an indiscriminate response that previously characterized Russian strategy. In these two attacks, the combination of pinpoint counterterrorism with previously discussed international law principles suggests greater sensitivity to blowback.

VII. INDIA

This section addresses intelligence gathering in the context of terror arising in Pakistan and the northwestern Indian states of Jammu and Kashmir.

A. KARGIL CONFLICT

In May of 1999, Pakistan crossed the Line of Control (the mutually agreed-upon boundary between India and Pakistan) and invaded India in the area commonly referred to as Kargil. The resulting skirmishes, which lasted through the summer, killed 474 Indian military personnel and wounded an additional 1,109.[39] The "Kargil Conflict" garnered international attention primarily because of India's and Pakistan's mutual nuclear capability. Though concerns of a nuclear standoff never materialized, the conflict brought to the forefront issues surrounding Indian state security. While not an act of terrorism, but an armed attack by a sovereign state, the incident contributed to widespread review and analysis regarding India's intelligence agencies. As India readily admitted in the aftermath of the conflict, the attack came as a total surprise to the Indian government.

In response, India created the Kargil Committee, which released a report addressing how Pakistan was able to move troops into Indian territory without

39. Harinder Baweja, *Nineteen Years After a Hard-Fought Victory in Kargil, is India Better Prepared Today?*, Scroll.in, July 26, 2018, *available at* https://scroll.in/article/887936/nineteen-years-after-a-hard-fought-victory-in-kargil-is-india-better-prepared-today (last visited February 19, 2024).

the Indian government's detection. The Committee announced that all government agencies charged with intelligence gathering had failed in their mission.

The report determined that the technological weakness of the Indian intelligence community made the prevention of conflicts difficult.[40] The committee found serious lapses in the "collection, collation, and assessment of intelligence" that had "no mechanism for tasking the agencies, monitoring their performance, and reviewing their records to evaluate their quality. Nor is there any oversight of the overall functioning of the agencies."[41] In short, the committee perceived that the lack of technology available to recognize the deployment of troops into the Kargil region, coupled with the lack of an organized approach to intelligence gathering within India's government, made prevention of the Kargil Conflict and future similar attacks difficult, if not impossible.

Issues to Consider

1. What are the similarities and differences between the Kargil Report and the 9/11 Commission?
2. How does the Indian government address "source intelligence" failure?
3. Is there an effective way to organize the intelligence agencies within the executive branch?
4. If SIGINT is unavailable and HUMINT is limited, what alternative measures can be developed?
5. India is forced to develop counterterrorism strategy in response to the actions of another sovereign nation; what are the limits of intelligence gathering when the focus is a nation rather than a terrorist organization?
6. If Kashmir is disputed territory to which both India and Pakistan lay claim, what is the danger in aggressively developing human intelligence sources there?

Similar to how 9/11 and the Spanish train station bombings drew attention to failings of the United States' and Spain's intelligence gathering, respectively, Pakistan's attack in Kargil highlights failings in India's intelligence gathering and analysis. A 2002 paper addressed the Kargil Conflict and echoed the Kargil Committee's discovery of issues endemic to Indian Intelligence Agencies.[42] The paper cited the following problems:

> Lack of control: The Indian situation is characteristic of a highly bureaucratized and politicized outside control and a loose, largely undefined set of rules

40. *Id.*
41. *Id.*
42. Surinder Rana & Dr. James J Wirtz, *Kargil Conflict A Systemic and an Intelligence Failure,* Center for Contemporary Conflict (Sept. 2002).

governing the inner functioning of intelligence agencies. There is no legal, constitutional or legislative control of intelligence in India.

Lack of coordination: Indian intelligence agencies are known to be working at cross-purposes, without any visible lack of coordination.

India's political establishment also focused on heightened terrorist activity in Jammu and Kashmir and thus ruled out major armed incursion. Indian intelligence agencies had continued to direct their efforts based upon prevailing national threat perception in the early 1999, which did not foresee Kargil. Hence, if there was a failure the entire system had failed.[43]

B. 2006 MUMBAI TRAIN BOMBING

On July 11, 2006, a series of 7 explosions killed at least 174 people on crowded commuter trains and stations in the Indian financial capital of Mumbai. The victims, like many of those in the 9/11 attacks, were middle-class business persons. The bombing of seven trains, during rush hour traffic in Mumbai, also revealed similar vulnerabilities within Indian intelligence networks. Not only did the act reflect significant SIGINT and HUMINT failings, but India's unfocused response reflected poor intelligence. As the report below indicates, weak intelligence capabilities can frequently result in abuse and frustration in and among the general populace.

> Teams of armed officers continued with their mass round-ups yesterday, with further raids on a number of shanty towns around Bombay. So far they have detained more than 1,300 men, but the police face mounting public criticism at their failure to arrest anyone involved in the terror network that is believed to have been living in India's financial capital for at least three months.[44]

More importantly, and similar to Russia's historical experience in Chechnya, poor intelligence sends a message to civilians and terrorists alike that the state is unable to prevent the attacks.

Issues to Consider

1. Is India's intelligence-gathering ability inherently limited by the Pakistani threat?
2. Why should a constant threat limit domestic intelligence gathering?
3. Is the "wall" referred to in the 9/11 Commission relevant to the Indian experience?

C. 2008 MUMBAI ATTACKS

Arguably, the most significant intelligence failure in India occurred when ten Pakistani men associated with the terror group Lashkar-e-Tayyiba rampaged

43. *Intelligence Failure Led to Kargil,* Rediff.com, February 12, 2003, *available at* https://www.rediff.com/news/2003/feb/12kargil.htm (last visited February 19, 2024).

44. Daniel McGrory, *Train Bombers "Funded by British Businessmen,"* Bombay, July 17, 2006, *available at* https://www.thetimes.co.uk/article/top-ten-articles-online-monday-july-17-9nh2mtwmw9q (last visited February 19, 2024).

through Mumbai over the course of four days. A series of attacks took place at the Chhatrapati Shivaji Terminus rail station, Cafe Leopold, Cama and Albless Hospital, Nariman House (a Jewish community center), and Taj Mahal Palace and Tower Hotel, killing approximately 200 people and wounding many more.

Issues to Consider

1. Should different standards for determining invasion of privacy be applied to threats emanating from different sources (international/Pakistan; domestic/Sikhs; disputed/Kashmir)?
2. What are the similarities and differences between the U.S. response to 9/11 and India's response to Kargil?

Without providing military commanders and decision makers an accurate assessment, intelligence officials have not fulfilled their responsibility. India recognized the need for the development of broad-based intelligence gathering capabilities. The examples discussed in this section largely draw attention to systemic and institutional weaknesses. How India continues to revamp its intelligence services while coping with legislative restrictions and facing complex threats will significantly affect operational counterterrorism measures in years ahead.

VIII. SPAIN

A. REORGANIZATION

The 2004 Madrid train bombing exposed overwhelming HUMINT and SIGINT failures in Spain's intelligence community. The intelligence gathering and analysis picture in Spain remains unclear.

According to the Spanish Criminal Code, the government "must obtain court approval before searching private property, wiretapping, or interfering with private correspondence."[45] The antiterrorist law gives discretionary authority to the Minister of the Interior to act prior to obtaining court approval in "cases of emergency."[46] In spite of statutory authorization to conduct wiretapping surveillance, the Spanish authorities failed to monitor conversations of those involved in planning the train station bombing. Spanish authorities' failure to monitor conversations indicated a misperception regarding the desire and ability of Islamic terrorists to commit an attack. Reports, such as the one below, suggest that Spain may be reorganizing the intelligence community's use of SIGINT.

---

45. *Country Reports on Human Rights Practices for 1995, Spain,* U.S. Department of State, *available at* https://www.refworld.org/docid/3ae6aa3e1c.html (last visited February 19, 2024).

46. *Country Reports on Human Rights Practices 2000,* U.S. Department of State, released by the Bureau of Democracy, Human Rights, and Labor, Feb. 23, 2001, *available at* https://2009-2017.state.gov/j/drl/rls/hrrpt/2000/eur/875.htm (last visited December 25, 2023).

Defence Conceals a Satellite Spy Station in the Sierra of Madrid

Jan. 28, 2003[47]

Although it seems surprising, telephone taps in Spain were not regulated until roughly a year ago, when the National Intelligence Centre laws were passed. With this new legislation Spanish spies—wary since such scandalous cases as that of the CESID tapping—have to obtain authorisation to interfere in the communications of a Spanish citizen from a High Court judge. But they also have the obligation the spy on and analyse the so-called "signal traffic" of a strategic nature, as has already been mentioned. This means that they can spy on international communications, provided that the taps do not affect Spanish citizens.

Nevertheless, it is surprising to observe how, coinciding with the approval of the NIC laws, the Ministry of Defence created the Armed Forces Intelligence Centre. Oddly, the AFIC is not regulated by any law, nor will it be in the future. Official defence sources confirm that a ministerial order will be published that will simply be limited to specifying the internal organisation of the Centre, but nothing else. Last December, the minister Federico Trillo made a pact regarding the Strategic Defence Review with the PSOE, the Spanish Socialist Party, that envisaged enabling "the process of rationalising the intelligence capabilities of the Defence, Army and Navy Staff, initiated with the creation of the Armed Forces Intelligence Centre."

The same document also mentions that "in order to face up to terrorism coming from beyond our borders, it will be necessary to make use of the capabilities of the Armed Force." Trillo emphasised, before the Congress Defence Committee, that military intelligence will only be orientated towards the cases of "a military threat abroad" and the "theatre of intelligence." However, he also acknowledged that the AFIC will not operate separately from the NIC, since its director Jorge Dezcallar will coordinate its activities. This aspect had already been established in the NIC Act, where it states that one of the missions of its directors is to "maintain and develop (. . .) the collaboration with the information services of the State Security Forces and Bodies and the organs of the civil and military administration that are relevant for intelligence objectives."

But while the NIC is authorised by law to spy on so-called "signal traffic," it is very possible that this institution has delegated the presumed espionage activities that are carried on at the Fresnedillas-Navalagamella base and the Conil chalet to the Army. This is because if a Spanish citizen falls through the "cracks" in the system, albeit by accident, the NIC would be breaking the law that obliges it to obtain prior authorisation to make taps from the High Court. Nevertheless, intelligence sources confirm that the concealed Conil de la Frontera operation continues in the hands of the NIC, that inherited it from the CESID. So, the Spanish intelligence agency could be acting against the the law if it also spies on Spanish citizens from there.

47. *Available at* http://cryptome.org/echelon-es.htm (last visited March 14, 2010).

With respect to the alleged tapping carried out at Fresnedillas, the same sources assures us that the installation was never under the control of CESID, but rather was run by the army. This detail would confirm the thesis that CIFAS is currently coordinating the activities that are carried on there. It seems clear that this would be the case because, if military officials are spying on a Spanish citizen, although they may not have intentionally intercepted his communications, nobody would have to give explanations before the courts or before Parliament as a result of this infringement of the fundamental rights to the inviolability of communications.

Years before, CESID had carte blanche to do what it wanted and it did so. It is now very possible that the NIC activities are more controlled thanks to the laws that regulate its functioning. But there is also the AFIC that can be entrusted with doing the "dirty work." Thus, we are in the same position as before, with the sole difference that the intelligence services have changed their name.

Issues to Consider

1. If Spanish authorities view terrorism through the prism of the criminal law paradigm, how can actionable counterterrorism intelligence be gathered?
2. Given Spain's determination that counterterrorism is criminal in nature, how do Spanish intelligence-gathering operations differ from those of the United States, Israel, and Russia?

According to a variety of Spanish government reports and media sources, Spain has become "the gateway to Europe for North Africans."[48] Successful intelligence gathering by the Spanish authorities depends upon an ability to infiltrate the immigrant or transient communities that support such attacks. The following excerpt highlights Spain's attempt to control this situation.

> The profile of Melilla, Ceuta and Andalucia, as "hosts" to Islamist terrorist activities, demonstrates the degree to which various terrorist groups have penetrated mainstream Spanish cities and populations. Several significant counterterrorism operations in 2005 (resulting in the arrest of approximately 85 individuals) netted an al Qaeda cell with a nucleus in Andalucia, as well as GSPC members dispersed throughout southern Spain. Of significance, Spanish police arrested a Moroccan national, Bahbah El H. (last name not available) in Nerja, Malaga, who had formerly been the imam of a mosque in Ceuta. It is also important to note that the "first Spanish Taliban," Hamed Abderrahaman

48. *See* Kathryn Haahr, *Emerging Terrorist Trends in Spain's Moroccan Communities,* 4 Terrorism Monitor, May 4, 2006, *available at* https://jamestown.org/program/emerging-terrorist-trends-in-spains-moroccan-communities/ (last visited December 25, 2023); Rebecca Williams, *Spain Becomes New Migrant Gateway to Europe from Africa*, Sky news, August 25, 2017, *available at* https://news.sky.com/story/spain-becomes-new-migrant-gateway-to-europe-from-africa-11004404 (last visited February 19, 2024).

Ahmed, was from Ceuta. He spent two years at Guantanamo Bay on suspicions of being an "enemy combatant" allied to al Qaeda.

As a result of the increasing presence of Islamists in the enclaves and Andalucia, Spanish security authorities have deployed counterterrorism agents to Ceuta, Melilla and other cities in southern Spain. As part of their activities, they have stepped up efforts to identify Islamic extremists among the thousands of Spanish Muslims who attend mosques in the two enclaves and Andalucia. According to press reports, the Spanish security services have monitored all of the mosques in Ceuta and Melilla and "analyzed the number of Muslims who attended them, as well as the profile of each of the adherents"

(El Mundo, November 24, 2001; El Pueblo de Ceuta, December 20, 2005). Spanish security officials continue to worry that members of al Qaeda will take advantage of the clandestine immigration pipeline route by inserting terrorists to make their way to either the enclaves or to the Spanish mainland. To prevent this, the Directorate General of National police recently advertised 357 posts for anti-terrorist officers to monitor potential Islamists in areas where the presence of Muslim immigrants is well known, such as Melilla, Ceuta, Granada, Malaga and Alicante.[49]

Issues to Consider

1. Much like the challenge Russian authorities face in Chechnya, Spanish authorities face the difficulty of infiltrating traditionally closed immigrant or transient communities. How can they overcome this difficulty?
2. How should Spain develop a network of sources that provides actionable intelligence?
3. In the aftermath of the Madrid train bombing, are civil liberties more likely to be breached?
4. Does the fact that the perpetrators of the train bombings resided in Spain prior to the attack suggest that Spanish intelligence-gathering operations should be significantly different than those implemented in the United States?

Islamic fundamentalists living in Spain carried out the Madrid train bombings. Similar to the 2005 London train bombings, the 2007 attack on the Glasgow airport, and the plan in 2006 to simultaneously blow up 13 commercial airline jets on trans-Atlantic routes, the train bombing was conducted by al Qaeda terrorists who were living in the country legally. According to a Spanish government report:

> The group that carried out the 11 March attacks was not linked directly to al Qaeda or any other international terrorist network, although its members claimed to be al Qaeda followers. The group consisted of legal residents of

49. *Id.*

Madrid, mostly of Moroccan origin, who had gradually come to embrace the radical ideology of international jihad, mainly based on information found on radical Islamist websites. They financed their operations through common criminal activities, such as shoplifting, theft and narcotics trading. The material used in the 13 improvised explosive devices was procured within Spain.[50]

B. SPAIN AND INTELLIGENCE GATHERING

Prior to the train station bombing, the Spanish authorities' primary human intelligence gathering was directed towards Basque terrorism. Initially, the Spanish government responded to the train attack on the assumption that ETA was responsible and ignored the possibility that Islamic terrorists were responsible for killing 191 people.

The attack reflects the operational capability of terrorists, both in planning and execution. It also points to a massive intelligence failure similar to 9/11. Analysts failed to predict the train bombings, suggesting a need to develop a network of sources in the relevant communities and to monitor, via electronic surveillance, suspected terrorists planning additional attacks in Spain.

Issues to Consider

1. What legal and institutional changes should be made in the aftermath of the Spanish intelligence failure?
2. What lessons regarding intelligence gathering can be learned from the experience of other nations?
3. Does an intelligence failure of this magnitude require restructuring existing intelligence mechanisms?
4. Does such an attack justify changing domestic laws?
5. What are the standards necessary to obtain authorization to interfere in the communications of a Spanish citizen from a High Court judge?

IX. CHINA

In addition to gathering basic intelligence deemed essential for purposes of public order and national security, Chinese intelligence officials target specific domestic groups. In this regard, their methods are similar to the other surveyed nations. However, in contrast—both philosophically and practically—the Chinese model is based on traditional information gathering methods such as human intelligence and also what has been termed "subtle spying" based on obtaining information a "little bit at a time"[51] from alternative sources.

50. *Lessons Learned from Recent Terrorist Attacks: Building National Capabilities and Institutions,* NRC Conference Ljubljana, Slovenia, Chairman's Report, *available at* http://www.nato.int/docu/conf/2005/050727/ (last visited October 8, 2010).

51. Paul Moore, *China's Subtle Spying,* N.Y. Times, Sept. 2, 1999.

In studying China's intelligence methods, the U.S. Commission on China noted that a common tactic used by China was to encourage foreign scientific experts to attend conferences in China as means to gather information. That is, in addition to traditional sources, the Chinese intelligence community also relies on external sources to provide information, contributing to a more complete intelligence picture.

The Ministry of State Security and Military Intelligence Department of the People's Liberation Army primarily gather intelligence. The Ministry of State Security is the civilian intelligence agency with responsibility for foreign and domestic security and intelligence operations. In addition, it has a role in counterintelligence, often engaging in surveillance and suppression of groups considered opposing government policy; these groups include dissidents and ethnic groups.[52] The Ministry of State Security uses the news media as cover, often sending agents abroad as correspondents for state news agencies.

A. USE OF THE INTERNET FOR INTELLIGENCE

INTEGRATED NETWORK ELECTRONIC WARFARE: CHINA'S NEW CONCEPT OF INFORMATION WARFARE

Deepak Sharma April 2010[53]

Network-Centric Warfare (NCW) now commonly called Network-Centric Operations is a universal military doctrine or theory of war. It seeks to translate an information advantage, enabled in part by information technology, into a competitive war fighting advantage through the robust networking of well informed geographically dispersed forces. To achieve tenants of NCW a robust and reliable multi-layered communication network for flow of information and integration of sensors, shooters and command and control elements, is an essential requirement of any force of the future.

The government of the People's Republic of China (PRC) is a decade into a sweeping military modernization program that has fundamentally transformed its ability to fight high tech wars. The Chinese military, using increasingly networked forces capable of communicating across service arms and among all echelons of command, is pushing beyond its traditional missions focused on Taiwan and toward a more regional defence posture. This modernization effort, known as informationization, is guided by the doctrine of fighting "Local War Under Informationized Conditions," which refers to the PLA's ongoing effort to develop a fully networked architecture capable of coordinating military operations on land, in air, at sea, in space and across the electromagnetic spectrum.

52. *China's Algorithms of Repression,* Human Rights Watch (May 1, 2019) https://www.hrw.org/report/2019/05/01/chinas-algorithms-repression/reverse-engineering-xinjiang-police-mass (last visited March 13, 2024).

53. *Available at* https://www.idsa.in/system/files/jds_4_2_dsharma.pdf (last visited December 25, 2023).

Issues to Consider

1. What are the costs and benefits of computer-intensive intelligence gathering?
2. Is signal intelligence a substitute for human intelligence?
3. What, if any, limits can be imposed on signal intelligence (with respect to privacy)?
4. Does signal intelligence pose a threat to national sovereignty?
5. Do the methods mentioned by the U.S. Commission on China suggest effective intelligence-gathering?

B. TARGETING CHINESE DISSIDENT GROUPS

The Office for Foreign Propaganda/State Council Information Office manages sensitive news stories and guides the Chinese media during major events, especially those affecting ethnic minorities and internal violence. The following report discusses the government's influence on sources and online censorship.

Media Censorship in China

Beina Xu and Eleanor Albert Feb. 17, 2017[54]

More than a dozen government bodies review and enforce laws related to information flow within, into, and out of China. The most powerful monitoring body is the Communist Party's Central Propaganda Department (CPD), which coordinates with General Administration of Press and Publication and State Administration of Radio, Film, and Television to ensure content promotes party doctrine. Ng says that the various ministries once functioned as smaller fiefdoms of control, but have recently been more consolidated under the State Council Information Office, which has taken the lead on internet monitoring.

The Chinese government employs large numbers of people to monitor and censor China's media. Experts refer to an October 2013 report in a state-run paper, the *Beijing News*, which said more than two million workers are responsible for reviewing internet posts using keyword searches and compiling reports for "decision makers." These so-called "public opinion analysts" are hired both by the state and private companies to constantly monitor China's internet. Additionally, the CPD gives media outlets editorial guidelines as well as directives restricting coverage of politically sensitive topics. In one high-profile incident involving the liberal Guangdong magazine *Southern Weekly*, government censors rewrote the paper's New Year's message from a call for reform to a tribute to the Communist Party. The move triggered mass demonstrations by the staff and general public, who demanded the

54. *Available at* https://www.cfr.org/backgrounder/media-censorship-china (last updated February 17, 2017).

resignation of the local propaganda bureau chief. While staff and censors reached a compromise that theoretically intended to relax some controls, much of the censorship remained in place.

The Chinese government deploys myriad ways of censoring the internet. The Golden Shield Project, colloquially known as the Great Firewall, is the center of the government's online censorship and surveillance effort. Its methods include bandwidth throttling, keyword filtering, and blocking access to certain websites. According to Reporters Without Borders, the firewall makes large-scale use of Deep Packet Inspection technology to block access based on keyword detection. As Ng points out, the government also employs a diverse range of methods to induce journalists to censor themselves, including dismissals and demotions, libel lawsuits, fines, arrests, and forced televised confessions.

Issues to Consider

1. What are the risks of targeting one group?
2. Does limiting the media aid or hinder China? How?

X. COLOMBIA

A. INTRODUCTION

The Administrative Security Department (DAS), has, until recently, been Colombia's main intelligence-gathering organization. Created in the early 1950s and reorganized in 1960, it has been responsible for providing security to individuals, police services for the judiciary, and counterintelligence services against both domestic and foreign threats.

B. INTELLIGENCE SCANDAL

In 2008, the Colombia media revealed that DAS had been gathering intelligence on politicians, human rights groups, journalists, clergy, unions, and Supreme Court justices. The operation was revealed when a news magazine obtained an intercept of a phone call between an attorney and the Supreme Court justice investigating President Uribe's supporters' ties to paramilitary death squads. The surveillance consisted of tapping phones, reading emails, watching people's homes, studying people's routines, and supplementing gathered information with banking, immigration, and driver's license records. The surveillance focused on individuals and families, even going so far as to investigate which schools children attended.

The operation's goal was aimed at undermining the activities of individuals perceived to oppose the government. There was no indication that the operation was intended to investigate guerrilla ties or threats to national security.

2009 Human Rights Reports: Colombia

Mar. 11, 2010[55]

The law prohibits such actions; while the government generally respected these prohibitions in practice, there were notable exceptions by some intelligence agencies. The law requires government authorities to obtain a warrant signed by a senior prosecutor to enter a private home without the owner's consent unless the suspect has been caught in hot pursuit, and government authorities generally adhered to these regulations.

Government authorities generally need a judicial order to intercept mail or monitor telephone conversations, even in prisons. However, government intelligence agencies investigating terrorist organizations sometimes monitored telephone conversations without judicial authorization, although evidence obtained in such a manner could not be used in court.

Surveillance by the DAS of high court magistrates, journalists, human rights organizations and activists, opposition leaders, and the Vice Presidency prompted an investigation by the CTI. Press reports indicated DAS surveillance included physical monitoring of individuals and their families, phone and e-mail intercepts, and collection of personal and financial data. A CTI report described a twofold strategy to mount prosecutions against the victims of the surveillance and to disrupt human rights groups' activities through "offensive intelligence." According to a publication released by the National and International Campaign for the Right to Defend Human Rights, examples of DAS harassment included operations involving diverse attacks, setups, and death threats. Former DAS director Jorge Noguera and deputy director Jose Narvaez were under investigation for colluding with paramilitary members to instigate the murders of three unionists, a college professor, and a journalist. The Prosecutor General's Office launched a separate investigation into the wiretapping scandal, and 34 DAS employees were under investigation, 10 of whom, including four directors, were detained. Investigations into the surveillance continued at year's end.

The government continued to use voluntary civilian informants to report terrorist activities and identify terrorists. Some national and international human rights groups criticized this practice as subject to abuse and a threat to privacy and other civil liberties. In the August report of the UN secretary-general on children and armed conflict, the UN called on the government to ensure children were not used for military intelligence purposes, noting this practice puts children at risk of retaliation by illegal armed groups. The FARC publicly justified its February 4 massacre of eight Awa indigenous persons as retaliation for collaboration with the military.

In September 2009, the government announced that the DAS would be dismantled to create a new agency that would focus on intelligence and counter-intelligence involving national security. In an interview the new

55. *Available at* https://2009-2017.state.gov/j/drl/rls/hrrpt/2009/wha/136106.htm (last visited December 25, 2023).

director, Filipe Munoz, stated that he had been taking steps including stricter controls of wiretaps, firing over 120 people who were involved in the scandal, and promoting a new intelligence law.[56] He stated that had been taken decision that were politically costly and unpopular in order to do the right thing for the country and to limit the expansive power that DAS had gained. He noted "It has been difficult to focus on reforms with so many scandals emerging. Don't forget that since I started, we've not only dealt with illegal wiretaps but also the resurgence of cases of alleged DAS involvement in the deaths of [presidential candidates] Luis Carlos Galan, Carlos Pizarro and Bernardo Jaramillo, even a bomb placed aboard an Avianca airliner. All of which is to remind people that these problems involving DAS and insufficient controls didn't arise yesterday."[57]

Issues to Consider

1. How do scandals impede future intelligence gathering?
2. Would strict rules governing how intelligence is gathered aid or hinder national security and individual rights?
3. What is the impact of targeting individual leaders, or branches of the government, on national security?

56. Chris Kraul, *Colombia Spy Chief Works to Clean Up Agency,* L.A. Times, Apr. 22, 2010, *available at* http://articles.latimes.com/2010/apr/22/world/la-fg-colombia-das-qa-20100423 (last visited June 12, 2010).

57. *Id.*

CHAPTER 8

INTERROGATION OF TERRORISTS

I. INTRODUCTION

Custodial detention of terrorism suspects inevitably involves a meeting between the detainee and the interrogator. Both represent a larger entity: the terrorist is usually part of a terrorist organization, and the interrogator represents the state. Whether or not the interrogation setting balances legitimate civil liberties and the state's equally legitimate security needs, either in the immediate aftermath of a terrorist attack or when an intelligence report indicates a detained suspect has information regarding a planned attack, is the focus of this chapter. A variety of guidelines, court decisions, statutes, and international and domestic laws outline the limits of interrogation.

How are interrogators expected to receive critically needed intelligence from suspects who know the rules of the game and understand the interrogator has limited means available with which to extract the information? The interrogator must attempt to gather, quickly and under stressful conditions, important information that may prevent an attack. Under such circumstances, may the threat of an attack justify exceptions? Perhaps the interrogator's chain of command has suggested—implicitly or explicitly—that bending the rules is acceptable when lives are *potentially* at stake. The circumstances surrounding an interrogation are visceral because an interrogation usually takes place in a small, pressure-filled room, soaked with sweat and anxiety.

ISSUES TO CONSIDER

1. Who determines if and whether the situation warrants an exception?
2. What are the criteria for determining the circumstances that justify interrogation methods going beyond the norm?
3. What is, or should be, the norm?

The interrogator determines the focus of the interrogation. The detainee—whether experienced or inexperienced—constantly attempts to determine what the interrogator knows. The detainee must also gauge whether one of his associates (or someone he believed to be an associate) has betrayed him by collaborating with the authorities or by implicating him. If he has been implicated, then his capability to negotiate with the interrogator has been compromised. Since the interrogation—very much like the classic prisoner's dilemma—is largely a guessing game, the interrogator must keep the detainee off guard to elicit the essential information.

Acceptable interrogator methods are essential to this discussion. Whether the seven surveyed nations distinguish between terrorism and the criminal law is relevant to understanding how each nation defines the limits of interrogation. If the relevant paradigm is criminal law, then the detainee is entitled to protections guaranteed within the nation's criminal code. If the detainee is not subject to criminal law, then a state may conceivably relax restrictions otherwise imposed on the interrogator.

Loosening restrictions may result in significant violations of detainee rights. Furthermore, loosening restrictions does not guarantee that the information received is accurate, reliable, and operationally or legally actionable. Incorrect information received in the course of an interrogation not only negatively affects the particular investigation, but, if provided to law enforcement, may contribute to critical misallocation of limited resources. Inaccurate or incorrect information may also lead to wrongful convictions and imprisonment of innocent parties.

These issues are not only the essence of this chapter but are—in conjunction with intelligence—the heart and soul of counterterrorism. How interrogations are conducted define societies: whether decision makers and the public adopt an "anything goes" attitude or a "self-imposed restraints" approach is critical to determining how a nation balances competing interests. In the U.S. criminal law paradigm, interrogation limits have been clearly articulated by the Supreme Court. In the Prisoner of War paradigm, Geneva Convention protections extended to the captured soldier exclude the holding of a trial, unless the individual is suspected of having committed a war crime or a crime in captivity. The captured soldier is required to provide to his captors only his name, rank, and serial number.

In 1984 the United Nations adopted the Convention Against Torture (CAT);[1] 173 nations are presently signatories, and 9 have yet to ratify the treaty. With the exception of India, all of the surveyed nations have ratified the CAT. The preamble to the Convention highlights the concern regarding torture:

> **The States Parties to this Convention**
> Considering that, in accordance with the principles proclaimed in the Charter of the United Nations, recognition of the equal and inalienable rights of all

---

1. Convention Against Torture or Other Cruel, Inhuman, or Degrading Treatment or Punishment, Dec. 10, 1984, 14 U.N.T.S. 85, 23 I.L.M. 1027 (entered into force June 26, 1987) [hereinafter Convention Against Torture].

members of the human family is the foundation of freedom, justice and peace in the world,

Recognizing that those rights derive from the inherent dignity of the human person,

Considering the obligation of States under the Charter, in particular Article 55, to promote universal respect for, and observance of, human rights and fundamental freedoms,

Having regard to article 5 of the Universal Declaration of Human Rights and article 7 of the International Covenant on Civil and Political Rights, both of which provide that no one may be subjected to torture or to cruel, inhuman or degrading treatment or punishment,

Having regard also to the Declaration on the Protection of All Persons from Being Subjected to Torture and Other Cruel, Inhuman or Degrading Treatment or Punishment, adopted by the General Assembly on 9 December 1975

Desiring to make more effective the struggle against torture and other cruel, inhuman or degrading treatment or punishment throughout the world, have agreed as follows. . . .[2]

II. INTERROGATION: LIMITS AND CONSIDERATIONS

The "ticking time bomb" has been mentioned frequently in the context of terrorism-related interrogations, suggesting the following scenario: a terrorist organization is planning a major attack that, if successful, would result in the deaths of thousands of innocent civilians. According to this scenario, law enforcement officials have detained an individual believed to possess information capable of foiling the plan were he to divulge the necessary information. Some scholars posit such a scenario might serve as a justifiable exception to international law and domestic legislation outlawing torture.[3] The argument propounded by Alan Dershowitz[4] suggests that in the context of a ticking time bomb, a judicial warrant should be issued enabling an exception to the prohibition on torture.

While the fact pattern is perhaps feasible from a "Hollywood" perspective, according to professional interrogators the chances of detaining *the one* individual capable of foiling such a plan are close to zero. As will be discussed later, the Israel High Court of Justice criticized the General Security Services' (today, Israel Security Agency) liberal use of the expression "ticking time bomb," which had become a dangerous catch-all phrase.[5]

2. *Id.*

3. *See* Phillip N.S. Rumney, *Is Coercive Interrogation of Terrorist Suspects Effective: A Response to Bagaric and Clarke,* 40 U.S.F. L. Rev. 479 (2006).

4. Alan Dershowitz has been the leading advocate of the so-called "torture warrant," whereby a detainee may be tortured under court order in severe circumstances. Similarly, the "ticking time bomb" has been cited as justifying an exception to the no-torture rule. *See* Alan M. Dershowitz, *The Torture Warrant: A Response to Professor Strauss,* 48 N.Y.L. Sch. L. Rev. 275 (2004).

5. H.C. 5100/94, Public Comm. Against Torture in Israel v. State of Israel & General Sec. Serv., ¶16, *available at* http://www.derechos.org/human-rights/mena/doc/torture.html (last visited July 10, 2010).

While the phrase was perhaps convenient from the perspective of the intelligence services, the Court believed it inevitably contributed to civil rights violations.

In determining the limits of interrogation, the efficacy of torture must be examined. That is, does torture work, and is it justified from an operational perspective? In analyzing torture and detention, one must note that the interrogation paradigm is not limited solely to the actual questioning of the detainee. Rather, interrogation must be understood in its wider context, from the moment the individual is brought to a detention center and the doors are literally and figuratively closed behind him. For example, the U.S. interrogation methods in the aftermath of 9/11 included mistreatment both by prison guards and interrogators: the former captured in the now infamous pictures from Abu Ghraib; and the latter in using interrogation measures that included water boarding. For example, Khalid Sheik Mohammed, one of the principal 9/11 planners, was water boarded over 150 times. President Obama's Executive Order (2009) forbade implementation of previously authorized aggressive interrogation measures and eliminated the exception to those techniques carved out for non-military personnel in the 2006 Military Commissions Act.

Issues to Consider

1. In a democracy, who is responsible for determining the limits of interrogation?
2. How should we monitor interrogators?
3. How should the "ticking time bomb" be defined?
4. Should society adopt a "don't know, don't tell" policy with respect to interrogations?
5. What is the acceptable loss of life in the no-torture proposition?
6. Should the limits of interrogation under criminal law be applied to interrogation in counterterrorism?

One must understand the universality of this dilemma. While cultural differences exist from country to country and from legal regime to legal regime, the basic moral quandary must be addressed by the leadership of each country: what are the limits of interrogation of detainees suspected of involvement in terrorism?

III. UNITED STATES

Reported instances of torture during interrogation in the Abu Ghraib detention facility received much attention:

> Seven members of the U.S. Armed Forces have been convicted . . . for severe violations committed at Abu Ghraib scandal. Graner is the only soldier still imprisoned in connection with the case. The Pentagon cleared four of five top

officers overseeing prison policies, and operations of wrongdoing. One brigadier general was relieved of her command and given a written reprimand.[6]

Interrogation policies implemented by the Bush administration violated both the Geneva Convention and U.S. domestic law. In a memo written by Assistant Attorney General Jay S. Bybee to White House General Counsel Alberto Gonzales, Bybee stated that Geneva Convention protections do not pertain to the detainees.[7]

Two independent investigations, the Schlesinger commission and an internal Army review, contain important and disturbing information regarding torture and mistreatment of prisoners in Afghanistan, Iraq, and Guantanamo.[8] While U.S. law forbids torture, the Bybee memo—combined with subsequent statements and actions by the Bush administration—created a climate where basic violations of human rights were acceptable, if not encouraged.

When ratifying CAT, the U.S. Senate made the Convention subject to its own definition of torture:

> [I]n order to constitute torture, an act must be specifically intended to inflict severe physical or mental pain or suffering and that mental pain or suffering refers to prolonged mental harm caused by or resulting from: the intentional infliction or threatened infliction of severe physical pain or suffering; the administration or application, or threatened administration or application, of mind altering substances or other procedures calculated to disrupt profoundly the senses or the personality; the threat of imminent death; or the threat that another person will imminently be subjected to death, severe physical pain or suffering, or the administration or application of mind-altering substances or other procedures calculated to disrupt profoundly the senses or personality.[9]

The Bybee memo addressed the relationship between international and domestic law with respect to defining torture in the context of the war on terror.

> You have asked for our Office's views regarding the standards of conduct under the Convention Against Torture and Other Cruel, Inhuman and Degrading Treatment or Punishment as implemented by Sections 2340-2340(A) of Title 18 of the United States Code. As we understand it, this question has arisen in the context of interrogations outside the United States. We conclude below that Section 2340(A) proscribes acts inflicting, and that are specifically intended to inflict, severe pain or suffering, whether mental or physical. Those acts must be of an extreme nature to rise to the level of torture within the meaning of Section 2340(A) and the Convention. We further conclude that certain acts may be cruel, inhuman or degrading but still not produce pain and suffering of the requisite intensity to fall within Section 2340(A)'s proscription against

6. Daniel Nasaw, *Report Vindicates Soldiers Prosecuted over Abu Ghraib Abuses, Lawyers Say,* Guardian. Co. UK., Apr. 22, 2009.

7. *See* Memorandum from Jay S. Bybee, Assistant Attorney General, to Alberto R. Gonzales, Counsel to the President and William J. Haynes II, General Counsel for the Department of Defense, Re: Application of Treaties and Laws to al Qaeda and Taliban Detainees, January 22, 2002, *available at* http://www.washingtonpost.com/wp-srv/nation/documents/012202bybee.pdf (last visited December 30. 2023) (on file with author).

8. *See* James Ross, *Hold Officials Responsible,* USA Today, August 27, 2004, *available at* http://www.hrw.org/english/docs/2004/08/27/usdom9275.htm (last visited December 30, 2023).

9. *Quoted in* Sanford Levinson, *Brutal Logic,* Village Voice, May 18, 2004, at 27.

> torture. We conclude by examining possible defenses that would negate any claim that certain interrogation methods violate the Statute. . . .
>
> To violate Section 2340 (A) the statute requires that severe pain and suffering must inflicted with specific intent. In order for a defendant to have acted with specific intent, he must expressly intend to achieve the forbidden act. . . .
>
> Here, because Section 2340 requires that the defendant act with the specific intent to inflict severe pain, the infliction of such pain must be the defendant's precise objective. . . . If the defendant acted knowing that severe pain or suffering was reasonably likely to result from his actions, but no more, he would have acted only with general intent.[10]

William J. Haynes, the General Counsel of the Department of Defense, wrote the following regarding interrogation measures:

> Specifically, with regard to Category I techniques, the use of mild and fear related approaches such as yelling at the detainees is not illegal because in order to communicate a threat, there must also exist an intent to injure. . . .
>
> With regard to Category II methods, the use of stress positions such as the proposed standing for four hours, the use of isolation for up to thirty days and interrogation the detainees in an environment other than the standard interrogation booth are all legally permissible so long as no severe physical pain is inflicted and prolonged mental harm intended, and because there is a legitimate governmental objective in obtaining the information necessary that the high value detainees on which these methods would be utilized possess, for the protection of the national security of the United States, its citizens, and allies.
>
> With respect to the Category III advanced counter-resistance strategies, the use of scenarios designed to convince the detainee that death or severely painful consequences are imminent is not illegal for the same aforementioned reasons that there is a compelling governmental interest and it is not done intentionally to cause prolonged harm.[11]

While American soldiers were court-martialed for abusing civilians, their actions were clearly the result of government policy. The following report submitted to the United Nations further indicates how U.S. policy shaped and enabled such abuse.

Torture by the United States

The World Organization for Human Rights USA, Jan. 2005[12]

III. Introduction

In particular, through legal memoranda prepared at the highest levels of the U.S. Government, official sanction has been given to carrying out torture for the purpose of detaining and obtaining information from suspected terrorists that presumably might prevent future or imminent acts of terrorism from

---

10. Memorandum for Alberto R. Gonzales *Re: Standards of Conduct for Interrogation under 18 U.S.C. Section 2340-2340(A), available at* http://www.washingtonpost.com/wp-srv/nation/documents/dojinterrogationmemo20020801.pdf (last visited December 30. 2023).

11. William J. Haynes II, *Action Memo on Counter-Resistance Strategies, available at* http://www.washingtonpost.com/wp-srv/nation/documents/dodmemos.pdf (last visited December 30, 2023).

12. The Status of Compliance by the U.S. Government with International Convention Against Torture and Other Cruel, Inhuman and Degrading Treatment or Punishment *submitted to* United Nations Committee Against Torture, January 2005, *available at* http://www2.ohchr.org/english/bodies/hrc/docs/ngos/wohr.pdf (last visited March 20, 2010).

taking place. Among the specific acts of torture and violations of CAT that have taken place are . . . the following:

- severe physical and psychological abuse of detainees in Abu Ghraib prison in Iraq, and in other detention and interrogation facilities in that country, Afghanistan, and Guantanamo Bay, Cuba;
- "rendition to torture" to other countries for purposes of interrogation of hundreds of individuals suspected of terrorist ties, including at least one known U.S. citizen, Ahmed Abu Ali, who has been detained in Saudi Arabia for over 17 months at the request of the U.S. government, and one Canadian citizen, Maher Arar, who was sent to Syria by the United States for over a year after being detained by U.S. authorities while in transit to his home country of Canada;
- indefinite, arbitrary detention, without a lawful determination of status other than the President's designation of their being "unlawful enemy combatants," of more than 600 detainees in the Guantanamo Bay, Cuba military base;
- execution by torture and other unlawful, extra-judicial means of upwards of 37 detainees being held for interrogation purposes;
- use of unlawfully constituted military tribunals to prosecute suspected terrorists and to keep them detained and subject to interrogation for prolonged periods; and
- maintenance of an undetermined number of "ghost" detainees in secret facilities without charges being filed against them, and without their whereabouts or status being reported to any recognized authorities.

Issues to Consider

1. What benefits would policy makers seek to achieve from practices of torture and detainee abuse?
2. How would the effectiveness of this policy be determined?
3. How is the reliability of information received from torture-based interrogation to be assessed?
4. Did 9/11 justify the policy articulated by the memos?
5. What controls should be imposed on guards and interrogators?
6. What is the long-term impact of a torture-based interrogation regime?

According to a Council of Foreign Relations report:

Lawrence Shoup, The Council on Foreign Relations Helps Shape Imperial Strategy

The Council on Foreign Relations Debates on Torture, Mar./Apr. 2006[13]

. . . The abuse, torture, and murder at Abu Ghraib and Guantanamo Bay, Cuba ("Gitmo") have been most reported on, but what is most revealing about both locations and the "Salt Pit" U.S. torture center in Afghanistan is the central

13. *Available at* http://www.thirdworldtraveler.com/Foreign_Policy_Institutions/CFR_ Debates _Torture.html (last visited March 21, 2010).

role of the CIA in all three places. Major General George R. Fay's investigative report on Abu Ghraib pointed out that the CIA was actually in charge of interrogation/torture at that facility and that they "poisoned the atmosphere" there. The "Salt Pit" was a CIA-run camp and the CIA was also very active at Gitmo. Some of their techniques caused deaths, with over 100 detainees dying in U.S. custody over the past several years, most of them murdered by U.S. personnel. Despite these homicides and over 400 criminal investigations of misconduct, only a few low level U.S. soldiers have been tried, convicted, and sentenced to prison terms. The CIA, while most responsible, has been completely exempt from any independent investigations, let alone any real accounting. The chilling fact is that the CIA is entirely above the law.

Many of these CIA torture techniques were codified much earlier in a secret 1963 torture instruction book called KUBARK Counterintelligence Interrogation. These torture techniques have been spread by the CIA throughout the world over the past 40 years, resulting in an epidemic of torture worldwide.

A September 2005 Human Rights Watch report based on interviews with active duty soldiers in the elite 82nd Airborne Division occupying part of Iraq found that military commanders demanded that lower ranking soldiers get intelligence from detainees, without giving guidelines about what was allowed in terms of interrogation techniques. The report found that the torture of detainees at the 82nd Airborne's base in Iraq (called FOB Mercury) took place almost daily from September 2003 to April 2004. It concluded that, since no full scale investigation had taken place and no one had been punished, such torture was probably still continuing today. Detainees captured by the 82nd were held in tents separated from the rest of the base by concertina wire for several days prior to being released or sent to Abu Ghraib. In these tents detainees were tortured to get information under the direction of officers from the military intelligence unit.

A summary of the Human Rights Watch report, based on U.S. soldiers' own testimony, stated that techniques used included: "severe beatings (in one observed incident, a soldier reportedly broke a detainee's leg with a baseball bat), blows and kicks to the face, chest, abdomen, and extremities, and repeated kicks to various parts of the detainees' body; the application of chemical substances to exposed skin and eyes; forced stress positions . . . sometimes to the point of unconsciousness; sleep deprivation; subjecting detainees to extremes of hot and cold; the stacking of detainees into human pyramids; and the withholding of food (beyond crackers) and water." The torture of detainees became so widespread and accepted that it became a means of "stress relief" for soldiers who were welcomed to the tents to beat up or otherwise abuse detainees. If a detainee suffered a broken bone from such beatings, then an army physician's assistant was called in to cover up the beating and agree that the detainee was injured during capture. Military intelligence officers approved of the beatings because they believed that it demoralized the detainees, making it easier to get intelligence from them. Officers and soldiers of the 82nd who wished to behave honorably and tried to report what was happening to superior officers to stop these outrages were told to keep their mouths shut and not risk their careers.

Since investigations about the behavior of other important U.S. military units in Iraq have not been conducted, we do not know if other divisions and units are also guilty of similar torture and abuse of detainees, but it would be surprising if this were not the case, since this problem is epidemic.

In the immediate aftermath of 9/11, the United States defined the "limits of interrogation" extremely broadly. The administration based this policy on the assumption that, other than basic guarantees, detainees are not entitled to Geneva Convention protections. The result was a policy that directly led to the abuses described above.

In the spring of 2009, the most comprehensive accounting of torture during the Bush administration was released by the Obama administration. The Obama administration decided not to prosecute CIA officials for their role in torturing detainees, stating it wanted to move away from a dark and painful chapter in U.S. history.

A. THE SLIPPERY SLOPE OF STANDARDS

International law provisions, particularly the Geneva Conventions, accord detainees certain protections. The Bush administration's initial approach of granting only basic, minimum rights was overwhelmingly discredited by independent observers and subsequently modified by the White House. While terrorists are not considered prisoners of war, Part II, Article 13 of the Geneva Convention relative to the treatment of Prisoners of War guarantees detainees protections:

> Prisoners of war must at all times be humanely treated. Any unlawful act or omission by the Detaining Power causing death or seriously endangering the health of a prisoner of war in its custody is prohibited, and will be regarded as a serious breach of the present Convention. In particular, no prisoner of war may be subjected to physical mutilation or to medical or scientific experiments of any kind which are not justified by the medical, dental or hospital treatment of the prisoner concerned and carried out in his interest.
>
> Likewise, prisoners of war must at all times be protected, particularly against acts of violence or intimidation and against insults and public curiosity.
>
> Measures of reprisal against prisoners of war are prohibited.[14]

In addition, CAT specifically and explicitly prohibits abuses documented above, which would qualify as torture under its definition:

> Any act which by severe pain or suffering, whether physical or mental, is intentionally inflicted on a person for such purposes as obtaining from him or a third person information or a confession . . . or intimidating or coercing . . . when such pain or suffering is inflicted . . . with the consent or acquiescence

---

14. Geneva Convention (III) Relative to the Treatment of Prisoners of War, *opened for signature* Apr. 12, 1949.

> of a public official . . . it does not include pain or suffering arising only from, inherent in or incidental to lawful sanctions.[15]

The Army Field Manual 34-52 has also established clear guidelines for U.S. military personnel:

> U.S. policy expressly prohibits[s] acts of violence or intimidation, including physical or mental torture, threats, insults, or exposure to inhumane treatment as a means of or aid to interrogations. Such illegal acts are not authorized and will not be condoned by the US Army. Acts in violation of these prohibitions are criminal acts punishable under the [Uniform Code of Military Justice].[16]

Despite CAT, existing domestic legislation, and relevant Geneva Convention protections and obligations, the Bush Administration established the following guidelines for the harsh interrogation of detainees.

Kenneth J. Levit, The CIA and the Torture Controversy: Interrogation Authorities and Practices in the War on Terror

1 J. of Nat'l Sec. L. & Pol'y 341 (2005)[17]

Guidelines for Aggressive Interrogations

Which "harsher methods" have been approved? No documents have yet been declassified that show what techniques are used specifically by the CIA, but one can reasonably assume that the Agency has at least the same range of freedom as that given to the Department of Defense in interrogating unlawful combatants outside the United States. In a Department of Defense memorandum entitled Working Group Report on Detainee Interrogations in the Global War on Terrorism, military officials divided non-routine interrogation techniques into two broad categories. The first category contained 26 techniques, all recommended for approval. These included techniques with names like "Fear Up Harsh," "Rapid Fire," "Dietary Manipulation," "Environmental Manipulation," and "Isolation."

A second set of nine techniques was recommended for approval only "where there is a good basis to believe that the detainee possesses critical intelligence" and where the detainee has been determined to be medically suitable to withstand the technique. The report also calls for an "appropriate specified senior level approval [to be] given for use with any specific detainee" These nine "exceptional" techniques, advanced in the report as legal, are:

> Isolation: Isolating the detainee from other detainees while still complying with basic standards of treatment.
>
> Use of Prolonged Interrogations: The continued use of a series of approaches that extend over a long period of time (e.g., 20 hours per day per interrogation).

---

15. Convention Against Torture and Other Cruel, Inhuman or Degrading Treatment, or Punishment, *opened for signature* Feb. 4, 1985, art. 1.

16. *Quoted in* David E. Graham, *The Treatment and Interrogation of Prisoners of War and Detainees*, 37 Geo. J. Int'l L. 61 (Fall 2005).

17. *Available at* http://www.mcgeorge.edu/documents/publications/jnslp/05_Levit_Master _ c.pdf (last visited March 21, 2010).

Forced Grooming: Forcing a detainee to shave hair or beard. (Force applied with intention to avoid injury. Would not use force that would cause serious injury.)

Prolonged Standing: Lengthy standing in a "normal" position (non-stress). This has been successful, but should never make the detainee exhausted to the point of weakness or collapse. Not enforced by physical restraints. Not to exceed four hours in a 24-hour period.

Sleep Deprivation: Keeping the detainee awake for an extended period of time. (Allowing individual to rest briefly and then awakening him, repeatedly.) Not to exceed 4 days in succession.

Physical Training: Requiring detainees to exercise. . . . Assists in generating compliance and fatiguing the detainees. No enforced compliance.

Face Slap/Stomach Slap: A quick glancing slap to the fleshy part of the cheek or stomach. These techniques are used strictly as shock measures and do not cause pain or injury. They are only effective if used once or twice together. After the second time on a detainee, it will lose the shock effect. Limited to two slaps per application; no more than two applications per interrogation.

Removal of Clothing: Potential removal of all clothing; removal to be done by military police if not agreed to by the subject. Creating a feeling of helplessness and dependence. This technique must be monitored to ensure the environmental conditions are such that this technique does not injure the detainee.

Increasing Anxiety by Use of Aversions: Introducing factors that of themselves create anxiety but do not create terror or mental trauma (e.g., simple presence of dog without directly threatening action). This technique requires the commander to develop specific and detailed safeguards to insure detainee's safety.

In response to the Working Group Report, Defense Secretary Rumsfeld sent a directive to the Commander of the U.S. Southern Command specifically accepting a number of the techniques endorsed in the report, but not the nine exceptional tactics. Rather, the Secretary directed that, in the event that the eight exceptional tactics are warranted, the Commander "should provide [the Secretary], via the Chairman of the Joint Chiefs of Staff, a written request describing the proposed techniques, recommended safeguards, and the rationale for applying it with an identified detainee.

The guidelines just described concern interrogation methods used by the Department of Defense, not necessarily the CIA. One can expect a similar degree of latitude, however, for detainees under the control of the CIA, especially since it appears that the CIA is expected to manage interrogations of senior terrorist leaders.

Issues to Consider

1. What risks did the Bush administration assume when the guidelines for aggressive interrogations were developed and implemented?
2. What is the fallout from developing a policy that violates international and domestic law?

3. Are violations of international and domestic law acceptable in the face of terrorism?
4. Does a major terrorist attack justify waiving the limits of "coercive interrogation"?
5. What assumptions regarding the efficiency, effectiveness, and efficacy of torture did the Bush administration make?
6. How are questions of morality resolved in the torture scenario?
7. What were the operative advantages attached to the Haynes and Bybee memos?
8. Did actionable intelligence result from this policy advocated by these memos?
9. What are the implications of the Department of Defense Directive being limited only to DoD personnel?

B. CHANGES WITH THE OBAMA ADMINISTRATION

While President Obama articulated an intention to close Guantanamo and end torture practices, as of this writing, Guantanamo remains open, and unsubstantiated press reports suggest harsh interrogation measures are still in effect.

Obama & Counterterror: The Ignored Record

Human Rights Watch, Feb. 5, 2015[18]

Obama has done little better when it comes to his vow to close Guantánamo. The good news is that the president has refused to bring any new detainees to Guantánamo. In his six years in office, terrorism suspects captured abroad have been delivered instead to regular federal courts for trial. So Obama has stayed true to his vow to treat Guantánamo as a problem that he inherited rather than one that he compounds.

Under Obama, the number of detainees has fallen—from 241 when he took office to 127 today, including twenty-eight released in 2014. However, despite a recent flurry of efforts, there has been no real progress toward shutting down the facility, which annually costs the American taxpayer roughly $3 million per detainee. All but a few of these men have been held in Guantánamo for over a decade without even being charged with a crime, let alone being tried.

The detainees can be divided into four broad groups. The first, and most prominent, are the five suspects in the planning of the September 11 attacks, as well as two others who have been charged with specific crimes and three who have been convicted, two by guilty pleas and one by an uncontested trial. Early in Obama's presidency, initially with his backing, Attorney General Eric

18. *Available at* https://www.hrw.org/news/2015/02/05/obama-counterterror-ignored-record (last visited February 19, 2024).

Holder sought to have the September 11 case tried in federal court in lower Manhattan. If the trial had been held as planned, it would probably have long been completed and, in view of the respect accorded the New York federal courts, widely seen as fair.

However, those plans were scuttled in the face of opposition from New York's then Mayor Michael Bloomberg and a host of mostly Republican senators and representatives, who said they were worried about the alleged security risk and contended that it was inappropriate to try the suspects in civilian rather than military court. It didn't matter to them that the New York authorities had a long history of prosecuting mafia dons, drug kingpins, and even World Trade Center terrorists without incident. Nor did it matter that Khalid Sheikh Mohammed and his September 11 codefendants were eager to portray themselves as warriors for whom a military trial is desirable rather than the "mere" murderers that a civilian trial would imply.

Instead, the prosecutions for September 11 and a handful of other cases have been pursued in Guantánamo before military commissions—a jerry-rigged institution that is being built and tested even as it attempts to handle one of the highest-profile cases of the century. That is also where a second group of twenty-three detainees are to be prosecuted, but none of them has even been charged despite, in many cases, having spent nearly thirteen years in detention.

The commissions have not fared well. Many of their problems stem from the Obama administration's decision to keep classified all evidence about the CIA's use of torture against six of the seven defendants currently being tried—a decision now being questioned by the military commission judge in light of publication of the Senate report on CIA torture. That approach has made it difficult for defense counsel to challenge the evidence. In addition, lax rules on the use of hearsay seem designed to allow the prosecution to avoid having to call interrogators as witnesses. Rules also permit the introduction of evidence that results from torture, as well as coerced testimony so long as the evidence comes from a witness and not a suspect. As one new legal issue after another requires adjudication, the military commissions have been subject to repeated delays, making them unlikely to complete (or perhaps even begin) the trials for taking part in the September 11 attacks before Obama leaves office.

The administration has determined that a third group of fifty-nine Guantánamo detainees do not pose a threat that would justify continued detention. Of these, fifty-two are from Yemen, but the administration has refused to release them on the grounds that the security situation in Yemen is too volatile—even though there seem to be few if any restrictions placed on other recently released detainees. Of the other seven, some cannot be returned to their home country for fear of persecution; but no other country has been found to take them. Efforts to resolve these cases are underway and should be vigorously pursed.

The administration has designated a fourth and final group of thirty-five detainees "too dangerous" to release but says either that there is insufficient evidence to prosecute them or that they have not committed a chargeable crime. In the meantime, they languish in Guantánamo, without ever receiving a trial or a fair opportunity to contest any evidence against them. Even if some might pose a risk if released, so do many other people around the world who are free to go about their business unless they commit actual crimes. If they pose a risk, moreover, there is no reason why they cannot be the subject of surveillance after they are released. Why do these few dozen prisoners remain in Guantánamo?

The answer seems to lie not in security but politics. The difference between risks to Americans from the Guantánamo detainees and risks posed by countless others is what might be called the Willie Horton problem. If a random person somewhere in the world commits an act of terrorism, that is a tragedy, but Obama has no special political responsibility for it other than the general duty of all presidents to try to safeguard Americans. But if a Guantánamo detainee released by Obama commits an act of terrorism, Obama would be held responsible in the same way that Michael Dukakis was famously tarred, with devastating political effect, for having allowed weekend furloughs to a number of convicts including the murderer Willie Horton, who then raped a woman. . . .

C. LOOKING FORWARD

The Bush administration's efforts to push the "legal envelope" resulted in serious violations of human and civil rights, well-documented abuses that resulted in limited actionable intelligence and potentially irreversible damage to America's foreign policy and image in the Middle East. The White House attempted to redefine the limits of interrogation and to authorize torture from a legal and policy perspective. In a series of memos, White House lawyers authorized illegal interrogation measures, including waterboarding. The actions of interrogators in Abu Ghraib resulted in humiliation, degradation, and ultimately, in at least one case, murder. Any questions of effectiveness must be weighed against this reality.

As Guantanamo Bay is still active over 20 years later, critics have continued to call on the Biden Administration to close the facility once and for all. The abuse and violations of civil rights are still occurring, and the U.S. has refused to accept any real accountability for the horrors it has committed since the war on terror began.[19]

IV. ISRAEL

In the aftermath of the 1967 Six-Day War, Israel occupied the West Bank, the Gaza Strip, the Golan Heights, East Jerusalem, and the Sinai Peninsula. As a result, 392,700 Palestinians living in the West Bank and the Gaza Strip were

19. *20 Years of US Torture—and Counting*, Human Rights Watch, January 9, 2022, 12:01 AM, *available at* https://www.hrw.org/news/2022/01/09/20-years-us-torture-and-counting (last visited February 19, 2024).

under Israel Defense Forces occupation. Between the years 1967-1987, the occupation was relatively tranquil; the Intifada of 1987-1993, which directly led to the Oslo Peace Process, marked the first time that Palestinians in the West Bank and Gaza Strip committed widespread terror attacks against the IDF, Jewish settlers living in the territories, and Israelis living in Israel proper.

How Israel responded, and in particular, what interrogation measures were developed and implemented by the General Security Services (GSS)—today known as the Israeli Security Agency (ISA)—comprise the focus of this section. The ISA is the government agency charged with preventing terrorism in Israel. It does so in a number of different operational manners; one of the most important is the interrogation of Palestinians suspected of involvement in terrorism or believed to have knowledge either of future terrorism acts or of individuals involved in terrorist activity. The ISA director is under the direct control of the Prime Minister and works in close cooperation with the IDF, but is not in the IDF's chain of command.

The following report, written by the Israeli human rights organization B'Tselem, provides an inside look into how ISA (then referred to as the GSS) interrogates suspected terrorists.

Stanley Cohen & Daphna Golan, The Interrogation of Palestinians During the Intifada: Ill-Treatment, "Moderate Physical Pressure" or Torture?

B'Tselem—The Israeli Information Center for Human Rights in the Occupied Territories[20]

The General Security Services ("Shin Bet" or "Shabaq," today called Israel Security Agency) is responsible for security matters and counter-intelligence within Israel and the Occupied Territories. It is directly responsible to the Prime Minister and not subject to any other external control or scrutiny either by a regular Government Ministry or a Knesset Committee. . . .

Article 78 of the Order provides that immediately following arrest, a person may be detained for up to 18 days without coming before a court. This is Stage One. (In East Jerusalem, according to Israeli Law, the period is 48 hours. Our description below concentrates on the Territories.) At the end of this 18 day period, the detainee must be released if he/she has not been charged, unless a judge extends the period. In practice, the Shin Bet (directly or through the police) usually requests this extension and the military judges almost automatically comply. . . .

During this initial period of detention after arrest, the detainee may in theory be interrogated by one of three bodies: (1) military personnel; (2) regular police; or (3) G.S.S. We concentrate on the G.S.S., which is responsible for the bulk of the interrogations of Palestinian suspects both in Israel and the Territories.

20. *Available at* www.btselem.org/Download/199103_Torture_Eng.doc (last visited June 25, 2010).

G.S.S. interrogation takes place in separate wings or blocks located in detention-centers/prisons which in the Territories are controlled by the I.D.F. or Prison Service and in Israel (in Petah Tikva or the Russian Compound in Jerusalem, for example) by the police. These wings are under the effective control of the G.S.S, Army, police, and prison staff claim that they are not permitted to enter (nor is the International Committee of the Red Cross). In practice (as our research shows) these other bodies do have contact (for example, in escorting the detainee). In legal terms, however, the detainee remains in the formal custody and responsibility of the army or regular Israeli police or prison authority.

The legal provisions for any supervision over G.S.S. interrogations or for dealing with any complaint by detainees (or their lawyers) of any abuses, are not clear. G.S.S. agents do not normally appear in court. After the interrogation, the suspect is handed over to the police investigator who takes down a confession as presented to the court. Requests for extension of detention are also made by the police. At this point, there are two main contexts in which complaints about abuses may appear:

First, in the rare cases where signs of ill treatment are visible when the suspect appears in court, a judge might record this in the protocol, but usually only after a formal complaint by the defense attorney. The police or State Prosecutor can justifiably claim no knowledge or responsibility for earlier stages. Military court judges do not normally deal with complaints and refer them to other authorities.

Second, there is the formal procedure known as a "trial within a trial." When the accused's confession during interrogation is the main or only evidence, then a plea of "not guilty" in court is tantamount to alleging that the confession was obtained by improper methods and is therefore invalid and inadmissible as evidence. This calls for conducting a "trial within a trial" on the question of the admissibility of the confession. This forum becomes, in essence, the trial itself dealing with the credibility of the evidence and, by implication, of the G.S.S. Allegations thus can be raised both about the process of interrogation and whether the G.S.S. is telling the truth about its circumstances. . . .

The special status of the G.S.S. can, therefore, lend itself to abuses in the interrogation process that are difficult to control. No law established the G.S.S. in the first place, nor does it have any clear legal authority in which to operate. It relies wholly upon the authority of other agencies—the police, the prison service, the army, the courts—which provide physical space, cooperation and legal cover. It does not have its own hierarchy of supervision or public accountability. Interrogators are anonymous at all stages, not just in the interrogation itself but in the court. . . .

A. SELF-IMPOSED RESTRAINTS

Over the years, Palestinians interrogated by the ISA have reported the use of torture; Palestinian, international, and Israeli human rights groups have filed numerous petitions to the High Court of Justice in support of such claims.[21] In response, the ISA has consistently denied torturing Palestinian detainees.[22]

The Israeli Supreme Court sitting as the High Court of Justice addresses these issues in the case below. By imposing limits on interrogation measures, the Court establishes clear guidelines for ISA interrogators.

Public Comm. Against Torture in Israel v. State of Israel

HCJ 5100/94 (1994)

This decision opens with a description of the difficult reality in which Israel finds herself security wise. We shall conclude this judgment by re-addressing that harsh reality. We are aware that this decision does not ease dealing with that reality. This is the destiny of democracy, as not all means are acceptable to it, and not all practices employed by its enemies are open before it. Although a democracy must often fight with one hand tied behind its back, it nonetheless has the upper hand. Preserving the Rule of Law and recognition of an individual's liberty constitutes an important component in its understanding of security. At the end of the day, they strengthen its spirit and its strength and allow it to overcome its difficulties. This having been said, there are those who argue that Israel's security problems are too numerous, thereby requiring the authorization to use physical means. If it will nonetheless be decided that it is appropriate for Israel, in light of its security difficulties to sanction physical means in interrogations (and the scope of these means which deviate from the ordinary investigation rules), this is an issue that must be decided by the legislative branch which represents the people. We do not take any stand on this matter at this time. It is there that various considerations must be weighed. The pointed debate must occur there. It is there that the required legislation may be passed, provided, of course, that a law infringing upon a suspect's liberty "befitting the values of the State of Israel," is enacted for a proper purpose, and to an extent no greater than is required. (Article 8 to the Basic Law: Human Dignity and Liberty.)

Deciding these applications weighed heavy on this Court. True, from the legal perspective, the road before us is smooth. We are, however, part of Israeli society. Its problems are known to us and we live its history. We are not isolated in an ivory tower. We live the life of this country. We are aware of the harsh reality of terrorism in which we are, at times, immersed. Our apprehension is that this decision will hamper the ability to properly deal with terrorists

21. *Israel: Amnesty International Updated Submission to the UN Universal Periodic Review (UPR),* Amnesty International, 17th Session of the UPR Working Group, October – November 2013.

22. B'Tslem, *Torture During Interrogations: Testimony of Palestinian Detainees, Testimony of Interrogators,* November 1994, *available at* https://www.btselem.org/publications/summaries/199411_torture_during_interrogations (last visited February 19, 2024); B'Tselem, *Absolute Prohibition: the Torture and Ill-Treatment of Palestinian Detainees,* May 2007, *available at* http://www.btselem.org/English/Publications/Summaries/200705_Utterly_Forbidden.asp (last visited February 19, 2024).

and terrorism, disturbs us. We are, however, judges. Our brethren require us to act according to the law. This is equally the standard that we set for ourselves. When we sit to judge, we are being judged. Therefore, we must act according to our purest conscience when we decide the law. The words of the Deputy President of the Supreme Court, Justice Landau, speak well to our purposes:

"We possess proper sources upon which to construct our judgments and have no need, and while judging, are forbidden from, involving our personal views as citizens of this country in our decisions. Still, great is the fear that the Court shall be perceived as though it had abandoned its proper place and descended to the midst of public debate, and that its decision making will be obstructed by one side of the population's uproar and by the other side's absolute and emotional rejection. In that sense, I see myself here as someone whose duty is to decide according to the law in all cases legally brought before the Court. I am strictly bound by this duty. As I am well aware in advance that the public at large will not pay attention to the legal reasoning, but to the end result alone. And that the Court's proper status, as an institution above partisan debates, risks being harmed. What can we do, as this is our function and role as judges."

The Commission of Inquiry pointed to the "difficult dilemma between the imperative need to safeguard the State of Israel's very existence and the lives of its citizens, and preserving its character—that of a country subject to the Rule of Law and holding basic moral values." The Commission rejected an approach suggesting that the actions of security services in the context of fighting terrorism, shall take place in the recesses of the law. The Commission equally rejected the "ways of the hypocrites, who remind us of their adherence to the Rule of Law, while ignoring (being willfully blind) to what is being done in practice." The Commission elected to follow a third route, "the way of Truth and the Rule of Law." In so doing, the Commission of Inquiry outlined the dilemma faced by Israel in a manner both transparent and open to inspection by Israeli society.

Consequently, it is decided that the order nisi be made absolute, as we declare that the GSS does not have the authority to "shake" a man, hold him in the "Shabach" position (which includes the combination of various methods, as mentioned in paragraph 30), force him into a "frog crouch" position and deprive him of sleep in a manner other than that which is inherently required by the interrogation. Likewise, we declare that the "necessity" defence, found in the Penal Law, cannot serve as a basis of authority for the use of these interrogation practices, or for the existence of directives pertaining to GSS investigators, allowing them to employ interrogation practices of this kind. Our decision does not negate the possibility that the "necessity" defence be available to GSS investigators, be within the discretion of the Attorney General, if he decides to prosecute, or if criminal charges are brought against them, as per the Court's discretion.

Military commanders and intelligence community officials criticized the decision for curtailing the state's ability to conduct operational counterterrorism. Nevertheless, the former President of the Supreme Court, Aharon Barak, argued that liberal democratic states must have "self-imposed restraints." In the context of interrogations, the significance is clear—past measures violating the detainee's basic rights should not be used.

Issues to Consider

1. What does it mean to enable interrogators to operate in the "twilight zone"?
2. What are the legitimate operational goals of an interrogation?
3. How is "appropriate pressure" operationally defined?
4. How is the "necessity defense" defined and implemented?
5. What are the recommended criteria for determining when the detainee will not cooperate and the interrogation must be stopped?
6. What is the significance—from an interrogation perspective—of denying the detainee the right to meet with an attorney?
7. What criteria should be established for preventing client-attorney meetings?
8. What should the standard of judicial review be for determining whether or not to prevent a detainee from meeting with an attorney in the context of counterterrorism?

How are rights to be protected when interrogators believe that the detainee possesses information vital to an ongoing investigation or relevant for immediate operational purposes? The High Court's decision in 5100/94 established clear parameters with which interrogators must comply.

Interrogation regulation is, by definition, a nebulous situation, particularly when the relevant interaction takes place in a small room with only two or three people present who have diametrically opposed interests under extremely stressful conditions.

There is little doubt that the High Court of Justice ruling imposes restrictions on the interrogation methods, limiting violations of individual rights. In contrast to the Bush administration's memorandums, which established a legal regime enabling torture, the HCJ opinion articulated an interrogation regime predicated on limits.

B. OPERATION CAST LEAD

The Report of the UN High Commissioner for Human Rights investigated IDF during the Gaza Conflict, which included the military action known as Operation Cast Lead. During the course of the operation, which took place from December 2008 to January 2009, Palestinian residents of the Gaza Strip were detained and interrogated. The Report details mistreatment of detainees, including reports of shackling, severe beatings, foul conditions, and solitary confinement. The hypothetical below highlights the dilemma facing interrogators.

Operational Hypothetical

Recently, there has been an increase in significant terror attacks in your country. These attacks have resulted in the deaths of 50 innocent civilians in the last month. You have been asked to develop an operational plan to prevent these attacks. According to intelligence reports, the attacks have been carried out both by individuals who previously lived in your country and those who entered specifically for the purpose of carrying out these attacks. A number of individuals (from both categories) have recently been detained, some caught in the act, others based on intelligence information and ongoing interrogations. To that end, the questions below represent operational dilemmas for counter terrorism decision makers.

1. How do you develop a policy that balances the civil rights of the individuals that are attacking you with your interest in preventing additional loss of innocent lives?
2. If you had the option to arrest and detain a large group—including not only those who attacked you, but also those who may be innocent—would you detain all of them? What would be your criteria for determining who to interrogate?
3. What further interrogation techniques would you authorize to prevent attacks or locate additional terrorists?

Human Rights in Palestine and Other Occupied Arab Territories: Report of the United Nations Fact Finding Mission on the Gaza Conflict

A/HRC/12/48. ¶1109-22, Sept. 15, 2009

On the morning of 5 January, shortly after the ground operations began, an estimated 40 Israeli soldiers broke into several homes, including that of AD/ 01,[23] who described to the Mission how 65 persons, several of whom were holding white flags, were made to assemble in the street. The soldiers separated the men from the women. The men were made to line up against a wall and strip to their underwear. AD/01 indicated that any attempt to resist the soldiers was met with physical force, resulting in injuries.

Approximately 20 minutes later, they were taken into a house owned by Mr. Khalil Misbah Attar, where they were detained for a day, the men still separated from the women. The house had been struck by a number of missiles that morning and was badly damaged. Witnesses indicated to the Mission that the house was at that time being used by the Israeli armed forces as a military base and sniper position.

At around 10 p.m., all of the men were handcuffed behind their backs with plastic restraints and blindfolded. The men, 11 women and at least seven children below the age of 14 were taken on foot to al-Kaklouk located south of the American School, one to two kilometers away. Many of the men remained in their underwear, exposed to the harsh winter weather. Al-Kaklouk is very close to Israeli military artillery and tank positions, and while the detainees were held here at least one tank was engaged in frequent firing.

AD/01 told the Mission that, on arrival at al-Kaklouk, everyone was asked to clamber down into trenches, which had been dug to create a pit surrounded by a wall of sand, about three metres high. There were three such pits, each of which was surrounded by barbed wire. They were estimated to cover about 7,000 square metres ("six or seven *donums*") each. . . . AD/01 described how they were assembled in long single files, rather than massed together, and

23. AD/01, and other similar initials, indicate a pseudonym for a witness.

held in these pits, in the open air and exposed to cold temperatures for three days (till 8 January). Each pit accommodated approximately 20 people. They were forced to sit in stress positions, on their knees and leaning forward keeping their heads down. They were monitored by soldiers and were not allowed to communicate with each other. They had no access to food or water on the first day of their internment, and were given a sip of water and an olive each to eat on the second and third days of their detention (6 and 7 January). They had limited access to toilet facilities. The men had to wait for two to three hours after asking before they were allowed to leave the pits to relieve themselves and sometimes were able to remove their blindfolds for the purpose. A few of them were told to relieve themselves inside the pit, behind a small mound of sand. They stated that it was culturally too difficult for the women to seek permission to relieve themselves and they did not ask.

AD/01 states that some tanks were inside the pit with at least one tank positioned at the eastern end. While the people were held there, the tank facing inland each day sporadically fired on the houses along the road opposite the site. . . .

AD/01B and AD/01C recounted that on 8 January, the women and children were released and told to go to Jabaliyah. The men were transferred to military barracks near the northern border, identified as the Izokim Barracks. At the Izokim barracks, the men were detained in pits similar to but smaller than those in al-Kaklouk. They continued to be exposed to the cold temperature, rain and the constant sound of tank movement overhead. The witnesses have described to the Mission the experience of continued and prolonged exposure to the sound of this tank movement as disorienting and creating feelings of futility, isolation, helplessness and abject terror. . . .

The men were held handcuffed and in their underwear in the Izokim barracks overnight. They were questioned intermittently, mostly on details and locations of Qassam rockets, the tunnels and the whereabouts of Hamas parliamentarians. According to statements made to the Mission, they were beaten during the interrogation and threatened with death and being run over by tanks. . . .

On 9 January, the men were taken to a prison in Israel, identified by one witness as the Negev prison, where they remained until 12 January. They were detained in one section of the prison, alternating between being held in isolation and in shared cells, and were subjected to harsh interrogation, often by two people dressed in civilian clothes. Interrogation focused on the identification of Hamas tunnels and arms as well as the whereabouts of Gilad Shalit.

AD/01B and AD/01C recounted that they were shackled to a chair with plastic strips and interrogated several times, with AD/01B stating that he was made to strip naked during an interrogation. He was kept in solitary confinement where a soldier would come intermittently during the day, and slam the cell door open and shut, exposing him to extremely cold temperatures. AD/01C stated that during the first interrogation he was verbally threatened and in the subsequent two he was blindfolded and beaten. He was made to stand up and face the wall, following which his face was smashed against the wall several times before he was severely beaten (kicked and punched) on his back and buttocks.

Requests for clothing were denied. During the interrogation the detainees were informed that they were "illegal combatants" and that they had no protection under the Geneva Conventions. They had limited access to food, water and sanitation. Their morning meal was a bottle-cap-sized piece of bread with a drop of marmalade. The evening meal, if provided, consisted of rotting sardines and cheese on mouldy bread.

AD/01C described the experience of being detained, stripped and shackled as one of abandonment, desperation, suffocation and isolation. He continues to experience discomfort where he was beaten and is unable to sit and sleep comfortably.

AD/01C stated that while in Negev prison an additional group arrived. They were kept separately in the second section. The exact number of detainees in the second group is unknown, although AD/01C indicated to the Mission that the second group was smaller.

On 12 January, nine people including the witnesses were blindfolded, handcuffed and transported to the Erez border. AD/01 described to the Mission how they were subjected to harsh interrogation at Erez and made to strip completely. Several hours later they were told to run into Gaza, to look straight ahead and not to look back.

AD/01 states that all 65 detainees from the original group taken from al-Atatra to Israel were eventually released. Some members of his family were detained afterwards, but not in the original group of 65. At the time of writing, three of these remain incarcerated in various detention facilities of the Israel Prison Service. An unknown number remain in prison facing charges of being illegal combatants and members of al-Qassam Brigades. The first hearing was scheduled to be held in August in Israel (exact date not known). Several prisoners were still in detention in August 2009 with approval from Israeli courts.[24]

Issues to Consider

1. What are the implications of using harsh interrogation measures during operations?
2. Using the standard of credibility, reliability, veracity, and timeliness of information, how is actionable intelligence received?
3. How does the High Court of Justices decision reflect on the most recent reports of Operation Cast Lead interrogation measures?
4. Does the inability to use torture or other methods impede national security?

V. RUSSIA

Interrogation methods in the Soviet Union were the subject of enormous international concern; the KGB (*Komitet Gosudarstvennoy Bezopasnosti*) was widely

24. B'Tslem, *Without Trial: Administrative Detention of Palestinians by Israel and the Incarceration of Unlawful Combatants Law, available at* https://www.btselem.org/publications/summaries/200910_without_trial (last visited December 31, 2023).

accused of constantly violating basic rights of detainees. Former detainees, human rights groups, and other nations regularly condemned KGB interrogation methods. Those interrogated included political dissidents, religious leaders, and enemies of the state; interrogation methods ranged from long-term imprisonment after show-trials to torture and death.

Relevant to this chapter is the question of whether individuals suspected of involvement in terrorism are interrogated in accordance with criminal law and granted its protections, or whether they are treated as non-soldier combatants.

With the fall of the Berlin Wall in 1989 and the collapse of the Soviet Union in 1992, the international human rights community expressed hope—if not optimism—that interrogation methods of the new Russian government would significantly differ from that of the former Communist regime.

A. RUSSIA'S CRIMINAL CODE

While no single provision of the Russian Criminal Code specifically addresses the interrogation limits of terrorist suspects, Article 205 defines the crime of terrorism:

Article 205. Terrorism

1. Terrorism, that is, the perpetration of an explosion, arson, or any other action endangering the lives of people, causing sizable property damage, or entailing other socially dangerous consequences, if these actions have been committed for the purpose of violating public security, frightening the population, or exerting influence on decision-making by governmental bodies, and also the threat of committing said actions for the same ends, shall be punishable by deprivation of liberty for a term of eight to twelve years.
2. The same deeds committed:
   a. by a group of persons in a preliminary conspiracy;
   b. abolished
   c. with the use of firearms shall be punishable by deprivation of liberty for a term of eight to fifteen years.
3. Deeds stipulated in the first or second part of this Article, if they have been committed by an organized group or have involved by negligence the death of a person, or any other grave consequences, and also are associated with infringement on objects of the use of atomic energy or with the use of nuclear materials, radioactive substances or sources of radioactive radiation or sources of radioactiveradiation, shall be punishable by deprivation of liberty for a term of fifteen to twenty years or by deprivation of liberty for life.

Note: A person who has taken part in the preparation of an act of terrorism shall be released from criminal responsibility if he facilitated the prevention of the act of terrorism by timely warning governmental bodies, or by any other method, unless the actions of this person contain a different corpus delicti.[25]

25. A full copy of the Russian Criminal Code is available at http://publication.pravo.gov.ru/Document/View/0001201607070042 (last visited December 31, 2023).

Article 302 defines the limits of interrogation within this criminal framework.

Article 302. Compulsion to Give Evidence

1. Compulsion to give evidence used with regard to a subject, defendant, victim, or witness, or coercion of an expert, a specialst to make a report or to give evidence through the application of threats, blackmail, or other illegal actions, by an investigator or a person conducting inquests, shall be punishable by deprivation of liberty for a term of up to three years.

2. The same act, joined with the use of violence, mockery, or torture, shall be punishable by deprivation of liberty for term of two to eight years.

Do these limits indicate that individual terrorist suspects are interrogated in accordance with the criminal law paradigm? Furthermore, does this paradigm guarantee protection of individual rights? The following United Nations Committee Against Torture report delineates general protections afforded people convicted of crimes under Russian Federation laws.

United Nations, Report of the Committee Against Torture

July 27, 2018[26]

The Committee against Torture this afternoon concluded its consideration of the sixth periodic report of the Russian Federation on the efforts made by the State party to implement the provisions of the Convention against Torture.

Introducing the report, Mikhail Galperin, Deputy Minister of Justice of the Russian Federation, noted that Russia had made a lot of progress in amending legislation on the penitentiary system and criminal justice, in order to achieve full protection of the rights of detainees and convicted persons, and to enhance their detention conditions. There were prohibitions and limitations on the use of force by correctional personnel, especially when it came to pregnant women, persons with disabilities, and minors. In addition, the authorities had organized further professional training on human and civil rights in the agencies of the Ministry of the Interior, with a particular focus on ensuring that the police did not use excessive force when managing demonstrations. There was ongoing training on the cases of the European Court of Human Rights pertaining to the Russian Federation.

In the ensuing discussion, the Committee Experts expressed concern that the Russian definition of torture was not in full compliance with the Convention, adding that there was reliable information that torture was practiced widely in the country, and indicating the need for a robust criminalization of torture. They further inquired about safety inside of the country's justice system, complaints of torture, fundamental legal safeguards, access to legal counsel from the very outset of the arrest, access to a medical doctor, registration of detainees, video surveillance, administrative detention, violence

26. *Available at* https://www.ohchr.org/en/press-releases/2018/07/committee-against-torture-examines-russian-federations-report (last visited August 14, 2023).

against women in detention, organization of prison medical services, the high rate of death in custody, and non-refoulement. Other issues raised concerned the activities of the Russian military police in Syria and Ukraine, the Ombudsperson of the Russian Federation, functioning of the Public Oversight Committees which monitored detention places, plans to establish a national mechanism for the prevention of torture, reprisals against human rights defenders, excessive use of force, discrimination and violence against minorities, serious human rights violations in the North Caucasus region, Russian jurisdiction in Transnistria, and compensation for victims of torture. . .

Issues to Consider

1. Does Russian legislation impose restraints on interrogators?
2. What is the impact of a lack of definitions with respect to the rule of law in the context of interrogations?
3. How are detainees to be protected if torture is not unequivocally defined?
4. Are self-imposed limits possible in this paradigm?
5. What protections are extended to a detainee in accordance with Russian legislation?
6. Are judicial holdings more effective protections than legislation?

B. TORTURE IN CHECHNYA

Before the current war with Ukraine, the issue of torture in Russia primarily concerned the treatment of Chechens.

Torture by Personnel of the Second Operational Investigative Bureau (ORB-2)

Human Rights Watch[27]

ORB-2 was established in 2002 and formally charged with detecting, preventing and suppressing actions by organized criminal groups.

Human Rights Watch interviewed several dozen people who were detained and tortured at ORB-2 premises between 2004 and 2006, as well as their relatives and lawyers; they consistently told of ORB-2 personnel coercing confessions under brutal ill-treatment and torture; denying detainees access to lawyers of their choice; preventing medical documentation of signs of torture by denying access to doctors and keeping detainees in custody until the signs of torture fade and, if suspects sought to renounce their coerced

27. *Available at* http://hrw.org/backgrounder/eca/chechnya1106/2.htm#_Toc150776963 (last visited December 31, 2023).

confessions after they were transferred to remand custody, subjecting them to further ill-treatment as punishment and to force them to stand by the original statements.

In cases we researched, ORB-2 personnel seized persons, usually young males, from their homes, places of work, or the streets without identifying themselves or providing a warrant or any explanation. They then brought the detainees to the ORB-2 temporary detention facility and immediately started interrogating them.

In almost all cases, the detention was officially registered only after several days. During this time detainees' families had no information on their relatives' whereabouts, and the ORB-2 personnel interrogated the detainees in the absence of a lawyer, or with the participation of a lawyer appointed by ORB-2 personnel. According to the interviewees, the appointed lawyers ignored their complaints about torture—although they saw the torture marks on their clients' bodies—and instead encouraged them to accept the charges.

During interrogations, ORB-2 personnel subjected the detainees to severe beatings, torture with electric shocks, suffocation, and threats or imitation of sexual violence. Most interviewees told Human Rights Watch that during these interrogations, which lasted for many hours, they were forced to confess to serious crimes, such as multiple murders or terrorist attacks, as well as to name other people allegedly involved with the rebel movement. In some cases, the confession had been prepared beforehand by the interrogators and contained exact dates, places, and identities of the victims. In other cases, the detainees themselves had to "choose" a crime and invent details that the interrogators would then record.

Once the confession was obtained and signed, the detainee was kept in the ORB-2 temporary detention facility for several days or sometimes weeks to allow any signs of torture, such as bruises or burns, to fade. The investigators would then transfer the accused to the remand prison (SIZO-1) in Grozny, where they stayed until and during trial.

The report above suggests not much is new with respect to Russian interrogation methods. Similar to what was revealed in Soviet-era accounts, Russian interrogators subject Chechen detainees to torture and other basic violations of civil and political rights. According to applicable legislation, terror suspects are subject to the traditional criminal law paradigm. However, available reports indicate a torture-based paradigm has been consistently implemented and imposed in contravention to both international and domestic law.

The critical question is whether these interrogation methods directly or indirectly contribute to Russia's operational counterterrorism efforts. The answer is not clear.

Issues to Consider

1. In determining effectiveness, has Russia accrued benefits from the policy of torturing detainees?

2. What is the significance of "fabricated criminal charges" in this context?
3. What advantages can be gained from compelling detainees to sign confessions?
4. Are interrogations that employ torture a reasonable response to terrorism?
5. Does the use of torture suggest a weakness on the part of the Russian authorities?

VI. INDIA

This section analyzes how Indian police officials interrogate those arrested in the aftermath of terrorist attacks. The limits of lawful interrogation in India have been statutorily regulated in a number of legislative acts; however, a discussion of India's interrogation policies cannot be divorced from geopolitical realities. As discussed throughout the casebook, India is confronted with three separate, yet connected, terrorist threats: internal, internal-external, and external. To that end, the government's flexibility in conducting operational counterterrorism is restricted. What needs to be examined is whether those limitations extend to the interrogation setting.

A. INTRODUCTION

The following excerpt, penned by R.K. Abichandani, a judge on the High Court of Gujarat, demonstrates the legal limits of interrogation under Indian law. Furthermore, it hints at the challenges Indian authorities face when balancing the rule of law with the requirement to adequately protect the state and its citizens.

R.K. Abichandani, Custodial Dignity

High Court of Gujarat[28]

The arrest of a person suspected of crime does not warrant any physical violence on the person or his torture. But, when the captive exercises his fundamental right to silence against self-incrimination (Art. 20(3)) during his interrogation, the police often abuse their authority by use of criminal force to extort information. The tyrannical way of custodial interrogation that exposes the suspect to the risk of abuse of his person or dignity has prompted the Supreme Court to ordain that interrogation should not be

28. *Available at* https://gujarathighcourt.nic.in/hccms/sites/default/files/articles_files/Custodial%20Dignity.pdf (last visited December 31, 2023).

accompanied with torture or use of "third degree" methods. (Kartar Singh v. State of Punjab, (1994) 3 SCC 569.) The constitution as well as the statutory laws condemn the conduct of any official in extorting a confession or information under compulsion by using any third degree methods. A confession to police officer cannot be proved as against a person accused of any offence (Sec. 25 Evidence Act) and confession caused by threats from a person in authority in order to avoid any evil of a temporal nature would be irrelevant in criminal proceedings as, inter alia, provided in Sec. 24 of the Evidence Act. Sections 330 and 331 of the Indian Penal Code provide for punishment to one who voluntarily caused hurt or grievous hurt to extort the confession or any information which may lead to detection of an offence or misconduct. The expression "life or personal liberty" in Article 21 includes a guarantee against torture and assault even by the State and its functionaries to a person who is taken in custody and no sovereign immunity can be pleaded against the liability of the State arising due to such criminal use of force over the captive person. As held by the Supreme Court in D.K. Basu v. State of W.B. (1997) 1 SCC 416 "custodial torture" is a naked violation of human dignity and a degradation which destroys, to a very large extent, human personality. It is a calculated assault on human dignity and whenever human dignity is wounded, civilization takes a step backwards—flag of humanity must on each such occasion fly half-mast. The convicts, undertrials, detenues and other persons in custody cannot be denied the precious right of the right to live with human dignity included in the expression "life or personal liberty," except according to the procedure established by law by placing such reasonable restrictions as are permitted by law. Any form of torture or cruel, inhuman or degrading treatment would fall within the inhibition of Art. 21, whether it occurs during investigation, interrogation or otherwise. Using any form of torture for extracting any kind of information would neither be right nor just nor fair and would therefore offend Art. 21. A crime-suspect can indeed be subjected to a sustained and scientific interrogation in accordance with law but he cannot be tortured or subjected to third-degree methods or eliminated with a view to elicit information, extract confession or derive knowledge about his accomplices, weapons etc. "State terrorism" is no answer to combat terrorism.

Issues to Consider

1. Does the constant threat of terrorism mean that India *should* have relaxed protections for terrorist suspects?
2. Should the various protections provided to terrorist suspects in India differ depending on the type of terror they are accused of?
3. Indian law proscribes use of the "third degree." Is this position tenable, or has Indian law curtailed investigatory techniques so extensively that the authorities have no choice but to break the law?

B. REPORTS OF CUSTODIAL ABUSE

Human rights organizations have repeatedly claimed that detainees in Indian custody have been regularly subjected to torture. The complaints focus on detainees arrested on suspicion of involvement in criminal and terrorism offenses alike; to that end, terrorism-related torture allegations have particularly emphasized interrogations in Jammu and Kashmir.

2022 Country Report on Human Rights Practices: India

U.S. Department of State, 2023[29]

The law prohibits torture and other abuses, but there were credible reports that government officials employed them. The law does not permit authorities to admit coerced confessions into evidence, but some nongovernmental organizations (NGOs) reported authorities used torture to coerce confessions. Authorities allegedly also used torture to extort money or as summary punishment. The government authorized the National Human Rights Commission (NHRC) to investigate rape cases involving police officers. By law the NHRC may also request information regarding cases involving the army and paramilitary forces, but it has no mandate to investigate those cases. NGOs reported NHRC statistics undercounted the number of rapes committed in police custody. Some rape victims were unwilling to report crimes due to social stigma and fear of retribution if the perpetrator was a police officer or official. There were reports police officials also refused to register rape cases.

There were reports that police beatings of prisoners resulted in custodial deaths (see section 1.a.). There were reports of abuse in prisons by guards and inmates, as well as reports of rape of detainees by police.

According to human rights NGOs, police used torture, other mistreatment, and arbitrary detention to obtain forced or false confessions. In some cases, police reportedly held suspects without registering their arrests and denied detainees sufficient food and water.

In April police filed criminal charges against Station House Officer Tilak Dhari Saroj under the Prevention of Children from Sexual Offences Act and suspended him from duty for the custodial rape of a minor in Uttar Pradesh. The victim was at the police station to register a rape complaint against four individuals when she was allegedly raped by Saroj. The girl's aunt allegedly trafficked her to four individuals who took her to neighboring Madhya Pradesh where they sexually assaulted her. Police arrested Saroj, the survivor's aunt, and the four individuals accused of assaulting her.

In June five policemen were charged for the custodial abuse of Rehan Shah in Uttar Pradesh. Police were interrogating Shah regarding his alleged involvement in a cow slaughter case. Shah's family alleged police severely beat him,

---

29. *Available at* https://www.state.gov/reports/2022-country-reports-on-human-rights-practices/india (last visited August 21, 2023).

administered electric shocks, and inserted a plastic pipe in his rectum, releasing him to the family only after a bribe of 5,000 Indian Rupees (INR) ($60). According to media, police were not arrested in this case.

India's legislative and judicial branches are cognizant of the delicate balance required to conduct lawful and effective counterterrorism. Much of their focus has emphasized the requirement to carefully consider the legitimacy—and therefore, admissibility—of a suspect's custodial confession.

SOLIL PAUL, COUNTER-TERRORISM LAWS: THE SUPREME COURT ON CONFESSIONS

South Asia Terrorism Portal[30]

. . . It must also be clear that such presumption against the validity of custodial confessions stands rebutted only in extreme and grave times; only when existing laws fail to effectively tackle or successfully address pressing dangers to society and the nation. Even under such extraordinary circumstances, this is not to argue that custodial confessions be treated on par with non-custodial confessions, but rather, to acknowledge the 'suspect' nature of the former, and ensure that stringent safeguards be made an intrinsic part of the scheme of such laws, and that such safeguards be scrupulously observed so as to prevent the possibility of the extortion of any false confession.

These circumstances and the need for such safeguards have been clearly recognised and the Supreme Court in the POTA Case, noted:

> Parliament has explored the possibility of employing the existing laws to tackle terrorism and arrived at the conclusion that the laws are not capable. It is also clear to Parliament that terrorism is not a usual law and order problem.

Nevertheless, the Court emphasised, in the same breath, the need to balance the security concerns of the nation with well-established values of the civilized world, and warned:

> The protection and promotion of human rights under the rule of law is essential in the prevention of terrorism . . . If human rights are violated in the process of combating terrorism, it will be self-defeating. Terrorism often thrives where human rights are violated, which adds to the need to strengthen action to combat violations of human rights . . . The lack of hope for justice provides breeding grounds for terrorism . . . In all cases, the fight against terrorism must be respectful to the human rights.

This brings us to the crucial question: what safeguards does the law enact?

As already stated, the first and foremost precondition for any valid confession is mandated by Article 20(3) of the Constitution: "No person accused of any offence shall be compelled to be a witness against himself." In addition, Section 24 of the Evidence Act specifically bars confessions that may be the

---

30. *Available at* http://www.satp.org/satporgtp/publication/faultlines/volume16/Article2.htm (last visited March 21, 2010).

result of any inducement, threat or promise, from the courts' consideration. Thus any confession, be it custodial or non-custodial, to be accepted by a court of law, should not be "compelled," in other words, must be "voluntary." This means that counterterrorism laws have to primarily safeguard the voluntary nature of a confession and see to it that no form of compulsion is used against the accused while extracting a confession.

What would 'voluntary' mean or encompass in this context? The Supreme Court in Defender Pal Singh, after referring to a few legal dictionaries and cases clarified:

> the crux of making a statement voluntary is, what is intentional, intended, unimpelled by other influences, acting on ones own will, through his own conscience.

While upholding the constitutionality of Section 15, TADA Act, in Kartar Singh, the Supreme Court had enumerated specific guidelines

> to ensure that the confession obtained in the pre-indictment interrogation by a police officer . . . is not tainted with any vice but is in strict conformity with the well recognized and accepted aesthetic (sic) principles and fundamental fairness.

Issues to Consider

1. Does the threat of confessions obtained through torture justify the presumption that all custodial confessions are invalid?
2. Should torture utilized to obtain information from suspects be punished differently than sadistic torture?
3. Does India's long history of terrorism mean that aggressive counterterrorism methods should be viewed favorably?

C. INTERROGATIONS IN RESPONSE TO TERRORIST ATTACKS

As discussed above, India's interrogation methods and policies have been frequently criticized. The Indian Judiciary and Parliament have attempted to address these concerns by limiting the use of confessions and other inculpatory statements made by individuals during interrogation. Yet, questions persist with respect to both the extent to which authorities respect these limitations and the effectiveness of existing interrogation methods.

Much like Russia and Spain, India utilizes a criminal law model to classify terrorists. Promulgation and subsequent repeal of statutes reflect the realities of India's dilemma: aggressive counterterrorism tempered by internal and external considerations alike. Indian authorities may continue to develop alternative interrogation methods, such as narcoanalysis, or may implement enhanced measures—if not torture—as claimed in the aftermath of recent, significant terrorist attacks. What interrogation measures are implemented depends on the attack's severity, circumstances, and what group or nation is connected with the attack.

Issues to Consider

1. Does a suspect subjected to narcoanalysis give information voluntarily?
2. Should investigators, relying on traditional methods that fail to turn up useful evidence, be allowed to utilize techniques of questionable reliability in the hope that evidence will come to light?
3. Is it accurate to assume that individuals investigated for a crime will naturally make allegations that investigators abused them?
4. In a country as religiously divided as India, would it be more effective to have interrogators only question people who practice the same faith?
5. How does the Indian interrogation paradigm compare to the U.S., Israeli, and Russian models?
6. What circumstances, if any, justify enhanced interrogation techniques?

VII. SPAIN

As discussed in earlier chapters, Spain did not modify its existing criminal law paradigm in response to the Madrid train bombings. Rather, Spain responded to the attack as if it were a non-terrorist criminal act. This response, however, does not guarantee that authorities did not use more aggressive interrogation methods.

According to the Spanish criminal code, Spain does not have specific anti-terrorism laws; rather, terrorism is treated as an aggravated form of a crime. According to Spain's penal code, a terrorist offense is committed if the purpose of the act is to "subvert the constitutional order or seriously alter public peace."[31] However, Spain does deviate from its standard procedural laws when dealing with suspected terrorists.

Human rights organizations have accused Spanish law enforcement authorities of subjecting detainees to interrogations that violate international law norms and conventions. Complaints have addressed the interrogations of Spanish citizens suspected of involvement in ETA and other criminal activity. Detainees held incommunicado, primarily ETA suspects, report they were tortured or ill-treated by Civil Guards or police officers. The European Court of Human Rights examined the case of 15 Catalans suspected of being sympathizers of a Catalan independence movement: "The Catalans alleged they had been subjected to physical and mental torture and inhuman and degrading treatment on their arrest and in custody in Catalonia and at the Civil Guard

31. *Setting an Example? Counter-Terrorism Measures in Spain,* Human Rights Watch, Vol. 17, No. 1(D), January 2005, *available at* http://hrw.org/reports/2005/spain0105/spain0105.pdf (last visited October 8, 2010).

headquarters in Madrid in mid-1992."[32] Amnesty International also reported that a group of journalists who had been arrested were held incommunicado.[33] After being released, several of the detainees said they had been tortured by asphyxiation with a plastic bag, exhausting physical exercises, threats, and simulated execution.

Human Rights Watch has also issued critical reports about the custodial interrogation practices of Spanish authorities.[34] Following the 2004 Madrid train bombings, Human Rights Watch reported the following:

> Human Rights Watch gathered testimonies about the experience of nine 11-M (March 11, 2004 train bombings, referenced hereinafter as 11-M) suspects. Of these, two were held for five days before the official police statement was taken; five were held for four days; and the remaining two were held for two days. One suspect was held for nearly ninety-six hours before his statement was taken. In almost all cases, the lawyer was notified the same day the statement was to be taken; he or she was only told the detainee's name, and the time and place of the proceeding.
>
> The three 11-M defendants with whom Human Rights Watch spoke recounted that they had been questioned by police during the incommunicado period without the presence of their lawyer. Defendant X said he was illegally questioned nightly without a lawyer present, sometimes two or three times a night, for the four nights he spent in police custody. Defendants Y and Z both said they were each questioned once by the police during their incommunicado period. The girlfriend of a fourth defendant told Human Rights Watch that he had been interrogated every day while in police custody.[35]

Human Rights Watch has further expressed concern that Spain's incommunicado detention policy creates conditions that facilitate the commission of torture or other forms of mistreatment of suspects in custody.[36] The need for medical examinations of suspects in custody has been recommended as a safeguard against torture or mistreatment while in custody.

> Under Spanish law, all detainees in police custody have the right to an examination by a forensic doctor. As described above, the November 2003 reform of the LEC [Spain's Code of Criminal Procedure] added the right of incommunicado detainees to request a second forensic examination. This reform, however, falls short of compliance with the CPT [European Committee for the Prevention of Torture] and the Human Rights Committee's recommendations, as it still does not allow the detainee to be examined by a doctor of his or her own choice.[37]

According to Spanish law, those suspected of committing a crime have the right to be informed immediately, in an understandable manner, of his or her rights and the grounds for the arrest (Art. 520(2)). All detainees have the

---

32. *Id.*
33. *Id.*
34. *Id.*
35. *Id. at* 32-33.
36. *Id.* at 34.
37. *Id.*

right to choose a lawyer and to request that the lawyer be present during any interrogations (Art. 520(2)(c)). "Detention in police custody should last 'no longer than the time strictly necessary to carry out the investigations aimed at establishing the facts'; the detainee must be released or brought before a judicial authority within seventy-two hours" (Art. 520(1)).[38] While incommunicado detention is allowed by law, the following must be addressed: whether according to Spanish law a detainee may be tortured or whether there are clear restrictions and guidelines delineating the limits of coercive interrogation. Furthermore, what branch of government guarantees that security and law enforcement officials will not violate statutory restrictions?

The concern expressed by Human Rights Watch over Spain's current anti-terrorism practices led to a series of recommended changes to Spanish policies. The central concerns pertain to the failure of Spain's Criminal Code and Code of Procedure to provide adequate safeguards against ill-treatment while suspected terrorists were in detention. The group has urged the Spanish government to ensure adequate safeguards for detainees in police custody by undertaking the following measures:

- All reports of ill-treatment during police custody should be fully investigated. Judges must act promptly to ascertain the veracity of all allegations of mistreatment that come to their attention, even when the forensic medical examinations do not reveal any physical abuse.
- The National Police and Civil Guard should ensure that all suspects in custody are treated with dignity. Measures designed to protect the physical integrity of suspects and others in the detention facility should be limited to those strictly necessary. In particular, the practice of holding suspects and presenting them in court without shoes should be abolished.
- Independent observers, including accredited nongovernmental and international organizations, should be allowed access to police stations to verify the material and physical conditions of detainees.

The Constitutional Court of Spain seeks to ensure that the recommendations of NGOs such as Human Rights Watch are duly implemented. As the supreme interpreter of the Spanish Constitution, the Court is responsible for the protection of fundamental rights and therefore has jurisdiction to hear individual appeals for protection against violations committed by any public power.

While Spain has been widely criticized for its treatment of ETA suspects, international concern has not been raised regarding interrogations conducted in the aftermath of the train station bombing. This seems to indicate that the Spanish authorities have not adopted more stringent interrogation methods used by the other surveyed nations.

---

38. *Id.*

Issues to Consider

1. In the context of terrorism interrogations, which branch of government is best suited for establishing guidelines for interrogators?
2. Is it appropriate that the courts or legislatures curtail the executive?
3. If the criminal law paradigm is implemented against terrorists, what should the limits of interrogation be?
4. What is the significance of domestic—rather than foreign-based—terrorism when developing an interrogation model?
5. Does the decision not to re-articulate the interrogation model after the Madrid train bombings suggest a "business as usual" approach?

VIII. CHINA

A. INTRODUCTION

In recent years, the issue of torture in China has become a subject of public concern and debate, particularly after several prominent wrongful-conviction cases came to light in 2005. The growing willingness of officials to acknowledge that Chinese scholars and journalists have been tortured in is a significant step forward. Chinese scholars and journalists are increasingly publishing detailed critiques of the criminal justice system, addressing issues including weak investigations, a lack of professionalism in the police, and confessions extorted by torture. Chinese officials and analysts have characterized torture as widespread.[39]

The government's willingness to acknowledge the pervasiveness of torture was confirmed when the Supreme People's Procuratorate (SPP) published *The Crime of Tortured Confession (Xingxun Bigong Zui)* in late 1997, which included China's first publicly released official statistics on criminal cases of torture-based confession. According to the report, there was an average of 364 cases of torture-based confession per year between 1979 and 1989, upward of 400 cases per year in the 1990s, and 241 persons who had died from torture over the two-year period of 1993-1994.

In light of this, the government has undertaken a number of measures to directly address torture as an interrogation measure. In August 2003, the Minister of Public Security, Zhou Yongkang, issued a set of unified regulations on law enforcement procedures for public security institutions entitled "Regulations on the Procedures for Handling Administrative Cases" which included procedures that defined police powers; imposed time limits for confiscation

39. 2005 Annual Report, Congressional-Executive Commission on China *available at* https://www.cecc.gov/publications/annual-reports/2005-annual-report (last visited February 19, 2024).

of property, investigations, and examination of suspects; and articulated legal means for gathering evidence.

In 2004, the Ministry of Public Security issued regulations prohibiting the use of torture and threats to gain confessions and initiated a nationwide campaign to improve criminal investigation capacity. In the same year, the SPP launched a nationwide campaign to crack down on officials who abuse their powers. The SPP announced in 2005 that eliminating interrogation through torture was a priority of its work agenda and instructed procurators that torture-based confessions cannot justify formal approval of arrests and that prosecutors must eliminate illegally-obtained evidence.

In addition to initiatives at the central level, several promising similar initiatives have occurred regionally. The Zhejiang provincial Public Security Department issued regulations regarding forced confessions stating that local police chiefs will be expected to resign in any district where there are more than two cases of forced confessions resulting in injuries, miscarriages of justice, or public order problems. In mid-April 2005, Sichuan law enforcement and judicial authorities issued a joint opinion prohibiting the use of illegally obtained evidence and required courts to exclude coerced statements and confessions if police could not provide a rational explanation of the alleged coercion or refused to investigate allegations of abuse. Furthermore, the Hubei provincial procuratorate, high court, justice department, public security bureau, and State security bureau issued regulations on criminal evidence, including the prohibition of testimonies acquired through torture-based confessions.

Practical measures have been introduced to eliminate torture, including audio and video recording in interrogation rooms, strengthening representation during the investigative and pretrial phase of the criminal process by placing lawyers on a 24-hour basis in pilot police stations, designing interrogation rooms that separate suspects from interrogators, and placing resident procurators in places of detention and near public security bureaus to supervise law enforcement personnel.

The UN Special Rapporteur has observed positive developments at the legislative level, including the planned reform of several laws relevant to the criminal procedure, intended to bring Chinese legislation into greater conformity with international norms, particularly the fair trial standards contained in the International Covenant on Civil and Political Rights (ICCPR) that China signed in 1998. The Special Rapporteur suggests that China might endeavor to increase transparency regarding the number of death sentences, as well as to consider legislation that would allow direct petitioning to the SPC in cases where individuals claim relief by lower courts, particularly in cases involving the use of torture and access to counsel.

B. CHINA AND GUANTANAMO

In 2002, the United States welcomed foreign interrogators from several countries including China, Libya, Jordan, Uzbekistan, and Tunisia to aid in interrogations of prisoners at Guantanamo.

Foreign Interrogators in Guantanamo Bay

Center for Constitutional Rights[40]

The U.S. allowed Chinese officials access to the Uighurs in Guantánamo as a diplomatic concession. China's human rights record is egregious, and Uighurs are one of the most persecuted groups in China. All of the Uighur prisoners are believed to have been interrogated by Chinese security forces while in Guantánamo.

Numerous Uighur prisoners in Guantánamo, including Ali Thabid, Bahtiyar Mahnut, Sabir Osman, and Huzaifa Parhat, were told by Chinese interrogators that they would be killed or imprisoned if the U.S. returned them to China. One Chinese interrogator even told prisoner Adel Abdul Hakim that he was "lucky" to be in Guantánamo because in a Chinese jail, he would be "finished." Uighur prisoner Abdusemet was threatened and deprived of sleep and food by Chinese interrogators.

Chinese officials told another prisoner that the Defense Department has given the Chinese information the prisoner had previously provided to U.S. interrogators about himself and his family, violating specific promises by U.S. interrogators that they would not provide this information to the Chinese. The Chinese also attempted to photograph this prisoner during his interrogation, and when he resisted, U.S. soldiers forcibly restrained him and held his head so that the Chinese could clearly photograph his face.

The U.S. government has consistently exploited the Uighurs' fear of torture and death at the hands of the Chinese. Prisoner Adel Noori reports that around January 2004, CIA or Defense Department officials threatened to send him to China unless he cooperated and spied on other non-Uighur prisoners in Guantánamo. When he refused, he was punished severely. Mr. Abdusemet also stated that an American who identified himself as a White House representative specifically threatened to send Mr. Abdusemet to China if he did not cooperate.

40. *Available at* https://ccrjustice.org/home/get-involved/tools-resources/fact-sheets-and-faqs/foreign-interrogators-guantanamo-bay (last visited February 19, 2024).

CHAPTER 9

DUE PROCESS

PART A – THE STATUS GIVEN TO TERRORISTS

I. INTRODUCTION

Much uncertainty remains regarding one of the seminal issues in terrorism: how to determine the rights and status of suspected terrorists and the appropriate judicial forum for trying suspected terrorists. Doing so requires, in part, resolving whether the terrorist defendant has the right to confront his accuser.

For example, in the context of American criminal and constitutional law, the Sixth Amendment guarantees a defendant the right to "be confronted with the witnesses against him." Granting that right to terrorist defendants potentially requires exposing both intelligence information and the means and methods by which it was received. However, the larger question—which shall be discussed in this chapter—is whether terrorists should be accorded the same rights as criminals or whether terrorism is a separate paradigm. The question is not abstract; the answer dictates what rights are to be extended to individuals defined as suspected terrorists.

How the paradigm is defined determines what court of law—if at all—a suspected terrorist is brought before. That is, if terrorism is defined as war, then terrorists are treated as prisoners of war; if terrorism is viewed in accordance with the criminal law paradigm, then suspected terrorists shall be accorded the same rights as traditional criminals; and if neither category is appropriate, then an alternative paradigm needs to be articulated.

Issues to Consider

1. Should terrorists be granted trials?
2. What should be the guiding principle in determining what judicial regime is appropriate for trying terrorists?
3. In determining which alternative regime to implement, what considerations and interests should be taken into account?
4. What issues and rights are at stake?
5. Should terrorists be granted the same rights as criminal defendants?
6. Should terrorists be treated as prisoners of war, who may not be brought to trial unless they are accused of having committed a war crime or of committing a crime in captivity?

II. UNITED STATES

A. MILITARY COMMISSIONS

In the aftermath of 9/11, the Bush administration concluded that Article III courts were inappropriate for trying terrorists and those who provided terrorists with safe harbor.[1] Administration officials argued that an alternate judicial regime was required to fight terrorism effectively. Accordingly, President Bush issued an Executive Order establishing military commissions.

Detention, Treatment, and Trial of Certain Non-Citizens in the War Against Terrorism

Military Order §1(a), November 13, 2001, 66 Fed. Reg. 57, 833 (Nov. 16, 2001)

By the authority vested in me as President and as Commander in Chief of the Armed Forces of the United States by the Constitution and the laws of the United States of America, including the Authorization for Use of Military Force Joint Resolution (Public Law 107-40, 115 Stat. 224) and sections 821 and 836 of title 10, United States Code, it is hereby ordered as follows:

Section 1. Findings

(a) International terrorists, including members of al Qaida, have carried out attacks on United States diplomatic and military personnel and facilities abroad and on citizens and property within the United States on

1. Article III Courts, defined by Article III of the U.S. Constitution, constitute the Supreme Court of the United States and the remaining courts of the judicial branch. Congress can vest these courts with jurisdiction to hear certain cases involving disputes between citizens of different states or countries.

a scale that has created a state of armed conflict that requires the use of the United States Armed Forces.

(b) In light of grave acts of terrorism and threats of terrorism, including the terrorist attacks on September 11, 2001, on the headquarters of the United States Department of Defense in the national capital region, on the World Trade Center in New York, and on civilian aircraft such as in Pennsylvania, I proclaimed a national emergency on September 14, 2001 (Proc. 7463, Declaration of National Emergency by Reason of Certain Terrorist Attacks).

(c) Individuals acting alone and in concert involved in international terrorism possess both the capability and the intention to undertake further terrorist attacks against the United States that, if not detected and prevented, will cause mass deaths, mass injuries, and massive destruction of property, and may place at risk the continuity of the operations of the United States Government.

(d) The ability of the United States to protect the United States and its citizens, and to help its allies and other cooperating nations protect their nations and their citizens, from such further terrorist attacks depends in significant part upon using the United States Armed Forces to identify terrorists and those who support them, to disrupt their activities, and to eliminate their ability to conduct or support such attacks.

(e) To protect the United States and its citizens, and for the effective conduct of military operations and prevention of terrorist attacks, it is necessary for individuals subject to this order pursuant to section 2 hereof to be detained, and, when tried, to be tried for violations of the laws of war and other applicable laws by military tribunals.

(f) Given the danger to the safety of the United States and the nature of international terrorism, and to the extent provided by and under this order, I find consistent with section 836 of title 10, United States Code, that it is not practicable to apply in military commissions under this order the principles of law and the rules of evidence generally recognized in the trial of criminal cases in the United States district courts.

(g) Having fully considered the magnitude of the potential deaths, injuries, and property destruction that would result from potential acts of terrorism against the United States, and the probability that such acts will occur, I have determined that an extraordinary emergency exists for national defense purposes, that this emergency constitutes an urgent and compelling government interest, and that issuance of this order is necessary to meet the emergency. . . .

Sec. 3. Detention Authority of the Secretary of Defense. Any individual subject to this order shall be—

(a) detained at an appropriate location designated by the Secretary of Defense outside or within the United States. . . .

Sec. 4. Authority of the Secretary of Defense Regarding Trials of Individuals Subject to this Order.

(a) Any individual subject to this order shall, when tried, be tried by military commission for any and all offenses triable by military commission that such individual is alleged to have committed, and may be punished in accordance with the penalties provided under applicable law, including life imprisonment or death. . . .

(c) Orders and regulations issued under subsection (b) of this section shall include, but not be limited to, rules for the conduct of the proceedings of military commissions, including pretrial, trial, and post-trial procedures, modes of proof, issuance of process, and qualifications of attorneys, which shall at a minimum provide for—

(1) military commissions to sit at any time and any place, consistent with such guidance regarding time and place as the Secretary of Defense may provide;

(2) a full and fair trial, with the military commission sitting as the triers of both fact and law;

(3) admission of such evidence as would, in the opinion of the presiding officer of the military commission (or instead, if any other member of the commission so requests at the time the presiding officer renders that opinion, the opinion of the commission rendered at that time by a majority of the commission), have probative value to a reasonable person;

(4) in a manner consistent with the protection of information classified or classifiable under Executive Order 12958 of April 17, 1995, as amended, or any successor Executive Order, protected by statute or rule from unauthorized disclosure, or otherwise protected by law, (A) the handling of, admission into evidence of, and access to materials and information, and (B) the conduct, closure of, and access to proceedings;

(5) conduct of the prosecution by one or more attorneys designated by the Secretary of Defense and conduct of the defense by attorneys for the individual subject to this order;

(6) conviction only upon the concurrence of two-thirds of the members of the commission present at the time of the vote, a majority being present;

(7) sentencing only upon the concurrence of two-thirds of the members of the commission present at the time of the vote, a majority being present; and

(8) submission of the record of the trial, including any conviction or sentence, for review and final decision by me or by the Secretary of Defense if so designated by me for that purpose.

When establishing the military commissions, the administration relied on the Supreme Court's holding in *Quirin*,[2] where the Court used three different terms (illegal combatant, enemy belligerent, enemy combatant) to refer to captured Germans. While the Court upheld President Roosevelt's decision

2. Ex parte Quirin, 317 U.S. 1 (1942).

to bring the German saboteurs before a military tribunal, the Court did not resolve the larger, far more crucial issue of defining the saboteurs. The Court stated that "we have no occasion now to define with meticulous care the ultimate boundaries of the jurisdiction of military tribunals to try persons according to the law of war."[3] In attempting to determine the *Quirin* Court's working definition for any one of those interchangeably applied terms, it was assumed that the Court was referring to an individual engaged in combat with the United States who, for whatever reason, was not a soldier as commonly understood.

The appellants in *Quirin* were German soldiers who lost their status when they *purposefully* discarded their uniforms. Unlike terrorists, who do not belong to a regular army, the Court seemingly applied this "working definition" to individuals who, by all accounts, had been soldiers but as a result of their actions lost their status. In doing so, they enabled the Court to hold they were not soldiers when captured, and thus not entitled to prisoner of war status.

By relying on *Quirin,* the Bush administration established an alternative judicial regime to try individuals because of an assumed involvement in 9/11. This alternative judicial regime was premised on two foundations: (1) the detainees were not prisoners of war and therefore could be brought to trial; and (2) the detainees were not entitled to traditional Article III protections afforded to defendants in the criminal law paradigm.

According to administration officials who testified before Congress, the fundamental purpose of the Presidential Order was to bring "justice to persons charged with offenses under the laws of armed conflict"[4] and to "target a narrow class of individuals—terrorists."[5]

Issues to Consider

1. Was the administration correct in asserting that Article III courts are not appropriate for trying the detainees?
2. What rights guaranteed to criminal law defendants were perceived as threatening to the administration's counterterrorism efforts?
3. What alternatives to Article III courts could the administration have developed without creating a new legal regime?
4. What were the policy considerations in developing the military commissions?
5. What were the operational considerations in developing the military commissions?
6. In determining which paradigm is applicable to counterterrorism, what factors need to be balanced?

---

3. *Id.* at 46, 63.

4. Testimony of The Honorable Michael Chertoff, Assistant Attorney General, Criminal Division, U.S. Dep't of Justice, November 28, 2001, *Department of Justice Oversight: Preserving Our Freedoms While Defending Against Terrorism, available at* http://scholarship.law.georgetown.edu/cgi/viewcontent.cgi?article=1095&context=cong (last visited October 8, 2010).

5. *Id.* (Testimony of The Honorable John Ashcroft, Attorney General, U.S. Dept. of Justice).

7. Are the rights of the defendant paramount, or does combating terrorism justify adjusting the rights traditionally accorded to defendants?
8. Is denying the defendant the right to confront an accuser indicative of a "slippery slope"?
9. How much can the criminal law process be altered in the context of counterterrorism?
10. Can the state risk introducing evidence in accordance with the rules of evidence?

Not everyone agreed with the Bush administration's rationale for establishing the military commissions. Criticism centered on the lack of an independent judiciary, the lack of an appeals process, the lack of a sentencing regime known to the detainee, the process by which counsel was assigned, and the ability of the prosecutor to submit classified evidence to the court that the defendant would not be entitled to review. The backlash suggested that determining the appropriate forum for trying suspected terrorists required closer examination of two related questions: what is the appropriate definition of those engaged in terrorism, and what rights should they be granted?

Joan Fitzpatrick, Military Commissions: Jurisdiction of Military Commissions and the Ambiguous War on Terrorism

96 A.J.I.L. 345 (2002)

Have the attacks of September 11 resulted in a shift from metaphorical war/actual crime control to actual armed conflict? The suggestion that international terrorists pose a criminal threat is met with impatience in some quarters, as if it somehow diminishes the magnitude of the events of September 11. Terrorist crimes arguably differ from other transnational crimes, in that they are politically motivated and pose a threat to national security. However, in democratic societies, crimes against national security—espionage, for example—are not generally handled by military commissions. The Military Order of November 13 appears to rest on a perception that the current terrorist emergency is legally of a warlike character, and not simply a danger to national security or suitable grounds for military involvement in law enforcement.

The order refers generally to individuals and groups involved in international terrorism, and to the necessity for the United States Armed Forces to respond to their threats, to subject suspected terrorists to military detention and trial, and to depart from "the principles of law and the rules of evidence generally recognized in the trial of criminal cases in the United States district courts" because of the "danger to the safety of the United States and the nature of international terrorism." Trial may be for violations of any "applicable laws."

If the war on terrorism is now to be conceived of as an international armed conflict, it is one of startling breadth, innumerable "combatants," and indefinite duration. The United States considers a wide variety of groups to be engaged in international terrorism, as reflected in the lists of foreign terrorist organizations adopted by the secretary of state. These groups include Aum Shinrikyo, Basque Fatherland and Liberty, the Kurdistan Workers' Party, the Liberation Tigers of Tamil Eelam, the Real IRA, and the Shining Path. The U.S. military provides support to some governments engaged in internal armed conflicts against listed groups, notably the Revolutionary Armed Forces of Colombia and the Abu Sayyaf Group in the Philippines. This war on terrorism will endure until all these groups, and others similar to them, are eradicated.

The criminal law process guarantees the accused, and subsequently the defendant, the following protections: (1) a presumption of innocence until proven guilty; (2) the requirement that evidence is submitted in an open court of law; (3) the right to confront witnesses; (4) the right to remain silent; (5) the right to appeal to an independent judiciary; and (6) the right to trial by a jury of peers. Perhaps the most important right granted by the criminal law process is the defendant's right to confront his accusers, thereby enabling cross-examination in open court. However, since counterterrorism is based on intelligence, the prosecution would be obligated to make intelligence sources available for cross-examination. The risk is extraordinarily significant—and potentially life-threatening—for sources who testify.

Adopting a paradigm that does not guarantee the defendant the right to confront witnesses enables the prosecution to base a case, either in whole or in part, on intelligence information. As an example—albeit one that was criticized by the Supreme Court in *Hamdi v. Rumsfeld*[6]—the United States attempted to introduce intelligence information via the Mobbs Declaration.[7]

> On remand, the Government filed a response and a motion to dismiss the petition. It attached to its response a declaration from one Michael Mobbs (hereinafter "Mobbs Declaration"), who identified himself as Special Advisor to the Under Secretary of Defense for Policy. Mobbs indicated that in this position, he has been "substantially involved with matters related to the detention of enemy combatants in the current war against the al Qaeda terrorists and those who support and harbor them (including the Taliban)." He expressed his "familiar[ity]" with Department of Defense and United States military policies and procedures applicable to the detention, control, and transfer of al Qaeda and Taliban personnel, and declared that "[b]ased upon my review of relevant records and reports, I am also familiar with the facts and circumstances related to the capture of . . . Hamdi and his detention by U.S. military forces."
>
> Mobbs then set forth what remains the sole evidentiary support that the Government has provided to the courts for Hamdi's detention. The declaration

6. Hamdi v. Rumsfeld, 504 U.S. 507 (2004).

7. The Mobbs Declaration is a statement supplied by a Department of Defense official, summarizing the intelligence information known to the authorities regarding the activities of a particular defendant. The material is used in detention hearings. In Israel, the classified information presented to the Judge regarding a defendant was previously referred to as "negative security material" and reflected the known intelligence based on HUMINT and SIGINT alike. The material was used for a variety of criminal law and administrative sanctions. The primary issues are the reliability of the source(s) and whether the material is corroborated.

> states that Hamdi "traveled to Afghanistan" in July or August 2001, and that he thereafter "affiliated with a Taliban military unit and received weapons training." It asserts that Hamdi "remained with his Taliban unit following the attacks of September 11" and that, during the time when Northern Alliance forces were "engaged in battle with the Taliban," "Hamdi's Taliban unit surrendered" to those forces, after which he "surrender[ed] his Kalishnikov assault rifle" to them. The Mobbs Declaration also states that, because al Qaeda and the Taliban "were and are hostile forces engaged in armed conflict with the armed forces of the United States," "individuals associated with" those groups "were and continue to be enemy combatants." Mobbs states that Hamdi was labeled an enemy combatant "[b]ased upon his interviews and in light of his association with the Taliban." According to the declaration, a series of "U.S. military screening team[s]" determined that Hamdi met "the criteria for enemy combatants," and "a subsequent interview of Hamdi has confirmed that he surrendered and gave his firearm to Northern Alliance forces, which supports his classification as an enemy combatant."[8]

In a series of memos, the Bush administration clearly articulated a position that those detained in the war on terrorism were not guaranteed Geneva Convention rights. Though the memos were later "corrected," the administration's initial response posited that the detainees were not entitled to full Geneva Convention protections; in other words, the administration determined they were not soldiers and therefore could be brought to trial.

According to the Geneva Convention,[9] captured soldiers must be returned to their home state upon the cessation of hostilities. Unlike war, where culmination is marked by an agreement between the warring states, cessation of terrorist hostilities is difficult to foresee. The lack of a foreseeable, agreed-upon end to the conflict directly affects the detainees' present and future status.

Unlike criminals, whose date of release is determined either by a judge or jury in their presence, enemy combatants, as defined by the Bush administration, are held in a black hole. In large part, this policy has been adopted by the Obama administration.

Issues to Consider

1. Under what circumstance is indefinite detention justifiable?
2. What are the dangers emanating from indefinite detention?
3. How does the state determine if the individual in indefinite detention represents a continued threat to the nation's security?
4. How much of a threat does the individual have to present in order to remain in indefinite detention, and what is the benchmark?
5. What government agency should be responsible for reviewing the status of the detainee? Should there be an independent review?
6. What act must an individual commit in order to be the recipient of these significantly reduced rights? Who decides?

---

8. *See Hamdi*, *supra* note 6, at 513.
9. Geneva Convention Relative to the Treatment of Prisoners of War art. 118, Aug. 12, 1949, 6 U.S.T 3316, 75 U.N.T.S. 135.

B. THE PRESIDENTIAL ORDER

In November 2001, President Bush issued a Presidential Order that did not clearly define the term "enemy combatant." According to Section 2 of the Order, the following individuals will be brought before the military commissions:

> (a) The term "individual subject to this order" shall mean any individual who is not a United States citizen with respect to whom I determine from time to time in writing that:
>
> (1) there is reason to believe that such individual, at the relevant times,
>
> (i) is or was a member of the organization known as al Qaeda;
>
> (ii) has engaged in, aided or abetted, or conspired to commit, acts of international terrorism, or acts in preparation therefore, that have caused, threaten to cause, or have as their aim to cause, injury to or adverse effects on the United States, its citizens, national security, foreign policy, or economy;
>
> (iii) has knowingly harbored one or more individuals described in subparagraphs (i) or (ii) of subsection 2(a)(1) of this order.[10]

According to the above, an enemy combatant may be defined as any individual, who *in any way, shape, or form* came in contact with any member of al Qaeda during any period of time with the intent of causing harm, *in the broadest definition of harm,* to the United States. An enemy combatant, as defined in the Presidential Order, is an individual who need not necessarily have been involved in an act of terrorism in the present; it is sufficient to have provided assistance in the past, even if minimal. Furthermore, the minimal degree required is not defined, leaving significant grounds for loose interpretation in determining whether an individual is an enemy combatant.

Issues to Consider

1. Is a broad definition of "enemy combatant" effective?
2. What are the risks of such a definition?
3. Does casting a wide net contribute to combating terrorism?
4. Should terrorists who have different positions/responsibilities be differentiated?
5. What level of intelligence needs to be submitted to determine if an individual is an enemy combatant?
6. What are the criteria for determining whether an individual is an enemy combatant?

10. *Id.*

The Court in *Quirin* failed to articulate who qualifies as an enemy combatant. Justice Stevens's dissent in *Rumsfeld v. Padilla*[11] addresses this issue:

> Whether respondent is entitled to immediate release is a question that reasonable jurists may answer in different ways. There is, however, only one possible answer to the question whether he is entitled to a hearing on the justification for his detention.
>
> At stake in this case is nothing less than the essence of a free society. Even more important than the method of selecting the people's rulers and their successors is the character of the constraints imposed on the Executive by the rule of law. Unconstrained Executive detention for the purpose of investigating and preventing subversive activity is the hallmark of the Star Chamber. Access to counsel for the purpose of protecting the citizen from official mistakes and mistreatment is the hallmark of due process.
>
> Executive detention of subversive citizens, like detention of enemy soldiers to keep them off the battlefield, may sometimes be justified to prevent persons from launching or becoming missiles of destruction. It may not, however, be justified by the naked interest in using unlawful procedures to extract information. Incommunicado detention for months on end is such a procedure. Whether the information so procured is more or less reliable than that acquired by more extreme forms of torture is of no consequence. For if this Nation is to remain true to the ideals symbolized by its flag, it must not wield the tools of tyrants even to resist an assault by the forces of tyranny.[12]

The need to develop standards for determining *when* and *why* an individual may be detained is ultimately more significant than *how.* A nation has a heavy burden when determining that an individual must be deprived of rights fundamental to the criminal law process.

The Supreme Court addressed the issue of the military commissions and enemy combatants in *Hamdan*:

> The commission's procedures . . . provide . . . that an accused and his civilian counsel may be excluded from, and precluded from, ever learning what evidence was presented during any part of the proceeding . . . the presiding officer decides to "close." Grounds for closure include the protection of classified information, the physical safety of participants and witnesses, the protection of intelligence and law enforcement sources, methods, or activities, and "other national security interests." Appointed military defense counsel must be privy to these closed sessions, but may, at the presiding officer's discretion, be forbidden to reveal to the client what took place therein. Another striking feature is that the rules governing Hamdan's commission permit the admission of any evidence that, in the presiding officer's opinion, would have probative value to a reasonable person. Moreover, the accused and his civilian counsel may be denied access to classified and other "protected information," so long as the presiding officer concludes that the evidence is "probative" and that its admission without the accused's knowledge would not result in the denial of a full and fair trial.[13]

---

11. Rumsfeld v. Padilla, 542 U.S. 426 (2004) (Stevens, J., dissenting).
12. *Id.*
13. Hamdan v. Rumsfeld, 548 U.S. 557, 560 (2006).

In further evaluating the procedures for the military commissions, the Court held that: "Even assuming that Hamdan is a dangerous individual who would cause great harm or death to innocent civilians given the opportunity, the Executive nevertheless must comply with the prevailing rule of law in undertaking to try him and subject him to criminal punishment."[14]

Issues to Consider

1. What standards of proof are applicable when determining who is an enemy combatant?
2. How engaged must the individual be in order to be classified as an enemy combatant?
3. Is a time limit appropriate in determining when the individual was last engaged?
4. What mechanisms enable the suspected terrorist to state his case?

Amos N. Guiora, American Counterterrorism: The Triangle of Detention, Interrogation and Trial

Magna Carta Institute's Symposium, Towards a Global Legal Counter-Terrorism Model: Transatlantic Perspectives, 2010

The Obama Administration has an extraordinarily full plate of demanding decisions. With respect to counterterrorism, the President must address core issues and resolve long simmering dilemmas. While examining the actions of the Bush Administration is important, resolving existing conundrums is essential. In that vein, as these lines are being written, the Administration announced on November 13, 2009 that it would prosecute Khalid Shaikh Mohammed, the self-described mastermind of the Sept. 11 attacks, in a Manhattan federal courtroom, a decision that ignited a sharp political debate but took a step toward resolving one of the most pressing terrorism detention issues. The decision, announced by Attorney General Eric H. Holder Jr., could mean one of the highest-profile and highest-security terrorism trials in history would be set just blocks from where hijackers for Al Qaeda destroyed the World Trade Center, killing nearly 3,000 people. Mr. Holder said he would instruct prosecutors to seek death sentences for Mr. Mohammed and four accused Sept. 11 co-conspirators who would be tried alongside him. But while the civilian system would handle those cases, he said five other detainees would be prosecuted before a military commission. Mr. Holder said he was confident that the men would be convicted, and other administration officials said they had ample legal authority to keep classified information secret. They also suggested that they could continue to detain anyone deemed to be a combatant under Congress's authorization to use military force against Al Qaeda. . . .

14. *Id.* at 563.

Similarly, terrorists are distinct from soldiers; the latter are part of the nation-state's military whereas the former belong to non-state entities. According to the Geneva Conventions, a soldier must meet a four part test: conduct himself in accordance with the laws of war, carry his weapon openly, wear readily visible insignia and belong to a chain of command. Of those four, the only relevant criterion to terrorism is a hierarchy that some terrorist organizations have created. Clearly, terrorists—in the main—do not carry their weapons openly (e.g., suicide bombers) nor wear readily distinguishable apparel that distinguishes them from the civilian population. Most importantly, terrorists deliberately target innocent civilians in a willful effort to advance their cause. Whereas soldiers are trained to distinguish between innocent civilians and combatants, terrorists do not distinguish between categories of potential targets. In essence, while soldiers are taught to kill but not to be killers, terrorists do not burden themselves with such hair splitting.

III. ISRAEL

Israel has historically applied a two-track approach to Palestinians suspected of having committed acts of terrorism. Following the June 1967 Six-Day War, the Israel Defense Forces established military courts in the West Bank and the Gaza Strip for the purpose of trying Palestinians suspected of committing acts of terrorism.

Military judges are appointed by military commanders who have command responsibility over the West Bank and the Gaza Strip; military prosecutors are similarly appointed. Palestinians are represented before the courts by civilian defense attorneys, comprised of Palestinians and Israelis alike.

Palestinians brought before the Court are initially interrogated by the Israel Security Agency (ISA), and afterwards by the Israel police. The charge sheet, based either on the individual's confession or testimony of others, is submitted to the Court by the military prosecutor; the case is heard by a panel consisting of either one or three judges, depending on the severity of the charges. The trial is conducted according to Rules of Criminal Procedure and Evidence akin to those in Israeli civilian courts. If convicted, the defendant may appeal to the Military Court of Appeals; the prosecution may appeal if the Court has acquitted the defendant.

The second track that Israel has implemented for people suspected of having committed acts of terrorism is administrative detention. Administrative detentions, unlike the criminal process, are not punitive. Rather, an individual is detained if available intelligence indicates the individual is involved in the preparation of a *future* attack, and the information gathered cannot be made public, both because of a need to protect the informant and the means used to gather the information. In such instances, a senior IDF Commander will sign an administrative detention order upon receipt of a recommendation from the ISA and a legal opinion from an IDF Legal Advisor. The legal opinion will analyze the intelligence information and attempt to gauge whether the High Court of Justice will deny a petition, should the detainee file one.

Administrative detentions are codified in Article 85 of the Defense Emergency Regulations Act (1945). The detention period is for renewable six-month spans, subject to independent judicial review. There is no statutorily determined time period limiting the number of detentions. Renewability requires demonstrating the detainee continues to present a viable security threat. In the overwhelming majority of cases, the basis for extension of the initial detention order is the *same* intelligence that had served as the basis for the military commander's initial decision.

Issues to Consider

1. When does intelligence information become too far removed to justify continued detention?
2. How significant must the information be in order to justify both the initial detention and its extension?
3. How great of a threat must the individual continue to present for the information to still be valid?
4. From the state's perspective what are the advantages of administrative detention compared to criminal prosecution?
5. What is the significance of Israel's two-track approach in the context of determining the rights and status of the detainee?

Administrative detention has been heavily criticized[15] for a number of reasons. The criticism has primarily concentrated on two issues: the detainee's inability to confront his accuser and the resulting "fishing expedition" his lawyer is required to conduct. However, unlike the initial U.S. Military Commission mechanism established by the Presidential Order, the Military Commander's decision regarding the administrative detention of an individual is subject to independent judicial review by the High Court of Justice.[16]

A. TRIALS OF DETAINEES

Trials can take place in either of two different venues: civilian courts or IDF military courts (distinct from a court martial, which only tries soldiers).

An overwhelming majority of Palestinians accused of terrorist acts are tried in the Military Court, even if the act was committed in Israel proper (pre-1967 borders). The primary reason for this is substantive: if the act was planned in the West Bank, the participants reside in the West Bank, and the terrorist activities occur primarily in the West Bank, then Military Courts are deemed to have jurisdiction over the matter.

15. *See, e.g.*, Orna Ben-Naftali & Sean S. Gleichgevitch, *Missing in Legal Action: Lebanese Hostages in Israel*, 41 Harv. Int'l L.J. 185 (2000), Eitan Barak, *With the Cover of Darkness: Ten Years of Games with Human Beings as "Bargaining Chips" and the Supreme Court*, 8 PLILIM 77, 80-81 (1999) (Heb.).

16. HCJ 5784/03, Salama v. IDF Commander in Judea and Samaria; HCJ 3239/02, Marab v. IDF Commander in the West Bank.

The judicial trial process is similar to the U.S. criminal system, except there is no jury: the defendant is innocent until proven guilty, the state submits a charge sheet, and—similar to courts in large U.S. cities—over 90 percent of defendants plead out.

Akin to the constitutionally guaranteed right in the United States to confront the accuser, secret intelligence information cannot be submitted to the court for the purpose of conviction. However, it can be the basis for a suspect's initial detention and remand extension. In Israel, a suspect who has been arrested must be brought before a judge within 24 hours. In the West Bank, as amended in 1997, a suspect can be held for up to eight days without seeing a judge.[17]

Issues to Consider

1. Should there be a term limit for administrative detentions?
2. What is the appropriate process for determining what classified information should be made available to the detainee?
3. After an individual has been administratively detained, what should the process be for evaluating if the criminal law process can be utilized?
4. Does a two-track approach achieve the goals of protecting the state and guaranteeing basic rights to the detainee?
5. What are the advantages of defining the detainee as an enemy combatant rather than as a criminal?
6. What safeguards need to be institutionalized to ensure that the enemy combatant is guaranteed basic rights?

B. APPLICATION

On April 14, 2002, the Israel Defense Forces arrested Marwan Barghouti, the head of the Tanzim, a militant wing of Arafat's Fatah organization in the West Bank. Barghout challenged the jurisdiction of the Court to try his case, arguing:

1. The authority of the State of Israel to try Palestinians who attack Israelis was negated upon the signing of the Oslo Accords.
2. The rules of international law reject Israel's right to try the Defendant, since he is a freedom fighter opposing occupation. All forms of opposition have been defined as legitimate, including the use of violent force. If such a fighter is apprehended, he is to be defined as a prisoner of war and not as a criminal.
3. The Defendant was kidnapped from Ramallah by IDF soldiers contrary to the Oslo Accords and international law.

17. Military Order 378. In Israel, according to section 9.3.3 of the penal code a detainee must be brought before a judge within 24 hours.

4. The Defendant holds immunity negating the right of the State of Israel to put him on trial.
5. The indictment is political and constitutes an indictment against the entire Palestinian people.[18]

Though Barghouti was a resident of the West Bank, a politically-based decision was made to bring him to trial in an Israeli civilian court rather than in the West Bank Military Court. Judge Zvi Gurfinkel's holding is equally applicable either to a military or civilian court, since it clearly articulates the status and rights of a detainee arrested and tried before a court of law in the context of "armed conflict short of war."

State of Israel v. Marwan Barghouti

Ruling by Judge Zvi Gurfinkel, Dec. 12, 2002

District Court of Tel Aviv and Jaffa Criminal Case No. 092134/02

The Defendant claims that he is to be considered a prisoner of war, and, accordingly, the Occupying Power is forbidden to prosecute him under criminal law.

The Defendant is not to be considered a prisoner of war.

Terrorists who attack a civilian population do not fall within the framework of "lawful combatants" entitled to the status of "prisoners of war," since they do not meet the conditions, in accordance with international law, that a lawful combatant is required to meet. The heads of the Palestinian terror organizations, of whom the Defendant is one, systematically violate the rules of war.

International law distinguishes between two groups of combatants who undertake hostile actions against the State of Israel.

The first group of elements that undertake hostile actions against the State comprises persons who are part of regular armies that engage in combative actions against the State of Israel in accordance with the rules of war.

Combatants who act within the framework of this group and are apprehended receive the status of prisoners of war. Prisoners of war are not prosecuted in accordance with criminal law for their participation in combative actions, provided that they acted in accordance with the rules of war. If, however, they acted contrary to the rules of war, they may be prosecuted on account of war crimes.

In order for a combatant to be recognized as prisoner of war, he must meet four cumulative conditions as established in the Third Geneva Convention of 1949 (Article 4(2)):

> The first condition is the presence of a commander responsible for his subordinates.

18. State of Israel v. Marwan Barghouti, Ruling by Judge Zvi Gurfinkel, Dec. 12, 2002, *available at* http://www.mfa.gov.il/MFA/MFAArchive/2000_2009/2002/12/State%20of%20Israel%20vs%20Marwan%20Barghouti-%20Ruling%20by%20Jud (last visited October 8, 2010).

> The second condition is the presence of a fixed distinguishing sign that may be identified from a distance.
>
> The third condition is that combatants must carry their weapons openly.
>
> The fourth condition is that the actions undertaken must be in accordance with the rules and customs of law.

Regarding the Defendant, three of the four conditions are not met.

The field staff, commanders and perpetrators of actions did not bear a fixed distinguishing sign, and accordingly could not be identified from a distance.

The weapon they carried was not overt—on the contrary. The explosives were placed in belts carried by the perpetrators on their bodies, under their clothes, and the weapons were concealed until the moment when they were suddenly revealed at the place of the attack.

The acts of resistance were not managed in accordance with the rules of war, which prohibit injury to civilians; rather, the combat was directed against civilians, including women and children, passengers on buses, shoppers in markets, persons walking in the streets of the city, persons sitting in cafes and eating in restaurants, passengers in cars and pedestrians. None of these are actions that are undertaken by army combatants; these are acts of mass murder against civilians, women, men and children who are not engaged in combat and are not armed, on their way to schools, homes and places of work, while walking, eating or engaging in recreation.

The conditions established in international law in the above-mentioned Geneva Convention must be met cumulatively, and since three of the four conditions were not met, it must be determined that the Defendant is not a legal combatant, and accordingly is not a prisoner of war. Rather, he engaged in acts of murder against persons who are not party to combative actions, causing mass injury to civilians in their places of residence and gathering.

The second group of combatants identified by international law is referred to as "unlawful combatants." This group comprises the members of terrorist organizations and enemy forces that take part in acts of terror and hostility against Israelis and Israel, but who, in apprehension, are not entitled to the status of prisoners of war.

International law distinguishes, by way of a central and fundamental value, between combatants and civilians. One of the most important goals of the rules of war is to ensure that those injured during war shall be solely enemy combatants, while the civilian population shall be afforded protection and shall not be injured.

In order to implement this distinction, great importance is attached to the ability to distinguish between a combatant and a civilian during combat.

In his book, Dinstein notes that "if combatants can disappear within a civilian public, any civilian within that public will be considered a combatant and will suffer the consequences accruing therefrom." In his opinion, this is the central reason for the distinction between lawful combatants, who act in accordance with the rules of law, and unlawful combatants, who do not wear uniforms, or do not carry their weapon openly or who attack civilians. In so doing, they blur the distinction between combatant and civilian, and also endanger the population among whom they operate.

Accordingly, international law negates the right of unlawful combatants to enjoy the status of prisoners of war.

Regarding these combatants, Dinstein notes: "These unlawful combatants may be prosecuted and punished with the full severity of the law. The protection of the rules of law is denied to them, and accordingly they are subject to the usual criminal sanctions in national law. The unlawful combatant is prosecuted on account of a usual offense before the national court."

This distinction by international law between lawful and unlawful combatants is based on a very large number of documents, and in addition is anchored in international practice and employed by other armies around the world, such as the US army and the German army.

As stated above, the Defendant is an unlawful combatant and may be prosecuted under criminal law for deliberate injury to innocent civilians.

Moreover, even if we assume that the Defendant is a (lawful) combatant—and it is evident that he is not—the deliberate injury of innocent civilians is considered a violation of the rules of war in accordance with international law, and he may be prosecuted under criminal law for war crimes. The jurisdictional authority in such a case is granted to the state in whose territory the offense is committed.

In his book Dinstein further notes that in the case of an unlawful combatant who is also a war criminal, the apprehending power has the choice of prosecuting him for a normal criminal offense—murder, in the case of the Defendant—or for an offense relating to the violation of the rules of law, such as injury to civilians.

The Defendant attempts to seize on the Geneva Convention in order to argue that the State of Israel does not have the authority to try him as an unlawful combatant for the offenses of murder. However, consistent regard for the Geneva Convention reveals that a combatant is forbidden to attack civilian targets and civilians. Moreover, Article 48 of the Complementary Protocol of the Geneva Convention from 1949 states that constant caution must be undertaken when managing military operations in order to avoid injury to civilians.

The Defendant's actions, as well as the actions of the field commanders subordinate to him, and those actually executing the attacks, were undertaken against a civilian population within the territories of the State of Israel and within the territories of Judea and Samaria. The actions were perpetrated among a civilian population, which was used as a hiding place and as cover for planning, organizing and executing the acts of terror and killing.

The central objective of the actions of the Defendant and his subordinates is to injure and murder innocent Israeli citizens who are present in an area in which no combat is taking place. These are civilians who were pursuing an ordinary way of life, like any other person, in an area populated by an innocent civilian population that does not constitute a part of the array of combatants.

This policy of terror, the goal of which was to injure as many civilians as possible, is utterly prohibited under international law. The rules of law note the obligation to exercise maximum caution in order to prevent injury to civilians.

The Defendant's method of combat is, in the clearest possible manner, contrary to the most basic rules of law, and accordingly he is not entitled to enjoy the protections afforded under international law to combatants who act in accordance with the rules of war.

We have seen that there is no impediment in terms of the rules of law to the prosecution of the Defendant in accordance with criminal law in the State of Israel.

Issues to Consider

1. Does Judge Gurfinkel's holding articulate the most effective judicial regime for balancing the rights of the individual with the legitimate rights of the state?
2. Does Judge Gurfinkel's opinion suggest any restrictions or limitations on a detainee's rights in the context of a judicial process?
3. How does Judge Gurfinkel's opinion compare with Justice O'Connor's in *Hamdi?*
4. Does Judge Gurfinkel adequately and sufficiently address Barghouti's rights?
5. In comparing and contrasting the judicial regimes available in Israel, does the court adequately protect the defendant's rights?

The Israeli two-track approach—criminal trials and administrative detentions—is subject to robust judicial review. In determining which option is appropriate for a particular detainee, judicial oversight exercised by the High Court of Justice is a significant factor in the executive's decision-making process. The two-tiered approach is intended to protect a number of different constituencies: the defendant, the public, and the intelligence source.

IV. RUSSIA

In analyzing what paradigm Russia implements, two questions are relevant: how is the conflict defined, and how does that definition impact public debate and legislation? While the Constitutional Court in the Constitutionality of the Presidential Decrees and the Resolutions of the Federal Government concerning the Situation in Chechnya[19] never expressly used the term "non-international armed conflict," it did state that the Geneva Convention Additional Protocol II should have been applied by the parties.[20]

19. Judgment of the Constitutional Court of the Russian Federation of July 31, 1995 on the Constitutionality of the Presidential Decrees and the Resolutions of the Federal Government concerning the Situation in Chechnya.

20. Sobraniye Zakonodatelstva Rossiyskoy Federatsii # 33, Art.3424, 14 August 1995; Bakhtiyar Tuzmukhamedov, *Chechnya and the Laws of War,* Crimes of War, October 1999, *available at* http://www. crimesofwar.org/expert/chech-tuzmuk.html (last visited October 8, 2010).

According to a U.S. State Department report in 2003:

> Russia passed several new antiterrorism laws, began implementing previously passed legislation, and facilitated effective interdiction of terrorist finance flows by becoming a full member of the Financial Action Task Force (FATF). In February, the Russian Supreme Court issued an official government list of 15 terrorist organizations, the first of its kind in Russia and an important step toward implementation of counterterrorism statutes. Following the promulgation of the list, the 15 organizations were prohibited from engaging in any financial activities.[21]

Nevertheless, according to the Russian penal code, terrorists are considered criminals, subject to a specific category within the criminal justice system.

> The Russian Criminal Code categorizes the following offenses as criminal: terrorism, hostage-taking, hijacking of an aircraft, sea vessel, or train, organization of an illegal armed unit, attempts on the life of a State or public figure, and attacks on person or agencies enjoying international protection.
>
> The Code provides that serious criminal offences are pre-meditated actions for which the maximum punishment does not exceed 10 years, imprisonment. Particularly serious pre-meditated actions carry a maximum punishment of ten years' imprisonment or more. The Russian Criminal Code states that the punishment for "terrorism" is imprisonment for a period of from 5 to 10 years, for a period of from 8 to 15 years in cases with aggravating circumstances and for a period of from 10 to 20 years in cases with especially aggravating circumstances.
>
> Russian legislation establishes increased liability for recruiting and training of terrorists and the financing of terrorist activities and organizations. Pursuant to the Criminal Code of the Russian Federation, persons who recruit, train or finance terrorists may be considered accessories to a criminal offence and prosecuted. Inducing a person to commit a terrorist offence (by recruiting the person) constitutes incitement and the perpetrator is held liable under the Criminal Code. If a person has facilitated the commission of a terrorist offence by means of advice, directions, the provision of information, that person may be considered an accomplice to the offence. The liability of such a person is stipulated in the relevant article of the special section of the Criminal Code.[22]

A Chechen, Islan Mukaev, was sentenced in a Daghestan Court to a 25-year prison term for allegedly participating in the execution of six captured Russian soldiers. In May 2005, one of the participants in the Beslan school massacre was prosecuted in Vladikavkaz, the North Ossetian capital. The defendant, Nur-Pashi Kulayev, was charged with nine crimes, including terrorism, murder, and banditry. According to press accounts, one of his two attorneys had only been practicing law for two weeks prior to being appointed by the State.[23]

---

21. *Available at* http://www.globalsecurity.org/security/library/report/2004/pgt_2003/pgt_2003_31621pf.htm (last visited February 20, 2024).

22. National Laws and Measures for Counter-Terrorism and Regulation of Biology, Depaul University, College of Law, *available at* https://via.library.depaul.edu/lawfacpubs/1079/ (last visited February 20, 2024).

23. Douglas Birch, *Admitted Militant Goes on Trial in Russian School Hostage Case,* The Baltimore Sun, May 18, 2005, at 10A.

> Prosecutors Gnl Nikolai Shepel and Maria Semisynova sought life imprisonment on behalf of 1343 plaintiffs. The trial judge is Tamerlan Aguzarov, and Kulayev is defended by Umar Sikoyev and Albert Pliyev, the latter of which had only practised law for 2 weeks prior to being appointed by the state. His defence lies in the claim that he was one of the recruited Chechnyans who were told they would be attacking a military checkpoint, and had no foreknowledge their target was the Beslan school; he was reportedly among several of the militants who argued in favour of capturing the local Beslan police station instead. While no witnesses have claimed he shot any of the victims, several have testified that he ran around the gymnasium shouting curses and threatening to shoot various hostages with his assault rifle—though Kulayev testifies that he was only given the firearm to carry because his leaders didn't want any of their weapons left lying around where hostages could seize them.
>
> He has testified that Polkovnik smashed his cellphone in rage, stating that Russian forces were unwilling to negotiate, and that the bloodbath started when Russian snipers killed two hostage-takers that were carrying detonators for the explosives strung around the gymnasium. Polkovnik then shot three of the militants including the two female suicide bombers who had objected to the scholastic target, detonating their bombs. Nur-Pashi was supposed to be shot himself, by his brother Khan on orders from Polkovnik, but Khan refused.[24]

In June 2004, the Federation Council approved amendments to the Criminal Code that established maximum sentences for terrorism-related crimes. There was an unsuccessful attempt to change the punishment system after Beslan: in January 2005, the State Duma rejected amendments enabling punishment of terrorists' relatives.

Issues to Consider

1. Is the criminalization of terrorism the appropriate response to the Chechen conflict?
2. Do criminal courts offer the most effective response to terrorists committing acts such as those committed at Beslan and the Moscow opera?
3. Would the Israeli two-track approach be applicable to Russia?

Implementation of methods extending beyond the criminal law paradigm suggests recognition that the traditional approach is ineffective. The United States, post-9/11, instituted the military commissions as an alternative paradigm that was widely criticized; the Israeli approach—particularly administrative detention policy—is considered a serious violation of detainee's rights because the right to confront the accuser is denied.

24. *Available at* http://en.wikipedia.org/wiki/Nur-Pashi_Kulayev (last visited February 20, 2024).

In spite of particularly violent terrorist attacks, the Russian approach has been to consistently categorize terrorists as criminals rather than as "enemy combatants." Yet, documents reveal that Russian forces have *not* treated Chechen terrorists as criminals in the zone of combat.[25] Accordingly, the question of whether Russia considers Chechens engaged in combat with Russian forces as criminals, enemy combatants, or terrorists requires a multiple response.

Once caught, a Chechen fighter is brought to trial similar to a traditional criminal and is subject to the relevant sections of the Russian penal code. As described above, the criminal law process includes a prosecutor, defense attorney, judge, and the right to confront the accuser.

Unlike criminal defendants suspected of having committed a serious crime, though, Chechen terrorists are subjected to human rights violations in combat. The Russian approach is similar to the American and Israeli approaches of engaging terrorism in the zone of combat. However, as articulated by the military commissions, the terrorist defendant is provided a full criminal process.

United States Department of State: 2009 Human Rights Report: Russia

Bureau of Democracy, Human Rights, and Labor, Mar. 11, 2009[26]

Trial Procedures

Trials typically are conducted before a judge without a jury (bench trials). The defendant is presumed innocent. The defense is not required to present evidence and is given an opportunity to cross-examine witnesses and call defense witnesses. Defendants who are in custody during the trial are confined to a caged area and must consult with their attorneys through the bars. Defendants have the right of appeal.

The law provides for the use of jury trials for a limited category of "especially grave" crimes, such as murder, in higher-level regional courts.

During the year the ECHR on multiple occasions found the country in violation of provisions of the European Convention on Human Rights with regard to trial procedures. In 2008, the latest year for which statistics were available, the court found 159 violations by the country involving the right to a fair trial and 20 violations involving proceedings that exceeded a "reasonable" length of time.

25. *See Worse Than a War,* Human Rights Watch Backgrounders, March 2005, *available at* http://hrw.org/backgrounder/eca/chechnya0305/ (last visited October 8, 2010); *Russia,* Human Rights Watch, Human Rights Overview, January 2006, *available at* http://hrw.org/wr2k6/pdf/russia.pdf (last visited October 8, 2010); *Briefing—Torture, "Disappearances" and Alleged Unfair Trials in Russia's North Caucasus,* Amnesty International, September 30, 2005, *available at* https://www.amnesty.org/es/wp-content/uploads/2021/06/eur460392005en.pdf (last visited March 15, 2023); *Violations Continue, No Justice in Sight,* Amnesty International, July 1, 2005, *available at* https://www.amnesty.org/fr/wp-content/uploads/2023/05/eur460292005en.pdf (last visited March 15, 2024).

26. *Available at* https://2009-2017.state.gov/j/drl/rls/hrrpt/2009/eur/136054.htm (last visited March 15, 2024).

There has been a trend to further limit the use of jury trials. In December 2008 the State Duma enacted, and the president signed, a law providing that certain crimes, including terrorism, espionage, hostage taking, and mass disorder, would be heard by panels of three judges rather than by juries. Supporters of the legislation justified it on the grounds of the war on terrorism and juries' alleged incompetence to judge cases involving terrorism, espionage, and state security. They also alleged that clan relations in the North Caucasus made it impossible to empanel objective juries there. Although the competence of jury trial participants, including advocates for both parties and to some extent judges, remained a serious concern to domestic and international observers, critics described the legislation as a violation of the constitution and a major step backwards in the protection of individual liberties.

No further action was taken during the year on a draft law introduced in the State Duma in December 2008 that would substantially expand the definitions of espionage and treason. The draft law caused serious concern among some lawyers, human rights activists, and government officials who claimed that, if enacted, the law would provide virtually unfettered discretion to security forces to charge almost anyone who had any contact with foreign governments or international organizations or persons with treason. In February, after consulting with the newly reconstituted Presidential Council on Human Rights, President Medvedev announced that the draft law would be revised to reflect these concerns. The law had not been discussed further by year's end.

Issues to Consider

1. Does the Russian mixed approach suggest that, in reality, the Chechen fighter is considered an enemy combatant?
2. What is the significance or benefit to the state using a mixed approach?
3. If the terrorist can be engaged in combat and similarly be subject to a full criminal trial, is describing him as a criminal accurate?
4. Would the establishment of military tribunals, such as Guantanamo, improve Russia's counterterrorism efforts?
5. Does the terrorist benefit from the criminal law process and the guaranteeing of rights that are not incorporated in the enemy combatant paradigm?
6. Does an avowed policy of defeating terrorism suggest that the enemy is defined as an enemy combatant and not as a criminal?

V. INDIA

For most of its history, India has applied the criminal law paradigm rather than developing or implementing an enemy combatant paradigm. On March 26, 2002, however, the Indian parliament passed the Prevention of Terrorism Act

(POTA). POTA, which replaced the Terrorist and Disruptive Activities (Prevention) Act (TADA), articulated a new Indian approach regarding terrorism. The central question in our discussion here is whether the Special Terror Courts established by POTA were an attempt to develop a hybrid system similar to Israel's administrative detention, or to develop a system more akin to U.S. policy post-9/11.

The Prevention of Terrorism Act, 2002

March 28, 2002, Act No. 15 of 2002, Chapter 4[27]

The POTA Special Courts

(1) The Central Government or a State Government may, by notification in the Official Gazette, constitute one or more Special Courts for such area or areas, or for such case or class or group of cases, as may be specified in the notification.

(2) Where a notification constituting a Special Court for any area or areas or for any case or class or group of cases is issued by the Central Government under sub-section (1), and a notification constituting a Special Court for the same area or areas or for the same case or class or group of cases has also been issued by the State Government under that sub-section, the Special Court constituted by the Central Government, whether the notification constituting such Court is issued before or after the issue of the notification constituting the Special Court by the State Government, shall have, and the Special Court constituted by the State Government shall not have, jurisdiction to try any offence committed in that area or areas or, as the case may be, the case or class or group of cases and all cases pending before any Special Court constituted by the State Government shall stand transferred to the Special Court constituted by the Central Government.

(3) Where any question arises as to the jurisdiction of any Special Court, it shall be referred to the Central Government whose decision in the matter shall be final.

(4) A Special Court shall be presided over by a judge to be appointed by the Central Government or, as the case may be, the State Government, with the concurrence of the Chief Justice of the High Court.

(5) The Central Government or, as the case may be, the State Government may also appoint, with the concurrence of the Chief Justice of the High Court, additional judges to exercise jurisdiction of a Special Court.

(6) A person shall not be qualified for appointment as a judge or an additional judge of a Special Court unless he is, immediately before such appointment, a sessions judge or an additional sessions judge in any State.

(7) For the removal of doubts, it is hereby provided that the attainment, by a person appointed as a judge or an additional judge of a Special Court, of the

27. *Available at* http://www.satp.org/satporgtp/countries/india/document/actandordinances/POTA.htm#4 (last visited April 4, 2010).

age of superannuation under the rules applicable to him in the service to which he belongs, shall not affect his continuance as such judge or additional judge.

(8) Where any additional judge or additional judges is or are appointed in a Special Court, the judge of the Special Court may, from time to time, by general or special order, in writing, provide for the distribution of business of the Special Court among all judges including himself and the additional judge or additional judges and also for the disposal of urgent business in the event of his absence or the absence of any additional judge. . . .

25. Jurisdiction of Special Courts

(1) Notwithstanding anything contained in the Code, every offence punishable under any provision of this Act shall be triable only by the Special Court within whose local jurisdiction it was committed or, as the case may be, by the Special Court constituted for trying such offence under section 23.

(2) If, having regard to the exigencies of the situation prevailing in a State,—

> (a) it is not possible to have a fair, impartial or speedy trial; or
>
> (b) it is not feasible to have the trial without occasioning the breach of peace or grave risk to the safety of the accused, the witnesses, the Public Prosecutor and a judge of the Special Court or any of them; or
>
> (c) it is not otherwise in the interests of justice, the Supreme Court may transfer any case pending before a Special Court to any other Special Court within that State or in any other State and the High Court may transfer any case pending before a Special Court situated in that State to any other Special Court within the State.

(3) The Supreme Court or the High Court, as the case may be, may act under this section either on the application of the Central Government or a party interested and any such application shall be made by motion, which shall, except when the applicant is the Attorney-General of India, be supported by an affidavit or affirmation.

26. Power of Special Courts with Respect to Other Offences

(1) When trying any offence, a Special Court may also try any other offence with which the accused may, under the Code, be charged at the same trial if the offence is connected with such other offence.

(2) If, in the course of any trial under this Act of any offence, it is found that the accused person has committed any other offence under this Act or under any other law, the Special Court may convict such person of such other offence and pass any sentence or award punishment authorised by this Act or such rule or, as the case may be, under such other law.

27. Power to Direct for Samples, etc.

(1) When a police officer investigating a case requests the Court of a Chief Judicial Magistrate or the Court of a Chief Metropolitan Magistrate in writing

for obtaining samples of handwriting, finger-prints, foot-prints, photographs, blood, saliva, semen, hair, voice of any accused person, reasonably suspected to be involved in the commission of an offence under this Act, it shall be lawful for the Court of a Chief Judicial Magistrate or the Court of a Chief Metropolitan Magistrate to direct that such samples be given by the accused person to the police officer either through a medical practitioner or otherwise, as the case may be.

(2) If any accused person refuses to give samples as provided in sub-section (1), the Court shall draw adverse inference against the accused. . . .

29. Procedure and Powers of Special Courts

(1) Subject to the provisions of section 50, a Special Court may take cognizance of any offence, without the accused being committed to it for trial, upon receiving a complaint of facts that constitute such offence or upon a police report of such facts.

(2) Where an offence triable by a Special Court is punishable with imprisonment for a term not exceeding three years or with fine or with both, the Special Court may, notwithstanding anything contained in sub-section (1) of section 260 or section 262 of the Code, try the offence in a summary way in accordance with the procedure prescribed in the Code and the provisions of sections 263 to 265 of the Code, shall so far as may be, apply to such trial:

Provided that when, in the course of a summary trial under this subsection, it appears to the Special Court that the nature of the case is such that it is undesirable to try it in a summary way, the Special Court shall recall any witnesses who may have been examined and proceed to re-hear the case in the manner provided by the provisions of the Code for the trial of such offence and the said provisions shall apply to and in relation to a Special Court as they apply to and in relation to a Magistrate:

Provided further that in the case of any conviction in a summary trial under this section, it shall be lawful for a Special Court to pass a sentence of imprisonment for a term not exceeding one year and with fine which may extend to rupees five lakh.

(3) Subject to the other provisions of this Act, a Special Court shall, for the purpose of trial of any offence, have all the powers of a Court of Session and shall try such offence as if it were a Court of Session so far as may be in accordance with the procedure prescribed in the Code for the trial before a Court of Session.

(4) Subject to the other provisions of this Act, every case transferred to a Special Court under section 25 shall be dealt with as if such case had been transferred under section 406 of the Code to such Special Court.

(5) Notwithstanding anything contained in the Code, but subject to the provisions of section 299 of the Code, a Special Court may, if it thinks fit and for reasons to be recorded by it, proceed with the trial in the absence of the accused or his pleader and record the evidence of any witness, subject to the right of the accused to recall the witness for cross-examination. . . .

31. Trial by Special Courts to Have Precedence

The trial under this Act of any offence by a Special Court shall have precedence over the trial of any other case against the accused in any other court (not being a Special Court) and shall be concluded in preference to the trial of such other case and accordingly the trial of such other case shall remain in abeyance.

32. Certain Confessions Made to Police Officers to Be Taken into Consideration

(1) Notwithstanding anything in the Code or in the Indian Evidence Act, 1872 (1 of 1872), but subject to the provisions of this section, a confession made by a person before a police officer not lower in rank than a Superintendent of Police and recorded by such police officer either in writing or on any mechanical or electronic device like cassettes, tapes or sound tracks from out of which sound or images can be reproduced, shall be admissible in the trial of such person for an offence under this Act or the rules made thereunder.

(2) A police officer shall, before recording any confession made by a person under sub-section (1), explain to such person in writing that he is not bound to make a confession and that if he does so, it may be used against him: Provided that where such person prefers to remain silent, the police officer shall not compel or induce him to make any confession.

(3) The confession shall be recorded in an atmosphere free from threat or inducement and shall be in the same language in which the person makes it.

(4) The person from whom a confession has been recorded under subsection (1), shall be produced before the Court of a Chief Metropolitan Magistrate or the Court of a Chief Judicial Magistrate along with the original statement of confession, written or recorded on mechanical or electronic device within forty-eight hours.

(5) The Chief Metropolitan Magistrate or the Chief Judicial Magistrate, shall, record the statement, if any, made by the person so produced and get his signature or thumb impression and if there is any complaint of torture, such person shall be directed to be produced for medical examination before a Medical Officer not lower in rank than an Assistant Civil Surgeon and thereafter, he shall be sent to judicial custody.

33. Power to Transfer Cases to Regular Courts

Where, after taking cognizance of any offence, a Special Court is of the opinion that the offence is not triable by it, it shall, notwithstanding that it has no jurisdiction to try such offence, transfer the case for the trial of such offence to any court having jurisdiction under the Code and the Court to which the case is transferred may proceed with the trial of the offence as if it had taken cognizance of the offence.

34. Appeal

(1) Notwithstanding anything contained in the Code, an appeal shall lie from any judgment, sentence or order, not being an interlocutory order, of a Special Court to the High Court both on facts and on law.

Explanation.—For the purposes of this section, "High Court" means a High Court within whose jurisdiction, a Special Court which passed the judgment, sentence or order, is situated.

(2) Every appeal under sub-section (1) shall be heard by a bench of two Judges of the High Court.

(3) Except as aforesaid, no appeal or revision shall lie to any court from any judgment, sentence or order including an interlocutory order of a Special Court.

(4) Notwithstanding anything contained in sub-section (3) of section 378 of the Code, an appeal shall lie to the High Court against an order of the Special Court granting or refusing bail.

(5) Every appeal under this section shall be preferred within a period of thirty days from the date of the judgment, sentence or order appealed from: Provided that the High Court may entertain an appeal after the expiry of the said period of thirty days if it is satisfied that the appellant had sufficient cause for not preferring the appeal within the period of thirty days.

POTA was heavily criticized. On September 17, 2004, it was announced that the Act would be repealed.[28]

Sachin Mehta, Repeal of POTA—Justified

LegalServiceIndia.com[29]

The developments after the enactment of the POTA, including the responses received by the POTA review committee show that the POTA is worse then TADA. POTA provides for criminal liability for mere association or communication with suspected terrorists without the possession of criminal intent (Section 3(5) of the POTA). Section 4 of POTA is similar to Section 5 of TADA in laying out a legal presumption that if a person is found in unauthorized possession of arms in a notified area, he/she is automatically linked with terrorist activity. Section 48(2) provides for the option of pre-trial police detention for up to 180 days. As under the TADA, where 98% of the cases never reached the trial stage, this Section 48(2) could also be misused by the police by keeping an accused for long periods of detention without charge or trial. Special courts for trials are established under POTA which are given the discretion to hold trials in non-public places, like prisons, and to withhold trial records from public scrutiny, thus preventing the independent monitoring of special court sessions. Section 32 provides that confessions made to police officers are to be admissible in trial, which has increased the possibility of coercion and torture in securing confessions.

The provisions contained under the POTA were mostly contained in existing laws, except those, which were contained in the Criminal Procedure Code,

28. Human Rights Watch: Human Rights News, *India: POTA Repeal a Step Forward for Human Rights: Government Should Dismiss All POTA Cases*, September 22, 2004, *available at* http://hrw.org/english/docs/2004/09/22/india9370.htm (last visited October 8, 2010).

29. *Available at* http://www.legalservicesindia.com/articles/pota.htm (last visited October 8, 2010).

the Indian Penal Code, the Evidence Act or the Constitution of India. The Act effectively undermines the fundamental tenet of the criminal justice system by putting the burden of proof on the accused. But the Act also had some provisions, which were not attacked for being against human rights. These provisions stated that Confessions must be recorded within 48 hours before a magistrate, who will send the accused for a medical examination if there is a complaint of torture. Further a legal representative of the accused can be present for part of the interrogation. Moreover police officers can be prosecuted for abusing their authority. The POTA also provided that victims could be paid compensation.

In addition, fault was found with POTA for discarding "the fundamental right of [the] accused to due process and [a] presumption of innocence. Persons arrested under POTA could be held for 30 days before authorities had to produce them in a special court of law."[30] POTA also allowed for the admission of evidence that would otherwise not be allowed in a criminal trial.

> The Supreme Court has convicted and sentenced to life three Jamait-ul-Mujahidin militants, including Ashiq Hussain Faktoo, who were acquitted by a Jammu TADA court of the charge of killing human rights activist H.N Wanchoo in 1992. Allowing an appeal filed by the CBI against their acquittal, a Bench of Mr. Justice S.N. Variva and Mr. Justice B.N. Agrawal took a diametrically opposite view on the admissibility of the evidence in the case based solely on the confessional statements of the three militants recorded under Section 15 of TADA. The TADA court had rejected the evidence on four counts. Firstly, the police official concerned did not ask the accused whether they were making the confessional statements voluntarily. Secondly, the CBI SP did not tell the accused that the confessional statement could be used against them as evidence. Thirdly, the statements were recorded in Hindi which was not the official language of the court and lastly, the SP did not ask the accused whether they wanted to add or subtract anything from their confessional statements. After going through the confessional statements of the three accused, the Supreme Court was of the opinion that all procedures, which the TADA court thought were not followed, were actually scrupulously followed.[31]

Issues to Consider

1. Do the multiple threats faced by India compel the country to the adoption of the criminal law model?
2. Would the implementation of either the American or Israeli dual approach satisfactorily protect the rights of Indian detainees?
3. What policy considerations justify adopting a judicial regime that minimizes detainees' rights?

---

30. Kranti Kumara, *Repeal of India's Draconian Anti-Terrorism Law,* November 27, 2004, *available at* http://www.wsws.org/articles/2004/nov2004/ind-n27.shtml (last visited October 8, 2010).

31. *3 JuM Ultras Get Life Term for Murder,* The Tribune (Chandigarh, India), February 3, 2003, *available at* http://www.tribuneindia.com/2003/20030203/nation.htm#4 (last visited October 8, 2010).

POTA's repeal suggests that the Indian government responded to international criticism of draconian powers granted to state authorities. These powers enabled the state to implement measures extending beyond the traditional criminal law paradigm. The measures were reflective of a hybrid system that included aspects of the criminal law paradigm incorporating special measures directly affecting the rights of the individual detainees. The hybrid paradigm implemented by India for a short period of time has, in essence, been replaced by the traditional criminal law paradigm.

Whether India will maintain the criminal law paradigm is unclear. For example, after the Mumbai train bombing of 2006, 19 suspects were brought to trial before a special court instead of regularly constituted courts.

Issues to Consider

1. Do special courts suggest that the defendant is more of an enemy combatant than a criminal defendant?
2. Are special courts sufficiently able to ensure the rights of a criminal defendant?
3. Does the convening of a special court suggest the adoption of an Israeli or American dual-track approach, or an alternative model?
4. Does a special court suggest a speedier trial at the expense of judicial caution and detainee rights?
5. What rights will be most susceptible to violations if a regular criminal law court does not hear the trial?

VI. SPAIN

Spain views terrorism as a criminal matter whereby terrorists are tried in courts of law established in accordance with the Spanish penal code. In addition, "(U)nder Spanish law, terrorism is classified as a crime that can be prosecuted even if it is alleged to have been committed in another country."[32]

Candiido Conde-Pumpido Touron, Judicial Response to Terrorism: National Venues, The Spanish Model

10th International Judicial Conference in Strasbourg from 23 to 24 May[33]

. . . Terrorism does not constitute a form of war in the strictest sense, but rather a form of crime, whilst possessing specific characteristics which set it apart from ordinary crime. As political insurrections or coups d'etats, it is a threat to society: its intention is to change the existing political situation through

32. Chris Johnston, *9/11 Terror Suspects on Trial in Spain,* Times Online, April 22, 2005, *available at* https://www.thetimes.co.uk/article/911-terror-suspects-on-trial-in-spain-ps6xb6nnf27 (last visited March 15, 2024).

33. *Available at* https://www.coe.int/en/web/portal/home (last visited February 20, 2024).

violence. It is the terrorists who present their crimes as methods of war, whilst directing their attacks against civilian victims. It is the role of democratic governments, in their fight against terrorism, to decide whether they can accept this claim or whether they prefer to treat terrorists as perpetrators of a specific kind of crime.

In Spain, the fight against terrorism is not undertaken in a bellicose way, but as a specific chapter in the fight against crime, independent of the political problems it poses and which cannot be left to one side. This is why criminal law and the courts are essential instruments in the fight against terrorism.

2. In our country, an indictment on terrorist offences comes under the jurisdiction of the Assize Court, called the Audiencia Nacional, a specialised body of jurisdiction, based in Madrid, whose jurisdiction covers all offences committed throughout the whole of the national territory. It is an ordinary court, a civil tribunal made up of professional judges, members of the judiciary, appointed by the Judicial Service Commission in compliance with predetermined legal criteria, who are irremovable and answerable only to the law. The tribunal is independent from the executive and, hence, the government exerts no influence upon it whatsoever. In no circumstances are such prosecutions left to ordinary juries, given the risks involved.

There are fundamentally three advantages of this specific jurisdiction: (1) centralisation, the criteria can thus be unified and some distance be taken from the place of the conflict; (2) specialisation, enabling a more in-depth knowledge of the problems surrounding the prosecution of terrorist acts and improving efficacy and (3) security, which can be stepped up as protection is concentrated around one single site and a limited number of judges.

The judicial investigation of terrorist trials is carried out by the central investigative tribunals which are also specialised bodies based in Madrid with jurisdiction over the whole of Spain. They are responsible for directing and supervising the police investigation, gathering evidence in preparation for the judgment and authorising methods to counterterrorism which may restrict fundamental freedoms such as, for example, searches of places of residence and telephone tapping.

The judicial investigation also enjoys a clear advantage compared to other regimes: depositions, made with every guarantee of confidentiality before the judge and in the presence of the defence lawyers, can be used as evidence for the judgment in cases where the witnesses are unable to appear in court as they have died, are abroad or in an unknown location, as quite frequently happens in complex trials dealing with terrorism or organised crime.

The decision handed down by the tribunal of the Audencia Nacional is subject to appeal in the Supreme Court in the same conditions as any other ruling, whereas appeals on points of law come under the criminal chamber, of which I am a member, with no specialisation.

3. The procedural rules are basically the same as in ordinary prosecutions, respecting the guarantee of the right to a defence and the principle of the presumption off innocence. The rules of evidence are identical.

Until 1988, there was special legislation in place but since then (LO 4/1988 of 25 May), matters linked to terrorism are dealt with by the Penal Code and the ordinary Criminal Procedural Code. This does not imply that we are no longer according terrorism the special treatment it deserves, as the law is the most precious tool of a state based on the rule of law in facing up to the manifestations of crime; as terrorist behaviour is a very specific form of crime, it is necessary to apply the law in order to establish specific investigative means or ways in which to preserve evidence.

The respect of constitutional guarantees is not incompatible with efficacy and this is possible if the penal and procedural instruments are adapted in the best way possible to the challenges thrown up by the fight against terrorism.

Issues to Consider

1. Is a modified criminal law process more effective than a hybrid paradigm?
2. Does the Spanish system better preserve basic rights of a detainee than the Israeli two-track approach?
3. Does the Spanish system facilitate the development of an enemy combatant paradigm?
4. How would the U.S. Supreme Court rule on the Spanish approach?

VII. CHINA

Similar to the other surveyed nations, China has adopted the criminal law paradigm regarding terrorism-related crimes defined as endangering national and public security. To that end, terrorism has been incorporated into the criminal code, thereby defining terrorist actions as criminal acts. In 2005, China amended the criminal code to include punishment for terrorism and for financing terrorism, in explicit terms.

According to Article 120 of the Chinese criminal code:

> Whoever forms or leads a terrorist organization shall be sentenced to fixed-term imprisonment of not less than three years but not more than 10 years; other participants shall be sentenced to fixed-term imprisonment of not more than three years, criminal detention or public surveillance.
>
> Whoever, in addition to the crime mentioned in the preceding paragraph, commits other crimes of homicide, explosion, or kidnap shall be punished in accordance with the provisions on combined punishment for several crimes.[34]

Article 120(a) specifies that financing a terrorist organization is to be punished as a crime:

34. Chinese Criminal Code art. 120.

Whoever provides funds to any terrorist organization or individual who engages in terrorism shall be sentenced to fixed-term imprisonment of not more than five years, criminal detention, public surveillance or deprivation of political rights, and shall also be fined; if the circumstances are serious, he shall be sentenced to fixed-term imprisonment of not less than five years, and he shall also be fined or his property shall be confiscated.

Where a unit commits the crime mentioned in the preceding paragraph, it shall be fined, and the persons who are directly in charge and the other persons who are directly responsible for the offence shall be punished in accordance with the provisions of the preceding paragraph.

Issues to Consider

1. Given the nature of the threat China faces, is the criminal law paradigm appropriate?
2. What are the costs and benefits in applying the criminal law paradigm to a country the size of China?
3. Do the threats China faces more closely resemble the threats faced by Israel, Russia, or India (regardless of size)?
4. Given the complexity of Chinese society, would a two-track approach be more realistic or effective?
5. Does the possibility that Uyghurs benefit from external influence (Pakistan) affect what model is adopted (akin to how India addresses influence from Pakistan)?
6. Does the criminal law paradigm lock the state into one model when flexibility—given circumstances—might be more beneficial to the state?

Thematic Compilation of Relevant Information Submitted by China; Article 14 UNCAC Prevention of Money-Laundering China (Sixth Meeting)[35]

Major Practices in China for Preventing Money-Laundering

A regime against money laundering and terrorism financing has been gradually established in China since 2003, which centers on the "one law and five decrees," and now largely covers requirements of international standards for building a national antimoney laundering and anti-terrorism financing legal system in different countries. China's anti-money laundering regulatory authorities, in line with the new international standards against money laundering, are engaged in in-depth practice of risk-based antimoney laundering approaches, for the purposes of improving the legal regulatory system and the risk control mechanism in this field.

35. *Available at* https://www.unodc.org/documents/corruption/WG-Prevention/Art_14_Prevention_of_money-laundering/China.pdf (last visited September 2023).

Improvement of the Anti-Money Laundering Legal System

Up till now, China's anti-money laundering and anti-terrorism financing legal system mainly comprises the following: i) laws, such as the Criminal Law, Anti-money Laundering Law, Decisions of the National People's Congress on Strengthening Antiterrorism Work and Interpretations of the Supreme People's Court on Applicable Laws for Cases of Money Laundering and Other Criminal Cases; ii) regulations, such as Antimoney Laundering Regulations for Financial Institutions, Administrative Measures for Financial Institutions on the Reporting of Large-value or Suspicious Transactions, Administrative Measures for Financial Institutions on the Reporting of Transactions Suspicious of Terrorist Financing, Administrative Measures for Financial Institutions on Customer Identification and Preservation of Records on Customer Identification Information and Transactions, and Administrative Measures for the Freezing of Assets Suspicious of Terrorist Activities; iii) normative and policy documents, such as Administrative Measures for Payment Institutions on Anti-money Laundering and Antiterrorism Financing Issues, Measures for Financial Institutions on Anti-money Laundering Supervision and Administration (Trial) and other supporting systems.

VIII. COLOMBIA

In 2003, Colombia enacted an antiterrorism law according to the which the armed forces are allowed to arrest, interrogate, and detain suspects for up to 36 hours and to search homes and obtain intelligence information without a warrant or any judicial oversight. The New Code of Criminal Procedure allows criminal judges in specialized circuits to try an individual who, during an armed conflict, either carries out or conducts indiscriminate or excessive acts. These acts, according to the Code, include targeting a civilian population or threatening the population for purposes of intimidation. The perpetrator, if found guilty, is to be sentenced for 15 to 25 years, fined, and banned from exercising any public right for 15 to 20 years. Below are the specific articles from this Code that pertain to terrorism.

New Code of Criminal Procedure of Colombia

Articles 144, 182, 343, 345, and 348

Article 144. Acts of terrorism.

Any person who, on the occasion of or in the course of, an armed conflict, engages in, or orders the commission of, indiscriminate or excessive attacks or makes the civilian population a target of attacks, reprisals or acts or threats of violence with the principal objective of terrorizing the civilian population, shall be liable, by that act alone, to a term of imprisonment of between fifteen (15) and twenty-five (25) years, a fine of between two thousand (2,000) and forty thousand (40,000) times the minimum statutory monthly wage, and loss of rights and public functions for a period of between fifteen (15) and twenty (20) years.

Article 182 of the Penal Code provides for a term of imprisonment of between one and two years for anyone who forces another person to do, condone or fail to do anything, a penalty that will be increased by between one third and one half (article 183) when the objective pursued by the perpetrator is of a terrorist nature.

Article 343. Terrorism.

Any person who provokes or maintains the population, or a segment of the population, in a state of anxiety or terror through acts that endanger the lives, physical integrity or the freedom of the persons or buildings or means of communication, transport, processing or conveyance of fluids or motive power, making use of means capable of causing destruction, shall be liable to a term of imprisonment of between ten (10) and fifteen (15) years and a fine of between one thousand (1,000) and ten thousand times the minimum statutory monthly wage, without prejudice to the penalty to which he or she is liable for the other offences committed in connection with such conduct.

If the state of anxiety or terror is caused by a telephone call, a magnetic tape, a video, a cassette or an anonymous letter, the punishment shall be from between two (2) and five (5) years and a fine of between one hundred (100) and five hundred (500) times the minimum statutory monthly wage.

Article 345. Management of resources linked to terrorist activities.

Any person who manages money or assets linked to terrorist activities shall be liable to a term of imprisonment of between six (6) and twelve (12) years and a fine of between two hundred (200) and ten thousand (10,000) times the minimum statutory monthly wage.

Article 348. Instigation to commit an offence.

Any person who publicly and directly incites another person or persons to commit a specific offence or type of offence shall be liable to a fine.

If the act is engaged in for the purpose of committing the crimes of genocide, enforced disappearance, extortive kidnapping, torture, forcible displacement or homicide or for terrorist purposes, the penalty shall be a term of imprisonment of between five (5) and ten (10) years and a fine of between five hundred (500) and one thousand (1,000) times the minimum statutory monthly wage.

In response to the Code's enactment, criticism emerged that focused particularly on the broad powers granted to the government and on the drastically reduced rights of the individual, which have led to the misuse of counterterrorism measures.

Colombia: Misuse of Counter-Terrorism Measures to Prosecute Protesters Threatens Human Rights, Say UN Experts

UN Human Rights Office of the High Commissioner, March 2023

UN experts today called on Colombia to stop misusing counter-terrorism measures and serious criminal offences, such as terrorism, to prosecute individuals for taking part in protests against government policies.

The experts urged authorities to ensure that any charges brought forward comply with international law and human rights standards. "The use of such egregious charges to prosecute violent conduct during protests poses a serious threat to the promotion and protection of human rights and fundamental freedoms and to the legitimacy of international counter-terrorism frameworks and laws," the experts said. "It has a chilling effect and encourages vilification campaigns against protest movements in the country."

Information received by the experts indicate that 228 individuals who took part in the protests of 2021 have been charged with serious offences, including terrorism and conspiracy to commit crimes, for which some are facing more than 22 years in prison. More than 180 demonstrators remain in prison or are under house arrest, despite legal provisions that allow for the release of people arrested in connection with the protests so they could await their trial in liberty. The detainees include peaceful protesters and young people who allegedly damaged public and private property, engaged in violent and destructive acts.

"We strongly condemn any violence during protests," the experts said. "While we recognise the State's responsibility to respond to violence, including by investigating, preventing and dissuading such acts, violent individuals among peaceful demonstrators must be dealt with fairly and in accordance international human rights standards," they said.

The experts expressed concern about reports of stigmatisation and judicial harassment of human rights defenders, reporters and defence lawyers prosecuted in the context of these proceedings.

They stressed that decisions on whether to prosecute, hold in pre-trial detention, convict or award damages to protesters must meet the requirements of necessity, proportionality and non-discrimination under international human rights law. "Prison sentences for non-violent protest activity and the exercise of human rights, including freedom of peaceful assembly and freedom of expression, are always disproportionate, and therefore incompatible with international human rights law," the experts said.

In Colombia, legislation that involves constitutional reform or fundamental human rights must be approved by the Constitutional Court of Colombia before becoming law. In August 2004, the Constitutional Court declared the anti-terrorism law unconstitutional due to procedural irregularities that occurred during the approval of the law by the Colombian Congress.[36]

IX. CONCLUSION

The United States, in the immediate aftermath of 9/11, defined suspected terrorists as enemy combatants, thereby enabling their detention in Guantanamo Bay, Abu Ghraib, and "black sites." The enemy combatant paradigm created by the United States allowed for violations of the Geneva Conventions. Such a model has not been adopted by the other surveyed nations. Or, if it has been adopted, then it has subsequently been revised.

While the war on terror paradigm has evolved with policies and administrations, the underlying rationales have remained the same.[37] Russia and China have adopted a criminal law paradigm with respect to suspected terrorists, however, that paradigm has not been applied to operational counterterrorism. India has largely implemented a criminal law paradigm, though a special court has been created, and suspected terrorists have been brought to trial before that forum. Spain has consistently adhered to a criminal law paradigm, only extending the time a detainee can be held in incommunicado detention. Israel has created a twin-track approach—criminal trial and administrative detention—thereby granting the state broader detention powers based both on criminal law and administrative sanctions. Colombia, in response to multiple threats (akin to threats faced by India), has implemented a paradigm that enables the state to bring suspected terrorists to trial before courts that are not regularly constituted.

PART B – PROSECUTION AND THE RIGHTS OF TERRORISTS

I. INTRODUCTION

There are four viable forums for trying suspected terrorists: domestic criminal courts, military commissions, domestic national security courts, and international courts. While criminal courts are predicated on existing domestic judicial regimes, military commissions and national security courts represent alternatives created especially to address the specific threat of terrorism. As discussed earlier, some nations try suspected terrorists exclusively before existing criminal courts, while others implement a two-track system that utilizes both

36. *Colombia Rule of Law Impunity Summary and Recommendations Thematic Report,* International Commissions of Jurists (2005), *available at* https://www.icj.org/wp-content/uploads/2012/05/Colombia-rule-of-law-impunity-summary-and-recommendations-thematic-report-2005-eng.pdf (last visited May 6, 2024).

37. Lisa Hajjar, *The Counterterrorism War Paradigm versus International Humanitariian Law: The Legal Contradictions and Global Consequencess of the US "War on Terror,"* 44 Law & Social Inquiry 4 (2019).

domestic courts and military commissions. The United States and Israel utilize a two-track approach, providing decision makers the flexibility to determine which judicial regime is most appropriate for a specific defendant. National security courts represent a "hybrid" model, trying only suspected terrorists while providing defendants greater rights than existing military commissions do, without extending the full panoply of rights guaranteed by domestic courts. No terrorist has, to date, been brought to trial before an international court.

Deciding which judicial forum is relevant depends on defining the status of the particular detainee. If a terrorist-defendant is defined as a traditional criminal, then he is entitled to full rights and protections guaranteed by the criminal law paradigm. However, if terrorists are not defined as criminals, then existing laws may not be applicable because certain rights inherent to the criminal law paradigm may be withheld from the terrorist-defendant.

Trying terrorists in an international court would signify the internationalization of counterterrorism. Rather than each surveyed nation bringing defendants to trial before a domestic court, an international tribunal would bring an individual accused of terrorism to trial. Such a court could be a treaty-based terror court or a tribunal[38] similar to the International Criminal Court or a combination of domestic and international courts.

This chapter analyzes the three domestic alternatives through the lens of the U.S. judicial system. Nevertheless, the options—existing domestic courts, military commissions, and specially constituted national security courts—are relevant to the other surveyed countries and can, therefore, be applied by analogy. To that end, unlike previous chapters which have emphasized a comparative, global perspective, this chapter focuses on the United States while addressing an issue that is also relevant to the other six nations. A treaty-based terror court is analyzed by examining the ramifications of an international approach to counterterrorism.

Issues to Consider

1. What is the most appropriate role for the courts?
2. What legal regime guarantees rights and protections for the defendant while protecting society's interests?
3. What criminal law punishment theory is most relevant to terrorism?
4. What is the fundamental purpose in bringing terrorists to trial?

38. William Carmines has put forth such a recommendation, along with a 50-page treaty. The International Terrorism Tribunal (ITT) idea, generally speaking, would be a treaty-based tribunal formed by like-minded nations united to combat international terrorism by trying international terrorists. It gives the ITT jurisdiction to try international terror suspects detained by member states. That is, once a party to this treaty, a member state should not try a suspected terrorist in a domestic court. In fact, once the suspect is arrested and detained on international terror charges (including, but not limited to, the actual conducting of terrorist activity, as well as threat, financing, and harboring of such terrorists), the suspect then, within seven days unless an extension applies, must be transferred to the ITT's Administrative Counsel for further detention, pre-trial hearings, interrogation, and potential prosecution.

Accused terrorists have been brought to trial before domestic courts (U.S., Israel, Russia, India, Spain, Colombia, and China), military commissions and military courts (U.S. and Israel), and special terrorism courts (India and Colombia). If the right to confront the accuser is preserved and otherwise-guaranteed rights are similarly protected, then special courts need not be established. Conversely, if the full panoply of rights guaranteed by the criminal law process is not extended to terrorists, but the right to trial is protected, then alternative judicial regimes, including national security courts, are viable options.

II. DOMESTIC JUDICIAL REGIMES

A. ARTICLE III COURTS

One of the primary considerations in determining where to try a suspected terrorist is ascertaining whether a particular judicial forum facilitates balancing legitimate national security considerations with equally legitimate individual rights. The essay below articulates specific reasons why Article III courts may not be the appropriate forum for post-9/11 detainees.

Walid Pharess, Moussaoui, Wrong Court, Wrong Debate?

Foundation for Defense of Democracies, May 4, 2006[39]

Should we be surprised by the watershed debate following Zacarias Moussaoui's trial ending? Not really. The jury rendering of its recommendation is not unusual throughout the American legal war with Terrorism: For the five years court struggle to try al Qaida members and other terrorists in the U.S. legal structure hasn't been working. After the classroom, America's courtroom is too alien to the conflict. In short Moussaoui's case is not the only one to display a systemic crisis, all other cases did and will continue to do. My take on it, as an analyst of past and future terror wars, can be simplified: The terrorists are processed in the wrong courts and our debate on this legal process is the wrong debate.

Let me be clear from the beginning: The issue I am raising is not about the death sentence or life in prison sentencing. That part should have been the last stage in the debate: The one that seals the sentencing logic, not the discussion that makes the debate. The *Moussaoui* trial is not about the principle of common criminal sentencing per se; it is about criminalizing Terrorism and its root ideologies. Here are few points that make my analytical case:

1. Zacarias Moussaoui's personal life is not a main factor in determining this particular mass crime, but one of the factors that could lower the punishment, if incriminated. If he had a bad childhood or other

39. *Available at* http://www.defenddemocracy.org/index.php?option=com_content&task=view&id=11782128&Itemid=102 (last visited July 20, 2010).

negative factors that affected his clarity of thinking, it should be considered as elements of clemency in the case of extreme sentencing, but not the foundations of the case evaluation. For 9/11 and the war it was part of, was not a personal vendetta by M. Moussaoui against the U.S. Government, but an al Qaida genocidal war against the American people. This and other similar cases aren't a private affair between individuals—with some bad luck—and U.S. policies with consequences on national security. By his own admitting, M Moussaoui is a member, call him Jihadist or not, of a Terrorist organization. He shouldn't be tried in a U.S. Court system designed to process common crimes instead of war crimes.

2. The victims of September 11, 2001 weren't selected by al Qaida, or the perpetrators—personally. The men, women and children massacred throughout that day of infamy are the targets of a Terror war on America not vandalism on two towers in New York and a large building in Washington. Terrorism could have targeted other high rises and objectives in different cities. The matter is not an individual vendetta between Moussaoui and the 3,000 persons killed. America was targeted as a nation for the purpose of genocide. As a massacred collectivity, the victims of 9/11 belong to the nation not to their relatives. As individuals the victims are profoundly mourned by all Americans and above all by their survivors. So who tried al Qaida on behalf of the nation?
3. Moussaoui is part of machinery larger than himself. In the 9/11 planning process, he is not a sole mechanism acting individually. He was executing orders by al Qaida and had the intention of carrying them out. His relation to the massacre is not pragmatic but mechanical. Hence the judicial process of finding out if he caused or not, the process of specific deaths of 9/11 is not the issue: For he has openly admitted, and it was proven, that he was part of the machinery put in place to perpetrate the massacre. That he slipped, failed or missed his opportunity is only one fact within a greater reality: his commitment to achieve the mass-killing and his participation in a chain of event that led to it, even if he didn't walk through the last part of the horror.
4. More seriously is the current system ability to process the Terror cases: Per my own experience and open documents available, most of the players in a current courtroom setting are often unable to absorb the density of the confrontation. The Jury, made of ordinary citizens, generally do not comprehend the ideology of the Jihadists, hence can't make a strategically educated decision, not on the sentencing process but on the essence of the war crime at hand. U.S. Judges are highly capable of controlling the procedure in their courtrooms but haven't been enabled by the system to try a war with Jihadi terror, if not specialized in Salafism, Khumeinism and other movements' strategies, thinking process or even tactics. Prosecutors as well are thrown into battles of ideas beyond their basic training. In the *Moussaoui* case, the jury asked for a dictionary, refused by the judge. The question deserves an answer.

5. As for the defense lawyers, and I was one in the past, in the absence of specialized courts, they would twist history and geopolitics to achieve a legitimate goal: win their case. But instead of focusing on proving the innocence of their clients and distancing him/her from the enemy, they tend to defend the ideology of their client, putting themselves in the wrong side of the war their nation is victim of.

These above five facts and many more to develop in the future constitute the basis of US failure in the courts' processing of Jihadism-related Terror cases. What is needed for future successes is the following:

a. That Congress identifies the ideologies of the Terrorists. Simply speaking: educate the jury, the judges, the prosecutors and the defense attorneys, as to who is the enemy and what is its ideology. The rest should flow as American justice at its best, impartial and fair.

b. As in France and Spain, train "Counter-Terrorism Judges." From Paris to Madrid, the tools needed to decide on procedures deemed appropriate to prosecute and ultimately try the Terrorists at war with democracies are present. A similar training could provide the Justice Department with "Counter Terrorism Prosecutors." In a sum, all players in the courtroom must at some point be acquainted with what they will have to reflect on, in Terrorism cases.

Moussaoui feels he won all the way, even if he got life in prison. He played the martyrdom card till his audience nauseated. He then played his personal life card till he obtained the mitigating factor. He played it tight, close, and smartly. His colleagues brought down towers five years ago, but Moussaoui administered another type of strike against his foes: Defeating them through their own system.

What the courtroom in Virginia missed in its trial of the decade was the factory that produced Moussaoui's mind. A life sentence is not necessarily a bad choice in democracies, or the wrong message to send when needed, if the nation the jury came from is enabled to cast a death sentence on the ideologies of hatred.

Issues to Consider

1. Is there a risk of allowing a terrorist-defendant to manipulate a trial in this structure?
2. Should a judge provide more leniency to a terrorist-defendant than to a criminal-defendant regarding courtroom conduct?
3. Are jury trials appropriate for terrorist-defendants? Should existing judicial regimes be adhered to regardless of the circumstances?
4. How should self-representation be addressed?
5. Is the dilemma regarding which forum is appropriate for terrorist-defendants primarily legal or political?
6. What should the factors be in determining whether the pre-existing judicial paradigm is effective and appropriate?
7. How should the effectiveness of an alternative paradigm be judged?

B. UNITED STATES MILITARY COMMISSIONS

President Bush's November 2001 Presidential Order, known as Detention, Treatment, and Trial of Certain Non-Citizens in the War Against Terrorism, established military commissions for the express purpose of trying individuals suspected of involvement in terrorism. Premised on a belief that the existing civilian judicial paradigm was insufficient with respect to the threat posed by terrorism, the administration chose to eschew Article III courts.

With respect to the debate surrounding the establishment of the military commissions, Professor Linda Dickinson's interpretation of the administration's motives is particularly insightful:

> Despite the availability of legal arguments, however, those supporting the Administration's actions have justified them primarily in the language of policy. They have made clear that they view law—at least the typical legal protections afforded defendants in criminal trials—to be a nuisance (or, worse, a danger) in the context of fighting terrorism. They contend that the normal principles governing adjudication of criminal responsibility ought to be suspended for several reasons. First, such trials take a long time and cost a great deal of money. Thus, they argue that trials of untold numbers of terrorists in civilian courts would be inefficient. Second, civilian trials would present risks to civilian judges and jurors, who might be targeted by terrorists in retaliation for their decisions. Third, they argue that there is no need to protect rights of people who are, after all, international terrorists. For example, they contend that it is ludicrous to suggest that we should have read al Qaeda members their Miranda rights before apprehending them in the caves at Tora Bora. Fourth, the evidence available to convict terrorists does not necessarily fit the strict evidentiary requirements, such as the chain of custody requirement or the hearsay rule, applicable in civilian courts. Indeed, much of the evidence is secret, we are told, and could compromise national security if it came to light in a public trial. Furthermore, public trials are subject to capture by grandstanding defendants who might use the process to air their views and thereby undermine the fight against terrorism. Fifth, it is alleged that indefinite secret detentions and military commissions give the government, and in particular the Executive branch, needed control over the process. In short, the view is that we cannot afford much law here. Stern measures are needed for violent times.[40]

In the aftermath of the Order's issuance, the Department of Defense issued rules, procedures, and instructions heavily favoring the prosecution in regards to rules of evidence, burden of proof, right to counsel, admissibility of classified information, right to confront the accuser, preponderance of the evidence required for conviction, sentencing guidelines, and flexibility with respect to what crimes the defendant may be charged with. In establishing the commissions, the administration circumvented constitutional guarantees and privileges articulated in Article III; the fact that baselines articulating what cases are suitable for prosecution were not developed is telling.[41]

---

40. Laura A. Dickinson, *Using Legal Process to Fight Terrorism: Detentions, Military Commissions, International Tribunals, and the Rule of Law,* 75 S. Cal. L. Rev. 1407 (2002).

41. Private correspondence with senior official; e-mail on record with author.

The following excerpt highlights criticisms of the military commissions that still hold true today; the comments are relevant to the commission and other judicial regimes created for the singular purpose of trying terrorist-defendants.

Jennifer Trahan, Trying a Bin Laden and Others: Evaluating the Options for Terrorist Trials

24 Hous. J Int'l L. 475 (2002)

Absence of Standard Trial Procedures

Aside from questioning the legality of using military commissions, another issue is whether, as a policy matter, the circumstances justify subjecting foreign defendants accused of terrorism to trials lacking certain safeguards provided in federal district courts (or, for that matter, most likely in trials before international tribunals). Military commission trials will (a) not afford the accused a jury trial; (b) not be governed by the Federal Rules of Evidence; (c) not be open to the public in certain circumstances; (d) not require unanimous support for convictions, except for death sentences; and (e) not permit appellate review to an independent court.

. . . While using military commissioners in place of jurors to hear cases before a military commission has been upheld as constitutional, the replacement of the jury seems unnecessary in terrorism trials. The United States may have at least two reasons not to use jurors: (a) concerns with juror safety and (b) concerns that juries may inappropriately acquit. Neither argument is persuasive. While security would obviously need to be stringent for a jury trial of suspected al Qaeda terrorists, similar trials have successfully occurred in the past, and the United States apparently is willing to try Zacarias Moussaoui in federal district court. Although fears of additional terrorism are legitimate, they should not drive U.S. decisions regarding the administration of justice. Moreover, it is unclear that terrorism concerns would be greater for a federal court trial as opposed to a trial by military commission. The argument of inappropriate acquittal by juries should be afforded little weight given the enormity of crimes committed on September 11.

The other significant procedural changes—such as eliminating the requirement of unanimity for conviction and sentencing (at least in non-death penalty cases) and eliminating normal appellate review—seem designed only to facilitate quick guilty convictions. While there is a legitimate national interest in convicting guilty terrorists, that interest should be weighed against damage to the rule of law and concerns about convicting innocent persons. Obviously, it is difficult to answer the question of whether convicting terrorists is such a high priority that the United States should abandon due process protections, normally considered central to our justice system.

In *Hamdan,*[42] the Supreme Court held that President Bush lacked congressional authorization to establish the commissions. The Court, in finding several deficiencies, held that the commissions' procedures violated basic fair trial standards established by the Geneva Conventions of 1949. According to the Court, the Geneva Conventions mandated humane treatment of all persons held by the U.S. in the "conflict with al Qaeda." The main thrust of the criticism was that "[t]he military commissions invalidated by the Court in *Hamdan* substantially deviated from regular court-martial practice and were thus found to have not been authorized by Congress. . . ."[43]

In response to *Hamdan,* Congress enacted the Military Commissions Act of 2006,[44] which purported to "facilitate bringing to justice terrorists and other unlawful enemy combatants through full and fair trials by military commissions, and for other purposes."[45]

The Act established a Combatant Status Review Tribunal to determine whether a detainee can be categorized as an "alien unlawful enemy combatant" under Section II of the Act. Criteria for this review are taken from the Detainee Treatment Act of 2005 and referenced in Section 10 of the Act. The Tribunal is made up of three neutral officers, one of whom is a judge advocate and another who, as senior ranking officer, is President of the tribunal. Detainees may testify, call witnesses, and introduce additional evidence. After the hearing, the Tribunal conducts a closed-door session to decide whether the detainee is properly held as an enemy combatant. The criteria for when other "competent tribunals" may review this status determination are specified in the Detainee Treatment Act of 2005, which essentially limits review to the United States Court of Appeals for the District of Columbia Circuit.[46]

1. The Geneva Convention and Rights Denied by the Act

A gap exists between the rights granted in criminal trials conducted by the military and rights accorded unlawful enemy combatants in military commissions. James G. Stewart makes the distinction clear:

> While an accused in a court-martial is protected from the admission of an involuntary statement, the unlawful enemy combatant before a military commission is only protected against statements obtained by cruel, inhuman or degrading interrogation, and then only if the interrogation occurred after the enactment of the Detainee Treatment Act of 2005. While the accused in a court-martial has the right to be warned before any interrogation of the nature of the accusation against him or her, as well as of his or her right to not make a statement concerning the offence and that any statement he or she

42. Hamdan v. Rumsfeld, 548 U.S. 557 (2006).

43. Jack M. Beard, *The Geneva Boomerang: The Military Commissions Act of 2006 and U.S. Counter-terrorism Operations,* 101 Am. J. Int'l L. 56 (2007), at 58.

44. Military Commissions Act of 2006, or Senate Bill 3930, signed September 22, 2006.

45. Military Commissions Bill, *available at* http://www.nytimes.com/2006/09/28/opinion/28thu1.html?ex=1317096000&en=3eb3ba3410944ff9&ei=5090&partner=rssuserland&emc=rss/ (last visited February 20, 2024).

46. Detainee Treatment Act of 2005, Section (e)(2)(A), *available at* http://jurist.law.pitt.edu/gazette/2005/12/detainee-treatment-act-of-2005-white.php (last visited February 20, 2024).

> does make may be used as evidence in a court-martial against him or her, the unlawful combatant has only the right to be free from irrelevant and degrading questions at a military commission. Under the UCMJ, a suspect or an accused can terminate interrogation at any time by requesting counsel, while the only provision of the Military Commissions Act that provides defence [sic] counsel does so only after the swearing of charges. In an obvious effort to protect military intelligence and security based interrogations and ensure that they remain effective in obtaining information from unlawful enemy combatants, the Congress created a criminal system that is far less supportive of any right against self-incrimination or right to counsel.[47]

Under the Act, the detainee is protected from cruel, inhumane, or unusual treatment while in custody or while under the physical control of the United States, regardless of the detainee's nationality or physical location. Nevertheless, as initially established, prosecutors may use evidence obtained under varying degrees of coercion, though this is expressly prohibited by the Geneva Conventions.[48]

Furthermore, the prosecution does not have to give the detainee prompt or detailed notice of the nature and cause of the charges against him.[49] In military commissions, pretrial hearings and investigations are severely limited compared to those in the courts-martial system.

Under the Act, detainees are explicitly denied the right to a speedy trial, meaning they may be held for indefinite periods without a finding of guilt.[50] Furthermore, case precedent is non-existent. The use of hearsay is specifically addressed:

> A noteworthy departure from American jurisprudence in the potential rules for the military commissions is a new process for the admissibility of hearsay evidence. Unlike the MRE, which mirror the general prohibition against hearsay with numerous exceptions of the Federal rules, the military commissions adopt a curious burden-shifting approach for hearsay evidence that does not fit under one of the enumerated exceptions. The proponent of the hearsay must give advance notice to the opposing party of their intention to admit hearsay evidence that includes the particulars of the hearsay evidence, including how it was obtained, and provides that party with fair opportunity to "meet" the evidence. The opposing party then has the burden of showing that the evidence is unreliable or lacking in probative value in order to have the evidence excluded.[51]

Another frequently repeated critique is the Act's failure to define "competent tribunal." The U.S. Army Field Manual[52] requires a board of no less than

---

47. James G. Stewart, *The Military Commissions Act of 2006 Inconsistency with the Geneva Conventions,* 5 J. Int'l Criminal Justice 19 (2007), at 56-57.

48. Beard, *supra* note 43, at 59.

49. Guénaël Mettraux, *Comparing the Comparable: 2006 Military Commissions v. The ICTY,* 5J. Int'l Criminal Justice 59 (2007), at 62.

50. Richard V. Meyer, *When a Rose Is Not a Rose: Military Commissions v. Courts-Martial,* 5J. Int'l Criminal Justice 48 (2007), at 59.

51. *Id.* at 56.

52. Section 27-10.

three officers to determine if a person is a prisoner of war. Article 5 of the Third Geneva Convention grants all belligerents protection until their status is determined by a competent tribunal.[53] However, the Act expressly revokes Article 5 and grants rights only to *lawful*, not unlawful, military combatants:

> (g) Geneva Conventions Not Establishing Source of Rights—No alien unlawful enemy combatant subject to trial by military commission under this chapter may invoke the Geneva Conventions as a source of rights.[54]

In other words, the Act restricts invocation of the Geneva Conventions when a detainee petitions for the writ of *habeas corpus*.[55] This provision applies to all cases pending at the time the Act was enacted, as well as to all future cases.

Michael C. Dorf, Why the Military Commission Act Is no Moderate Compromise

FindLaw, Oct. 11, 2006[56]

The Constriction of the Writ of Habeas Corpus

There is, of course, an answer to that question, but it is not a pretty one: Perhaps the enemy will be kept guessing because the Administration does not actually intend to abide by the provisions of the MCA or DTA. After all, no alien can sue to enforce these provisions, and thus violations may never come to light. And that's before the President construes the MCA even more narrowly in a signing statement, as he is wont to do.

To be sure, if the government provides someone declared to be an enemy combatant with a combatant status review tribunal (CSRT), then the DTA authorizes judicial review of that determination. And the MCA does amend the DTA for the better in one important respect: Whereas the DTA only authorized civilian judicial review of CSRT determinations for detainees at Guanta-namo, under the MCA, a person held by the United States pursuant to a CSRT anywhere in the world can appeal the CSRT's ruling to a civilian federal court. But, there is no statutory requirement that the government ever utilize a CSRT-and absent a CSRT ruling, there is no access to civilian court.

Thus, under the terms of the DTA as amended by the MCA, there would be no access to a civilian court whatsoever, even if the detainee were held within the United States, so long as the government determined that he or she were an unlawful enemy combatant by some means other than using a CSRT.

---

53. Third Geneva Convention, Article 5, October 1950, *available at* https://www.un.org/en/genocideprevention/documents/atrocity-crimes/Doc.32_GC-III-EN.pdf (last visited March 15, 2024).

54. *Id.* at §984b(g).

55. *Id.* at §5(a).

56. *Available at* https://supreme.findlaw.com/legal-commentary/why-the-military-commissions-act-is-no-moderate-compromise.html (last visited March 15, 2024).

2. Military Commission Act 2009

In October 2009, Congress passed the Military Commission Act of 2009, which replaced the Bush-era Military Commission Act of 2006. The 2009 Act was the last amendment made and includes changes to the rules governing military commission proceedings, in particular evidentiary rules and rules regarding defense resources. Although the Obama administration failed to resolve the conundrum of whether to shut down the Military Commissions permanently, the 2009 Act reformed the 2006 Act. The reforms—while granting defendants additional rights—have continued to fail to satisfy the human rights community in the Trump and Biden administrations.

The Failed Military Commissions

The Center for Victims of Torture, July 2023[57]

As Professor David Luban has described, since their founding, "the Military Commissions have been dogged by one scandal after another, beginning as early as 2004 when a veteran Marine Corps prosecutor withdrew because he became convinced that he would have to present evidence obtained through torture. There was the hearing blacked out to observers by someone unknown to the judge, the moment the CIA black sites were mentioned; there was the interpreter detailed to the defense team who had previously worked for the CIA at a black site; there were the microphones disguised as smoke detectors installed in attorney-client interview rooms; and the prohibition on defense counsel doing independent investigations of the torture program; and so many more."

More recently, prosecutors in the military commissions attempted to use evidence obtained from torture against men whom the United States tortured—a clear violation of long-settled law.

To date, there have been a total of nine convictions in the military commissions, most through plea agreements with the defendants. Several of the convictions have been overturned in whole or in part on appeal, mostly by U.S. federal courts. Only one of those convictions is final.

There are three cases currently ongoing in the commissions, including United States v. Khalid Sheikh Mohammed, et al.—the prosecution of the men alleged to be most responsible for the September 11, 2001 attacks. None of those five cases has yet gone to trial.

Brig. Gen. John Baker, chief defense counsel for the military commissions from 2015 through 2021, testified before Congress in December 2021 to the commissions' failure:

"Justice delayed is justice denied. But the injustice meted out by the Guantánamo military commissions to the defendants, public, and victims extends far beyond mere delay. These delays are the direct result of government

57. *The Failed Militarry Commissions*, The Center for Victims of Torture, last updated July 19, 2023, *available at* https://www.cvt.org/what-we-do/advocating-for-change/legacy-of-us-torture/the-failed-military-commissions/ (last visited February 20, 2024).

decisions that have corrupted the process from its outset, and that make any just or satisfying future outcomes of commission cases—in the form of legitimate convictions and fair sentences—unlikely if not impossible. Allowing the military commissions to proceed in their current form will thus result at very best in many more years of agonizing delay, and at worst in verdicts that—following those years of delay—are overturned on appeal. To be blunt, the government is gambling with the victims' real need to achieve closure in some form. That is unconscionable."

"At the heart of the commissions' problems," Gen. Baker continued, "is their original sin, torture." He added, "More specifically, the government's fear that the truth will become public is what has most undermined the commission processes."

Colleen Kelly, whose younger brother, Bill Kelly Jr., was killed in the North Tower of the World Trade Center on September 11th, echoed Gen. Baker's remarks:

"[I]n May of 2012—more than a decade after 9/11—five men were arraigned. Today, another nine years and seven months later, a trial has not even begun. Instead, family members have heard years of argument in pretrial hearings. While these hearings have produced no legal justice for 9/11, they have revealed the shocking role of torture in undermining the 9/11 prosecution. Instead of learning how and why the attacks were carried out, and who was responsible for doing what, family members have followed seemingly endless litigation largely concerned with the defendants' torture by government agents and the government's attempts to keep that information from coming to light."

Issues to Consider

1. How should a proper judicial forum be identified?
2. What are the reasons the U.S. has failed to develop a consistent judicial paradigm policy?
3. What are the practical effects of MCA 2006 and MCA 2009?
4. What defendant rights are the most important to protect?
5. Does the lack of consistent decision making reflect an inability to determine terrorist status and rights?
6. From the initial military commissions premised on troubled case law, the administrations have denied detainees basic constitutional protections; what are the strategic consequences of this failure?

III. INTERNATIONAL COURTS

In addition to comparing the relative merits of civilian (Article III) courts and military commissions for terrorist-defendants, one must weigh the possibility of internationalizing the judicial process. Unlike war crime defendants who have been brought to trial before tribunals, terrorist-defendants have almost exclusively been brought to trial before domestic courts, aside from the rare ad hoc Special Tribunal for Lebanon explicitly established to investigate and prosecute on major terrorist incidents, although it was largely determined by Lebanese criminal law.

While not authorizing the implementation of an international judicial regime to prosecute terrorists, the 15 member-nations of the United Nations Security Council adopted Resolution 1373 (Sept. 28, 2001), which mandated the following:

> On 28 September 2001, acting under Chapter VII of the United Nations Charter (concerning threats to international peace and security), the Security Council adopted Resolution 1373 (2001), reaffirming its unequivocal condemnation of the terrorist attacks which took place in New York, Washington, D.C., and Pennsylvania on 11 September 2001, and expressing its determination to prevent all such acts. Resolution 1373 also established the Counter-Terrorism Committee (CTC), made up of all 15 members of the Security Council. The CTC monitors the implementation of resolution 1373 by all states and tries to increase the capability of states to fight terrorism. The CTC is an instrument to monitor the implementation of resolution 1373. The CTC is not a sanctions committee and does not have a list of terrorist organizations or individuals.

Establishing an international tribunal primarily for the purpose of trying terrorist-defendants would deviate greatly from current domestic judicial regimes, which embody both sovereignty and national counterterrorism. In domestic judicial paradigms, the only considerations are the specific nation's goals, laws, and moral values. The central question here is whether or not the internationalization of terror trials enhances counterterrorism while, admittedly, minimizing sovereignty.

Would an international judicial regime better serve the interests of nations that purport to seek similar goals on a global scale? The relative advantages and disadvantages of bringing terrorists to trial before an international court are underscored in the following excerpt.

Peter Golding, The Transformation of Counter Terrorism

USAWC Strategy Research Project, April 9, 2002[58]

International Problem

Though domestic courts are not monolithic in their judicial regime, the defendant—regardless of which regime is adopted—is tried either by that country's national court system or in a military court established by that nation in its capacity as an occupying power. The authority for each of these judicial systems is therefore, a single nation's sovereign power. The only considerations are that nation's goals and means for achieving them in a judicial setting.

Although these terrorists targeted the United States on 11 September 2001, countering terrorism effectively is an international problem. The problem is international in scope because the terrorist network is itself international in

58. *Available at* https://apps.dtic.mil/sti/tr/pdf/ADA400955.pdf (last visited March 15, 2024).

scope; the continuing threat these terrorists pose is not confined to the Untied States. The victims of 11 September 2001 were not only United States citizens, but citizens of many countries. Indirectly, the terrorists' attacks affected all nations, thus the community of nations together ought to coalesce and deal with the terrorism problem. United Nations Security Council Resolution 1368 "calls on all states to work together to bring justice to the perpetrators." Indeed, Mary Robinson United Nations High Commissioner for Human Rights said, "No one can argue that this isn't a crime against humanity."

Arguments Against Using an International Court

Practical Reasons

As the International Criminal Court does not yet exist, to pursue an ad-hoc International Court would necessitate developing court procedures, rules of evidence, standards of proof (beyond a reasonable doubt, clear and convincing, preponderance of the evidence or some other standard). As different countries have different procedures and traditions, for example the common law adversarial tradition versus the civil law inquisition tradition, establishing the ground rules could consume months if not years in simply creating the court. Furthermore, who would determine the rules and the selection of the judges? Would it be just the United States, or the combatants in the war in Afghanistan, or NATO or the United Nations?

For example, the crime of conspiracy could impose substantial difficulties from the point of view of the United States. It appears clear that the United States government is treating conspiracy to commit the terrorism on 11 September 2001 as a capital crime. However, most countries, including our European allies, would be unlikely to support the notion of conspiracy to commit murder as being a capital crime.

Proposals to develop and establish an international terror court have drawn attention to potential obstacles, including the appropriate rules of evidence, particularly the right to confront the accuser; the right to self-representation; and determining whether the scope of the court's jurisdiction should include both domestic and international terrorism. Attempts to punish guilty individuals by sentencing them to death also stands out as a major source of conflict. The Presidential Order established the death penalty for those convicted by a military commission convened in Guantanamo Bay. European nations are unanimously opposed to the death penalty and have refused to extradite terror-suspects to Guantanamo Bay, although extraditions have been made for terrorist-defendants tried in US domestic courts.

Yet perhaps the most difficult issue remains the definition of terrorism. As discussed previously, there are over 260 definitions worldwide, and while a working definition has been offered for this book, the international community continues to be divided regarding what, exactly, constitutes terrorism. A universal legal definition of terrorism has been debated especially following the Special Tribunal for Lebanon's judgement finding a customary international law of "transnational terrorism" yet there is still no agreement regarding an existing universal definition of terrorism.[59] If nations cannot agree upon the very entity compelling the need for an international tribunal, then they will unlikely be able to settle other disagreements regarding the appropriate judicial processes.

A. BARRIERS TO INTERNATIONAL TRIBUNALS

Professor Michael Newton's analysis, excerpted below, emphasizes the definitional quandary inherent to the establishment of international tribunals and suggests that the failure to agree on terms may be the largest stumbling block.

Michael A. Newton, International Criminal Law Aspects of the War Against Terrorism

79 U.S. Naval War College International Law Studies 323 (2003)

Modern international law embodies a significant body of law and practice that empowers domestic states to adjudicate terrorist crimes. Recent arguments, however, have postulated that an internationalized enforcement mechanism is warranted simply by virtue of the international nature of the problems posed by transnational terrorism. International law often evolves in response to perceived weaknesses in the normative structure that are highlighted by current events. This is the pattern for the post-September 11 wave of thinking about the linkage between international terrorism and an internationalized trial process. Given the inability of domestic forums to eradicate transnational terrorism, it is understandable that the aftermath of September 11 saw a ground-swell of support for the creation of an international judicial forum to prosecute such terrorists. Even as they acknowledge that national courts are the backbone for the systematic prosecution of international terrorists, some scholars have pointed out that an international forum would "symbolize global justice for global crimes."

However, this strain of thought is merely the current incarnation of an older set of discarded ideas. Despite nearly a century of discussion and debate, the nations of the world have not agreed on a comprehensive definition of terrorism, which is the obvious cornerstone of any international forum with jurisdiction over transnational terrorist acts. States instead shifted from a universal and general approach towards cooperative efforts to define and criminalize specific manifestations of terrorism through specific multilateral treaties which bind signatory states to proscribe and punish such acts using domestic systems.

As a logical corollary, states have repeatedly rejected proposals for an over-arching international tribunal charged with prosecuting crimes of transnational terrorism. The repeated formal rejections of terrorism as an

59. E4J University Module Series: Counter-Terrorism, Module 4: Criminal Justice Responses to Terrorism, United Nations Office on Drugs and Crime, July 2018, *available at* https://www.unodc.org/e4j/en/terrorism/module-4/key-issues/defining-terrorism.html (last visited February 20, 2024).

international problem that should be addressed in supranational judicial forums date back to the League of Nations era. In 1926, the International Congress of Penal Law recommended that the Permanent Court of International Justice "be competent to judge individual liabilities" incurred as a result of crimes considered as international offenses "which constitute a threat to world peace." This proposal died on the vine of international diplomacy.

The cries for an international tribunal imply that an international response is always appropriate for crimes grounded in international law that shock the conscience of mankind, which in turn implies an unseemly assertion that domestic prosecutions are always inappropriate and unfair. While terrorism is widespread, and may be impossible to eradicate, the compelling motivations that have required the formation of international forums in other contexts are notably absent.

In other words, despite the inherent difficulty of investigating and prosecuting international terrorists, there is no culture of impunity because one or several sovereign states will always have jurisdiction, political will, and a very strong motivation to prosecute that particular set of terrorists when there is available evidence sufficient to sustain conviction of persons who are within the substantive and personal jurisdiction of the sovereign state. Creation of an international forum specifically designed to respond to crimes of terrorism would be a wholly new development in the field of international criminal law because it would be the first time that an international forum was created solely due to the nature of the crimes committed. If the nations of the world are committed to combating the core problem of transnational terrorism, the best place is in the domestic forums of affected states. This approach will accomplish the most in the long term to ensure that the rule of law is strengthened and justice is done.

Issues to Consider

1. If one man's freedom fighter is another man's terrorist, can the international community articulate an agreed upon definition of terrorism?
2. How should the death penalty controversy be resolved?
3. What are the benefits for like-minded nations to establish an international terror court?
4. Is terrorism sufficiently international to justify the establishment of an international judicial regime?
5. If Chechen terrorists have different goals than the terrorists responsible for the Madrid train bombings, would an international terror court be the appropriate forum for their respective trials?
6. What is the appropriate reach of an international terror court in regards to: the doers, the financiers, the providers of safe haven?

B. STATES, EVIDENCE, AND THE RIGHTS OF THE ACCUSED

The establishment of an international terrorism tribunal requires addressing evidentiary issues, particularly the admissibility of classified intelligence information. The testimony of Gerald Gahima, former judge for the War Crime Chamber of the Court of Bosnia-Herzegovina, before the United States House Armed Services Committee explains how the various war crimes tribunals have struck a crucial balance between the rights of nations to use classified information and the rights of defendants to confront their accusers.

TESTIMONY OF GERALD GAHIMA BEFORE THE US ARMED SERVICES COMMITTEE

July 26, 2006[60]

The rules of both the ICTR and the ICTY recognize the legitimacy of national security concerns of states assisting the two tribunals. It was understood and was provided for in the tribunals' rules of procedure and evidence that the sensitive nature of some of the assistance provided by states to the tribunals might preclude the conduct of public proceedings and or require restrictions on the submission of certain types of evidence. Rule 54(F) of the ICTY and ICTR's Rules of Evidence and Procedure ("RPE") were specifically constructed to address national security concerns of this nature. According to the rule, a state having concerns over the national security impact of a public hearing shall "file a notice of its objection not less than five days before the date of the hearing" and may request in camera or ex parte proceedings, or the use of documents submitted in redacted form accompanied by an affidavit signed by a senior official explaining the reasons for the document's restrictions.

Not every piece of information is subject to disclosure or exclusion based on national security. According to Rule 70(B) of both Tribunals on the production of evidence,

If the Prosecutor is in possession of information which has been provided to him on a confidential basis and which has been used solely for the purpose of generating new evidence, that initial information and its origin shall not be disclosed by the Prosecutor without the consent of the person or entity providing the initial information and shall in any event not be given in evidence without prior disclosure to the accused.

If rules of procedure of international criminal courts permit states which have assisted them to seek orders for the non-disclosure of information which might jeopardize their national interest, the availability of such remedies (the use of summaries and redactions of classified information, in camera proceedings and ex parte proceedings, etc.) in proceedings in U.S. courts trying suspected terror suspects would not by analogy violate international standards of fair trial.

60. *Available at* http://www.globalsecurity.org/security/library/congress/2006_h/060726-gahima.pdf (last visited July 20, 2010).

Issues to Consider

1. What are the benefits of trying terrorists in an international tribunal?
2. Should nation-states relinquish the right to try terrorists in a domestic criminal law court?
3. How should the lack of a unifying definition of terrorism be resolved?
4. Is international cooperation enhanced by international tribunals?

The development of an international tribunal would require nations, including the seven that have been surveyed, to make significant legal and policy decisions regarding counterterrorism. If the goal is to contribute to international cooperation in responding to global terror threats, then tribunals—whether existing tribunals such as the ICC or special terror tribunals—are an appropriate response. Conversely, if nation-states seek to punish terrorists who have attacked its citizens, then a domestic court paradigm—either civilian courts or military commissions—may be a more effective venue.

The policy ramifications of the globalization of counterterrorism are not insignificant. Establishing an international terror court requires nation-states to accept cooperation as not only a theme, but also a reality. The decision to establish such a tribunal is ultimately not a legal issue but rather a policy consideration requiring decision makers to implement a universal model in response to global terrorism.

Laura A. Dickinson, Using Legal Process to Fight Terrorism: Detentions, Military Commissions, International Tribunals, and the Rule of Law

75 S. Cal. L. Rev. 1407 (2002)

Terrorism is a transnational problem that spans virtually the entire world, and strong multilateral efforts are required if it is to be contained. The Al Qaeda network alone draws on the nationals of multiple countries who leave their homes to train in terrorist camps in host countries such as Afghanistan, Somalia, Sudan, and the Philippines, and who are then sent to target countries such as the United States, where they live in cells, waiting to be deployed.

Immediately following the September 11 attacks, the United States drew on the support of numerous countries around the globe in efforts to combat terrorism. On the day after the attacks, the UN Security Council issued a resolution strongly condemning the attacks and recognizing "the inherent right of individual or collective self-defence in accordance with the Charter." Shortly thereafter, the Security Council issued another resolution, explicitly invoking its authority under Chapter VII of the United Nations Charter, referring to the previous resolution's recognition of the right to self defense, reaffirming the need to combat by "all means" terrorist acts threatening international peace and security, requiring states to take steps to block terrorist finances and end any state support for terrorism, and calling on states to increase cooperative intelligence-gathering and law enforcement efforts.

An international legal process would help to build on these cooperative efforts. First, as discussed in more detail below, an international process would likely have greater legitimacy internationally than the proposed military commissions or even domestic trials within the United States. If other governments perceive the United States as acting fairly and with appropriate deference to international norms, they are more likely to continue as active members of a coalition to combat terrorism. Second, even beyond the question of perceived legitimacy, the international proceeding itself, by involving participants from many countries, would strengthen both formal and informal intergovernmental networks and institutions.

An international proceeding would involve participants from many nations in the prosecution and punishment of terrorism suspects, which would give those nations a stake in the process, lead to the development of a cadre of governmental, intergovernmental, and nongovernmental personnel with expertise in addressing the problem of terrorism, and foster channels of communication and collaboration among them.

In order to see how an international process helps to create a context for the development of intergovernmental networks, we can look at the problem of secret evidence. Critics have charged that an international process offers the greatest potential for damaging leaks, which will make countries reluctant to provide the intelligence information needed at trial. Due to the transnational nature of terrorism, however, information-sharing is absolutely essential, and countries will refuse to disclose information only at their peril, with or without an international legal process. Indeed, as UN Security Council Resolution 1373 recognizes, enhanced multilateral information-sharing is an intrinsic part of any serious effort to contain terrorism. In tracking down and locating Al Qaeda suspects, the United States has already relied considerably on intelligence provided by other countries.

To be sure, the United States might well be reluctant to disclose, even to a group of intelligence officials operating under conditions of secrecy, certain information that would be necessary to convict Al Qaeda operatives, if members of the panel included representatives from governments deemed less trustworthy. The circle of governments to which we might be willing to disclose such information could well be, and perhaps should be, quite narrow. Indeed, we may not even trust certain other countries enough to give credence to the information received from them, let alone enough to give them additional material. Nonetheless, there can be no doubt that information-sharing is already occurring and that it is necessary in the fight against terrorism. Moreover, even a multilateral panel with representatives from only a few countries would be an improvement over a purely unilateral approach.

Issues to Consider

1. What are the policy implications of establishing international tribunals?
2. How should "effective" be defined in the judicial paradigm with respect to terrorism?

IV. NATIONAL SECURITY COURTS

Some critics suggest that neither system currently in place in the United States—military commissions and Article III courts—can effectively try suspected terrorists, and therefore a national security court, or domestic terror court, should be created.

Amos N. Guiora, Creating a Domestic Terror Court

48 Washburn L. J. 617 (2009)

. . . As an absolutely critical first step, President Obama *must* articulate criteria for determining—via a person-specific vetting process—which of the detainees presents a current or future threat to America's national security. Those deemed to present a threat must be brought to trial; those deemed not, must be released. Although the logistics of releasing thousands of detainees is a daunting task, it must not-under any circumstances- justify their continued detention. As the former President of the Israeli Supreme Court, Aharon Barak, once commented, "logistical requirements should never stand in the way of personal freedom."

There is one important caveat to this ironclad rule that requires careful consideration: What is the correct decision when the *only* information available against a particular detainee is classified information and therefore no judicial process is feasible? There are, I suggest, three options: (1) outright release of the individual in spite of the available information; (2) continued, indefinite detention thereby prolonging violation of constitutional rights; or (3) creation of an administrative detention paradigm, borrowing from the United Kingdom or Israeli models, subject to statutorily mandated periodic review by an independent judiciary.

. . . Detainees present a definitional challenge primarily because they are neither traditional criminal defendants nor prisoners of war as defined by international law. It is important, however, to define "detainee" not only to ensure their established rights, but also to articulate additional rights. I propose that "post-9/11 detainees" are "individuals suspected of involvement in terrorism." This term gives us a starting point toward creating a hybrid paradigm. This hybrid paradigm will contribute to resolving the difficult task of balancing legitimate national security concerns with the equally legitimate rights of the individual suspects. . . .

. . . The DTC [Domestic Terror Court] itself will be a restructured Foreign Intelligence Surveillance Act (FISA) court thereby enabling it to adjudicate guilt and innocence in addition to its primary statutorily mandated responsibility of considering governmental wire tap warrants. This added responsibility obviously will require the appointment of a significant number of additional judges to the FISA bench. The current FISA structure is clearly inadequate to support the increased needs inherent in the establishment of a DTC. These judges will be drawn from the pool of sitting United States District Court judges, as is the current practice, and the president will need to nominate, subject to Senate confirmation, new judges who will sit on the DTC. The DTC will have, in addition to considering wire tap requests, three primary responsibilities: (1) to rule on remand requests, from detention to indictment;

(2) to determine whether to hold the defendant for trial based on the charging documents and evidence presented at a preliminary hearing; and (3) to adjudicate guilt or innocence.

One of the critical—and admittedly problematic—features of the DTC is the manner in which the government's interest in protecting legitimate national security concerns will be balanced against the obligation to simultaneously ensure the rights of individual suspects, particularly with respect to the right to confront an accuser. The DTC will not provide suspects with the same level of constitutional protection as traditional Article III courts. This measure will enable the government to keep intelligence information classified. Nevertheless, significant measures will be taken to ensure that the information received by the DTC is weighed by the bench in a manner intended to benefit the defendant, precisely because he is absent.

Although the evidence is presented by the prosecution and a member of the intelligence community, by applying a strict four-part test in weighing the submitted information, the judge will wear two hats: one as the court and the other as defense counsel. The information and the source must be held to be: (1) reliable; (2) viable; (3) valid; and (4) corroborated. If the intelligence meets the four-part test, then and only then is it admissible and available for use against the defendant at trial. However, a defendant's conviction may not be based solely on confidential intelligence information. This evidence may only be used to support an existing body of evidence known to the defendant and his counsel and introduced in open court proceedings. In every case, the sitting judge will make all decisions as to the admissibility of evidence while viewing the evidence in a light most favorable to the defendant.

Similarly, the sitting judge may determine through *in camera* review of intelligence evidence that introducing the information in open court proceedings does not pose a threat to national security. In these cases, the judge gives the prosecution the option of declassifying the information and presenting it in court or proceeding to trial without such evidence.

If a defendant is convicted in the DTC, sentencing will proceed just as in traditional courts with maximum and minimum sentencing terms. Furthermore, sentencing will not, under any circumstance, involve the death penalty. Appeals will be filed directly to the United States Court of Appeals.

A Critique of "National Security Courts"

The Constitution Project, June 23, 2008[61]

Advocates of national security courts that would try terrorism suspects claim that traditional Article III courts are unequipped to handle these cases. This claim has not been substantiated, and is made in the face of a significant—and growing—body of evidence to the contrary. A recent report released by Human Rights First persuasively demonstrates that our existing federal

61. *Available at* https://www.americanbar.org/content/dam/aba/administrative/law_national_security/critique_ofthe_nat_security_crts_updated_signers.pdf (last visited March 15, 2024).

courts are competent to try these cases. The report examines more than 120 international terrorism cases brought in the federal courts over the past fifteen years. It finds that established federal courts were able to try these cases without sacrificing either national security or the defendants' rights to a fair trial. The report documents how federal courts have successfully dealt with classified evidence under the Classified Information Procedures Act (CIPA) without creating any security breaches. It further concludes that courts have been able to enforce the government's Brady obligations to share exculpatory evidence with the accused, deal with Miranda warning issues, and provide means for the government to establish a chain of custody for physical evidence, all without jeopardizing national security.

Of course, our traditional federal courts have not always done everything that the government would like them to do. They are, after all, constrained by well-established constitutional limits on prosecutorial power. For example, no federal court would permit the prosecution to present witnesses without protecting the defendant's constitutional right to confront those witnesses against him or her. Nor would a federal court permit the prosecution to rely on a coerced confession in violation of a defendant's Fifth Amendment right against self-incrimination. But creating a new set of courts would not repeal existing constitutional rights. Conversely, to the extent that the existing rules are not constitutionally compelled, ordinary federal courts (or Congress, where applicable) can modify them when it is shown that the modification is necessary to accommodate the government's legitimate interests.

Most importantly, there is the intrinsic and inescapable problem of definition. Whereas the argument for specialized courts for tax and patent law is that expert judges are particularly necessary given the complex subject-matter, proposals for specialized courts for terrorism trials are based on the asserted need for relaxed procedural and evidentiary rules and are justified on the ground that terrorists do not deserve full constitutional protections. This creates two fundamental constitutional problems. First, justifying departures from constitutional protections on the basis that the trials are for terrorists undermines the presumption of innocence for these individuals. Second, if a conviction were obtained in a national security court using procedural and evidentiary rules that imposed a lesser burden on the government, then the defendant would be subjected to trial before a national security court based upon less of a showing than would be required in a traditional criminal proceeding. The result would be to apply less due process to the question of guilt or innocence, which, by definition, would increase the risk of error. And, if the government must make a preliminary showing that meets traditional rules of procedure and evidence in order to trigger the jurisdiction of a national security court, such a showing would also enable it to proceed via the traditional criminal process.

National security courts for criminal prosecutions are not just unnecessary; they are also dangerous. They run the risk of creating a separate and unequal criminal justice system for a particular class of suspects, who will be brought before such specialized courts based on the very allegations they are contesting. Such a system undermines the presumption of innocence for these defendants, and risks a broader erosion of defendants' rights that could spread to traditional Article III trials. It was Justice Frankfurter who wrote that "It is a fair summary of history to say that the safeguards of liberty have frequently been forged in controversies involving not very nice people." Committee members strongly believe that the shadow of terrorism must not be the basis for abandoning these fundamental tenets of justice and fairness.

In addition, these proposals are alarmingly short on details with respect to the selection of judges for these national security courts. Although there is a history of creating specialized federal courts to handle particular substantive areas of the law (e.g., taxation; patents), unlike tax and patent law, there is simply no highly specialized expertise that would form relevant selection criteria for the judges. Establishing a specialized court solely for prosecutions of alleged terrorists might also create a highly politicized process for nominating and confirming the judges, focusing solely on whether the nominee had sufficient "tough on terrorism" credentials—hardly a criterion that lends itself to the appearance of fairness and impartiality.

None of the above is to deny that there is a class of individuals who may be tried in appropriate military tribunals. Persons captured by the U.S. military as part of an armed conflict have traditionally been subject to military jurisdiction under the laws of war. This principle is well-established, but it has long coexisted with the complementary principle that only individuals who are properly subject to military jurisdiction under the laws of war may be so tried. Military tribunals may not try offenders or offenses unless they are encompassed by traditional laws of war.

Just as there is no need to establish national security courts to replace traditional Article III courts, so too there is no need to create such tribunals to handle cases that would normally be tried by military courts. Individuals should be tried either in our traditional criminal justice system or in properly constituted military courts.

V. CONCLUSION

The four options discussed—domestic criminal courts, military commissions, international tribunals, and national security courts—represent very diverse approaches to bringing terrorists to justice. Again, how nations balance diametrically opposing rights of the individual and the state represents the essential dilemma facing decision makers and jurists. By adopting a traditional criminal law approach, the state is guaranteeing the terrorist-defendant full rights and privileges, *potentially* at the cost of losing prosecutorial power. Conversely, by adopting a domestic military court, the state establishes a judicial framework that facilitates prosecution at the cost of denying the defendant universally accepted rights.

To balance these competing interests, each nation has adopted different approaches to policy, operations, intelligence gathering, and the appropriate use of information gathered from detainees. These issues are directly related to the judicial paradigm adopted by each of the seven surveyed nations; any sustainable international paradigm would require some level of consensus regarding these different approaches.

How should the seven surveyed nations go forward? In the United States, amending FISA legislation so that suspected terrorists might be brought to trial before a special FISA court could resolve legal ambiguity. Such congressional initiative might enable suspects to be tried before a civilian court competent in issues specific to terrorist trials. As the *Moussaoui* trial clearly demonstrated, traditional Article III courts are ill-equipped for such trials. Individuals suspected of involvement in terrorism could be heard before a bench trial, without a jury, to allow the introduction of intelligence information that would not be made available to the defendant or counsel. While this would violate the Sixth Amendment right to confront the accuser, a court specifically trained in reading and analyzing the reliability of intelligence information would satisfy a balancing test whereby the state could introduce such information subject to strict judicial scrutiny by an independent court. Clearly, the U.S. is still struggling in deciding where and how to try terrorist suspects.

The judicial approaches adopted by Russia and India indicate that these nations prefer to apply a criminal law paradigm in which terrorists are brought before a civilian court. At the same time, these countries employ aggressive operational counterterrorism methods in contrast to traditional law enforcement. In other words, both Russia and India treat terrorists as a distinct entity in an operational sense, but as criminals once the suspected terrorists are caught. These countries have come under severe criticism due to widespread allegations of human rights violations.

China's and Colombia's implementation of the criminal law paradigm extends to their policy regarding the proper judicial forum for suspected terrorists.

The Spanish government, on the other hand, treats terrorists as criminals in both the operational and judicial regimes. But Spain's traditional law enforcement is unique in that it allows for incommunicado detention, which has also been the subject of international criticism. Nevertheless, three of the surveyed countries—Russia, India, and Spain—have largely resisted the adoption of a second judicial tier established by the United States and Israel.

Israel has the most fully developed two-track judicial approach to terrorism in that defendants may be brought either to court for a full criminal trial or detained administratively subject to independent judicial review. A terrorist defendant brought to trial in a military court is provided full criminal rights and protections akin to the judicial process before a civilian court; in administrative detention, the detainee is not entitled to confront his accuser.

Implementation of methods extending beyond the criminal law paradigm suggests a recognition that the traditional approach is inapplicable, but careful analysis of *how* each paradigm has been implemented hints at overreach and tweaking rather than at a consistent legal policy. All of the seven surveyed nations articulate—subtly or clearly—a realization that terrorists are somehow *different* than common criminals. How different and how to articulate the difference are issues with which nations continue to struggle. That struggle has resulted in policy inconsistency, ambiguity, and violations of human rights.

CHAPTER 10

FUTURE CHALLENGES TO COUNTERTERRORISM

In Chapter 1 there were references to the January 6 attack on the U.S. Capitol, the attack on the Tree of Life Synagogue, the two attacks on the mosque in Christchurch, and the Jewish Underground (Israel). Despite the differences between the four, sufficient linkage exists amongst them to serve as the basis for a discussion seeking to understand the future face of terrorism. While prognostication is invariably a risky undertaking, decision makers must do just that in order to define threats, risks, and opportunities, and to ultimately gauge how and where to allocate limited resources.

The assessment with respect to domestic extremism/terrorism has a direct relationship to the balance between free speech and incitement. This reality was made dramatically clear before, during, and after the events of January 6. It is not an exaggeration to suggest that were it not for the words (if not actions) of President Donald J. Trump, what unfolded inside the Capitol and its immediate environs would not have occurred. The question regarding the limits of freedom of speech is particularly acute when examining domestic extremism in a democracy.

Exacerbating the complexity of the discussion is the encouragement, tolerance, and justification of domestic extremism by national leaders. While particular leaders' political leanings may resonate with extremist actors—for example, President Trump with regards to the January 6 mob or Prime Minister Yitzhak Shamir with regards to the Jewish Underground in Israel[1]—those very extremist actions undermine the society with whose protection the leaders are tasked by law to uphold. Rather than condemning violent actions by domestic actors which resulted in loss of life, injury, and destruction of property,

1. Hannah Brown, *The Jewish Underground, More than 30 Years Later*, Jerusalem Post, July 4, 2018, 11:17 PM, *available at* https://www.jpost.com/israel-news/culture/the-jewish-underground-more-than-30-years-later-561672 (last visited February 20, 2024).

both President Trump and Israeli Prime Minister Shamir[2] took a different tack. This, obviously, was not their approach to external attacks, which they both understood as a direct threat on national security.

That same consideration of internal and external threats applies to the limits to which the state can intrude on privacy; this is particularly relevant in considering the legal application of sophisticated technological surveillance. What is considered to be tolerable and legitimate in the face of terrorism from "across the border" is more prone to resistance when the limits are imposed on domestic actors. That is, then, the great challenge facing decision makers confronting domestic terrorism.

While the requirement to protect the public is of the uppermost importance, the state's responsibility is to ensure public order. Furthermore, democracies strive to structure themselves in accordance with state power limits and with the requirement to balance legitimate, competing interests. That tension—for there is no more fitting word—which is difficult enough when the attackers are akin to bin Laden, is accentuated when the actor is a citizen of the nation state who is committed to a domestic extremist ideology that justifies killing innocent fellow citizens.

This, after all, is what happened in Charlottesville, Pittsburgh, Christchurch, and Washington, D.C. Given the impact of these events, and the powerful questions they raise in regards to the relationship between law, morality, and the effectiveness of operational counterterrorism, leaders and counterterrorism experts must recognize the power and impact of domestic terrorism.

The challenge regarding resource allocation and prioritization is an essential aspect of proactive operational counterterrorism. Determining how/where to spend valuable resources must take into consideration powerful competing interests. Those considerations are complicated, given the need to protect civil rights and liberties. However, in many ways, that sensitivity, while understandable, can serve to limit the scope of domestic operational counterterrorism. The inherent reluctance to go "too far" in addressing terrorism is less acute when the threat is from outside.

Given the scope and intensity of domestic extremism, this political, social, and cultural reality can be understood as limiting the reach of the state in its efforts to protect the public. The instinctual rallying around the flag in response to an attack from "outside" does not occur when the perpetrators look and talk like people from the "inside." This reality poses limits on decision making when determining proactive and reactive measures. In democracies, the assumption that civil rights be preserved and protected can have unintended consequences from the perspective of the intelligence and security agencies mandated with public safety.

The public perception of the trammeling of otherwise guaranteed rights is magnified when the nation state spends extraordinary amounts of resources on technology. While there is no doubt regarding the important role of technology in proactive operational counterterrorism, concern regarding possible

2. *Yitzhak Shamir*, Israel Prime Minister's Office, last updated May 23, 2019, *available at* https://www.gov.il/en/departments/people/shamir (last visited February 20, 2024).

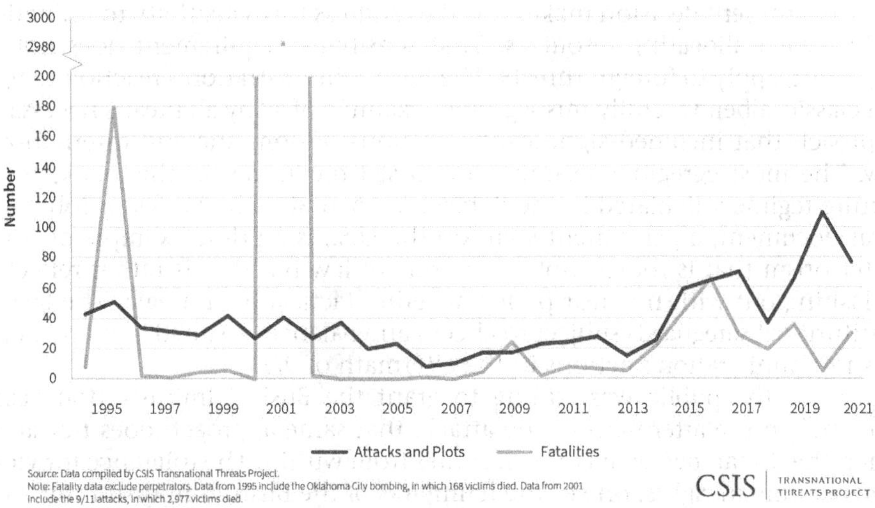

U.S. Terrorist Attacks and Plots and Fatalities, 1994-2021[3]

misuse resulting in illegal surveillance as well as unjustified and unwarranted invasions of privacy is often articulated. Those criticisms cannot be easily dismissed, nor should they be.

While protecting the public is a primary obligation of the nation state, no less important is respecting individual rights. The fact that an individual's ideology is extremist is not, in and of itself, cause for deliberately limiting the right to free speech and other guaranteed rights, whether by the judiciary or by relevant laws. In the age of social media, guaranteed anonymity, and the literally unlimited range of speech, the question of the limits of free speech is particularly pressing.

That issue is more acute when the target of surveillance is a domestic threat as compared to a global threat. Regardless of the country, the public largely accepts that public safety requires the need to keep a border safe from external threats. However, that same understanding does not necessarily carry over to the need to protect from identified—much less unidentified—domestic threats, even though the risk they pose may be substantial. When the potential threat is not fully identified, the risks to individual rights are significant, given the potential for "fishing" expeditions by the security community. That is a reality that repeats itself, with negative consequences all but guaranteed in advance.

---

3. *Pushed to Extremes Domestic Terrorism amid Polarization and Protest*, U.S. Terrorist Attacks and Plots and Fatalities, 1994-2021, data compiled by CSIS Transnational Threats Project, *available at* https://www.csis.org/analysis/pushed-extremes-domestic-terrorism-amid-polarization-and-protest (last visited February 20, 2024).

Government decision makers need to address this sensitivity to individual rights when allocating resources. That sensitivity requirement does not, in large part, apply to foreign threats. The Bush Administration's reaction to 9/11 is a classic, albeit woefully misbegotten, example of a "by all means necessary" approach that included significant violations of domestic and international law. The most egregious example, discussed previously in this book, is the torture regime articulated in the Bybee Memo, drafted by Professor John Yoo. That document, a permanent stain on the U.S., is a prime example of counterterrorism that is rooted not in the rule of law but that is rather reflective of lashing out with no clear policy, whether tactical or strategic. The lack of institutional safeguards subject to checks and balances resulted in many of the Bush Administration's actions in the aftermath of 9/11.

While the public was willing to grant the Bush Administration "carte blanche" in the aftermath of the attack, that same approach does not apply when the threat, perceived or real, comes from within. The tolerance for violations of human rights, one of the hallmarks of the Bush Administration, does not carry over to domestic policy.

A caveat is in order: this is not to suggest that civil rights have not been violated in the U.S. when organizations challenge mainstream society. A casual perusal of how the FBI, under former director J. Edgar Hoover, violated the rights of civil rights leaders, including—but not limited to—Dr. Martin Luther King Jr., speaks for itself. That similarly applies to violations of the civil rights of those protesting U.S. involvement in the Vietnam War. While public reactions were, in the main, muted in the face of these violations, calls for the protection of rights, whether constitutionally guaranteed or protected by a nation's judiciary, will be an all but inevitable reality that decision makers need to confront.

Even in the aftermath of the events of January 6, regardless of the severity of what occurred in the U.S. Capitol, the rights of the suspects were protected. There is no indication that law enforcement considered any short-cuts, or other measures, that would have impacted guaranteed rights. That same model does not apply, as made clear after 9/11, when the threat, or attack, is not domestic in origin.

The differences in responses, however, must not serve to minimize or downplay domestic threats, which as discussed in this book must be recognized as significant. The tension lies in the question of how decision makers, going forward, can most effectively react to domestic threats without over-stepping boundaries, distinct from previous eras in U.S. history. This same dilemma of balancing rights in the face of domestic extremism-terrorism also applies to the other countries surveyed in this book.

While perhaps politically uncomfortable for certain national leaders to address nationalism/extremism, responsible leadership requires the same verve be paid to combating domestic and international threats. "Political considerations be damned" must be the motto, even if the actors are aligned, regardless of the extent, with elected officials. Leaders must act and speak forcefully in the face of domestic extremism; a symbiotic relationship—regardless of its extent—between actors and politicians cannot justify a "kid glove" approach.

Overreaction, as previously referenced, is similarly harmful. However, a deliberately (one assumes) understated response to domestic extremism/terrorism affiliated with right-wing nationalism is also dangerous because it fails to sufficiently articulate the threat, much less serve as a deterrent to future actors. This is no less dangerous than overreactions which violate otherwise guaranteed rights. The tension in how to most effectively, and legally, balance rights with appropriate responses and deterrents is one of the critical issues this book has addressed. The complexity in doing so is exacerbated when the issue at hand is domestic terrorism.

For example, in the aftermath of the "Unite the Right" rally in Charlottesville, Virginia in August 2017—an event in which Heather Heyer was killed by a white nationalist[4]—President Trump downplayed the actions of those responsible.[5] That same approach of downplaying the actions of extremists defined then Israeli Prime Minister Yitzhak Shamir, who minimized the terrorist acts of the Jewish underground—whose actions, had they succeeded, could have engulfed the region in a religious war. The ultimate plan of the Jewish underground was to destroy what is considered in Islam to be the second most holy site, located in Jerusalem.[6] It is hard to over-state the impact of this planned attack. Referring to them (in Hebrew) as "good boys" was as harmful as Trump's "some very fine people on both sides" regarding the Charlottesville "Unite the Right" rally. Moral equivocation is perhaps politically effective but sends the absolute wrong message from an operational counterterrorism perspective.

Given the impact of domestic terrorism, decision makers—regardless of their political inclinations and leanings—will need to clearly and consistently articulate the threats posed by domestic terrorists. While 9/11 provided President Bush the opportunity to articulate great anger at bin Laden, both Trump and Shamir took the opposite tack toward domestic threats.

The failure to condemn extremists is irresponsible (politics notwithstanding) and can be understood as encouraging domestic terrorists, particularly when a national leader, as was the case with January 6 and the Jewish underground, is sympathetic to the cause. In response to the Christchurch mass shootings in March 2019, New Zealand Prime Minister Ardern's emotional response was very different from Trump's and Shamir's.[7] Trump's response

4. Press Release, U.S. Dep't of Justice, Ohio Man Sentenced to Life in Prison for Federal Hate Crimes Related to August 2017 Car Attack at Rally in Charlottesville, Virginia June 28, 2019, *available at* https://www.justice.gov/opa/pr/ohio-man-sentenced-life-prison-federal-hate-crimes-related-august-2017-car-attack-rally (last visited February 20, 2024).

5. David Jackson, *Trump Defends Response to Charlottesville Violence, Says He Put It 'Perfectly' with 'Both Sides' Remark*, USA Today, April 26, 2019, 1:51 PM, *available at* https://www.usatoday.com/story/news/politics/2019/04/26/trump-says-both-sides-charlottesville-remark-said-perfectly/3586024002/ (last visited February 20, 2024).

6. Zena Al Tahhan, *Who Are the Jewish Groups Who Enter Jerusalem's Al-Aqsa Compound?*, Al Jazeera, April 12, 2023, *available at* https://www.aljazeera.com/news/2023/4/12/who-are-jewish-groups-entering-al-aqsa-mosque (last visited February 20, 2024).

7. Charlotte Graham-McLay, *'Her Tears Were Real': Survivors of Christchurch Attack Weigh Up Jacinda Ardern's Legacy*, Guardian, January 25, 2023, 2:00 PM, *available at* https://www.theguardian.com/world/2023/jan/25/christchurch-attack-survivors-on-jacinda-ardern-legacy-as-new-zealand-pm (last visited February 20, 2024).

to the Tree of Life shooting was reflective of his political perspective on self-protection and the death penalty.[8] However, distinct from his reaction to Charlottesville, he did not attempt to explain away the act by engaging in victim blaming.

What do we learn from this?

More than anything, that national leaders must—notwithstanding countervailing instincts—put aside their political leanings in the face of domestic terrorism and understand the threat posed by extremists to public order and safety, even if those extremists are their natural political base. That nuance is perhaps less required in the face of an external threat, but is of the greatest importance when the actor is, perhaps literally but certainly figuratively, the next-door neighbor. Clear, unconditional condemnation is essential not only because of the loss of life, but also—no less importantly—to signal zero tolerance of domestic extremism.

There is a natural tension between extremism and speech.

While acts of domestic terrorism—Charlottesville, January 6, Tree of Life, Christchurch, Assassination of Prime Minister Rabin, and many others—must be condemned in the strongest language possible, freedom of speech must be respected in accordance with national laws and relevant judicial holdings. There are, obviously, significant differences in how different countries interpret freedom of speech and how the question of incitement is resolved.

Israeli case law has a broad tolerance for the freedom of speech. Even in the aftermath of the 1995 assassination of then Prime Minister Rabin by Yigal Amir, a religious right-wing extremist, the Attorney General failed to prosecute rabbis who had incited Amir. That was notwithstanding the unbridled—if not unhinged—daily incitement directed at Rabin, leaving little doubt as to the speakers' intention.

The venom, including a religious ceremony calling for Rabin's murder,[9] was palpable. More than that, it was part and parcel of life in Israel after Rabin signed the Oslo Peace Process, seeking to resolve the decades-long Israeli-Palestinian conflict. Rabin was regularly referred to as a "traitor";[10] his picture was photo-shopped in the likeness of the SS,[11] and bumper stickers calling for

8. Caroline Kelly, Ray Sanchez & Liz Stark, *Trump Says Pittsburgh Synagogue Should Have Had Armed Guards*, CNN Politics, October 28, 2018, 12:45 AM, *available at* https://edition.cnn.com/2018/10/27/politics/trump-jba-death-penalty-pittsburgh/index.html (last visited February 20, 2024).

9. *Assassination in the Middle East: Jewish Mystic Put a Curse on Rabin, Magazine Reports*, L.A. Times, November 5, 1995, 12:00 AM, *available at* https://www.latimes.com/archives/la-xpm-1995-11-05-mn-65263-story.html (last visited February 20, 2024).

10. The same word is used today in Israeli as a criticism of those demonstrating against the Netanyahu government's judicial "reform"; in full disclosure, the author is an active participant in the demonstrations.

11. *SS Uniform Photo Defames Rabin*, Chicago Trib., November 24, 1995, 12:00 AM, *available at* https://www.chicagotribune.com/news/ct-xpm-1995-11-24-9511250151-story.html (last visited February 20, 2024).

violence were widespread.[12] None of these facts convinced the State Attorney General to act.[13]

This is distinct from the U.S. Supreme Court decision in *Brandenburg v. Ohio,* which held that speech that incites can be limited.[14] The two approaches—one allowing unlimited speech, the other imposing limits—must be navigated by prosecutors, the defense bar, and courts. Social media, and the anonymity it guarantees, has imposed significant challenges to limiting incitement in accordance with *Brandenburg.*[15]

The questions posed by social media in the free speech/extremism debate are particularly relevant given social media's range, impact, and power. This is particularly important when considering the interaction between social media and the January 6 attack on the U.S. Capitol.[16] Notwithstanding speech that is "ugly" (with the caveat that beauty is in the eye of the beholder), tolerance of free speech is the sign of a vibrant and healthy democracy, discomfort be damned. That is, as we have seen, both a positive and a negative.

One of the principal tenets of a democracy is the freedom of speech. The balance-tension between this right and the fight against domestic terrorism is of great importance when decision makers consider operational measures and the extent to which otherwise guaranteed rights might be subject to limits, with the understanding such measures run up against the law. These measures are nevertheless of the balancing requirement, subject to checks and balances and separation of powers.

That consideration largely does not apply when developing measures to counter non-domestic terrorism/extremism. We recall that the Bush Administration largely looked askance at limits on state power imposed by international law, referring to international law as "quaint."[17] Such open disparagement defined the Bush Administration's approach to the rule of law in the aftermath of 9/11. The consequences have been previously referenced in this book; it is an open question whether clear violations of the law contributed to operational counterterrorism or, rather, reflected an instinctual response, reflecting a lack of preparation, understanding, nuance, and strategic thinking.

12. *Shamgar Commission Report on the Assassination of Prime Minister Yitzhak Rabin,* Ctr. for Israel Educ. (Roni Eshel, trans.), March 28, 1996, *available at* https://israeled.org/resources/documents/shamgar-rabin-assassination/ (last visited February 20, 2024).

13. In a meeting for a different book project, I was told by a senior Ministry of Justice official "it depends" regarding when speech crosses "the line." Given this was after the assassination, the answer was beyond disingenuous (or not), reflecting an absolute unwillingness to impose limits on speech that by any reasonable test was incitement.

14. 395 U.S. 444 (1969).

15. The author was subjected to online death threats after publication of a book about the Holocaust.

16. Peter Suciu, *Social Media Platforms and the Lessons of January 6,* Forbes, August 1, 2022, 1:06 PM, *available at* https://www.forbes.com/sites/petersuciu/2022/08/01/social-media-platforms-and-the-lessons-of-january-6/?sh=631f909f75c9 (last visited February 20, 2024).

17. *Attorney General Alberto Gonzales vs. Civil Liberties,* ACLU, June 11, 2007, *available at* https://www.aclu.org/documents/attorney-general-alberto-gonzales-vs-civil-liberties (last visited February 20, 2024).

While President Trump may or may not ultimately be held accountable for his words prior to January 6, many of those who acted on his words—whether directly or indirectly—have been prosecuted. This, then, is the dilemma facing U.S. national security officials addressing domestic extremism and terrorism in the years ahead: how to navigate the limits of free speech when considering the ruling in *Brandenburg,* recent domestic terrorist attacks, and the unwillingness of elected officials to criticize those whose ideology reflects—to what extent is always a matter of interpretation—their political beliefs and base.

How this dilemma is resolved will directly impact resource allocation and prioritization which, as we have previously noted, is predicated on assessment of intelligence information and the determination of what is a threat and how it should be addressed in accordance with the rule of law. That assessment is, as we come to understand, more nuanced and complicated when addressing domestic extremism as compared to an external threat.

TABLE OF CASES

Principal cases denoted by italics.

INDEX